Deception, Intrigue, and the Road to War

Volume I

Deception, Intrigue, and the Road to War:

A Chronology of Significant Events Detailing

President Franklin D. Roosevelt's Successful Effort

to Bring a United America into the

War Against Germany

During the Second World War

(Volume 1 of 2)

by

Douglas P. Horne

Copyright © 2017 by Douglas P. Horne

All rights reserved under International and Pan-American Copyright Conventions.

ISBN-13: 978-0-9843144-5-4

Dedication

To the memory of Franklin Delano Roosevelt:

Savior of his country from 1933-1936,

Defender of Western Civilization from 1940-1945,

And Champion of Freedom.

A prince, wrote Machiavelli, must imitate the fox and the lion,

for the lion cannot protect himself from traps,

and the fox cannot defend himself from wolves.

One must therefore be a fox to recognize traps,

And a lion to frighten wolves.

---James MacGregor Burns,
author of **The Lion and the Fox**

Men seek to avoid being deceived less than they seek to avoid being injured by deception. They detest illusion not so much as the noxious consequences of certain types of illusion. In a similar, limited sense, men also want the truth; they welcome the agreeable, life-sustaining consequences of truth, are indifferent toward pure knowledge that brings no consequences, ***and are downright hostile toward possibly damaging and destructive truths*** [emphasis added].

---Friedrich W. Nietzsche, author of
"On Truth and Falsehood in the Extra-Moral Sense"
(from *Scapegoats,* by Edward L. Beach)

Table of Contents

Preface   xi-xxi

Introduction and Chronology   1-530

Conclusions   531-675

Bibliography   677-683

Retrospective Quotation   685

Afterword (A Critique of *A Matter of Honor*,   687-706
by Anthony Summers and Robbyn Swan)

Appendix A (Purported German Transcript of   707-714
Alleged Transatlantic Telephone Call between FDR
And Winston Churchill on November 26, 1941)

Appendix B (First Draft and "Final Text" of FDR's   715-724
War Speech to Congress on December 8, 1941)

Appendix C (FDR's War Speech to Congress 725-730

on December 8, 1941: *As Actually Spoken*)

Index 731-740

About the Author 741-742

Preface

In my own mind, this work is simply an historical monograph---albeit a book-length one. That is to say, its focus is very narrowly defined, and it is copiously footnoted and referenced, so that its readers will know exactly where I am coming from, and why. **It is my belief that studying this subject as a chronology, via a timeline, will prove unusually instructive.** Timelines shine a spotlight on likely (or certain) linkage between events, and lead to a fuller appreciation of causality in historical research. Linkages between events in the Pearl Harbor drama---that previous historians have been loath to acknowledge---are hard to deny when studying the events in a chronological continuum. The reader will surely note that I have been influenced, to a greater or lesser extent, by six of the most recent books about Pearl Harbor and America's entry into World War II: Robert Stinnett's *Day of Deceit;* George Victor's *The Pearl Harbor Myth; Scapegoats,* by the celebrated Edward L. Beach; *Days of Infamy,* by John Costello; *Betrayal at Pearl Harbor,* by Rusbridger and Nave; and finally, the encyclopedic *Pearl Harbor: The Seeds and Fruits of Infamy,* by Percy Greaves, Jr. I do not totally subscribe to the full thesis of either *Days of Infamy* or *Betrayal at Pearl Harbor;* disagreed in some instances with Stinnett's speculations in *Day of Deceit;* and also found the scurrilous anti-Churchill rhetoric and speculation in *Betrayal at Pearl Harbor* to be unsupported by facts---but nevertheless, I found useful historical material and insights in all six of these works. The July 1946 *Report of the Joint Congressional Committee on the Investigation of the Pearl Harbor Attack,* and its accompanying 39 volumes of *Hearings,* proved most useful, as did *The Campaigns of the Pacific War,* published in 1946 by the Naval Analysis Division of the U.S. Strategic Bombing Survey (Pacific). What I have tried to do in this book that I believe is new, is to interweave the differing threads of European war diplomacy; U.S.-Japanese diplomacy in the Pacific; the cataclysmic events of the war in Europe; the crucial American and British advances in codebreaking (and the intelligence provided, as it affected American-Japanese relations); and finally, American radio traffic analysis and radio direction finding in the Pacific, *into a unified whole, arranged chronologically,* so that the reader can more readily appreciate sequencing, and likely causality, within all of these spheres for the period 1938-1941.

This historical monograph is *not* about the tactical details of the planning for the Pearl Harbor attack, or about its execution, which was so tactically brilliant, but strategically flawed (in the sense that the Japanese did not return with third, or even fourth wave attacks to attack the exposed, above-ground oil storage tanks at Pearl Harbor, which were the "Achilles' heel" of the base; or the Pearl Harbor Naval Shipyard, and its four crucial drydocks and many machine shops; or the submarine base and its nearby repair facilities). The story of the masterful Japanese planning and training for the daring and complicated raid has been definitively documented by Gordon Prange in *At Dawn We Slept,* and the execution of the attack itself has been masterfully told by both Prange in *December 7, 1941,* and initially by Walter Lord, in *Day of Infamy.* Furthermore, examining whether or not Admiral Kimmel and General Short should be viewed as scapegoats, or as military commanders derelict in their duty, is not a goal of this work (although it will surely have an impact upon that long-running debate).

Nor does this monograph examine the long term, future ramifications of FDR's military and diplomatic policy during America's run-up to war (from September 1939 to December 1941) upon the future power of "the Imperial Presidency." This has been adequately---even exhaustively---covered by others. I have, however, expressed my impatience with the overly sanctimonious, collective hand-wringing, decades later, of those who have taken such umbrage at the way Franklin D. Roosevelt gathered tremendous powers unto himself as Chief Executive between Germany's attack on Poland in 1939 and Japan's attack on the United States late in 1941. If he had not done so, the world today would be very different, and decidedly not for the better. As I make abundantly clear in this work, I am profoundly grateful that FDR was so often a bold, forceful, determined, and also a patient and wily Chief Executive from 1939 to 1941, and it does not unduly trouble me that he repeatedly deceived the American people about his ultimate objective, which in hindsight is now so blatantly obvious---to enter the World War against Nazi Germany---and that he did so by publicly playing the role of a leader who was reluctantly being forced closer and closer to engaging in hostilities, against his will. The historians who have claimed that FDR bent or evaded the law in providing "all aid short of war" to Great Britain in 1940 seem to have forgotten that while Hitler's armies were rampaging through Holland, Belgium, and France, General Marshall's team of lawyers came up with a *legal justification* to transfer surplus military equipment through sale to third parties; and that Attorney General Jackson declared the Destroyers-Bases deal *to be legal* in August of 1940, before FDR proceeded with the swap. And of course, the enormous Lend-Lease program was *enacted by vote of Congress* on March 11, 1941---after lengthy debate and public hearings on the matter---so that can hardly be considered "bending or breaking the law." FDR, at the eleventh hour, feared that he might be impeached by Congress over the Destroyers-Bases deal, but as it turned out this never happened; Congress accepted FDR's report on his actions in the matter, after the fact, with only mild grumbling, because the Attorney General had blessed it, and the American people as a whole supported it. Yes, FDR outmaneuvered his powerful isolationist political opposition to successfully provide aid to Great Britain when it was crucial to do so---but exercising more political skill than one's opposition hardly constitutes breaking the law.

Franklin Roosevelt made a serious and prolonged attempt to educate the American people about the danger to Western civilization presented by Nazi Germany, and while he succeeded in persuading Americans to render all aid short of war to Great Britain and other nations opposing Fascist tyranny, he was markedly unsuccessful in his attempt to build an American consensus to voluntarily enter the war in Europe. This failure was not due to any lack of persuasive abilities, or effort, on his part. (Throughout 1941 public opinion polling showed that increasing numbers of Americans believed that eventually we would be forced to enter the war, but this was a far cry from a desire to *voluntarily* enter what was then viewed as "a European war.") President Roosevelt---rightly so, in my view---was unwilling to see the world dominated by victorious "bandit nations" who were intent upon looting the planet and trampling on human rights. And Roosevelt, as a politician, was always concerned with ends, not means. Given the stubborn and myopic refusal of the American people to budge on this crucial issue, FDR had no choice but to "engineer" America's entry into World War II by provoking hostile incidents that would drag us in. As I explain in this work, he was no doubt shocked and dismayed that the "incidents" in the autumn of 1941 (between the U.S. Navy and the German Kriegsmarine), during the undeclared war in the north Atlantic, did **not** incite a war fever and serve as the *casus belli* he had hoped for. But since they didn't, he then had no choice but to keep pressuring Japan, diplomatically and economically, until the Japanese let their emotions get the better of them and "made a mistake"---as FDR predicted and hoped they would---and committed the "first overt act of war" that Roosevelt so desperately desired to move American opinion over the threshold from peace to war.

Do I feel sorry for the Japanese? No, not at all---for they were clearly intent throughout the latter half of 1940, and all of 1941, upon continuing their predatory behavior in Asia by taking advantage of the war in Europe, and grabbing what they could for themselves in East Asia. (The philosophy in Japan during 1941 was "don't miss the bus"---that is, grab what we can to supplement our Empire in the Far East and make ourselves self-sufficient in resources, while Hitler's conquests in Europe have greatly weakened the colonial European powers--- Great Britain, France, and the Netherlands---in the Far East.) Once FDR froze Japanese financial assets in the U.S. at the end of July 1941, and thereby cut off the source of 90 per cent of its crude oil, Japan became firmly, irrevocably committed to striking south instead of north. The Japanese decided they had to take by force the oil their expansionist Empire needed---and which the U.S. would no longer sell them---from the Dutch East Indies; but the point is, they were always fully intent on going to war anyway (while Hitler was perceived to be winning in Europe) to expand their empire by conquest. All Roosevelt did with the oil embargo imposed in late July 1941 was ensure that the Japanese aggression would be channeled toward the *south* (with southeast Asia and the Dutch East Indies the ultimate prize), rather than the *north* (a settling of both old and recent scores with the beleaguered Soviet Union); and make it likely that when the Japanese did move, that they would also strike the United States with a strong overt blow, in an undeniable manner. FDR wanted Japan to "commit the first overt act" of war against the United States at the very beginning of its aggressive moves, in a way which would ***electrify, unify, and mobilize the American people for war***---he did <u>not</u> want to see Japan and the United States slowly drift toward war with each other in the months (or years) following a successful Japanese invasion and occupation of Southeast Asia, Malaya, and the Dutch East Indies. His biggest concern was that the Japanese might *only* attack Singapore and the Dutch East Indies, and not the United

States. Roosevelt knew that the Congress would not declare war on Japan for attacking Singapore and the Dutch East Indies alone, and he was worried that even a Japanese attack *solely on the Philippines*---a place out-of-sight, and out-of-mind, for most Americans---may not have stimulated a declaration of war by a wary and recalcitrant Congress in 1941. He knew for sure, however, that an undeniable and clear-cut Japanese attack on U.S. men-of-war at sea, or upon U.S. bases on U.S. soil in American territories overseas (Guam or Hawaii, for example), would provoke the strongest possible reaction in the United States. This, I have documented, was constantly on his mind from October of 1940 through December of 1941.

That Roosevelt initiated an undeclared naval war against Hitler in the Atlantic, in the autumn of 1941, is common knowledge today; that he deliberately provoked war with expansionist Japan---Germany's military ally---when he could not provoke a war with Hitler, can be persuasively demonstrated, and I believe I have done so in this work. (FDR did not "blunder into the wrong war" while preoccupied with the war in Europe; I have put this myth to bed forever.)

Much more controversial is my contention that FDR and a small number of key American military leaders probably---indeed, almost certainly---came to know very late in the autumn of 1941 (only within the two week period prior to the Pearl Harbor attack) that the Japanese were going to attack Hawaii, and in a stoic act of national self-sacrifice, steeled themselves to permit this to happen. The evidence here is circumstantial, but in my view quite persuasive, when viewed in its totality. There is too much smoke here, for there to be no fire. I have refused, on this issue, to engage in the collective denial about the Pearl Harbor attack that our mainstream historians, with their pack mentality, are so noted for; and I have refused to accept the stonewalling and denial of the NSA and its proxy historians. Too many historians have confused the results *actually obtained* by the Japanese in their Pearl Harbor attack, with the *likely expectations* by the naval establishment of the day, and even of President Roosevelt, in the event of such an attack on Hawaii.

President Roosevelt long hungered for a dramatic "incident" of unmistakable clarity (where the aggressor was clearly identified) that would plunge the United States into the World War *by uniting the population in its outrage,* and he had already proclaimed in private (when discussing his provocative "pop-up" cruises in Japanese controlled waters) that he was prepared to lose "one or two" ships, but not "five or six," in such a cause. So, knowing---commencing on November 26, 1941---that there was an attack force headed toward the Hawaiian Islands, and patiently allowing that blow to fall, in the belief that the damage would be middling, or moderate at best, *and* in the belief that the local commanders (Kimmel and Short) would put up a good fight (and not only severely punish the enemy, but in the process mitigate the damages incurred), is the correct way to visualize FDR's thinking prior to December 7th. The tired old mainstream historian complaint that "FDR would not knowingly have sacrificed all of the battleships in the Pacific Fleet, nor would he knowingly have accepted over 3,500 casualties (2,403 deaths and 1,178 wounded), because he loved the

Navy," is the wrong argument, and the wrong way to think about the matter. To repeat, this old argument wrongly conflates ***the results actually achieved by the enemy*** with the **expectations at the time** of what the enemy could achieve ***if he did attack,*** which are two entirely different things. Surely, President Roosevelt *did not* expect that a Japanese hit-and-run "raid" on Pearl Harbor would destroy 188 planes on the ground, and damage another 159; sink 4 of the Pacific Fleet's 9 battleships in one day (*Arizona, Oklahoma, West Virginia,* and *California*), and damage 4 other battleships in the Navy's Pacific Fleet "battle line" (*Nevada, Tennessee, Maryland, and Pennsylvania*)---or cause over 3,500 casualties. [The ninth Pacific Fleet battleship, *Colorado,* was on the West Coast at the time of the attack.]

And consider this: it is **undeniable** that President Roosevelt knew on December 7th that largely as a result of the Two Ocean Navy Act passed in July of 1940, the United States then had under construction 15 battleships, 11 fleet (large) aircraft carriers, 54 cruisers, 191 destroyers, and 73 submarines.[1] After all, it was he who stimulated this to happen, and pushed the bill through Congress, after the fall of France; so surely, this comforting knowledge was part of the calculus in "his forested mind" as he presumably assessed the overall impact of a prospective Japanese hit-and-run raid on Pearl Harbor. Such an attack, no matter how grievous, would not in any way constitute a threat to the existence of the United States---nor would it alter the inevitability of our future military predominance in the Pacific, given the Naval construction and aviation construction (50,000 planes per year was the target) already underway.[2]

---

[1] Parker, *A Priceless Advantage,* 37.

[2] Homer Wallin, author of *Pearl Harbor: Why, How, Fleet Salvage and Final Appraisal,* wrote (p. 36-37) that in 1937 Roosevelt announced the U.S. would build two new battleships, *North Carolina* and *Washington,* and modestly increased the size of the Army; that in 1938 Congress, at his request, appropriated funds for two more battleships and two new aircraft carriers; that in June of 1940 Roosevelt had asked Congress to fund the building of 50,000 planes per year (which Congress approved); that following the fall of France the President had asked Congress to appropriate 5 billion dollars for further increases in defense, which was granted on August 27, 1940; that Congress that summer authorized calling up the National Guard and Reserves to active duty; that in July 1940 forty more Naval warships were ordered by the Navy Department; that the Two Ocean Navy Act was approved that summer; that the first peacetime draft was commenced in September 1940 (and that although by a narrow margin---one vote---Congress had extended the term of service from one year to a year-and-a-half in August of 1941); and that during 1940 the following ships were ordered or authorized for the Navy: 6 Iowa-class battleships of 45,000 tons; 5 Montana-class battleships of 56,000 tons; 6 battle cruisers of about 27,000 tons; 11 aircraft carriers of 27,000 tons; 40 cruisers; 115 destroyers; 67 submarines; and many auxiliaries and small craft. (Note: only 4 Iowa-class battleships were completed; none of the Montana-class behemoths were built; and none of the battle cruisers were constructed.) While some of these ships were never built, increased numbers of other types were authorized later (for example, aircraft carriers). The point is that at the time of the Pearl Harbor attack, there was no reason to panic when one considered the numbers and types of ships that were under construction or authorized---and the fact that **none** of the Pacific Fleet's carriers were destroyed in the Pearl Harbor attack.

So---putting one's self in FDR's mind prior to December 7th, which is what this book attempts to do---allowing a Pearl Harbor attack to take place is actually not inconceivable at all (especially if one believed that the attacker would seriously stub his toe on the "American Gibraltar"), for a surprise Japanese raid on the fleet and shore installations at Oahu (U.S. territory, within easy reach of the American West Coast, *not* a faraway foreign commonwealth like the Philippines) <u>would have provided FDR with the perfect *casus belli* that he had been searching for</u>. Roosevelt at this time was thinking as Commander-in-Chief, and as the leading statesman among the surviving democracies: strategically, coldly, logically, and with detachment---as any general or flag officer does in war. ***The few had to be sacrificed so that the many could be saved, and so that a greater good could be accomplished.*** By the time I completed my manuscript, I was struck by the ruthless determination shown by Franklin D. Roosevelt to: (1) get America into World War II as a full-fledged belligerent; and (2) to find a way to do so that would permit him to take a *unified nation* with him, not one riven by controversy and fractious debate.

I believe FDR's abject state of shock on December 7th was driven not by surprise that the Japanese had attacked the U.S. (or even that Pearl Harbor was the target), but rather by the enormity of the air raid and the massive damage inflicted on what was truly viewed as America's "Gibraltar of the Pacific." No one in Washington understood the depth of how strategically unprepared we were to face the Japanese. Some of FDR's shock on December 7th was due to his failure to appreciate the extent of our strategic unpreparedness (the Army's air reconnaissance and air defense on the island of Oahu was appalling---operationally inept, and almost non-existent---and the Navy was shepherding and minimizing the use of most of its limited force of patrol planes for the expected offensive against Japan once the impending hostilities with Japan kicked off, and therefore had only devoted minimal numbers to offshore patrol); some to racist hubris (few white Americans or Europeans in positions of authority believed the Japanese were capable of building *very good* airplanes or training *excellent* pilots, and FDR was surely no different in this regard from other Western elites prior to the Pearl Harbor attack); and some was driven by the fact that (apparently) ONI believed that only **two** Japanese carriers were headed for Hawaii---<u>not the six that were actually employed</u>. [No one on the planet had yet amassed that many aircraft carriers into an offensive striking force of such unparalleled magnitude; prior to Pearl Harbor, the U.S. Navy's doctrine was still to employ carriers simply as scouting and screening forces for battleship task groups, not as the main offensive striking arm of the fleet.] Nor did the American Navy generally believe that aerial torpedoes could successfully be employed in the shallow waters of Pearl Harbor, and yet the ingenious Japanese Navy modified its existing aerial torpedoes so that they could be launched effectively and reliably in shallow water, within the known 40-foot depth limit of Pearl Harbor, instead of plunging to a depth of 75 feet or more, as our own aerial torpedoes did at the time. And certainly no one in the U.S. Naval establishment foresaw that the innovative Japanese Navy armaments experts would transform battleship armor-piercing projectiles, normally fired from the huge naval rifles on battleships, into armor-piercing bombs, and drop them from naval aircraft to penetrate the thick deck armor of battleships---and do so successfully, from a height of 10,000 feet. So in my view the causes of Franklin Roosevelt's abject shock on December 7, 1941 were many. His stunned frame of mind on December 7th, I believe, was entirely related to the **effectiveness** of the blow struck by the Japanese that day, certainly not by the fact that the Japanese were about to initiate a "southern war strategy," *nor by the location of the blow---in Hawaii.* On December 7, 1941, President Roosevelt temporarily believed himself undone by his war strategy and his own secret plans, and momentarily felt tremendous astonishment, guilt, shame, and burning embarrassment. He quickly recovered his balance, with the realization that the Pearl Harbor attack had succeeded beyond his wildest dreams in uniting the American people "in their righteous might;" and with the recognition that it would be a long war, and that America's overwhelming industrial capacity would surely, given time, prevail against the Axis. Hitler's Germany would now eventually be defeated, and without a successful Germany to challenge and/or distract the Allies, Japan had no chance of holding onto its conquests, or its empire. Roosevelt's sound and experienced judgment of the psychology of the American people was far superior to Admiral Yamamoto's, for Roosevelt knew that once the United States was clearly attacked by an aggressor nation, it would **never** "sue for peace," and allow that aggressor to keep its ill-gotten gains, no matter how severe were the initial setbacks at the beginning of hostilities. Neither Franklin Delano Roosevelt (a man who after all, had "beaten" polio by becoming President of the United States), nor the American people, were quitters---something that Admiral Yamamoto never understood, in spite of his three tours of duty in the United States.

But I'm getting ahead of myself, and the topic addressed in this work. The main theme of this monograph is that President Roosevelt was convinced by May of 1940 that the United States would eventually have to enter the war against Nazi Germany to guarantee Hitler's defeat, and that his foreign policy from that time, until the Pearl Harbor attack, was motivated by two goals: preventing the defeat of Great Britain (or of the Soviet Union, once Hitler turned on the USSR), and taking a united America into the war against Hitler. It is my firm belief that FDR's ratcheted-up pressure on Japan starting in mid-1941 was designed to prevent a Japanese attack on the weakened USSR by starving Japan of the oil it needed, and engaging in provocations in the Pacific, thereby forcing the Japanese to adopt the "southern" war strategy---thus preventing Japan from striking a crippling, and possibly fatal blow to Soviet Union. Roosevelt knew that the huge German and Soviet armies fighting on Germany's Eastern Front from late June, through December of 1941, were likely to decide the ultimate outcome of the war in Europe, more than any other single factor; and his goal after June 22, 1941 was to keep the USSR *in the war against Germany, and to prevent an early defeat of the Soviet Union.* (A Japanese invasion of Siberia in the autumn of 1941---the "northern" strategy being considered by Japan throughout the first half of 1941---would have prevented Stalin from transferring General Zhukov's 1.5 million men to the west in October; and without those fresh reinforcements to help defend Moscow, Hitler may have won an early victory in his war against the Soviet Union.) It is my further contention that once it became clear to FDR, in the autumn of 1941, that combat "incidents" during the U.S. Navy's undeclared war against German U-boats in the Atlantic were not sufficient to induce the American people to go to war against Germany, that Roosevelt clearly and intentionally instigated war with Japan ***through the adoption of a very hard diplomatic line in late November of 1941;*** and that his apparent decision to permit the ensuing Pearl Harbor attack to unfold, and land as an apparent "surprise blow," truly did constitute FDR's "back door to war" against Nazi Germany, as has been alleged elsewhere, by so-called "revisionist" historians, for decades. However, unlike virtually every other author who has made this allegation about Roosevelt's foreknowledge of the Pearl Harbor attack, I applaud FDR's vision, wily determination, sense of purpose, and patient pursuit of the correct strategy (taking a ***united*** country into World War II), and believe he was the right man, in the right place, at the right time. [Many of my leftist and libertarian friends will be unhappy with this viewpoint, but I ardently believe World War II was a special case, dictated by the overwhelming brutality and racism of Nazi Germany and Imperial Japan, and that therefore FDR's grand strategy was justified.] Regardless of each reader's own leanings as he approaches this work, I ask each of you to study the evidence in this book dispassionately, after setting aside any preconceptions, or bias, you may have---and that you then reconsider your views after a full and thorough examination of the contents of this book. Knowing our true history is much preferred, in my view, to engaging in willful denial.

A Short Note About the Many Pearl Harbor Investigations

There have been a total now of ten (10) separate investigations by various government officials and entities into the Pearl Harbor attack; nine of them took place between 1941 and 1946, and the most recent is the Dorn Report, issued on December 1, 1995. They are: (1) the investigation conducted by Secretary of the Navy Frank Knox immediately after the attack; (2) the five-member commission headed by Supreme Court Justice Owen J. Roberts, known as the Roberts Commission; (3) Admiral Thomas C. Hart's Investigation; (4) the Army Pearl Harbor Board; (5) the Navy Court of Inquiry; (6) the Clarke Investigation (Col. Carter W. Clarke); (7) the Henry C. Clausen investigation (ordered by Secretary of War Stimson); (8) the Admiral Henry K. Hewitt Inquiry; (9) the Joint Congressional Committee (JCC) on the Investigation of the Pearl Harbor Attack; and (10) the report of Undersecretary of Defense Edwin Dorn.

It is well beyond the scope of this book to attempt to summarize the ten investigations, but I will now recommend two books that do so admirably. *Scapegoats,* by Edward L. Beach (1995), summarizes the first 9 investigations very nicely in chapter 7; and *Kimmel, Short, and Pearl Harbor: The Final Report Revealed,* by Fred Borch and Daniel Martinez (2005), publishes the Dorn Report of 1995, explains the political context of the Dorn Report, and publishes a critique of that report written by a third party. In addition, Appendix A of the Joint Congressional Committee *Report* (p. 267-271) addresses items (2) through (8) above, and summarizes the nature of each investigation and the authority authorizing it in carefully neutral language, for those who may find the opinions expressed by Edward L. Beach about these investigations distracting, or unwelcome. As Beach points out in his book *Scapegoats,* most of the reference materials used by Pearl Harbor historians (especially quotes of statements by former government officials and military officers) come from the *Report* of JCC findings, or the supporting volumes of hearings and exhibits. Many of the quotes in my book of statements made by Stimson, Marshall, Stark, Turner, *et. al.*---even though often sourced to secondary works by other authors---originated with the JCC *Report,* or the accompanying 39 volumes of *Hearings,* published in July of 1946.

Endeavoring to Get the Names and Ranks of Key Players Straight

I have tried to record with precision the names and military ranks of the key American players in this drama, setting down for the reader their rank, as best I can determine, for the time I am writing about them, usually during 1940 or 1941. In a few instances, it has proven surprisingly difficult to pin down the actual rank (or correct name spelling) for certain American military officers, because the voluminous historical record of the Pearl Harbor event is replete with conflicts.

For example, the first name of **LCDR A. D. Kramer, USN,** the Navy translator and linguist on loan to OP-20-G in 1941---the Navy's man assigned to deliver **MAGIC** diplomatic intercepts to the President and the Navy brass---was *misspelled* in the film *Tora! Tora! Tora!* as "Alvin;" is spelled "Alwin" by Beach, Prange, Stinnett, Victor, and Toland; is spelled "Alwyn" by Greaves in his index (and as *both* "Alwin" *and* "Alwyn" in his text); and is also spelled "Alwyn" by Prados in his index also (but is spelled *both* ways---as both "Alwyn *and* "Alwin"---in *his* text)! Even the NSA, in different historical documents, spells Kramer's first name as both "Alwyn" and "Alwin." Because Percy Greaves, Jr. was the chief of the Minority (Republican) Staff for the Joint Congressional Committee investigating Pearl Harbor after the war in 1945-6, and "was there"---and because John Prados is such a respected military historian---**I have decided to go with "Alwyn,"** the spelling for Kramer's first name used in both of their indices. This was an "old-fashioned" name that I have never once encountered personally in my lifetime; therefore, I have gone with what appears to be the most "old-fashioned" spelling. (Furthermore, the use of "Alwyn" will prevent any possibility of mispronouncing or misspelling his name as "<u>Alvin</u>," as in the 1970 film mentioned above---a largely excellent docudrama about Pearl Harbor, with only a handful of relatively minor historical errors to its discredit.)

More serious dilemmas arise when trying to pin down the <u>ranks</u> of certain individuals in 1941. Most of the follow-on investigations (in 1944, 45, and 46) referred to their key witnesses using the ranks they held *at the time of each investigation,* which can be very misleading when trying to write about 1940 and 1941, since wartime promotion was so swift.

One of the three Directors of ONI in 1941 was **Alan G. Kirk.** Prados, in his only textual reference to Kirk, refers to him as a "Rear Admiral" when he was briefly the ONI Director; however, Victor, Beach, and Greaves all refer to Alan G. Kirk as a "Navy Captain;" Beach, in particular, refers to Kirk as a "senior Navy Captain." **In my text, I have opted to designate this ONI Director as "CAPT Alan G. Kirk,"** and *not* as a Rear Admiral. (He reached the rank of full Admiral during the war, and may have been promoted to the next step above Navy Captain---Rear Admiral---very soon after leaving ONI.)

Kirk's relief as the new Director of ONI was **Theodore S. Wilkinson.** He is referred to as a "Navy Captain" by Stinnett and Prange; but is identified simply as "Admiral" (a rather imprecise term that *may* refer to a full four-star Admiral, but *sometimes* serves as a generic, honorific description of either a Vice Admiral or Rear Admiral) by Prange (when quoting the Hewitt Hearing), by Victor, by Greaves, and in the crucial diary entry of December 6, 1941 made by the Dutch Naval Attache, Johan Ranneft. Wilkinson, as ONI Director in 1941, is referred to specifically as a "Rear Admiral" by Clausen, Prados, and Beach. That is persuasive to me. **I have therefore chosen to describe Theodore S. Wilkinson, the third ONI Director installed in 1941, as "Rear Admiral Wilkinson."** His predecessor, CAPT Kirk, lost his job in the fallout from a power struggle with the irascible and vindictive Director of War Plans, Rear Admiral Richmond K. Turner, which could explain why "Ping" Wilkinson, who was assigned to relieve Kirk immediately after commanding the battleship *USS Mississippi,* was promoted---in an attempt to level the playing field on the second deck in the Navy Building. (A battleship's commanding officer was always a Navy Captain---never an Admiral---but Wilkinson must have been promoted soon after relieving Kirk, or even simultaneous with that relief.)

The most difficult rank issue, which I do not have a definitive answer to, is in regard to the rank of President Roosevelt's new Naval Aide in 1941, **John R. Beardall.** Greaves refers to him simply as "Admiral;" CAPT Safford (the former OP-20-G himself) in 1944 referred to him as a "Rear Admiral," and so does Clausen; Prange refers to Beardall as a "Rear Admiral" (RADM) in his index, but as a "Navy Captain" in his text; Beach refers to Beardall as a "Navy Captain," as does Stinnett. I know for certain that his two predecessors at the White House were Navy O-6s---Captains---**so I have opted to side with Edward L. Beach, a Navy career man, and designate John R. Beardall as a Navy Captain in this book.** My sense is that this was probably his rank at the time of the Pearl Harbor attack, and that he may have been promoted to Rear Admiral soon after the U.S. entered World War II.

Finally, according to Stinnett, the Navy Far East Intelligence Specialist (Head of the ONI's Far East Division in 1941) and Japanese linguist, **Arthur H. McCollum,** was definitely a Commander in the Navy when he wrote his famous policy memo of October 7, 1940; however, in the December 6, 1941 diary entry of Dutch Naval Attache Johan Ranneft, he is referred to as "Capt. Mac Collum," which indicates to me that he had been promoted by that time from O-5 to O-6. It makes sense; if the new ONI Director (Wilkinson) was now a Rear

Admiral (instead of a Captain), it follows that a long-time Japanese language and intelligence expert, and the Head of ONI's Far East Division, would be promoted one step as well. But for purposes of simplicity, since I am unaware of the date of his promotion, **he will be referred to throughout most of this work as "CDR McCollum."**

As I concluded writing the above section about names and ranks, I came across Appendix B to the JCC *Report* published on July 20, 1946, titled: *"Names and Positions of Principal Army and Navy Officials in Washington and at Hawaii at the Time of the Attack Along With the Leading Witnesses in the Various Proceedings."* Clearly, this is the ultimate referee to any confusion the reader may encounter regarding names, ranks, and job functions of individuals who had a role in the Pearl Harbor drama; it is found on pages 273-281 of the JCC *Report*. Appendix B *does* confirm that the Chief of ONI was Rear Admiral Wilkinson (but does not clarify the ranks of his immediate predecessors); confirms that on December 7, 1941 Arthur McCollum *was indeed* a Navy Captain (O-6); but does *not* clarify the rank of FDR's Naval Aide, John R. Beardall, at the time of the Pearl Harbor attack; *nor* does it definitively resolve how to spell LCDR Kramer's first name (simply listing him as "Lt. Comdr. A. D. Kramer"). Interestingly, the head of OP-20-G, the "Father of Navy Cryptography," Laurance F. Safford, is listed in Appendix B as a Navy Captain (O-6) at the time of the Pearl Harbor attack, whereas he is almost universally referred to as "CDR Safford" in the literature. This implies to me that like CDR McCollum, he must have received a promotion from CDR to CAPT in 1941, shortly before the attack on Pearl Harbor.

For the convenience of Western readers, since this book is written from an unabashedly American perspective, and is intended primarily for an American and British audience, I have chosen to spell Japanese names in the American style, with the surname last---rather than Japanese style, with the surname written first. My apologies are extended to any purists who are irritated by this.

Deception, Intrigue, and the Road to War:

A Chronology of Significant Events Detailing

President Franklin D. Roosevelt's Successful Effort to Bring a

United America into the War Against Germany

During the Second World War

World War II, in its essence, is the story of three "have-not," resource-poor nations---Germany, Italy, and Japan---which nevertheless were determined to "have their place in the sun," and enjoy the fruits and prestige of colonial empires, just as other nations (most notably Great Britain, France, and the Netherlands) had for centuries. They chafed against the "status quo" so sanctimoniously insisted upon by countries with long-established empires (Great Britain, France, and the Netherlands), and by other nations rich in land and natural resources (most notably the United States). Germany, with its very strong and robust industrial base---and with its martial, Teutonic race hungering for revenge after the humiliation of the Versailles Treaty following the First World War---took the big gamble, rolled the dice, and upset the entire world order between 1936 and 1939 with its expansionist policies in Europe, exposing how unprepared for war were the Western powers, and the weakness of the systems established to uphold the status quo in international affairs. Japan, engaged in an imperialistic struggle-to-the-death with China since 1937 which it could not win, and from which it was unable to disengage, sought to take advantage of Germany's tremendously successful Western European offensive in May and June of 1940, and brazenly grab most of the mineral, food, and petroleum resources of Southeast Asia for itself while Germany, from afar, was critically weakening the British, French, and Dutch empires in Southeast Asia. The decisions and actions taken by Japan between July of 1940 and December of 1941 turned two totally different wars half a globe apart---the "last European war," and Japan's fratricidal war with China---into the first true worldwide conflict, the first true World War in terms of geography, participants, and the stakes. "Have-not" Italy hungered for a Mediterranean and African empire that would rival ancient Rome; "have-not" Germany initially hungered, first, for revenge over its defeat in World War I, and "correction" of European borders (i.e., acquisition of territories settled by German populations within other nations), but this quickly evolved into the Nazi blood-lust for huge amounts of territory in Eastern Europe and in European Russia, upon which Hitler and his regime placed its hopes for future empire, wealth, and power. Germany and Italy were both Fascist dictatorships, totally driven by the desires of their unchallenged, and all-powerful totalitarian leaders, Hitler and Mussolini. Japan, the biggest "have-not" of these three nations, was neither a democracy nor a dictatorship, but rather---beneath a thin veneer of democratic institutions---remained a feudal, warrior-dominated society that reached decisions through elite consensus; she was not a true Fascist nation ruled by one all-powerful leader, but her hunger for empire (and the resources and status she believed empire would bring) was just as strong as that of Germany and Italy, if not more so. There was a desperation behind Japan's drive for empire and resources that exceeded the simple greed of Germany and Italy; Imperial Japan, by sheer force of will, in record time, had ended centuries of isolation and embraced the industrial revolution---impoverishing itself in the process---in order to build and acquire a modern Navy and Air Force, and a large Army. Imperial Japan (a nation smaller than the U.S. State of California, and with fewer resources) was intent upon acquiring a colonial, resource-rich empire, and upon enjoying the perceived fruits of empire, and great-power status, like the nations Japan found itself confronted with after the United States forcibly ended its isolation, and forced Japan to join the modern world, in the mid-nineteenth century. Following the incredible success of Germany's Western offensive launched in May of 1940, these three "have-not" nations---impatient and scornful of the "status quo," Western liberal morality (used all too often, they believed, to simply justify and maintain existing empires acquired in the past by force), international diplomacy (which was perceived as a "rigged game"), and an Anglo-American dominated world economic system---set out to brazenly loot the planet, by force. As far as Japan's elites were concerned, it was "now or never," while the West was still in a weakened condition, and before the Western powers could mobilize their superior resources.

Let us now turn to President Franklin Delano Roosevelt, whose foreign policy in the run-up to Pearl Harbor this book is about. Hitler's invasion of Poland on September 1, 1939 brought about a declaration of war against Germany by Great Britain and France. (The policy of appeasement had failed, and Hitler's insatiable appetite for foreign territory---*lebensraum*---and his untrustworthiness, were finally recognized. While the declaration of war by Britain and France did nothing to save Poland, it was a formal recognition that Nazi Germany had to be stopped by force of arms, since diplomacy had failed.) Following several months of virtually no combat action between the Allies (Britain and France) and Germany, dubbed "Sietzkrieg" (or 'the sitting war') by the Germans, Hitler's armed forces suddenly occupied Denmark and Norway in April of 1940, and then in May of 1940, quickly overran the Netherlands and Belgium as they smashed their way into France, routing the Belgian Army, French Army, and the British Expeditionary Force in a remarkably successful military campaign which resulted in the defeat and partition of France, and the total isolation of Great Britain, before the end of June. Franklin Roosevelt was 58 years old, and well into the eighth (and presumably final) year of his presidency, when France fell and the British army was kicked off of the continent of Europe. (The primary unwritten rule of American presidential politics, set by George Washington's early example, was that U.S. Presidents, by tradition, did not serve more than two terms, or eight years in office.) The son of privilege and a fifth cousin of Theodore Roosevelt (who had been President from 1901-1909), FDR had served as

Assistant Secretary of the Navy during World War I under President Woodrow Wilson. Struck down by polio in 1921, and paralyzed for life from the waist down and unable to use his legs, Roosevelt soon proved to be a resilient survivor, and in 1928 was elected as Governor of New York. He had already earned a reputation for successfully combating the worst of the Great Depression in New York State, when he secured the Democratic nomination for President in 1932. He soundly defeated his "do-nothing" predecessor, Republican Herbert Hoover, and took office in March of 1933. His immediate task once in office was to prevent a total economic collapse in America, where unemployment was at 25 per cent, and the banking system was unsound. Foreign policy was not a priority for Franklin D. Roosevelt from 1933 to 1936.

Historian Ian Kershaw has painted some very good word-pictures of Roosevelt in his fine book *Fateful Choices: Ten Decisions That Changed the World, 1940-41,* from which I will quote liberally here. FDR proved a "shrewd and capable politician…His personal charm, seemingly relaxed style, good humour, and affable manner helped him persuade his friends and assuage his opponents on many occasions, as he wove his way through the political thickets. Some of his political enemies accused him of deviousness and duplicity. His supporters, on the other hand, admired his cleverness and skilful manoeuvering. He remained, for all his years in power, something of an enigma. 'His bewildering complexity,' it has been said [and here Kershaw quotes historian James MacGregor Burns], 'had become his most visible trait. He could be bold or cautious, informal or dignified, cruel or kind, intolerant or long-suffering, urbane or almost rustic, impetuous or temporizing, Machiavellian or moralistic.' Whichever way he was viewed, it could scarcely be doubted that by the time he faced the daunting questions of war and peace in the critical months of 1940-41, Roosevelt was the supreme master of the political scene in the United States." Kershaw continued: "Roosevelt's way of operating often gave the somewhat misleading impression of a lack of any systematic application. In fact, it spoke of a highly personal level of involvement based upon accessibility. The 'air of small town friendliness' that characterized the White House belied the fact that Roosevelt kept the reins of power very tightly in his own hands."

Kershaw's overview of the built-in conflict within the American political system, the checks and balances---most particularly, designed by the framers to limit Presidential power---is useful to review here, and to keep in mind, as one reads this monograph. It is a somewhat lengthy, but useful, discourse and tutorial: "The U.S. Constitution endows the President with wide powers, though it also imposes checks and balances on his executive authority. Most notably, the powers invested in the legislature and the judiciary were intended to limit presidential power and any abuse of it. The doctrine of the separation of powers foresaw the friction that was built into the relations between the President and the Congress."

Kershaw, an accomplished British historian and expert on the Nazi regime and the Holocaust, and a recent biographer of Hitler, continued with his outsider's incisive overview of FDR's political operating environment: "The duopoly between the President and Congress, the complex balance between the powers of each, inevitably produced a need for compromise, often arrived at through wearisome, time-consuming processes and intense lobbying. The absence of swift, perhaps impulsive, decision-making and apparent lack of governmental efficiency were generally regarded as the necessary price of freedom from overweening power. On the other hand, at times of international crisis---and the implications for the United States of the war in Europe and the increasing threat in the Far East certainly amounted to such---the need to negotiate crucial measures through an obstructionist Congress could prove not simply laborious, but weakening when urgent action was called for. Yet precisely at such times it was imperative that the President have national, not partisan backing. Roosevelt's caution, his reluctance to embrace the bold moves that his advisors sometimes advocated, reflected his pronounced sensitivity to the need to carry the country with him. And he was all too aware that the nation was divided on the decisive issue of American involvement in the European war---in favor of giving Britain more material support, certainly, but opposed by four to one to entry into the conflict. Roosevelt often showed consummate political skill in his dealings with Congress. He became, however, increasingly prepared to bypass Congress through use of his prerogative powers, sometimes ingeniously justified, in order to take action which might otherwise have been stymied or held up by protracted debate."

Kershaw continued: "Each President brings his own inimitable style to the exercise of power. Roosevelt was a man of bold ideas, though without a coherent ideology. He was prepared to experiment, then pull back if his initiatives proved unworkable. He exuded confidence, and his genial affability helped to convey his sense of pushing at the limits of the possible to those around him. He focused on ends, not means…He was impatient with formal bureaucracies, often seeing them as a challenge that he had to circumnavigate…His discursive approach to problems could prove an irritation to those in his entourage who favored more direct, forensic analysis. Stimson's impatience for action [beginning in June of 1940, Henry L. Stimson, a conservative interventionist Republican with prior experience as both Secretary of War and as Secretary of State, served as FDR's Secretary of War] and Roosevelt's caution and *ad hoc* improvisations led the Secretary of War to note with a tone of frustration that 'it literally is government on the jump' and that conversation with the President was 'like chasing a vagrant beam of sunshine around a vacant room.' Stimson, like others, did however, come to appreciate Roosevelt's ingrained shrewdness in engineering, at times through patience, wariness, and roundabout means, the passage of the measures he wanted to take. And no one mistook Roosevelt's caution for weakness. In the formulation of policy and in the taking of key decisions, there was no doubt in anyone's mind of Roosevelt's outright primacy."

Kershaw's tutorial concluded: "…The growing crisis from spring 1940 required more flexible and dynamic government. In the wake of the German triumph in Western Europe in May and June 1940, there was an urgent need to convert the nation to a defence footing. A belated, massive effort had to be taken to mobilize the economy for defence, and to rearm with all haste. And, since national security was bound up with the fate of Britain and France, the attempt had to be made to prevent the destruction of the western democracies. Roosevelt now started to function more as commander-in-chief than as President of a civil administration, centralizing the orchestration of defence in his own hands. He was careful to bypass Congress, without alienating it, using statutes from the First World War to create new defence agencies and avoid legislation, strengthening his own position in the process." This trend will be well documented in the forthcoming chronology and conclusion to this book.

FDR's cabinet during the second half of 1940 and throughout 1941 included many ardent interventionists who were impatient with what they perceived as Roosevelt's slow, cautious, and halting steps toward bringing America into the European war. These interventionists included the two Republicans Roosevelt had wisely added to his administration in June of 1940 during the near-panic in Washington following the rout of the British and French armies on the continent: newspaper publisher Frank Knox as the affable and energetic new Secretary of the Navy; and the experienced Henry L. Stimson, a man of firm principles and moral rectitude who had served previous Republican administrations in high office. These were shrewd political appointments that helped to create at least the appearance of a bipartisan foreign policy. Stimson became the strong-man in the cabinet among the interventionists; and he and Knox brought a much needed dynamism to America's rearmament program. As noted by Kershaw, "In Knox and Stimson, Roosevelt now had in position two men who favored a more forceful defence policy---indeed were considerably more hawkish than the President himself and ready to push him in a direction he often seemed reluctant to take." The other key interventionists in the Cabinet were the President's friend, Treasury Secretary Henry Morgenthau, who believed, like Stimson, that Nazi Germany could only be defeated if the resources of the United States were mobilized; and the fiery, emotional Secretary of the Interior, Harold Ickes. The Chief of Naval Operations, Admiral Harold ("Betty") Stark, was someone fully compliant with the President's wishes, who did not resent FDR's "hands on" approach to Navy policy; and the Chief of Staff of the Army, George C. Marshall, was a somewhat formidable figure because he was exceptionally able, personally austere, and had the reputation for speaking bluntly (and honestly) with his superiors, including the President himself. Marshall and Stimson quickly developed a close personal and professional relationship.

Counterbalancing the interventionists to some degree was Secretary of State Cordell Hull; while he detested Fascism, and took a strong line of condemnation against Japanese aggression, he was wary of taking actions that could serve as unnecessary provocations to the

Axis belligerents. As Kershaw states, "Roosevelt was content [author's note: in my view this was true before October of 1940, but not so much afterwards, especially from July-December 1941] to let the wary and experienced Hull deal with the Far East with minimal interference and to keep a fragile peace in the Pacific by avoiding provocation to the Japanese while refraining from action that might condone their war against China." FDR exerted a much more direct role in formulating and directing foreign policy in the Atlantic sphere. But even in the Far East, it was Roosevelt who controlled trade restrictions and issues of military deterrence, not Hull. There was little empathy between Roosevelt and the stern, moralistic, inflexible Tennessean who had been Secretary of State since 1933; FDR sometimes snubbed Hull by dealing directly on some initiatives with his Under-Secretary, Sumner Welles, a friend and confidant of the President.

Perhaps the only advisor who was truly close to the President was the Secretary of Commerce, Harry Hopkins, the primary proponent and defender of his New Deal economic policies, a man who had been with Roosevelt from the beginning of his presidency and who had an apartment in the White House. Hopkins had the President's ear on most matters, virtually unlimited access to FDR, and exerted influence far beyond his job title. Harry Hopkins---who, per Ian Kershaw, was "decried by opponents as a combination of Machiavelli, Svengali, and Rasputin"---was FDR's most trusted advisor. He is described by Kershaw as "…indefatigable, straight-talking with a knack of cutting to the heart of any issue, and utterly loyal to Roosevelt with 'an extrasensory perception' of his moods."

This completes my brief portrait of the essential *dramatis personae* who will appear and reappear throughout this work. It should also be mentioned that throughout much of 1940 and 1941, Roosevelt and America's foreign policy were the target of intense lobbying campaigns. The two principal interventionist lobbies (who publicly favored maximum aid to Great Britain, and privately even entering the European war when the time was right) were the Committee to Defend America by Aiding the Allies (founded in May 1940 by newspaper publisher William Allen White), and the east-coast based Century Club. America First, a counter-lobby to the Committee to Defend America by Aiding the Allies, was formed in early September of 1940 as the Presidential campaign heated up, and was an isolationist organization. The America First organization was strongest in the mid-west, and was centered in Chicago; most of its members were Republicans, and it was highly critical of Roosevelt's foreign policy. The America First position was that Hitler did not endanger the United States, and that giving aid to Britain would not only weaken the United States, but would eventually drag America into the European war. Its primary public spokesman was iconic aviator and hero Charles Lindbergh; with its many mass meetings and numerous sympathetic midwest newspapers and radio stations spreading its message, this minority movement (with which about one third of the country identified) had a disproportionate impact and influence in the U.S. during late 1940 and early 1941. The respective lobbying campaigns were fed not only by the catastrophe of Hitler's successful Western offensive in Europe in May and June, and by the drama of the Battle of Britain in August and September, but also by Franklin D. Roosevelt's unprecedented run for a third term as President, something that no one had ever done before. This, then, is the stage upon which the drama that unfolds in this chronology is set, and you now know the major players who shared the *domestic* stage with FDR. (You will read much about Winston Churchill in the chronology itself.) But what about President Roosevelt, the undecipherable sphinx who was President of the United States? The key question on everyone's mind from late July through early November of 1940 was: "Why is 'That Man in the White House' acting counter to the tradition established by George Washington and running for a *third term* as President? Is it to embroil us in the war in Europe, or to keep us out of war, by providing 'all aid short of war' to Great Britain?" What were his true concerns and motivations? What made him tick?

President Franklin Delano Roosevelt was an internationalist, who early-on, recognized the serious danger represented by a rearmed and aggressive Nazi Germany, and who foresaw with certainty by May of 1940, and possibly as early as September of 1939, the eventual need for America to fight Germany on the battlefield. But he was leading a nation that suffered from the illusion that it was protected from events in Europe and Asia by the Atlantic and Pacific Oceans; and whose citizenry was wary, and even cynical, about European politics because of its recent experiences during and following World War I---a nation which as a result, was overwhelmingly isolationist in sentiment. FDR was therefore loath to get out too much in front of public opinion in his attempt to enlist America in stopping Hitler. A previous misstep had cautioned him against this. His failed attempt to pack the Supreme Court in 1937 (and thereby eventually reverse its 1935 judgments that his principal New Deal programs were unconstitutional) was the result of political hubris---his court-packing scheme was launched in the confident flush of his 1936 landslide re-election victory---and following the failure of this attempt, and his equally embarrassing failure to exact revenge on his opponents during the 1938 mid-term elections, Roosevelt was determined never again to get out so far ahead of the public on any major issues. This very political mistake---proceeding boldly on a correct course of action without first educating the public and taking them with him---had led to President Woodrow Wilson's failure to persuade the Senate to ratify America's entry into the League of Nations following the end of World War I. As a result of America's withdrawal from European power politics at the end of World War I, the hope that "collective security" could successfully restrain aggression in the world was reduced; and unilateral efforts by the U.S. to restrain aggression during the 1930s were not taken seriously by the European powers.

Roosevelt, clearly recognizing throughout 1938 dictator Adolph Hitler's insatiable appetite for territorial expansion, and the high likelihood that he was intent upon a war of revenge and conquest (and appalled also by the appetites and behaviors of Fascist Italy and Imperial

Japan), saw a need for America to play a decisive role in the coming struggle to preserve civilization from the coming onslaught of Nazi barbarism. Germany's 1938 absorption first of Austria, and then of the Sudetenland in Czechoslovakia, caused FDR to be seriously concerned for the survival of the European democracies. So, freshly wounded by his struggles with Congress over the Supreme Court (which taught him that there were limits to his power, no matter how great his electoral victory in 1936), and mindful of the critical mistake of Woodrow Wilson in outdistancing public opinion (rather than first molding it, and taking the people with him in his quest for collective security), in 1939 Roosevelt embarked upon a serious, long-term effort to educate the American public about the interdependency of modern nations; the dangerous and misleading illusion of protection offered by the Atlantic and Pacific Oceans; and the danger to a stable world order and human rights posed by what he had branded the three "bandit nations"---Germany, Italy, and Japan. This patient effort to educate the U.S. public was only partially successful, for throughout 1941, while there was much sympathy for Great Britain's plight, and Americans shared a clear revulsion toward the behavior of Nazi Germany in Europe (and Japan in China), between 82 to 88 percent of the American people nevertheless consistently opposed going to war with Germany. Although Roosevelt's primary focus shifted in 1938 from domestic to foreign policy concerns, and even though he successfully persuaded and cajoled the American people (from mid-1940 through mid-1941) into providing "all material support short of war" to the nations defending themselves against Nazi and Fascist aggression, he clearly failed to develop a consensus that would have supported a declaration of war against Germany. Such an attempt, in late 1940 (with Great Britain standing alone and enduring heavy bombing of its cities by the German Luftwaffe), or even in the late summer and autumn of 1941 (after Germany had invaded the Soviet Union and had the USSR "on the ropes"), **would almost certainly not have passed in Congress,** and would have left FDR a failed, lame-duck President. This was made very clear to him by both the new science of public opinion polling, and by the loud voice of the isolationist movement (representing at its height about one third of the American people) and its many spokesmen in both the Congress and the national media. So, while many of his key cabinet advisors (knowing how imperative it was *not* to allow Great Britain or the USSR to "go under") advised him to declare war against Germany at various points throughout 1941, FDR would *not* request that Congress formally declare war against the Nazi regime, knowing that to request a declaration of war, and to fail in the attempt, would fatally weaken his Presidency. Equally unacceptable to Roosevelt was the specter of a knock-down, drag-out fight in Congress over a 'premature' war declaration that was out-of-step with the public mind. Public opinion polling made it clear that *even if he could* persuade Congress to declare war on Germany after a contentious debate, the measure would (at best) pass by only a small margin. This eventuality would have meant taking a seriously divided nation into war. ***That, to him, was a prescription for failure, and was to be avoided at all costs.***

Accordingly, FDR's successful effort from mid-1940, through early 1941, to commence sending all possible material aid to Great Britain, evolved in the autumn of 1941 into an undeclared war in the Atlantic Ocean against German submarines and surface raiders, ***in an attempt to provoke "an incident"*** (a shooting incident between the German Navy and the U.S. Navy) which would either provoke Hitler to declare war on the United States, or which the public would view as a *casus belli,* such as the mysterious explosion which sank the USS *Maine* in Havana Harbor in 1898, or the German torpedoing of the British ocean liner *Lusitania* during World War I. From January through November of 1941, Hitler steadfastly refused to "take the bait" and declare war on the U.S., either in response to America's strong material aid to Britain, or in response to naval incidents at sea. When three such duly anticipated "incidents" in the Atlantic, during the autumn of 1941, failed to incite a wary and cautious American public to go to war with Germany, ***provoking Japan to commit an act of war against the United States*** then became FDR's "next best option" for getting the United States into World War II.

It is now clear that commencing in October of 1940, Roosevelt's efforts to restrain Japan, and employ ***deterrence*** against further Japanese expansion, ***gradually evolved into a strategy to provoke Japan into committing an act of war against the United States,*** or at least into committing "mistakes" which would provide a *casus belli* in the Pacific. By signing the Tripartite Pact on September 27, 1940, Japan had formally become the third principal member of the Axis pact; as a result, it seemed that any overt attack on the U.S. by Japan would likely---by one means or another---eventually provide a "back door" for American entry into the war against Germany. Roosevelt's adoption of a strategy of ***provocation*** in the Pacific (vice mere ***deterrence***), which had first been suggested to him in October of 1940 by a strategy memo drafted within the Office of Naval Intelligence, took off in an accelerated fashion almost immediately after Hitler invaded the USSR on June 22, 1941. In July of 1941, Roosevelt became aware, via the American ability to break the highest-level Japanese diplomatic code, that Japan was definitely preparing for war (during this time of great opportunity when both the European colonial powers, and the USSR, were greatly weakened), and would soon strike ***either*** to the north in Siberia (against its traditional modern enemy, Russia), ***or*** move south, in an attempt to secure the mineral, food, and oil resources of Southeast Asia and the Dutch East Indies. (Already bogged down for four years in an exhausting war of attrition in mainland China, Japan did not have the resources to strike in both directions; it had to be either north, or south.) I agree with historian Waldo Heinrichs that Roosevelt placed his policy of provocation against Japan into high gear in July of 1941, in an attempt to ***prevent the Japanese from selecting the northern option,*** i.e., going to war against the Soviet Union. He knew that if Japan went to war against Russia it would likely cause the final collapse of the USSR, and he desired to prevent this at all costs, since the titanic struggle between Germany and the Soviet Union which began in June was likely, more than any other single factor, to decide the fate of Germany and the ultimate victor of

World War II. If Germany defeated the USSR, and gained access to its natural resources, then the downfall of Great Britain would only be a matter of time; and without a staging base in Great Britain, the U.S. could not hope to launch a bombing campaign against Germany, or an invasion of German-occupied France. Since the United States was providing about 90 per cent of Japan's oil in 1941, cutting off the sale of all crude oil to Japan in late July of that year forced Japan to abandon any possibility of pursuing its northern war option, and to opt for its southern strategy (where the main goal was to secure the oil in the Dutch East Indies). It was assumed (and correctly so) that Japan would view it necessary to attack the British colonies of Malaya and Singapore, and the American colony in the Philippines, in order to protect its new projected source of oil in the Dutch East Indies, since these British and American possessions lay athwart Japan's future lines of supply and communication with the islands we now call Indonesia. Roosevelt and his Cabinet learned definitively during September of 1941 that Japan had chosen the southern war option, and that Japan would *not* be going to war against Russia. As a consequence of this Japanese decision, in October of 1941, Joseph Stalin (who learned about the firm Japanese intention to invoke the southern option from his own source) shifted about 1.5 million troops from Siberia back to the area around Moscow, which proved instrumental in preventing the seizure of his capital by the Germans in December of 1941. Thus, Roosevelt's provocation of Japan in July of 1941 indirectly prevented the Germans from dealing a knockout blow to the USSR that year.

But successfully getting Japan to abandon the possibility of war with the Soviet Union, and to adopt its southern expansion strategy, did not necessarily answer the question: "Would a Japanese war against Western colonies in Southeast Asia and the Dutch East Indies provoke war with the United States?" Specifically, it was unclear whether the American people would demand a declaration of war against Japan if the Philippines were the only U.S. possession to be attacked. The U.S. had already granted the Philippines "Commonwealth Status," and agreed to grant the Filipinos their independence in the near future; most Americans did not, by any means, consider the Philippines a vital American interest.

Since FDR's principal goal was to get America into the fight against Nazi Germany, <u>he therefore continued his strategy of provoking Japan to commit acts of war directly against the United States, even after Japan decided not to go to war with the Soviet Union</u>. Roosevelt's continued provocation of Japan, it is my contention, was designed to provoke "incidents" between the armed forces of Japan and the U.S. military: unambiguous attacks on American troops, ships, and airplanes. A formal Japanese declaration of war on the U.S. would have served adequately to get the U.S. into hostilities against the Axis, but FDR knew that modern Japan had exhibited a propensity for surprise attacks **without an accompanying declaration of war,** which served his purposes even better---for a physical attack by the Japanese military <u>on the U.S. armed forces</u>, **preferably without any formal warning,** would serve better than a mere war declaration, in a diplomatic note, to unite the country and bring America into

World War II. The American people had not reacted as FDR had anticipated to German U-boat attacks in the autumn of 1941 on USS *Greer,* USS *Kearney,* and USS *Reuben James* in the Atlantic. Skittish about Roosevelt's obvious bias in favor of Great Britain, and mindful of the effect of the "Remember the Maine" *casus belli* that brought on the Spanish-American War in 1898, the American public seemed determined not to let isolated incidents between individual German U-boat commanders and individual American destroyer skippers drag America into World War II. Americans simply did not want to fight what appeared to be an invincible Germany, during 1940 and 1941. But FDR remembered that the American people had reacted sharply to Japan's intentional bombing and destruction of the American gunboat *Panay* in China, in 1937. He sensed, correctly, that a serious "incident" between the Japanese military and the U.S. military, if it occurred in an unambiguous manner---or preferably, a full-scale attack---might affect the country quite differently than had the three isolated incidents in the Atlantic between individual U.S. ships and German submarines.

What most Americans are unaware of today---and what no one but a few select officials and codebreakers knew at the time---is that in August of 1941, Hitler secretly promised the Japanese ambassador in Berlin that if Japan found itself in hostilities with the United States, he would wage war on America. Roosevelt learned of this that same month, via the broken Japanese diplomatic code (known as "Purple" by the Americans). The Tripartite Pact of September 1940 between Germany, Italy, and Japan was technically only a **defensive** pact, which guaranteed its members that if any one of them were *attacked by a third power (i.e., the U.S.),* the others would come to their aid. Hitler's secret promise to Baron Oshima in August of 1941 was significant, for it guaranteed that hostilities between the U.S. and Japan, even if initiated by Japan, would result in war between Germany and the United States. This promise, not known to the American public and completely believable (since it was made in secret, i.e., was not a mere treaty agreement or propaganda ploy, and was made to a highly trusted and respected Japanese ambassador with long-established, intimate access to the Nazi power elite), provided FDR with his true "back door" to the war he knew the United States *must fight* with Nazi Germany. Two months later, in October 1941, FDR became aware (through more diplomatic codebreaking) that Tokyo had instructed its consulate in Honolulu to report regularly on detailed information about U.S. naval ship movements **within Pearl Harbor,** including where specific ship types were moored when inport. This so-called "bomb plot" message was never shared with the Army or Navy commanders in Hawaii. (Furthermore, two high-ranking Naval officers in Washington who had unsuccessfully insisted on sharing it with the Hawaiian commands were summarily relieved and transferred out of Washington.) And even though Japan did not invade the USSR, and Stalin was able to successfully transfer 1.5 million troops from Siberia to Russia in October, Roosevelt continued to tighten the screws on Japan, diplomatically, throughout November 1941---delivering, in late November, a *defacto* ultimatum to Japan that he knew would be found unacceptable at just the moment when he was aware the Japanese government was approaching a self-imposed deadline for the commencement of the southern Pacific war.

The Japanese struck simultaneously all over Southeast Asia and the Central Pacific on December 7, 1941 American time (December 8, 1941 in the Far East). The American Cabinet and President knew from both the diplomatic codebreaking efforts, as well as intelligence reports of the disposition of Japanese forces, that war was imminent in late November/early December in the Pacific. Japan's southern strategy was known in Washington, and only the exact timing (and exact locations) of the blows in that region were uncertain. Furthermore, there exists today strong *circumstantial* evidence <u>that the very highest levels of the American leadership in Washington also knew that Hawaii was going to be a target</u>, even though the U.S. government has always officially denied foreknowledge of the Pearl Harbor attack. (The chronology below will present this evidence, in detail, and will be followed by a discussion of how much weight to assign to that evidence.) Diplomatic codebreaking revealed that the Nazi government <u>reiterated</u> to the Japanese Ambassador, in early December 1941, just prior to Japan's initiation of war all over Southeast Asia and against Pearl Harbor, its intention to make war on the United States should Japan and the U.S. find themselves engaged in hostilities. It seems clear, therefore, why Franklin D. Roosevelt did *not* ask Congress for a declaration of war against *both* Germany and Japan on December 8, 1941, the day after the Japanese attack on Pearl Harbor, the Philippines, Wake, Guam, and Midway: he knew that Hitler was going to solve his "Germany problem" for him, so FDR cautiously and prudently requested only a declaration of war on Japan. (If FDR had requested on December 8, 1941 that the Congress declare war **on Germany, as well,** <u>he might have fractured a united public, and drawn immediate suspicion upon himself</u>, since only Japan, and not Germany, had attacked the United States on December 7th.) And sure enough, on December 11, 1941---just four days after Pearl Harbor---Germany and Italy both declared war on the United States. FDR sent a request for a declaration of war against Germany and Italy to Congress that same night, and Congress immediately complied in kind. The desired lineup was now complete. Roosevelt's strategy to provoke Japan into moving south (instead of north) had succeeded beyond his wildest dreams: this strategy had *not only* kept Japan from attacking the USSR and therefore helped to keep Stalin in the war against Hitler, but FDR's series of provocations against Japan (diplomatic, military, and economic measures he knew Japan would not long tolerate) had provided his "back door" to war between the United States and Germany, the principal threat in the Second World War. Japan's direct assault on U.S. military forces had occurred in such a manner (without a prior declaration of war), and with such overwhelming force, that it presented Roosevelt with an American citizenry united in its rage, and determined to exact revenge; isolationism was dead on the morning of December 8, 1941. (There was only one dissenting vote in Congress when it declared war on Japan.) When Hitler declared war on the United States on December 11, 1941, an enraged and united public barely blinked. FDR had proven to be a master chess player, and had checkmated Adolf Hitler and the Axis by sacrificing some of his pawns (Wake and Guam), a knight (the Philippines), and a rook (the fleet at Pearl Harbor). And even though the U.S. had been required to passively absorb the first blow for his strategy to succeed---and in spite of the fact that this first blow was much worse than FDR had ever dreamed it would be---*war with Japan did not threaten the existence of the United States.*

Early in 1941, during joint contingency planning sessions between the U.S. and British military staffs in Washington, D.C., it was agreed that in the event of war between America and Great Britain on the one hand, and Germany and Japan on the other, that a "Germany first" strategy would be pursued, since Germany was the primary danger, from the standpoint of industrial plant and war-making ability. Despite the intense anger in America over the Japanese attack, and despite several setbacks early in the war in the Pacific (in which the United States suffered noteworthy military reverses), the "Germany first" strategy was confirmed at the Arcadia Conference in Washington in December '41-January '42. Throughout World War II---as planned---the European Theater of War received 85% of American war materiel, and the Pacific Theater received only 15%. This was made possible by the fact that America's industrial potential (before the war) was ten times that of Japan---a situation that only grew more disproportional as the war proceeded and the U.S. gradually imposed a very effective blockade around Japan, starving it of strategic materials. Roosevelt knew exactly what he was doing when he provoked Japan to make war on the United States, and history has borne that out. (While Japan had the world's third largest Navy in December of 1941, and arguably the world's *best trained* Navy at the time, it was a resource-poor nation with a middling industrial base, insufficient to conduct a long war against a strong opponent.) There was no other way to get a united American public into the war against Germany. And the horrific, violent, and brutal excesses of both the Nazi state and the Japanese Empire---their crimes against humanity, committed on a scale never before seen in human history---justify the strategy taken by Franklin D. Roosevelt in 1940 and 1941. Having tried to provoke war directly with Germany and failed, he successfully adopted his fallback plan and went to war with Germany through the "back door," *via a war he successfully provoked with Germany's ally, Japan*. Roosevelt has been variously described as "cold as ice" and completely detached emotionally from the people around him when he had to make difficult decisions, and many historians have correctly noted that he never completely shared his innermost thoughts with anyone; discouraged note-taking during cabinet meetings; and intentionally did not leave any written records of his private planning and strategy. His personality has appropriately been described as impenetrable. In the absence of such records, the chronology detailed below allows us to **infer** both his innermost thoughts, and his private strategy, as he dealt with the challenge of how to successfully counter the Axis threat during the years leading up to America's entry into the Second World War. In the words of historian Waldo Heinrichs, author of *Threshold of War* (p. vii), "By striving for comprehensiveness we may…gain a better understanding of the foreign policy of Franklin D. Roosevelt…this most elusive and dissembling of Presidents…".

CHRONOLOGY

Dates	Events	Remarks
September 18, 1931	Mukden Incident	The Kwantung Army, in Southern Manchuria to protect Japanese economic interests and citizens, stages a pretext (by setting off a small bomb on a railway line and blaming it on Chinese soldiers) to justify the invasion and seizure of Manchuria by Japan. This action is taken without the knowledge or permission of the Tokyo government, or of Army headquarters.
September 19, 1931 through February 27, 1932	The Japanese Army seizes both Southern and Northern Manchuria from Chinese Warlords. (The Japanese puppet state of "Manchukuo" is established in Manchuria on February 18, 1932.)	This action receives the belated blessings of both the Tokyo government, and of Army headquarters, once its success is realized. This acquiescence presages increasing control over Japanese foreign policy by the military. The public in Japan has more faith in the Army to solve the economic problems of the worldwide depression, than in despised and corrupt civilian politicians. Japan is a resource-poor, overpopulated nation which dreams of emulating European colonialism by establishing strong spheres of influence (i.e., an Empire) throughout Asia---principally, by dominating a weak China politically and economically.
September 1932	A League of Nations commission reported formally on the Manchurian Incident (the Lytton Report) and placed	The commission performed its work after China lodged a complaint with the League of Nations. The report was made public on October 2, 1932. Knowing the contents of the report ahead of time,

		all of the blame fully on Japan.	Japan recognized the puppet state of "Manchukuo" on September 16, 1932, before the report was released.
January 30, 1933		Adolf Hitler is appointed Chancellor of Germany by President Paul von Hindenburg.	The Nazi party never achieved a majority in the German parliament prior to this time, but it did win a plurality of the vote. After refusing the Vice-Chancellorship earlier, Hitler was finally given what he wanted by people who disliked him, but who thought they could control him.
February 1933		The League of Nations formally censures Japan and demands its withdrawal from Manchuria.	Forty (40) nations voted against Japan, one nation (Siam) abstained, and only Japan voted against the measure. Instead of withdrawing from Manchuria, Japan quits the League of Nations.
February 27, 1933		The German parliament building, the Reichstag, is mysteriously destroyed by fire.	The communists are blamed for the fire (which some historians assume was set by the Nazis), and are banned from politics.
March 4, 1933		Franklin D. Roosevelt is sworn in as the thirty second President of the United States	Roosevelt inherits a nation at the nadir of the worst depression in its history, with 25% of the work force unemployed; farm prices down 60%; with industry producing only half of what it had been producing in 1929; and with banks failing. He spends the next four years restoring confidence in the economy and the banking system through a series of vital reforms, based on extensive government regulation, experimental intervention, and stimulus programs. Four years later, in 1937, although unemployment remains high, productivity has increased; capitalism has been reformed; the government has provided numerous forms of assistance

		for the dispossessed and unemployed; and democracy in America, and indeed, the union itself, has been preserved. Roosevelt is an internationalist who strongly admires Woodrow Wilson, the U.S. President who founded the League of Nations following World War I. FDR believes throughout the 1930s that the best way to stay out of war is through international engagement, not through withdrawal from international affairs, and isolationism. (The vast majority of the American people, disillusioned and cynical after World War I, do not agree with him.) FDR's primary, and almost exclusive, focus during his first four years in office is naturally on domestic economic affairs, and not on international politics.
March 23, 1933	The Reichstag passes the Enabling Act in Germany, giving the Chancellor and his cabinet emergency powers.	After gaining the cooperation of other parties to ram this emergency legislation through the Reichstag by means of intimidation, the Nazis slowly squeeze them all out of existence over the next 4 months. The Enabling Act gives the cabinet and the Chancellor law-making powers, and emasculates the Reichstag, which henceforth is a rubber-stamp body.
July 14, 1933	The Nazi party becomes the sole legal political party in Germany.	As of this date, Adolph Hitler effectively becomes a dictator. (Some historians believe this occurred with the passage of The Enabling Act on March 23rd.)
June 30, 1934	"Night of the Long Knives"	Hitler carries out a bloody purge of the more radical, revolutionary members of his party who are members of the large, violent paramilitary group called the SA (i.e., the "brownshirts," or "storm

		troopers"), killing scores of people. He does this to mollify the Army (the Reichswehr) and the industrialists, who fear a social revolution. Hitler also uses this opportunity to kill off conservative opposition. (The Social Democrats and Communists had all been removed as threats in the spring of 1933.)
August 2, 1934	German President Paul von Hindenburg, long senile and in ill health, dies.	Upon the death of Hindenburg, the cabinet enacted a law making Hitler both Chancellor and President. In so doing, Hitler is made Head of State, in addition to being chief political leader in Germany. There is now no one left who can remove him from office legally.
August 14, 1934	By plebiscite, the German public approves the merging of the offices of President and Chancellor by a vote of 84.6%.	As Head of State, Hitler is now also Supreme Commander of the armed forces. Members of the armed forces are subsequently required to take a personal loyalty oath to Adolph Hitler (not to the state or to the constitution).
August 31, 1935	The Neutrality Act, passed by the U.S. Congress, is signed by President Roosevelt. Set to expire after 6 months, and stimulated by growing tensions between Italy and Abyssinia, it imposed a general embargo on the export of arms, ammunition, or implements of war with all parties in a war. It also declared that all Americans traveling on the ships of warring	This, the first in a series of laws enacted during the 1930s, was the response to a widespread belief in the United States that America was dragged into World War I unnecessarily by bankers and arms dealers for profit reasons. The goal of the Neutrality Acts was to prevent U.S. involvement in foreign wars by prohibiting trade in the implements of war with all belligerents, without distinguishing between the aggressors and the victims. Both the President and the Secretary of State were critical of the Neutrality Acts, believing that they would restrict the administration's ability to support its allies in various

	nations did so at their own risk. The act required the President to first declare that a state of war existed (and thus activate the law's provisions while identifying the belligerents), and to specifically define which materials were prohibited from export.	contingencies. Roosevelt and Hull would both have preferred powers to impose a discretionary arms embargo, discriminating against aggressors; and yet Roosevelt signed the original Act in 1935. Renewals and amendments meant that there were five pieces of neutrality legislation between 1935 and 1937, designed to prevent any recurrence of the circumstances that had led to American intervention in the First World War. (The Johnson Act, passed earlier in 1934, also prevented the granting of loans and credits to any nations that had defaulted on their war debts to the U.S. following World War I; this was specifically aimed at Great Britain.) Although Congressional support for the series of Neutrality Acts (in 1935, 1936, 1937, and 1939) was strong, it was insufficient to override a Presidential veto. FDR nevertheless signed them all into law because he felt he could not afford to alienate Southern Democrats, whose votes he needed for his legislative programs. With considerable reluctance, Roosevelt signed each of the Neutrality Acts into law. (Only the "cash and carry" amendment incorporated into the 1939 Act was welcomed by Roosevelt.)[1]
October 3, 1935	Italy invades Abyssinia (Ethiopia) after a long military buildup in its neighboring colonies, and an extended period of tensions and earlier	Great Britain sponsored a League of Nations arms embargo against Italy during the run-up to the invasion, which proved ineffective. However, strong moral censure by the League of Nations drove Italian dictator Benito Mussolini

---

[1] See *Wikipedia* entry titled: "Neutrality Acts of 1930s;" and Kershaw, *Fateful Choices,* 189.

	border clashes. The war ends on May 5, 1936, and Italy's conquered territory is merged with two nearby Italian colonies to form "Italian East Africa." Mussolini's declared intention is to build a New Roman Empire in the Mediterranean and North African regions.	into a close relationship with Hitler's Germany, a regime he had previously disliked and distrusted. (Mussolini's Italy had previously opposed Germany's interference in Austrian politics, and its observed desire to annex that nation, in 1934.) This failure to prevent an invasion of Ethiopia was a disaster for the concept of "collective security"---the League had only imposed an embargo without teeth, and had failed to take military action (such as blockading Italy or closing the Suez Canal)---and was the death knell of the League of Nations. (Italy would leave the League of Nations in 1937.)
February 29, 1936	The Neutrality Act (which was originally good for only 6 months) is extended for another 14 months, and one important provision was added which forbade all loans or credits to belligerents.	Roosevelt had invoked the Neutrality Act following Italy's invasion of Abyssinia (Ethiopia) in October of 1935.
March 7, 1936	**Germany occupies the Rhineland (a demilitarized zone following Germany's defeat in World War I) with troops, which had been forbidden by the Treaty of Versailles following World War I.** This open defiance of the Versailles Treaty had been preceded in March of 1935 by Germany's	Hitler had embarked upon immediate rearmament when he assumed office, in violation of the Versailles treaty, and none of the victorious powers did anything about it. **His occupation of the Rhineland (German territory bordering France) with a token military force was a bluff---he was prepared to withdraw if challenged by military force from France or England---but no one called his bluff.** (Germany had withdrawn from the League of Nations in 1933.) His

	announcement that it was building both an air force, and a large army through conscription; both acts were violations of the Versailles Treaty, yet the Western powers had failed to act, presumably emboldening Hitler.	successful remilitarization of the Rhineland effectively sounded the death knell of the remaining provisions of the Treaty of Versailles. This increased his willingness to take risks, and he correctly sensed great political weakness in the formerly victorious Western powers---a desire to avoid armed conflict at any cost.
July 17, 1936	The Spanish Civil War begins (and will not end until April 1, 1939).	The extremely brutal Spanish Civil War between the forces of the Left (the Republican government, which was strongly leftist and anti-clerical) and the Right (which was pro-Monarchy, Fascist, and had the strong support of the Catholic Church in Spain), resulted in the deaths of approximately 300,000 people, of which probably more than 120,000 were civilians executed by both sides. This civil war became, in a sense, a proxy war aided by foreign assistance, with the armed forces of first Germany, and then Italy, aiding the Right; and with weapons from the Soviet Union aiding the Left (the Republican government). Hitler enthusiastically ordered three major military operations to assist the Fascists in Spain, with forces eventually numbering about 12,000 men, and including a total of 600 planes, 200 tanks, and 1,000 artillery pieces. Determined not to be outdone by Hitler, Mussolini contributed at one point a maximum of about 50,000 troops, and Italy's support included a total of about 660 planes, 150 tanks, and 1,000 artillery pieces. The USSR ignored the League of Nations embargo (when few other League members would do so) and sold

		the Republican government 806 planes, 362 tanks, and 1,555 artillery pieces, many of them antique or obsolete models. Soviet troops numbered only about 700, but advisors and "volunteers" numbered between 2,000-3,000 men, while the activities of the NKVD (secret police) were pervasive. Thus, the Spanish Civil War became a testing ground for new German and Italian weapons, and allowed Hitler and Mussolini to blood their troops, while it allowed Stalin to plunder the gold reserves of the Spanish government in payment for his ageing and obsolete weapons. The German Luftwaffe's Condor Legion demonstrated to the world, for the first time, the horrors of mass terror bombing of civilians in cities.[2]
October 25, 1936	Italy and Germany sign a treaty of friendship.	On November 26, 1936, Italian dictator Mussolini, in referring to this treaty, proclaimed an "axis" between Rome and Berlin around which the other nations in Europe (and the world) would revolve. On May 22, 1939, this relationship evolved into an alliance, called the "Pact of Steel." Later still, on September 27, 1940, a third principal member would join the "Axis" when Germany, Italy, and Japan signed the Tripartite Pact, a defensive alliance aimed at keeping the United States out of World War II, and on the sidelines.
November 25, 1936	The "Anti-Comintern Pact" was signed between	This defensive *political* alliance against the Communist International (i.e., the

---

[2] See *Wikipedia* entry titled: "Spanish Civil War."

	Germany and Japan.	Soviet Union) was later joined by Italy on November 6, 1937, serving as a preview of the Tripartite Pact (the defensive *military* alliance aimed at the United States), which was to be signed on September 27, 1940.
May 1, 1937	**The latest Neutrality Act revision is signed by President Roosevelt.**[3] This version of the Neutrality Act included the provisions of the earlier Acts, this time without an expiration date, ***and extended them to cover civil wars as well.*** Furthermore, U.S. flag ships were prohibited from transporting any passengers or articles to belligerents, and U.S. citizens were prohibited from traveling on ships of belligerent nations.	The Neutrality Acts of 1935 and 1936 had not covered civil wars occurring within individual countries, where there was no formal declaration of war between independent states. As a result, several U.S. companies (Texaco, Standard Oil, Ford, General Motors, and Studebaker) had engaged in trade with the forces of the Right in Spain, and by 1939 Fascist General Franco, the eventual victor in Spain's civil war, owed these and other companies more than $100,000,000.00. A ***cash-and-carry provision*** designed by Roosevelt's advisor Bernard Baruch was added to the act, which permitted belligerents to purchase materials and supplies as long as the recipients arranged for the transport on non-U.S. flag ships and paid immediately in cash. This cash-and-carry provision was set to expire in two years, in May of 1939. Early in 1939, after Germany had gobbled up the

---

[3] In the PBS documentary *FDR,* historian Robert Dallek summarized Roosevelt's dilemma as he saw the danger from Nazi Germany, Italy and Japan growing: "Roosevelt, from the start of his Presidency, is troubled by Hitler, and privately, is deeply concerned, but he's not going to say anything in public [because] he knows the country is so opposed to anything that would involve it in European power politics. And so, he caters to the isolationist and pacifist sentiment in the country. But if he had had his druthers, he would avoid war not by retreating from international politics, but by participation in international politics. And so, it's a matter of method. He wants to avoid war, but the way to do it, he feels, is not to be isolationist, not to pass these Neutrality bills, but for the United States to be assertive and play a significant role in international power politics."

		remainder of Czechoslovakia in March, Roosevelt lobbied the Congress to have the two year cash-and-carry provision renewed (hoping to assist Great Britain and France in the event of a future war with Germany). He was rebuffed by Congress, and the two year provision lapsed.
July 7, 1937	**The Sino-Japanese War Begins** with the "Marco Polo Bridge Incident," and lasts until September 9, 1945, when Japan surrenders at the end of World War II. During the eight year war, about 3.22 million Chinese soldiers are killed; and over 9.13 million Chinese civilians are killed through collateral damage, and another 8.4 million civilians die from indirect results of the war. Approximately 396,000 Japanese soldiers and sailors are killed in the China conflict.[4]	The proximate cause of Japan's full scale war with China was a series of troop clashes throughout July 1937 between Japanese and Nationalist Chinese troops near the Marco Polo Bridge, near Peking (possibly instigated by Chinese Communist troops under Mao Tse-Dung). But the true, underlying cause was Japan's attitude that it was destined to dominate and exploit a fractured China, whose old, Feudal system had been cast aside with the success of its revolution in 1912. Since 1927 China had been in the midst of its own civil war (between the Nationalists under Chiang Kai-shek and the Communists under Mao Tse-Dung). Japan had defeated China earlier during its first modern war (the First Sino-Japanese War), in 1894-5, and since that time its policy had been to dominate China politically, militarily, and economically, exploiting China's resources (food, labor, and mineral ore).[5] There had been many "incidents" between the Japanese military and Chinese Warlords since 1931, none of which had escalated into full scale war.

---

[4] See *Wikipedia* entry: "Second Sino-Japanese War."

[5] Toland, *The Rising Sun,* 43-47.

		When Japan seized the Chinese city of Peking following the "Marco Polo Bridge Incident," the Chinese Nationalist Army under Chiang Kai-shek mobilized, and a full scale war ensued, beginning with horrific casualties and fierce fighting in and around the city of Shanghai.[6] Roosevelt (who favored the Chinese in their war against Japan) refused to invoke the provisions of the Neutrality Act in the Sino-Japanese War, citing the technicality that neither country had declared war. (The cash-and-carry provisions would primarily have benefited the Japanese, who had a large merchant fleet.) This enraged the isolationists in the U.S.; consequently, FDR prohibited American merchant ships from carrying arms to China, but permitted British ships to transport American arms to China. He then imposed a "moral embargo" on the export of U.S.-built aircraft to Japan.[7]
October 5, 1937	**FDR Makes His "Quarantine Speech," likening aggressor nations to a disease which had to be quarantined** to prevent its spread.[8] (It was greeted by howls of protest and alarm from the isolationists in the	Key passages from this speech include the following: "The present reign of terror and international lawlessness began a few years ago…and has now reached a stage where the very foundations of civilization are seriously threatened." He continued, "Without a declaration of war, and without warning or justification of any kind, civilians, including vast numbers of women and

---

[6] See *Wikipedia* entry titled: "Second Sino-Japanese War."

[7] See *Wikipedia* entry titled: "Neutrality Acts of 1930s."

[8] Hunt, ed., *The Essential Franklin Delano Roosevelt,* 141-144.

	United States, even though Roosevelt proposed no specific program or concrete actions in his address.)	children, are being ruthlessly murdered with bombs from the air…Nations are fomenting and taking sides in civil warfare in nations that have never done them any harm." Concluding, FDR summarized: "It seems to be unfortunately true that the epidemic of world lawlessness is spreading. When an epidemic of physical disease starts to spread, the community approves and joins in a quarantine of the patients in order to protect the health of the community against the spread of the disease." FDR had come to refer privately to Italy, Germany, and Japan as "the bandit nations."[9]
December 12, 1937	Aircraft of the Imperial Japanese Navy intentionally sink the American gunboat USS *Panay*, which was anchored in the Yangtze river outside the city of Nanking. The attack was captured on motion picture film by a newsreel cameraman, and witnessed by an Italian journalist who was onboard. A week earlier the British gunboat *Ladybird* had been shelled and seized by the Japanese Army.[10]	Two Americans were killed, including the Captain of USS *Panay,* and 43 crew members and five civilians were wounded. The Japanese Government formally apologized on Christmas Eve, and paid an indemnity of $ 2,214,007.00. While the Japanese claimed the incident was a mistake, U.S. military communications intelligence specialists in the Asiatic Fleet intercepted radio messages proving that the incident was intentional, and was planned.[11] U.S. Ambassador Joseph C. Grew initially feared the incident could rupture diplomatic relations between the U.S. and Japan, such was the anger in the United States. President Roosevelt was so angry that he initially considered a

---

[9] Dallek, *Franklin D. Roosevelt and American Foreign Policy,* 144-153.

[10] Ibid., 153-155.

		naval blockade to deny Japan of vital raw materials, but was quickly dissuaded by lack of British support.[12]
December 13, 1937	The "Rape of Nanking," a six week period of raping, looting, and murder by the Japanese Army, began on this date. (Somewhere between 20,000 and 80,000 women were raped by Japanese Army soldiers.)	After the fall of the Nationalist Chinese capital city on December 13th, the Japanese Army, out of control, in an orgy of rape, torture, and murder, wantonly butchered somewhere between 200,000 and 300,000 people. This event had a profound effect on world opinion.[13]
March 12, 1938	**Germany Annexes Austria in what Hitler calls the "Anschluss."**	Capitalizing on many, many months of agitation and propaganda, Nazi elements in Austria stage a coup on March 11, 1938, and cancel a planned referendum in which the Austrians were soon to vote to determine whether or not they wished to be annexed by Germany. [The Austrian Chancellor, Schuschnigg, who had been resisting Hitler's demands to share power with Austrian Nazis, was in favor of the referendum.] The next day, on March 12, 1938, Nazi military formations drive into Austria unopposed, and Hitler gloats in a public speech to adoring crowds in Vienna. Hitler has absorbed Austria (his birthplace) into Germany, and has begun to build the greater German Reich he wrote of in his autobiographical political tract, *Mein Kampf*. Aside from the emotional satisfaction this gives him---more

---

[11] Prados, *Combined Fleet Decoded,* 48-52.

[12] Toland, *The Rising Sun,* 48-50.

[13] Ibid., 50-51; and *Wikipedia* entry titled: "Nanking Massacre."

		importantly---Austria gives Germany access to key mountain passes into Czechoslovakia, his next target on the road to building his German Empire.
September 30, 1938	**The "Munich Pact,"** agreed to on September 29, 1938 and signed by England, France, Italy, and Germany in the early hours of September 30th, allows Germany to annex the Sudetenland, key areas around the borders of Czechoslovakia inhabited by ethnic Germans. Hitler claimed that this was his last territorial ambition in Europe. Czechoslovakia was not invited to participate in the four power discussions about its future, and was told by Great Britain that it would have to fight on alone against Germany if it did not accept the pact. The Czechs reluctantly bowed to reality by accepting the "Munich Dictat." This calculated giveaway, popular at the time in Great Britain and France, is now universally despised and recognized as the ultimate symbol of the failure of any and all policies of ***appeasement***. (Roosevelt was a	**The German Army immediately occupied the Sudetenland,** in which were located most of the rugged, mountainous defenses that the Czechs would have used to defend themselves if invaded. Hitler's diplomatic victory at Munich over timid British and French leaders, militarily unprepared and terrified of another European World War, was roundly hailed at the time by the relieved British and French publics, who did not want to go to war unless attacked. Hitler had loudly and often threatened war over Czechoslovakia, simultaneously fomenting Nazi agitation within the Sudetenland, while visibly moving large segments of his army up to the Czech border. He privately told his army that he would go to war if the British and the French did not give him the Sudetenland. The German military command structure had privately objected strenuously to Hitler's plans for war with the Czechs, telling him that it would precipitate a Second World War that Germany could not win. Key members of the German military secretly planned a coup against Hitler, providing the British and French would *not* cave in and grant him the Sudetenland, *and* if he still persisted and actually ordered war against Czechoslovakia. When Hitler triumphed at the Munich conference, the coup fizzled, and Europe missed its last chance to avoid World War II. Hitler was

"powerless spectator" of events at Munich, the leader of "an unarmed, economically wounded, and diplomatically isolated country."[14])

The British Prime Minister, Neville Chamberlain, first discussed the partition of Czechoslovakia with Hitler at Berchtesgaden on September 15th; Chamberlain then flew to Godesberg to again meet with Hitler on September 22nd; and Chamberlain's final journey, to Munich, took place on September 29th. Chamberlain returned to London on October 1st brandishing an Anglo-German head of state agreement pledging that the two nations would never go to war again, and claiming "peace with honor." The public reaction was one of relief and joy, and for a brief time Chamberlain was an international hero. MP Winston Churchill, who vociferously opposed the dismemberment of Czechoslovakia, emboldened by his success at Munich, and his military leadership was cowed into submission ever after. One of the lonely voices of dissent in Great Britain was an out-of-power conservative MP named **Winston Churchill,** who said to Parliament on October 5, 1938: ***"We have sustained a total and unmitigated defeat…All is over.* Silent, mournful, abandoned, broken, Czechoslovakia recedes into the darkness.** She has suffered in every respect by her association with the Western democracies and with the League of Nations, of which she has always been an obedient servant…We are in the presence of a disaster of the first magnitude which has befallen Great Britain and France. Do not let us blind ourselves to that. It must now be accepted that all the countries of Central and Eastern Europe will make the best terms they can with the triumphant Nazi Power…<u>there can never be friendship between the British democracy and Nazi Power, that Power which spurns Christian ethics, which cheers its onward course by a barbarous paganism, which vaunts the spirit of aggression and conquest, which derives strength and perverted pleasure from persecution</u>…*What I find unendurable is the sense of our country falling into the power, into the orbit and influence of Nazi Germany, and of our existence becoming dependent upon their goodwill or pleasure*…**we have sustained a defeat without a war,** the

---

[14] Rosen, *Saving the Jews,* 75.

	courageously struck a different note (at right), and correctly predicted that the Nazi state would soon violate the Munich agreement, and gobble up the remainder of Czechoslovakia. (It did so in short order, on March 14, 1939.)	consequences of which will travel far with us along our road…we have passed an awful milestone in our history, when the whole equilibrium of Europe has been deranged, and…*the terrible words have for the time being been pronounced against the Western Democracies:* **'Thou art weighed in the balance and found wanting.'**"[15] [Emphasis added]
October 16, 1938	**Winston Churchill (who is a mere member of Parliament and holds no national office at this time), addresses the American people via radio broadcast from London.** He had numerous social contacts among the rich and influential in America, and had been a traveling lecturer in the United States during the early 1930s. He was fairly well known to educated Americans, as a man of letters who had already had a distinguished political career, who had written (and lectured) about his many experiences in the Great War, and about his illustrious military ancestor, the Duke of	Churchill, whose mother was an American (and who had a lifelong love affair with the United States), sensing that American support will eventually be required to stop Hitler, attempts to educate and warn the American public about the recent events in Europe, saying: "I avail myself with relief of the opportunity of speaking to the people of the United States. I do not know how long such liberties will be allowed. The stations of uncensored expression are closing down; **the lights are going out;** but there is still time for those to whom freedom and Parliamentary expression mean something, to consult together…The American people have, it seems to me, formed a true judgment upon the disaster which has befallen Europe. They realize, perhaps more clearly than the British and French publics have yet done, the far-reaching consequences of the abandonment and ruin of the Czechoslovak Republic…The culminating question to which I have been leading is whether the world as we

---

[15] Churchill, ed., *Never Give In!,* 171-182; James, ed., *Churchill Speaks,* 653-662.

		Marlborough.	have known it…should meet this menace by submission or resistance…Europe lies at this moment abashed and distracted before the triumphant assertions of a dictatorial power…Far away, happily protected by the Atlantic and Pacific Oceans, you, the people of the United States…are the spectators…**We are left in no doubt where American conviction and sympathies lie; but will you wait until British freedom and independence have succumbed, and then take up the cause when it is three quarters ruined, yourselves alone?**…It is not in the power of one nation, no matter how formidably armed, still less is it in the power of a small group of men, violent, ruthless men…to cramp and fetter the forward march of human destiny…We must arm. Britain must arm. America must arm. If, through an earnest desire for peace, we [in Britain] have placed ourselves at a disadvantage, we must make up for it by redoubled exertions, and, if necessary, by fortitude in suffering…But I hold the belief that we have now at last got far enough ahead of barbarism to control it, and to avert it, if only we realize what is afoot and make up our minds in time…We need the swift gathering of forces to confront not only military but moral aggression; the resolute and sober acceptance of their duty by the English-speaking peoples, and by all the nations, great and small, who wish to walk with them."[16] [Emphasis added]

---

[16] Churchill, ed., *Never Give In!,* 182-185.

November 9-10, 1938	**"Kristallnacht"** (or "The Night of Broken Glass") takes place in Germany. Using the killing of a Nazi diplomat in France by a young Jew (Herschel Grynszpan) as a pretext, what came to be known as *Kristallnacht* was a modern pogrom, a well-orchestrated series of anti-Jewish riots and actions throughout Germany and the former Austria, in which Hitler unleashed his SA "storm troopers," the "brownshirts," who had been largely muzzled (to please the Army and the industrialists, who feared revolution) since the bloody purge of radical Nazi party members on June 30, 1934.	Antisemitic mobs smashed, looted, and burned Jewish businesses, homes, and most of Germany's synagogues (and destroyed all 21 Jewish synagogues in Vienna). Thousands of Jews were arrested and sent to concentration camps. After *Kristallnacht*, the Nazi regime levied an "atonement fine" of one billion Reichsmarks against Germany's Jews (thus adding insult to injury, making them pay for the damage done by others against them), closed all Jewish retail businesses, and announced the liquidation of real estate, securities, and industrial firms owned by Jews. Americans were outraged. President Roosevelt recalled the American ambassador in Berlin for consultations, and in a written public statement, said: "The news of the past few days from Germany has deeply shocked public opinion in the United States…I myself could scarcely believe that such things could occur in a twentieth-century civilization." No U.S. ambassador returned to Germany until after the end of the Second World War and the defeat and ouster of the Nazi regime. Roosevelt was the only important world leader to openly and strongly criticize Germany. While some called FDR's action a mere gesture, it was all he could do, short of breaking diplomatic relations (an action usually reserved for countries about to go to war with each other).[17]
March 15, 1939	**Germany invades and**	This heinous action by Adoph Hitler

---

[17] Rosen, *Saving the Jews,* 75-77.

	absorbs the remainder of Czechoslovakia (Prague, Bohemia, and Moravia); a silent, hateful, and embittered populace offers no armed resistance. The German Third Reich now includes all of the former nations of Austria and Czechoslovakia (except for two small portions of Czechoslovakia which had been taken by Poland and Hungary after Munich), and Hitler has absorbed these territories without firing a shot, through the use of bluff and intimidation.	forever proved the foolhardiness of accepting his public promises, or of taking any stock in treaties or written agreements signed with Nazi Germany. With this action, British Prime Minister Neville Chamberlain (the architect of appeasement at Munich) realized the error in his appeasement policy, and his egregious mistake in believing that Hitler was someone he could do business with. Accordingly, on March 31, 1939, Chamberlain publicly stated that the British government would unilaterally guarantee the territorial integrity of Poland, Germany's next presumed victim, and announced that France was joining in this guarantee.
April 14, 1939	President Roosevelt sends a strong diplomatic message---in effect, a sermon and a moral scolding---to Hitler (and forwards an identical message to Mussolini), and broadcasts it to the world, with powerful effect, the next day. The message asks Hitler to stop his course of conquest and to assure the nations of the world nearest to Germany (naming 31 other nations, specifically, by name) that they would not be invaded. Hitler	FDR did not have any illusions that his message would truly cause Hitler or Mussolini to change their behavior, but it was intended to put the dictators on the spot and to point out to the world (and the American public) that they did not have limited territorial aims, but were intending to conquer Europe: "…throughout the world hundreds of millions of human beings are living today in constant fear of a new war or even a series of wars…On a previous occasion I have addressed you in behalf of the settlement of political, economic, and social problems by peaceful methods, and without resort to arms. But the tide of events seems to have reverted to the force of arms. If such threats continue, it seems inevitable that much of

| | | responded in a speech to the Reichstag on April 28, 1939, "in a sarcastic harangue which elicited roars of malicious laughter from the assembled delegates." Hitler's response was also cleverly crafted to appeal to isolationists in America.[18] | the world must become involved in common ruin…Reports, which we trust are not true, insist that further acts of aggression are contemplated against still other independent nations…You have repeatedly asserted that you and the German people have no desire for war. If this is true there need be no war…Are you willing to give assurance that your armed forces will not attack or invade the territory or possessions of the following independent nations: Finland, Estonia, Latvia, Lithuania, Sweden, Norway, Denmark, the Netherlands, Belgium, Great Britain and Ireland, Portugal, Spain, Switzerland, Liechtenstein, Luxembourg, Poland, Hungary, Rumania, Yugoslavia, Russia, Bulgaria, Greece, Turkey, Iraq, the Arabias, Syria, Palestine, Egypt, and Iran?…I think you will not misunderstand the spirit of frankness in which I send you this message. Heads of great governments in this hour are literally responsible for the fate of humanity in the coming years…History will hold them accountable…"[19] Note: Regardless of the sarcasm evident in Hitler's reply[20] when he mocked Roosevelt's list of |

---

[18] Dallek, *Franklin D. Roosevelt and American Foreign Policy, 1932-1945,* 185-187.

[19] Hunt, ed., *The Essential Franklin Delano Roosevelt,* 152-155.

[20] In the PBS television documentary *FDR* (The *American Experience* series), Historian Robert Dallek explained why Hitler felt so free to mock Roosevelt to the world in his informal public reply to FDR's note: "In essence, he [FDR] was being told by Hitler, 'You're not a player in this world political game; we don't count you for very much; and we know that you have a big political headache. Your isolationists are not going to let you do anything; you have all these Neutrality laws; [and] if we go to war against Britain and France, you're not going to have a significant say in things.' And it, I think, it deepened his frustration. He knew it; he knew Hitler was right in that sense, at least for the moment."

		potential victims, Germany eventually invaded or attacked 13 of the countries on FDR's list.
June 1, 1939	The Imperial Japanese Navy introduces a major new operational code (initially called the "AN" code by the U.S. Navy, and called <u>Code Book D</u> by the Japanese Navy, it was also often referred to by American and British cryptanalysts as the five-digit code, or the five-numeral, i.e., "5-Num" code). **This fleet operational code would become more commonly known by the U.S. Navy as "JN-25."** Its formal description by the U.S. Navy became the <u>Imperial Navy General Purpose Fleet Code</u>.	A basic code book defined 33,333 5-digit code groups, each of which could represent a phrase, word, letter, or number. Later, after December 1, 1940, some were assigned two meanings, which increased the total number of 5-digit "words" to over 50,000. The code book was accompanied by, and used in tandem with, a 300 page book containing 50,000 5-digit *additive values,* which were always added to each of the five-digit "word" values from the basic code book---to further disguise them---prior to transmission by radio. This "superencipherment" always had to be stripped at the receiving end, before the text of each message could be decoded by its recipient. The cryptanalysts and linguists at Station US (or "NEGAT") in Washington, D.C. are initially assigned the sole responsibility for breaking JN-25 by OP-20-G (CDR Laurance Safford).
June 12, 1939	**President Roosevelt meets the King and Queen of England as they commence an unprecedented visit to America, hosting them in both Washington, D.C. and at his family estate in Hyde Park.** The public interest in the visit is intense due to the fact that such a state visit had never before	With Hitler making very loud noises about his demands in Poland, FDR sensed the coming of a large-scale European war, which if unchecked, would threaten to engulf all of civilization. While Roosevelt was no lover of the British Empire (he disliked its colonial/racial policies, and its opposition to free trade), he genuinely believed that solidarity with the British people during the coming war would be of paramount importance, since he correctly viewed the coming conflict as a

	happened since the American War of Independence (1776-1783), and the film media provided extensive coverage through newsreel footage.	fight to the death between dictatorship and democracy in the modern world. FDR sought to engender in the American public an increased kinship and affection for the British people through this visit. The symbolism of simply hosting the King and Queen of America's former colonial master and mother-country, in a time of great international peril when the British seemed headed for a showdown with Germany, was very powerful.
August 8, 1939	**Winston Churchill once again broadcasts to the United States from London, via radio.**	Churchill made one last attempt to awaken slumbering America to the dangers inherent in the world situation: "There is a hush all over Europe, nay all over the world, broken only by the dull thud of Japanese bombs falling on Chinese cities…the suffering Chinese are fighting our battle---the battle of democracy…If this habit of military dictatorships' breaking into other people's lands with bomb and shell and bullet, stealing the property and killing the proprietors, spreads too widely, we may none of us be able to think of summer holidays for quite a while…But to come back to the hush I said was hanging over Europe. What kind of a hush is it? Alas! It is the hush of suspense, and in many lands, it is the hush of fear…these German and Italian armies may have another work of liberation to perform. **It was only last year they liberated Austria from the horrors of self-government. It was only in March they freed the Czechoslovak Republic from the misery of independent existence. It is only two years ago that Signor**

Mussolini gave the ancient Kingdom of Abyssinia its Magna Carta…no wonder there is a hush among all the neighbors of Germany and Italy while they are wondering which one is going to be 'liberated' next…One thing has struck me as very strange, and that is the resurgence of the one-man power after all these centuries of experience and progress. **It is curious how the English-speaking peoples have always had this horror of one-man power…the Architects of the American Constitution were as careful as those who shaped the British Constitution to guard against the whole life and fortunes, and all the laws and freedom of the nation, being placed in the hands of a tyrant**…in Germany, on a mountain peak, there sits one man who…in a single day can plunge all that we have and are into a volcano of smoke and flame…If Herr Hitler does not make war, there will be no war. Britain and France are determined to shed no blood except in self-defense or in defense of their allies…Therefore, if war should come there can be no doubt upon whose head the blood-guiltiness will fall." Churchill had again cleverly (and truthfully) emphasized the common bonds between Great Britain and America, and reminded his audience of the odious nature of the two Fascist dictatorships, and of militaristic Japan.[21] [Emphasis added]

---

[21] Churchill, ed., *Never Give In!,* 191-194.

| August 23, 1939 | **The Molotov-Ribbentrop Pact is signed in Moscow.** Officially, this was titled the "Treaty of Non-Aggression Between Germany and the Soviet Union." The pact gave Germany the *defacto* go-ahead to invade and seize Poland without worrying about a hostile reaction from the USSR, Poland's immediate neighbor to the East. A secret protocol of the pact ceded the eastern half of Poland to the USSR following the imminent German invasion. Soviet dictator Joseph Stalin, in an appeasement gambit of his own, agreed to send key shipments of raw materials to Germany on a regular basis. (Ultimately, this appeasement did not work any better than the appeasement at Munich had.) | Hitler and Nazi Germany were much aggrieved that the Post World War I borders drawn up by the Treaty of Versailles had taken the Baltic city of Danzig away from Germany, and that Eastern Prussia had been separated from the rest of Germany by the "Polish Corridor." Hitler was demanding cession of the port of Danzig (officially a Free City, in which 95% of the inhabitants were German speakers); an extra-territorial highway between Germany and East Prussia through the Polish Corridor; and special treatment for the German minority in Poland. On the surface, these were the reasons for Germany's decisions to go to war. The deeper reasons were that Hitler, as revealed in *Mein Kampf* (his manifesto and blueprint for his future actions), had always intended to grab Poland to obtain both lebensraum (living space) and its rich farmlands. The farmlands of Poland (and later the Ukraine), in Hitler's mind, had always been targeted for absorption into his growing Third Reich. (They were to be freed up, post war documents reveal, by genocide---the intentional mass murder of the Polish and Soviet populations, who were considered subhumans by Nazi racist ideology.) The surprise signing of the non-aggression pact between foreign ministers Ribbentrop and Molotov stunned the British and the French, who had been attempting for many months to consummate a military alliance with the Soviet Union. Nazi Germany beat them to it, and the British and the French knew |

		on August 23rd that they would soon be embroiled in a war with Germany over its coming invasion of Poland.
August 24, 1939	President Roosevelt sends a last-ditch appeal to avoid war to Hitler during the Polish Crisis.[22]	Some key phrases follow: "To the message I sent you last April I have received no reply…I therefore urge with all earnestness…that the governments of Germany and of Poland agree by common accord to refrain from any positive acts of hostility for a reasonable and stipulated period…The people of the United States are as one in their opposition to policies of military conquest and domination. They are as one in rejecting the thesis that any ruler, or any people, possess the right to achieve their ends or objectives through the taking of action which will plunge countless millions of people into war and which will bring distress and suffering to every nation of the world, belligerent and neutral…". The message encouraged Hitler to solve his grievances over Poland through direct negotiation, or binding arbitration, or through conciliation through an impartial third party. Needless to say, it had no effect on Hitler, who was set on establishing a Eurasian German Empire, by conquest, in the middle of the world's largest land mass.
August 25, 1939	England and Poland sign the British-Polish Common Defense Pact.	This agreement officially consummated the public guarantee that Prime Minister Neville Chamberlain had given to Poland on March 31, 1939. It was Britain's immediate response to the Molotov-

---

[22] Hunt, ed., *The Essential Franklin Delano Roosevelt,* 167-168.

		Ribbentrop pact, and it set Hitler back on his heels a bit, causing him to delay the invasion of Poland from August 26th to September 1st.
September 1, 1939	Vice-Admiral **Isoroku Yamamoto** transfers from his prior post as Vice-Minister of the Navy to that of <u>Commander in Chief, Combined Fleet</u>---the one man in operational command of all Imperial Japanese Navy forces. The only man the CinC of the Combined Fleet had to answer to, operationally, was the Chief of the Naval General Staff. According to his biographer, Hiroyuki Agawa, author of *The Reluctant Admiral: Yamamoto and the Imperial Navy* (p. 193), Yamamoto's concept of attacking Pearl Harbor may have originated much earlier than officially credited. Although officially, from the standpoint of staff studies and orders given to subordinates, Yamamoto's idea of attacking Pearl Harbor at	Yamamoto left an indelible mark on history. He became the initiator and chief advocate of the Japanese attack on Pearl Harbor, which so forcefully transformed a reluctant and disunited United States populace into a fervent and united people bent on revenge, and determined to achieve absolute victory over the Axis in World War II. The irony of this situation lies in the fact that Yamamoto was a vocal opponent of Japan signing the Tripartite Pact with Germany and Italy (which nevertheless happened anyway in September 1940), and had, throughout his career, always opposed war with the United States. As a moderate, and because he was correctly perceived as the leader of the Navy's opposition to closer ties with Nazi Germany and Fascist Italy, he was hated by the "radical right" within the Japanese Army and Navy (especially the Army), and his life was therefore literally at risk while he was Navy Vice-Minister. Transferring him to the Combined Fleet as its Commander in Chief was, in the opinion of his biographer, done to save his life and keep him from being assassinated by right wing militarists. Yamamoto had been assigned to America three different times: from 1919-21 as a Commander, when he studied at Harvard; in 1923, as a Navy Captain traveling America and Europe on a nine-

the outset of a possible war with the United States began in January of 1941, it may have *unofficially* first been conceived of by Yamamoto as early as April or May of 1940, according to CAPT Shigeru **Fukudome**--- long before the daring and successful British attack on Italian battleships at Taranto Harbor in Italy, in November of 1940, with torpedo planes.

Former RADM **Fukudome,** in his monograph *"The Hawaii Operation"* (p. 5-9), found in David Evans' *The Japanese Navy in World War II,* wrote that for 30 years the Japanese Navy had been conducting staff studies of possible war against the U.S. Navy, and had always (until Yamamoto changed everything in January of 1941) planned on a passive defense, waiting for the U.S. Navy to approach Japanese waters through a string of massively fortified and well-defended island barriers. The traditional concept of how to fight

month reconnaissance mission; and again from 1926-28 (while still a Captain) as Naval Attache at the Japanese Embassy in Washington, D.C.

He had become a proponent of Naval aviation from 1924-1933 in a succession of aviation related assignments, ashore and afloat; had served as Commanding Officer of the aircraft carrier *Akagi* ("Red Castle"), which would later lead the attack on Pearl Harbor; and later had served as Commander of the First Carrier Division (again onboard *Akagi*). Promoted to Rear Admiral in 1930, in 1934 he became a Vice Admiral, and in 1936 he was appointed Navy Vice-Minister. He was promoted to full Admiral in 1940, *after* he had been appointed as Commander in Chief, Combined fleet.

Once the "necessity" (from the Imperial Japanese expansionist standpoint) of war with the United States became clear, he initiated staff consideration of the Pearl Harbor attack in January of 1941, and became the most passionate advocate of the attack on Pearl Harbor, as a means of securing the flank of the Japanese Navy so that it could successfully carry out its Southern Operations (against Southeast Asia, Malaya, and the Dutch East Indies) unimpeded for six months without harassment, and also as a means of destroying (so he hoped) the American will to fight. It is also ironic that someone who had spent so much time in the United States would so misjudge Americans that he thought he could

the U.S. Navy had been to seriously weaken it as it battled its way across the Pacific to relieve the Philippines, and to then overwhelm what was left of the U.S. Fleet in the "decisive battle" in waters relatively close to Japan (or nearby), reminiscent of the Battle of Tsushima Strait in 1905 between the Japanese and Russian fleets. The disadvantages of this traditional concept were that it would have yielded the initiative to the U.S. Navy, and that as time progressed, the balance of Naval strength between the two navies would greatly have favored the U.S., with its much stronger economy.

The strength of this concept was that it would have allowed Japan to first seize what it wanted in the Far East, *and would have required America to initiate hostilities.* In fact, this **psychologically and politically superior approach** was still favored by ADM Shigetaro **Shimada,** the discourage Americans from successfully prosecuting a long war with Japan---that he could destroy the American will to fight---*by launching a surprise attack on the United States.* Americans might well have been discouraged in a Pacific war with Japan (as we later were in a war of policy, and not necessity, in Vietnam) **if** President Roosevelt had embarked upon a *war of choice* against a Japan that *had never attacked the U.S.,* simply to prop up the *status quo* of the British and Dutch empires in the far East---and **if** the U.S. had never been subjected to a surprise attack by the Japanese Navy on a Sunday morning, while negotiations were still in progress in Washington, D.C. Yamamoto, who knew Japan could not win a long war against the United States because of the economic and industrial imbalance between the two nations, correctly predicted before the war that he would "run wild" for six months to a year if Japan fought the U.S., but that after that he could guarantee nothing. Japan's only hope of victory in a war with the U.S. was to secure a negotiated peace with America (allowing Japan to keep its conquests), after: (1) initially securing the resources it needed in the massive Southern Operation; (2) building up an impregnable, defensive island perimeter in the central and southwest Pacific; and (3) crushing the United States Navy with a series of quick victories at the outset of the war. What Yamamoto unaccountably failed to understand was that **a surprise attack on**

	Navy Minister at the time Japan went to war,[23] and was what President Roosevelt and Harry Hopkins truly feared at the time---namely, that Japan would **only** attack the British and Dutch in East Asia, and ***NOT*** attack the United States.	<u>the U.S.</u>---although it would have a high chance of *military* success---would ultimately be self-defeating, and would be a political and psychological disaster for Japan, because it would galvanize and electrify the previously divided and lethargic American populace, and would make a negotiated peace with Imperial Japan impossible for any American President.
September 1, 1939	**Germany invades Poland.**	**Most historians designate this date as the beginning of World War II.** (Others, looking farther backward, designate Japan's invasion and seizure of Manchuria in 1931 as the true beginning of the Second World War.) Over 55 million people will be killed, and the international structure of the world will be profoundly altered.
September 3, 1939	**England and France declare war on Germany.**	Although they have no troops in Poland with which to directly assist the Poles, the British and the French have finally

---

[23] Fukudome explained it this way in his monograph (Evans, *The Japanese Navy in World War II,* p. 6): **"Admiral Shigetaro Shimada, the navy minister at the time Japan went to war, wanted by all means to prevent the United States from becoming an enemy and taxed himself to find some means of enabling Japan to declare war only after the United States had opened hostilities. His idea was for Japan to declare war on Britain and the Netherlands, but to resort to arms against the United States only after being challenged by the latter."** Ultimately Shimada's traditional argument lost out to Yamamoto's for two reasons: because of Yamamoto's strong personality and iron will; and because the Japanese Navy's limited 2-year stockpile of oil would fast begin to run out in such a "wait-for-America-to-attack" scenario. This atmosphere of near panic about the dwindling oil stockpile (after late July 1941, when FDR imposed his oil embargo against Japan) created a consensus within the Imperial Navy that if war were inevitable with the United States, it had to commence <u>as soon as possible</u> while adequate supplies of petroleum were still on hand for offensive operations---and that if hostilities against the United States could not commence immediately while they were still operationally feasible, then war would have to be delayed for several years. Such a delay was inconsistent with the prevailing attitude within the Japanese government that Japan could not afford to "miss the bus"---namely, that it must expand its Empire in the Far East while the success of the Axis in Europe was seriously weakening the British and the Dutch in the orient.

		taken a crucial moral stand against the Nazi state's continuing expansion, and backed it up by committing their nations to stop Germany on the battlefield. As many military commentators have since pointed out, during the next six weeks, the British and French missed an unparalleled opportunity, for Hitler had gambled on their inaction and had committed the vast majority of his army to the war with Poland in the east; his back door, in the west, was virtually undefended. While the British and French were unprepared to go on the military offensive against Germany in 1939, they had stated categorically, with their declarations of war, that future negotiations of any kind with Nazi Germany were out of the question, recognizing that Hitler had an insatiable appetite, and that his word could not be trusted. Britain and France had staked the honor and the very survival of their countries on the need to stop Germany by force of arms.
September 3, 1939	Churchill makes his last speech as a back-bencher during the Parliamentary debate following Neville Chamberlain's declaration of war against Germany.	Some of his most pertinent remarks follow: "We must not underrate the gravity of the task which lies before us or the temerity of the ordeal, to which we shall not be found unequal. We must expect many disappointments, and many unpleasant surprises…**This is not a question of fighting for Danzig or fighting for Poland. We are fighting to save the whole world from the pestilence of Nazi tyranny and in**

		defense of all that is most sacred to man."[24] [Emphasis added]
September 3, 1939	**Winston Churchill is appointed First Lord of the Admiralty by Prime Minister Neville Chamberlain, and thus joins the British War Cabinet.**	Churchill's "wilderness years" are over. More than once, during the 1930s, he was considered washed-up, and was ridiculed for being on the wrong side of most of the major issues of the day. However, virtually alone, he had sounded frequent and public warnings against the danger of a rearming Germany since 1934, especially against the alarming growth of the German air force. Winston Churchill had been First Lord of the Admiralty prior to, and during Britain's entry into World War I, and his service in that arena in the previous European War, combined with his uncompromising attitude throughout the decade toward the dangers presented by Hitler's Germany, made him uniquely qualified to serve as the political head of the British Navy as hostilities commenced with Nazi Germany.
September 3, 1939	President Roosevelt delivers his Fireside Chat in response to the state of war now existing between allies Britain and France, and Germany. He carefully mixed themes of both isolationism and intervention in his speech, capturing the mood of the American people at the time, and was careful not	Key phrases in this address of mixed messages are: "For four long years a succession of actual wars and constant crises have shaken the entire world and have threatened in each case to bring on the gigantic conflict which today is unhappily a fact…You must master at the outset a simple but unalterable fact in modern relations between nations. **When peace has been broken anywhere, the peace of all countries everywhere is in danger.** It is easy for

---

[24] Churchill, ed., *Never Give In!,* 197-198.

	to get out too far in front of public opinion.²⁵	you and me to shrug our shoulders and say that conflicts taking place thousands of miles from the continental United States...do not seriously affect the Americas---and that all the United States has to do is to ignore them and go about its own business. **Passionately though we may desire detachment, we are forced to realize that every word that comes through the air, every ship that sails the sea, every battle that is fought, does affect the American future.** Let no man or woman thoughtlessly or falsely talk of America sending its armies to European fields. At this moment there is being prepared a proclamation of American neutrality...And I trust that in the days to come our neutrality can be made a true neutrality...I cannot prophesy the immediate economic effect of this new war on our nation, but I do say that no American has the moral right to profiteer at the expense either of his fellow citizens or of the men, the women, or the children who are living and dying in the midst of the war in Europe...We seek to keep war from our own firesides by keeping war from coming to the Americas. For that we have historic precedent that goes back to the days of the administration of President George Washington...**This nation will remain a neutral nation, but I cannot ask that every American remain neutral in thought as well. Even a neutral has a right to take account of facts. Even a neutral cannot be asked to close his

---

[25] Buhite and Levy, ed., *FDR's Fireside Chats,* 148-151.

		mind or close his conscience. I have said not once, but many times, that I have seen war, and that I hate war. I say that again and again. I hope the United States will keep out of this war. I believe that it will. And I give you assurance and reassurance that every effort of your government will be directed toward that end. As long as it remains within my power to prevent, there will be no blackout of peace in the United States." [Emphasis added] In retrospect, it can clearly be seen that Roosevelt had captured the national mood, which was both supportive of the Allies, and fearful of American involvement in war.
September 11, 1939	**President Roosevelt writes a personal letter to First Lord of the Admiralty and member of Chamberlain's War Cabinet, Winston S. Churchill, suggesting they commence a personal correspondence about the war.** (Roosevelt is well aware of his strong anti-Hitler stance during the 1930s, and decides to cultivate a personal relationship on the off chance that Churchill might become Prime Minister some day. This paid off just eight months later.) This letter is the first of almost 2,000 letters and written	FDR's letter reads as follows: "My dear Churchill: It is because you and I occupied similar positions in the World War that I want you to know how glad I am that you are back again in the Admiralty. Your problems are, I realize, complicated by new factors but the essential is not very different. What I want you and the Prime Minister to know is that I shall at all times welcome it if you will keep me in touch personally with anything you want me to know about. You can always send sealed letters through your pouch or my pouch. I am glad you did the Marlboro [sic] volumes before this thing started---and I much enjoyed reading them. With my sincere regards, Faithfully yours, [signed] *Franklin D. Roosevelt*." Churchill received permission from Chamberlain to carry out this most unusual correspondence with the Head of State of another nation, and responded

| | messages exchanged between them during World War II.²⁶ They | with alacrity. The two men first spoke by transatlantic telephone on October 5, 1939.²⁷ |

---

²⁶ Meacham, *Franklin and Winston,* xiv.

²⁷ Author Jon Meacham, in his incisive book *Franklin and Winston,* characterized succinctly the nature of what Eleanor Roosevelt called a "fortunate friendship," a tempestuous but intimate relationship that rallied the forces of light when darkness fell upon the world. As Meacham summarized, "Roosevelt and Churchill helped shape the way we live now. Four of the turning points of World War II---the American decision to support Britain in its struggle against Germany in the months before Pearl Harbor; the victory over the Germans in the North African desert, which kept the Middle East out of Hitler's hands; the development and control of the Atomic bomb; and the timing of the liberation of Europe---were largely products of their personal collaboration." Meacham continued, "The Roosevelt-Churchill story proves…that *it does matter* who is in power at critical points…". [Emphasis added] Meacham explains, "From the beginning Churchill thought victory required Roosevelt; after an initial period of uncertainty and skepticism, Roosevelt decided that Churchill was vital to the complete defeat of Hitler. From afar, and then face-to-face, they chose to believe in each other, fighting…to increase democracy's chances against totalitarianism and terror."

It was not always smooth sailing. As Meacham points out, "Mary Soames, Winston and Clementine Churchill's youngest and last surviving child, pointed out the complexities of the relationship by quoting a French proverb: 'In love, there is always one who kisses and one who offers the cheek.' Churchill was the suitor, Roosevelt the elusive quarry. Their friendship mirrored their private characters. With Roosevelt, Churchill was sentimental and shrewd. With Churchill, Roosevelt was cheerful and calculating. Churchill was warmer and more anxious for reassurances about Roosevelt's affection for him; Roosevelt cooler and more confident, alternately charming and distant." Continuing, Meacham again quoted Mary Soames: "My father's friendship and love were spontaneous and unmotivated. He was not complicated in his approach to people. He was trusting and very genuine. He could be wily if he had to, but it did not come naturally." In contrast, Meacham quotes what Harry Truman said about Roosevelt long after FDR's death: ***"He was the coldest man I ever met.*** He didn't give a damn personally for me or you or anyone else in the world as far as I could see. ***But he was a great President.*** He brought this country into the twentieth century." [Emphasis added] Meacham explained: "Their personal faults---**Roosevelt's duplicity,** Churchill's self-absorption---were at times *political virtues.* What could make Roosevelt a trying husband and a frustrating friend could make him a great President: <u>sometimes politicians have to pursue different courses at the same time and deceive those closest to them about what they are doing</u>." [Emphasis added] Meacham quotes columnist Walter Lippmann in expanding upon Roosevelt's ability to deceive and engage in duplicity when required: ***"Roosevelt was a wonderful finagler. He loved to take a complicated thing which involved a certain amount of deception---hornswoggling of people---and somehow get it done."*** [Emphasis added] The reader is enjoined to keep the above quotations in mind as he proceeds on this journey and studies Roosevelt's actions regarding his use of the Pacific Fleet, communications intelligence, and diplomacy during the run-up to the Pearl Harbor attack.

Meacham gets at the heart of the matter when he writes: "Roosevelt and Churchill became friends under the force of circumstance. From the invasion of Poland in 1939 to the Japanese attack on Pearl Harbor in 1941, Churchill begged for help from Roosevelt, who had to be convinced Britain was worth American trust and

	would also speak during several transatlantic telephone calls, and spent 113 days together during World War II.	
September 21, 1939	**FDR assembles a Special Session of Congress and urges repeal of the embargo provisions of the Neutrality Act.**[28] Clearly seeing that war was approaching in Europe, he had been trying since May of 1939 to get Congressional leaders to change the neutrality legislation to permit aid to countries resisting Axis aggression, with little success. A full-court press by Roosevelt in July had failed to get the Neutrality Act repealed or amended. However, the commencement of war in Europe on September 1, 1939, gave his appeals an added sense of urgency.	Pertinent excerpts follow: "Because I am wholly willing to ascribe an honest desire for peace to those who hold different views from my own as to what those measures should be, I trust that these gentlemen will be sufficiently generous to ascribe equally lofty purposes to those with whom they disagree. Let no man or group…assume exclusive protectorate over the future well-being of America, because I conceive that regardless of party or section the mantle of peace and patriotism is wide enough to cover us all." FDR then provided a summary of the drift of the world toward war, and of his warnings to the nation in this regard. He then spoke of mistakes made by the United States during its history in an attempt to avoid war: "Our next deviation…was the so-called Neutrality Act of 1935---only four years ago---an Act continued in force by the joint resolution of May 1, 1937, despite grave doubts expressed as to its wisdom by officials charged with the conduct of

---

treasure." He continued: "Roosevelt was the better politician, Churchill the warmer human being. When Hitler dominated the continent, staring across the English Channel, Churchill stood alone and stared back. Some respectable people in Britain would have cut a deal and let Hitler rule much of Europe. Defending liberty when others wavered, **Churchill held out long enough to give Roosevelt time to prepare a reluctant America for the fight** and then for global leadership. Together they preserved the democratic experiment." [Emphasis added]

[28] Hunt, ed., *The Essential Franklin Delano Roosevelt,* 173-180.

		foreign relations, including myself. **I regret that the Congress passed that act. I regret equally that I signed that act.** On July 14 of this year, I asked the Congress in the cause of peace and in the interest of real American neutrality and security, to take action to change that act. I now ask again that such action be taken in respect to…the embargo provisions. I ask it because they are, in my opinion, most vitally dangerous to American neutrality, American security and, above all, American peace. These embargo provisions, as they exist today, prohibit the sale to a belligerent by an American factory of any completed implements of war, but they allow the sale of many types of uncompleted implements of war, as well as all kinds of general materials and supplies. They, furthermore, allow such products of industry and agriculture to be taken in American flagships to belligerent nations. There in itself---under the present law---lies definite danger to our neutrality and our peace…Let us be factual, let us recognize that a belligerent nation often needs wheat and lard and cotton for the survival of its population just as much as it needs antiaircraft guns and antisubmarine depth charges…I seek a greater consistency through repeal of the embargo provisions…It has been erroneously said that return to that policy might being us nearer to war. I give to you my deep and unalterable conviction, based on years of experience as a worker in the field of international peace, that by repeal of the embargo the United States will more

probably remain at peace than if the law remains as it stands today. I say this because with the repeal of the embargo, this government clearly and definitely will insist that American citizens and American ships stay away from the immediate perils of the actual zones of conflict…I believe that American merchant vessels should, as far as possible, be restricted from entering war zones…The second objective is to prevent American citizens from travelling on belligerent vessels, or in danger areas…the third objective, requiring the foreign buyer to take transfer of title in this country to commodities purchased by belligerents, is also a result that can be attained by legislation…the fourth objective is the preventing of war credits to belligerents. This can be accomplished by maintaining in force the existing provisions of the law, or by proclamation making it clear that if credits are granted by American citizens to belligerents, our government will take no steps in the future to relieve them of risk or loss." The heart of his address then followed with these words: **"The result of these last two objectives will be to require all purchases to be made in cash, and all cargoes to be carried in the purchaser's own ships, at the purchaser's own risk."** Continuing, "Under present enactments…arms cannot be carried to belligerent countries by American vessels, and this provision should not be disturbed…To those who say that this program would involve a step toward

war on our part, I reply that it offers far greater safeguards than we now possess or have ever possessed, to protect American lives and property from danger. It is a positive program for giving safety. This means less likelihood of incidents and controversies which tend to draw us into conflict, as unhappily they did in the last World War…At this time I seek no further authority from the Congress…I see no compelling reason for the consideration of other legislation at this extraordinary session of the Congress. It is, of course, possible that in the months to come unforeseen needs for further legislation may develop but they are not imperative today…The facts compel my stating, with candor, that darker periods may lie ahead. **The disaster is not of our making; no acts of ours engendered the forces which assault the foundations of civilization. Yet we find ourselves affected to the core; our currents of commerce are changing, our minds are filled with new problems, our position in world affairs has already been altered. In such circumstances our policy must be to appreciate in the deepest sense the true American interest.** Rightly considered, this interest is not selfish. **Destiny first made us, with our sister nations on this hemisphere, joint heirs of European culture. Fate seems now to compel us to assume the task of helping to maintain in the Western world a citadel wherein that civilization may be kept alive."**
[Emphasis added]

November 4, 1939	**FDR signs into law the "cash and carry" provisions of the revised Neutrality Act.** As always, FDR was acting only as far as the public consensus would allow him to act; he was determined not to ever get out too far ahead of public opinion again, as he had with his court-packing scheme in 1937---for to do so would fatally weaken both his Presidency, and U.S. foreign policy, the fatal mistake of Woodrow Wilson after the end of World War I. A Gallup poll taken on October 22, 1939 indicated that ***95 per cent of Americans wanted to stay out of the war,*** but that ***62 per cent said yes*** when asked if "the United States should do everything possible to help England and France win the war, except go to war ourselves."[29] FDR had helped shape that public opinion himself, by requesting amendment of the Neutrality Act on September 21st. A huge majority of those polled	After Nazi Germany invaded the remainder of Czechoslovakia on March 15, 1939, Roosevelt had attempted to get the Congress to have the two year "cash and carry" provision (due to expire in May of 1939) renewed, and had failed. However, the German invasion of Poland on September 1st, and the declarations of war against Germany by England and France on September 3rd, radically altered the landscape of international affairs, and this time the President succeeded, following his Special Message to Congress on September 21st. Arms trade with belligerent nations was now legal for the first time in over four years, providing such trade was conducted on a "cash and carry" basis. This clearly favored Great Britain over Germany, since Britain had a large merchant marine, and Germany was a largely landlocked nation (with ocean access only in the Baltic), which was under blockade by the British Navy. The Neutrality Acts of 1935 and 1937 were repealed, and American citizens and ships were barred from entering war zones designated by the President. The isolationists had lost this round to Franklin D. Roosevelt, and were ever more alert to any perceived designs on his part to provide aid to Great Britain that would increase America's chances of getting dragged into the European war.

---

[29] Meacham, *Franklin and Winston,* 50.

	by Gallup in October, 85 percent, wanted Britain and France to win the war, and only 2 per cent favored a German victory. But in a poll taken by *Fortune* magazine in December 1939, <u>only 15 per cent of Americans wanted America to enter the war on the side of the Allies</u>, *even if Britain or France were losing the war.*[30]	
December, 1939	Cryptanalyst Lieutenant Commander Malcolm Burnett, Royal Navy, flies to Singapore to deliver a highly classified book of all of the "recoveries" made by GCCS (the British Government Code and Cipher School) of JN-25(a), the Japanese Navy's operational code, to the Far East Combined Bureau (FECB), Britain's cryptanalysis center in the Far East. FECB's intercept station (which could intercept all Japanese Navy radio messages originating in Japan) was located at Stonecutter's Island in Hong Kong, and the	The now-celebrated Eric Nave, the brilliant Royal Australian Navy Japanese linguist and cryptanalyst, had been loaned out to the British Royal Navy as a young junior officer in 1925 because of his unusual proficiency in Japanese, and established a very successful signals intelligence operation in Hong Kong that attracted the serious attention of the Admiralty in London by the end of 1927. He was transferred to GCCS in London early in 1928, and established the Japanese codebreaking section there. His tremendous success in breaking Japanese codes is well-documented in *Betrayal at Pearl Harbor,* the controversial 1991 book written by Nave and his co-author, James Rusbridger. In the autumn of 1937 Commander Nave was transferred from GCCS in London to the Far East Combined Bureau (FECB) in Hong Kong, to take advantage of the huge

---

[30] Shogun, *Hard Bargain,* 22.

FECB cryptanalysts had been moved in August of 1939 from Hong Kong to Singapore---inside the Naval Base---for security reasons, because of the escalating war between Japan and China.

Britain's Government Code and Cipher School was established in 1919, following World War I, as a civilian organization under the Foreign Office. Although it employed many officers on active duty, as well as civilians, its strength was that it was one unified organization. [In the U.S., the Army and the Navy each had their own codebreaking organizations---the Signals Intelligence Service (SIS) for the Army, and OP-20-G in the Navy, part of the Naval Communications organization. Both of these American cryptologic organizations distrusted each other, and

volume of Japanese Navy radio traffic intercepted at Stonecutter's Island. After FECB was relocated from Hong Kong to Singapore in the late summer of 1939, Nave began serious penetration of JN-25(a) in September, and likewise much progress was being made back at GCCS by the chief cryptanalyst at Bletchley Park, Brigadier General John Tiltman.[31] The progress at GCCS was so rapid that Lieutenant Commander Burnett, Nave's counterpart back at GCCS, in charge of the rapidly expanding Japanese section (employing about 300 people) at Bletchley Park [the new wartime home for GCCS commencing in late August 1939], was able to hand-carry the "recovered" portions of the basic JN-25(a) code book, additive tables, and instructions on how to use the unique "keys" in each enciphered message---i.e., instructions on how to use the current version of the additive table to decipher and strip away the superencipherment from each message---to FECB in Singapore, where there was a continuous, heavy flow of intercepted Japanese Navy messages from Hong Kong to work with. Following Burnett's arrival with these materials, the primary GCCS effort in decrypting JN-25 shifted to FECB. [Nave left Singapore in February of 1940, to return to his native Australia on

---

[31] John Tiltman's role in breaking JN-25 is not discussed in the book *Betrayal at Pearl Harbor* by Nave and Rusbridger; however, author Michael Smith, in his book *The Emperor's Codes,* gives Tiltman a significant amount of credit for understanding the basic structure of both Japanese Army and Navy encrypted operational codes, including JN-25(a), and Smith actually gives Tiltman overall credit for "breaking" JN-25. There can be no doubt that Nave also played a major role between September 1939 and February 1940, when ill health forced him to leave Singapore and FECB.

viewed their sister organization as a competitor---and withheld significant information from each other much of the time. Although cooperation increased markedly in 1940 and continued to improve throughout 1941, because of the partnership required to decrypt and translate the many daily **MAGIC** messages, inefficiencies were created by the Army and Navy duplication of effort, and sequestration of information, which reduced the overall efficiency of American codebreaking efforts.]

As explained in *Betrayal at Pearl Harbor* (p. 34), "In simple terms, GCCS had two functions. The public one was 'To advise as to the security of government codes and ciphers used by all government departments and to assist in their provision.' The secret one was 'To study the methods of cipher communications used by

medical leave, after he was declared unsuited for duty in the tropics. The RAN physicians would not let him return to Singapore, so he detached from the Royal Navy, remained in his native Australia, and established the Royal Australian Navy's own codebreaking unit in Melbourne.] The breakthrough in decrypting JN-25(a) by Tiltman at Bletchley Park and Nave in Singapore enabled both GCCS and FECB to read much of the Japanese Navy's JN-25 traffic on a current or "real time" basis until December of 1940, when the basic JN-25(a) code book was replaced by a more complex code book the U.S. Navy then designated as JN-25(b).[32] Eric Nave explained to his co-author James Rusbridger (*Betrayal at Pearl Harbor*) that JN-25 was not a difficult code to break---simply a very, very tedious one, that required a lot of labor (a large staff), tabulating machines (punch card sorters), and a large volume of message traffic to work with. It was a "book code" that was based on a basic dictionary, whose coded values for each word, or phrase, or number were superenciphered by the use of additive tables---a labor intensive, time-consuming manual process for both the radiomen of the Japanese Navy who had to encode each message, and for the foreign cryptanalysts who wished to decode each message. [OP-20-G in Washington had independently determined in November 1939 that JN-25 was similar to an old book code system

---

[32] Costello, *Days of Infamy*, 318-321; Rusbridger and Nave, *Betrayal at Pearl Harbor*, 88.

	foreign powers.' "	used by the American Army and Navy during the Spanish-American war of 1898, and by the British and French Navies in World war I.] Because JN-25 was *not* a machine code or cryptograph (such as the German **Enigma** later broken by GCCS, or the Japanese diplomatic code dubbed **Purple,** broken in September of 1940 by the Americans), the methods for breaking it were already well established by both the British and American signals intelligence services.[33]
February 9, 1940	The "Sumner Welles Peace Mission" President Roosevelt announces that he is sending Under Secretary of State Sumner Welles to Europe on a "fact-finding mission" to visit Italy, Germany, France, and England. (An earlier draft of the statement indicated that Welles would explore peace possibilities, but was likely altered to avoid angering isolationists in the United States, who objected strenuously every time FDR indicated a desire to involve the U.S. in European power politics.) FDR sensed an opportunity to see if there was any possibility to promote peace and avert	FDR made his announcement without even consulting the aging, moralistic, and increasingly inflexible Cordell Hull, the American Secretary of State; like many U.S. Presidents who have followed him, Roosevelt served as his own Secretary of State when it came to the truly big decisions involving foreign policy; Roosevelt relegated the "donkeywork" to Hull, and made the big decisions himself, often without prior consultation, or without fully explaining his true motives. Welles arrived in Italy on February 25, 1940, and visited Italy, Germany, France, Great Britain, and then France and Italy again, before returning to the United States. He spent 20 days visiting both the Foreign Ministers, and then the political leadership in each country. (Each foreign leader received a letter from Franklin Roosevelt delivered by Welles, except Hitler.) Other than sow confusion and resentment among various parties, his visit accomplished nothing

[33] Rusbridger and Nave, *Betrayal at Pearl Harbor,* 83-88.

	continued war during the pregnant pause known as the "Sietzkrieg" (the sitting war, or "phony war"), which followed Germany's conquest of Poland in the autumn of 1939 and full-scale war with the Western European nations in the spring of 1940.	and had no effect upon Hitler's plans to pursue active war in the West against the low countries and France, once Spring arrived and the winter rains stopped in Northern Europe.[34] But the "Sumner Welles Peace Mission," as it was informally known, allowed Roosevelt to claim (truthfully) that the United States had made one last effort to avert a larger conflagration in Europe, and to claim the moral high ground at home once the war resumed in earnest. While the Germans were unhappy about the amendments to the Neutrality Act pushed through by FDR, they still did not at this time take the United States seriously in the arena of European power politics, because of the small size of its Army and the power of the isolationist movement. Just as predicted in *Mein Kampf,* Hitler had continued the expansion of the Reich following FDR's peace note in April with the attack on Poland, and was preparing, from mid-October of 1939 throughout the first four months of 1940, for a war of revenge against Germany's traditional enemy, France. Welles visited Western Europe long after Hitler had given his military the order to prepare for an attack on France, at a time when only the weather, and the unpreparedness of the Wehrmacht, was causing a delay. The perceived opportunity for peacemaking seen by FDR and Welles was illusory, and without foundation. The die had already been cast.

---

[34] Gellman, Irwin F., *Secret Affairs,* 166-202.

April 8, 1940	The British Navy begins mining the coastal waters off Norway, in an attempt to deny Germany the Swedish iron ore which was transshipped via Norwegian ports.	This action had long been advocated by the First Lord of the Admiralty, Winston Churchill; it took him a considerable amount of time to achieve a consensus within the British government for taking this action to withhold vital raw materials from Germany. The British planned, in time, to land troops to garrison Norway in defense of a possible German invasion.
April 9, 1940	**Without warning, Germany occupies Denmark and launches a stealth invasion of Norway by sea.** The "Sitzkrieg" is over. Germany needed Denmark to take and supply Norway; and the Germans wanted Norway for the same reasons Great Britain wanted to deny it to them: Norway was Germany's supplier of iron ore, in great demand by its war machine.	Germany claimed at the time that its invasion of Norway was in response to the British mining of Norwegian waters the day before, but in actuality its attack had been planned long before the British action. While the British Navy sank many German destroyers and some cruisers, Germany successfully landed its troops, overcame initial resistance, and occupied Norway. Throughout April and May the British and French landed troops in Norway and fought with the German Army. The British and French operations were logistically hampered and tactically inept. This unsatisfactory example of warmaking against Germany resulted in the fall of the Chamberlain government in Great Britain, and in the ascendancy of Winston Churchill to the post of Prime Minister on May 10, 1940.
May 10, 1940	**Germany invades the Netherlands, Belgium, Luxembourg, and shortly thereafter, France.** The objective was to gain revenge for its defeat by France, and the allies of France, in World	*Winston Churchill is coincidentally asked to become Prime Minister by King George VI on the same day that Germany launches its blitzkrieg in the West.* (Chamberlain had resigned the day before, and after the Foreign Minister, Lord Halifax---Chamberlain's first choice--- turned down a chance to

	War I.	become Prime Minister, Chamberlain reluctantly offered the job of becoming leader of the Conservative party to Churchill. The King's invitation to Churchill to form a government made it official.) At the time, the King, most of the aristocracy, and many in Parliament considered Churchill a high risk choice for Prime Minister, and would have preferred Halifax to Churchill. While an eloquent elder statesman and a respected man of letters, Churchill was nevertheless widely distrusted as a politician by the establishment because he had twice switched political parties; and also because he had a reputation as a heavy drinker who was considered erratic, occasionally rash, and impulsive by many in the halls of government. His initial hold on power during the month of May---as the British and French Armies were being routed on the Continent---was tenuous, for many in the aristocracy (like Churchill's most serious rival in 1940, Lord Halifax) privately preferred to make a deal with Hitler in order to avoid invasion, and the subsequent loss of the British Empire, rather than fight what they viewed as a hopeless battle with what then appeared to be an invincible Nazi Germany, and see their country utterly destroyed, and then enslaved. After becoming Prime Minister, in an unprecedented move, Churchill appointed himself Minister of Defense, so as to be better able to control the conduct of the war.
May 13, 1940	**"Blood, Toil, Tears, and**	Memorable excerpts follow: "To form an administration of this scale and

Sweat"

Churchill addresses the House of Commons for the first time as Prime Minister. The timid mannerisms, demeanor, and spirit of Neville Chamberlain (who clearly did not have the temperament to be a successful war leader) had been replaced by those of a bulldog. There was a stunned silence in the House of Commons after the speech ended--- followed by a rare standing ovation.[35] However, as one historian (John Lukacs) has noted, many members of Churchill's own Conservative Party sat on their hands following this speech.[36] Many Conservatives believed, even at this time, that Churchill's government might be short-lived, and that the Conservative Party might replace him with another leader if the war on the Continent did not go well. (Churchill had not only been

complexity is a serious undertaking in itself, but it must be remembered that we are in the preliminary stage of one of the greatest battles in history, that we are in action at many other points in Norway and in Holland, that we have to be prepared in the Mediterranean, that the air battle is continuous and that many preparations…have to be made here at home. In this crisis I hope I may be pardoned if I do not address the House at any length today…I would say to the House, as I said to those who joined this government: **'I have nothing to offer but blood, toil, tears, and sweat.'** We have before us an ordeal of the most grievous kind. We have before us many, many long months of struggle and suffering. *You ask, what is our policy? I say, it is to wage war, by sea, land, and air, with all our might and with all the strength that God can give us; to wage war against a monstrous tyranny, never surpassed in the dark, lamentable catalogue of human crime. That is our policy. You ask, what is our aim? I can answer in one word: It is victory, victory at all costs, victory in spite of all terror, victory, no matter now long and hard the road may be; for without victory there is no survival.* Let that be realized; no survival for the British Empire, no survival for all that the British Empire has stood for, no survival for the urge and impulse of the ages, that mankind

---

[35] Churchill, ed., *Never Give In!*, 204-206.

[36] Lukacs, *Five Days in London*, 14.

	responsible for the Gallipoli disaster in World War I, but had been directing the Royal Navy when disaster befell Great Britain in Norway, the previous month.)	will move forward towards its goal. But I take up my task with buoyancy and hope. I feel sure that our cause will not be suffered to fail among men. At this time I feel entitled to claim the aid of all, and I say, 'Come then, let us go forward together with our united strength.'" [Emphasis added]
May 15, 1940	In a cable to Roosevelt, **Churchill requests 50 old World War I-era destroyers (then mothballed), and other arms, from the United States.** Subsequently, throughout the summer of 1940 (and indeed, up until the passage of the Lend-Lease Act in March of 1941), Secretary of the Treasury Henry Morgenthau becomes the focal point within the U.S. government for interfacing with the British purchasing mission, and for handling its multiplying requests for both arms sales and transfers; Morgenthau works closely with U.S. military leaders, particularly the new Army Chief of Staff, George C. Marshall, to evaluate and prepare responses to the British requests for military equipment. (France was defeated, and	Churchill, calling himself "Former Naval Person," wrote: "Although I have changed my office, I am sure you would not wish me to discontinue our intimate, private, correspondence." Churchill quickly got down to business: "As you are no doubt aware, the scene has darkened swiftly. The enemy have a marked preponderance in the air…the small countries are simply smashed up, one by one, like matchwood. We must expect, though it is not yet certain, that Mussolini will hurry to share the loot of civilisation. We expect to be attacked here ourselves, both from the air and by parachute and airborne troops in the near future, and are getting ready for them. If necessary, we shall continue the war alone, and are not afraid of that." Churchill continued, in the frankest manner, **"But I trust you realise, Mr. President, that the voice and force of the United States may count for nothing if they are withheld too long. <u>You may have a completely subjugated and Nazified Europe established with astonishing swiftness,</u>** *<u>and the weight may be more than we can bear</u>*. All I ask now is that you should proclaim non-belligerency, which would mean that you would help us with everything short of

	capitulated, too quickly for its requests to bear any fruit.)	actually engaging armed forces." Churchill then wrote, **"Immediate needs are first of all the loan of forty or fifty of your older destroyers,"** several hundred of "the latest types" of aircraft, along with antiaircraft guns and ammunition, and iron ore. But it was the destroyers, which would "bridge the gap between what we have now and the large new construction we put in hand at the beginning of the war," Churchill made clear, that were the greatest need. He would continue to urgently, almost desperately (and even bitterly), stress this point throughout June, July, and August, as FDR (who was operating during an election year, when he was about to run for an unprecedented third term as President) played surprisingly hard to get on this score. Churchill also asked for "a visit of United States destroyers to Irish ports," and *"to keep that Japanese dog quiet in the Pacific, using Singapore in any way convenient."* Churchill concluded, **"We shall go on paying dollars for as long as we can, but I should like to feel reasonably sure that when we can pay no more, you will give us the stuff all the same."**[37]
May 15, 1940	**FDR decides to keep the visiting U.S. fleet in Pearl Harbor indefinitely, as deterrence against any further Japanese mischief in the Far East.**	The bulk of the U.S. Navy's fleet at this time was in the Pacific Ocean, and homeported in southern California (at San Pedro and at San Diego); there was also an Atlantic Squadron homeported in Norfolk, a small Hawaiian Detachment, and a token Asiatic Fleet now

---

[37] Meacham, *Franklin and Winston,* 49-50; and Shogan, *Hard Bargain,* 15-16.

At this time FDR intended the move as one of ***deterrence,*** and not as a provocation. This action---directed on May 15th, in a Naval message from CNO Harold R. "Betty" Stark to CINCUS James O. Richardson---was clearly in response to Churchill's request to "keep that Japanese dog quiet in the Pacific," ***received the very same day by FDR.*** Neither Roosevelt nor Churchill wanted the Japanese to see the war in Europe as an opportunity to grab the resources of weakened European colonial possessions in the Far East, particularly with regard to the Dutch East Indies and its oil. [The Netherlands had just surrendered to Hitler when FDR made this deterrent move to prop up the status quo in the Netherlands East Indies and all of Southeast Asia.]

homeported in Manila. On April 29, 1940 Chief of Naval Operations (CNO) Harold Stark had first informed Admiral Richardson, Commander in Chief, U.S. Fleet (CINUS) that he might receive instructions to temporarily keep the fleet in Hawaii after the conclusion of its Fleet Problem XXI exercises. (The original schedule called for the Fleet to remain in Hawaii until May 9th, and to then depart and arrive back at its West Coast bases on May 17th). On May 4th, Stark confirmed to Richardson in a Naval message: "It looks probable but not final that the fleet will remain in Hawaiian waters for short time after May 9th." On May 7th, CNO cabled CINCUS a directive to issue a press release saying that the fleet would be staying in Hawaiian waters, and saying it was his own (Richardson's) idea (!). This same message from Stark also told Richardson: "Delay fleet departure Hawaiian area for about two weeks prior to end of which time you will be further advised regarding future movements." On May 15th, CNO cabled CINCUS the following guidance: "Present indications are that fleet will remain Hawaiian waters for some time. Hope to advise you more definitely next week." On May 22nd, Stark cabled Richarson: "Nothing more definite regarding movements [of] fleet." The fleet was never returned to its West Coast homeports, and to say that Admiral Richardson was unhappy would be an understatement. At the time Hawaii lacked the training facilities, industrial repair facilities, and fuel oil supplies necessary to support advanced basing of the U.S. fleet. Furthermore, repair ships and tugs needed to support the fleet were still on the West Coast. Richardson was subsequently instructed not to give any publicity to the fact that individual ships were departing to conduct previously scheduled overhauls in West Coast ports. On May 22, 1940 Richardson wrote a letter to Stark and asked him why the Fleet was now at Pearl Harbor, and what impact this would have on fleet training. Stark replied forthrightly in a letter dated May 27th: **"Why are you in the Hawaiian area?** *Answer:* **You are there because of the deterrent effect which it is thought your presence may have on the Japs going into the East Indies**…The above I think will answer the question: 'Why are you there?' It does not answer the question as to how long you will probably stay…Nobody can answer it just now. Like you, I have asked the question, and also---like you--- I have been unable to get the answer…You were not detained in Hawaii to develop the area as a peacetime operating base…". [Emphasis added] On June 22, 1940 Stark wrote: "Tentatively decision has been made for fleet to remain…where it is." It did, in spite of vociferous and repeated objection by CINCUS. Admiral Richardson would later twice meet with FDR (in July and in October of 1940), and personally complain that the U.S. fleet could not train adequately, or be properly maintained or provisioned, in Hawaii; this temerity would cost him his

			job. Richardson wrote in his memoirs that FDR and Hull were in error in assuming that moving the U.S. fleet to Pearl Harbor would act as a brake on Japanese intentions---as deterrence---citing an Army analysis written after World War II (with considerable hindsight) which claimed that rather than acting as a deterrent to Japanese adventurism in the Dutch East Indies and French Indochina, that the basing of the fleet in Hawaii was insufficient in and of itself to prevent Japanese expansion, and would only have deterred the Japanese if its government decided that it was *not* a bluff, i.e., if basing the fleet at Pearl Harbor was not inconsistent with other U.S. actions, and that if it *was* perceived as a bluff, that the Army in 1940 viewed this move as a potentially dangerous one, which presented the expansionists in Japan with two choices: either accept the challenge presented by the forward-basing of the fleet and back down---cease plans for expansion; or act in defiance and proceed with expansion by commencing hostilities on the most favorable terms possible.[38]
May 16, 1940		**FDR requests a massive increase in arms production from Congress; and he will follow in July with a request for a two-ocean Navy, which will also be readily approved.**	The panic was finally on in the United States, as the British and French armies fighting the Germans in Belgium and France were already in pell-mell retreat before the well-executed German advance, just 6 days after Germany launched its offensive in the West. FDR addressed a joint session of Congress,

---

[38] Richardson, *On the Treadmill to Pearl Harbor,* 307-333.

	Before the defeat of France, the Navy had under construction 52 warships and 62 auxiliaries. Afterwards, a geyser of money was forthcoming, and <u>by February of 1941, there were 368 warships and 338 auxiliaries under construction.</u>[39]	warning that "new powers of destruction" unleashed by "ruthless and daring" aggressors threatened the traditional American faith in the security provided by its two adjoining oceans. **He requested a *fivefold increase* in defense spending for 1940 (of 1.4 billion dollars); an increase in the Army from 280,000 to 1,200,000 men; and a jump in the production of military aircraft from 12,000 to 50,000 per year.**[40] These requests were quickly approved.
May 17, 1940 (Two sources consulted, Shogan and Davis, list the date of this cable as May 16th, but since Meacham's work is dedicated solely to the correspondence and relationship between FDR and Churchill, I have chosen to employ the date he cites, that of May 17th, which presumably is authoritative. Perhaps the cable	**FDR replies to Churchill's request for the 50 vintage destroyers and other weapons.** Some of FDR's advisors (notably Interior Secretary Harold Ickes and Under Secretary of State Sumner Welles) did not think highly of Churchill, disparaging him as a heavy drinker infused with "Dutch courage." Roosevelt, who remembered him as a cad from the one occasion when they had met in	"I have just received your message," Roosevelt cabled, "and I am sure it is unnecessary for me to say that I am most happy to continue our private correspondence as in the past." **FDR disappointed Churchill by declining his most urgent requests.** <u>Addressing the question of destroyers, Roosevelt reminded Churchill of his constitutional constraints:</u> ***"As you know, a step of that kind could not be taken except without the specific authorization of the Congress and I am not certain that it would be wise for that suggestion to be made to the Congress at this moment."*** FDR did state that he would try to arrange for "antiaircraft equipment and ammunition" and for "the purchase of

---

[39] Marolda, ed., *FDR and the U.S. Navy,* 95-96. Another historian, Waldo Heinrichs, summarized the massive increase in the size of the U.S. Navy when he wrote in *Threshold of War* (p. 10) that from May of 1940 through the end of the year, the following increases in Naval construction were authorized: nine new battleships (in addition to the eight previously ordered between 1937-1940); eleven aircraft carriers; three battle cruisers; eight heavy cruisers; thirty-one light cruisers, and 181 destroyers.

[40] Shogan, *Hard Bargain,* 73; Davis, *FDR: Into the Storm,* 548; and Heinrichs, *Threshold of War,* 10.

was drafted and released in Washington on May 16th, but not received by Churchill until May 17th. Sensitive cables of this nature could take many hours to be both transmitted, and then decoded at the receiving end.)	1918 (during World War I), seemed himself not to be sure what to think of Churchill's leadership ability, or Britain's chances of survival, at this time. Most of the people in FDR's administration sat on the fence during May and June waiting to see if the British would quickly fold, or whether they could and would fight effectively against Germany. While numerous people in the administration began to seek strategies for getting arms transferred to the British, and to compile lists of what could be sent, FDR and his advisors were waiting to see whether the British were worthy of receiving significant material aid. No one wanted to send precious weapons (even obsolescent ones) from a country that was already woefully unprepared for war itself, to a country that might be defeated in the near future.	steel" while promising to ponder the Irish ports question and to keep the fleet in Hawaii "for the time being."[41] [Emphasis added]
May 18, 1940	Winston S. Churchill	Churchill's son Randolph was home on

---

[41] Meacham, *Franklin and Winston*, 49.

		explains his overall war strategy to his son, Randolph: ***hold on, until we can drag the United States into the war.***	leave from his military unit on May 18, 1940 while the British and French armies on the continent were crumbling under attacks by the German army and air force. Randolph was sitting with his father while the Prime Minister was shaving, and the old man suddenly said: ***"I think I see my way through."*** Randolph asked his father (now Prime Minister and Minister of Defense) if he really believed Great Britain could avoid defeat (which seemed credible), or beat Germany (which seemed incredible), and his father replied: ***"Of course I mean we can beat them."*** Randolph later wrote (in 1963) that by this time his father had dried and sponged his face, and turned to his son with great intensity, saying: ***"<u>I shall drag the United States in.</u>"***[42] [Emphasis added]
May 19, 1940	**"Arm Yourselves, and Be Ye Men of Valour"** Holland had just fallen on May 15th, and the French army was in full retreat before the onslaught of the German army and air		**"I speak to you for the very first time as Prime Minister in a solemn hour for the life of our country, of our Empire, of our Allies, and above all, of the cause of Freedom.** A tremendous battle is raging in France and Flanders. The Germans, by a remarkable combination

---

[42] Ibid., 51; and Rushbridger and Nave, *Betrayal at Pearl Harbor,* 23. The full account of this intimate father-son conversation is quoted in *Betrayal at Pearl Harbor*. It was lifted verbatim from page 358 of *Their Finest Hour,* written by Churchill's official biographer, Martin Gilbert, and is titled "Randolph Churchill's Recollections, 18 May 1940: "I went up to my father's bedroom. He was standing in front of his basin and was shaving with his old-fashioned Valet razor. He had a tough beard and as usual was hacking away. 'Sit down, dear boy, and read the papers while I finish shaving.' After two or three minutes of hacking away he half turned to me and said: 'I think I see my way through.' I was astounded and said: 'Do you mean we can avoid defeat or beat the bastards?' He flung his valet razor into the basin, swung round, and said: 'Of course I mean we can beat them.' I replied: 'Well, I'm all for it, but I don't see how you can do it.' By this time my father had dried and sponged his face and turning round to me said with great intensity: 'I shall drag the United States in.'"

force. The commander of the British Expeditionary Force (BEF) in northern France and Belgium, Lord Gort, was preparing to retreat toward Dunkirk. It was in these circumstances that Winston Churchill made his first radio broadcast to the British people.[43]

of air bombing and heavily armoured tanks, have broken through the French defenses north of the Maginot Line, and strong columns of their armoured vehicles are ravaging the open country…they have penetrated deeply and spread alarm and confusion in their track…we must not allow ourselves to be intimidated by the presence of these armoured vehicles in unexpected places behind our lines…It would be foolish, however, to disguise the gravity of the hour…In the air---often at serious odds, often at odds thought hitherto overwhelming---we have been clawing down three or four to one of our enemies; and the relative balance of the British and German Air Forces is now considerably more favourable to us than at the beginning of the battle…**My confidence in our ability to fight it out to the finish with the German Air Force has been strengthened by the fierce encounters which have taken place and are taking place**…Is this not the appointed time for all to make the utmost exertions in their power? If the battle is to be won, we must provide our men with ever-increasing quantities of the weapons and ammunition they need. We must have, and have quickly, more aeroplanes, more tanks, more shells, more guns…Our task is not only to win the battle, but to win the war. **After this battle in France abates its force, there will come the battle for our Island---for all that Britain is, and all that Britain means.**

---

[43] Churchill, ed., *Never Give In!*, 206-209.

That will be the struggle. In that supreme emergency we shall not hesitate to take every step, even the most drastic, to call forth from our people the last ounce and the last inch of effort of which they are capable. *The interests of property, the hours of labour, are nothing compared with the struggle of life and honour, for right and freedom, to which we have vowed ourselves*…I have formed an administration of men and women of every party and of almost every point of view. We have differed and quarreled in the past; but now one bond unites us all ---**to wage war until victory is won, and never to surrender ourselves to servitude and shame, whatever the cost and the agony may be.** This is one of the most awe-striking periods in the long history of France and Britain. It is also beyond doubt the most sublime…side-by-side, the British and French peoples have advanced to rescue not only Europe but mankind from the foulest and most soul-destroying tyranny which has ever darkened and stained the pages of history. Behind them---behind us---behind the armies and fleets of Britain and France---gather a group of shattered States and bludgeoned races: the Czechs, the Poles, the Norwegians, the Danes, the Dutch, the Belgians---upon all of whom the long night of barbarism will descend, unbroken even by a star of hope, unless we conquer, as conquer we must; as conquer we shall…Centuries ago words were written to be a call and a spur to the faithful

		servants of Truth and Justice: '**Arm yourselves, and be ye men of valour, and be in readiness for the conflict; for it is better for us to perish in battle than to look upon the outrage of our nation and our altar.** As the will of God is in Heaven, even so let it be.' " [Emphasis added] Commencing with this speech, Churchill was speaking to two audiences: to the British people, and to the American people---and especially to Franklin D. Roosevelt. He had to persuade the American people, and especially Roosevelt, that the British people and the British nation were worthy of America's support. This is also the second consecutive speech in which Churchill seemed to be speaking directly to the aristocracy at home that did not trust him and which at this time was doubtful about fighting on against seemingly hopeless odds---telling them twice within one week that making a deal with Hitler was unacceptable; that the only road to survival was through victory; and that even death was preferable to a shameful surrender.
May 21-May 24, 1940	Churchill sounds an alarming note to FDR in a cable, and FDR responds with a secret diplomatic initiative designed to save the British Fleet should Churchill's government fall, and be replaced by a pacifist, defeatist regime determined to make peace with Hitler's Germany.	On May 21st, stung by FDR's refusal to provide the 50 old destroyers, and depressed by the success of the rapidly advancing German armies in France and Belgium---and no doubt filled with anxiety about the long-term prospects for the survival of his own tenuous government---Churchill sent Roosevelt the following gloomy and (to FDR) rather alarming message: "If members of the present administration were finished **and others came in to parley amid the**

ruins, you must not be blind to the fact that **the sole remaining bargaining counter with Germany would be the fleet,** and *if this country was left by the United States to its fate* no one would have the right to blame those then responsible if they made the best terms they could for the surviving inhabitants. Forgive me, Mr. President, putting this nightmare bluntly. Evidently I could not answer for my successors who in utter despair and helplessness might well have to accommodate themselves to the German will." [Emphasis added]

(The possible leaders of a pro-German government of accommodation in Great Britain might be one of the two prominent English Fascists about to be jailed by Churchill, or more likely, along the lines of what later happened in France, elder statesman Lloyd George. Later, in July of 1940, writer George Orwell predicted in his diary that if Britain was defeated, George would likely become the "Petain of England." Lloyd George had been Prime Minister during World War I, and in 1936 had visited Hitler and publicly called him "the greatest living German." In October of 1939, after Germany had defeated Poland, Lloyd George said openly in Parliament that Hitler's peace offer should be seriously considered. By 1940, Lloyd George had evolved from an open Hitler admirer, into a defeatist.)

On May 24th, FDR, unknown to the British (but not for long), began making secret overtures to the Canadian

		government of Prime Minister Mackenzie King. Roosevelt asked that King persuade the British Government to agree to send the British Fleet to Canada, in the event a defeated or cowed Great Britain was forced to make peace with a victorious Germany. FDR asked that Churchill *not be told* about the American origins of the proposal, and that it be pressed by Canada and the Dominions. King felt at the time that the United States was "trying to save itself at the expense of Britain" and suggested that Roosevelt should talk directly to Churchill about the matter.[44]
May 25, 1940	A highly classified report is prepared by the British Chiefs of Staff for the Cabinet titled: **"British Strategy in a Certain Eventuality."** The eventuality was the defeat of France and the British Expeditionary Force by Nazi Germany, which appeared imminent.	The report states in part: "We make two assumptions. A. That the United States of America is willing to give us full economic and financial assistance, *without which we do not think we could continue the war with any chance of success.* [Emphasis in original] B. That Italy has intervened against us." The authors of the report predicted that if France fell, Britain's ability to avoid defeat depended on three factors: (1) whether the morale of its people could withstand the anticipated air bombardment; (2) the ability of Britain to import essential commodities; and (3) Britain's capacity to resist invasion.[45]
May 26, 1940	FDR gives a Fireside Chat about the effects upon America of the war	Excerpts follow: "My friends…We are shocked by the almost incredible eyewitness stories that come to us, stories

---

[44] Lukacs, *Five Days in London,* 71-76; and *Finest Hour: The Battle of Britain* (PBS, 2003).

[45] Moss, *19 Weeks,* 127-128.

	in Europe, with the intention of reassuring Americans about both their present situation, and about action being taken in response to the war; it also served as a tutorial about the realities of a world at war, and a little bit of an "I told you so" lecture about the dangers of the modern world and the foolishness of isolationism in the era of the airplane and the submarine. In short, it was a speech designed for domestic consumption--- not a pep talk for the British or the French.	of what is happening at this moment to the civilian populations of Norway and Holland and Belgium and Luxembourg and France…There are many among us who in the past closed their eyes to events abroad---because they believed in utter good faith what some of their fellow Americans told them---that what has taken place in Europe was none of our business; that no matter what happened over there, the United States could always pursue its peaceful and unique course in the world. There are many among us who closed their eyes, from lack of interest or lack of knowledge; honestly and sincerely thinking that many hundreds of miles of salt water made the American hemisphere so remote that the people of North and Central and South America could go on living in the midst of their vast resources without reference to, or danger from, the other continents of the world. There are some among us who were persuaded by minority groups that we could maintain our physical safety by retiring within our continental boundaries…**I illustrated the futility---the impossibility---of that idea in my message to the Congress last week.** Obviously, a defense policy based on that is merely to invite future attack…And finally, there are a few among us who have deliberately and consciously closed their eyes because they were determined to be opposed to their government, its foreign policy and every other policy, to be partisan, and to believe that anything the government did was wholly wrong.

To those who have closed their eyes for any of these many reasons, to those who would not admit the possibility of the coming storm---to all of them the past two weeks have meant the shattering of many illusions. They have lost the illusion that we are remote and isolated and, therefore, secure against the dangers from which no other land is free. In some quarters, with this rude awakening has come fear, fear bordering on panic. It is said that we are defenseless. It is whispered by some that only by abandoning our freedom, our ideals, our way of life, can we build our defenses adequately, can we match the strength of the aggressors. I do not share those illusions. I do not share these fears. Today we are more realistic. But let us not be calamity-howlers and discount our strength." [Emphasis added] To reassure the public, FDR then proceeded to enumerate how the armed forces had been strengthened during the 7 years he had been in office (from the spring of 1933 to the spring of 1940): "The fighting personnel of the Navy rose from 79,000 to 145,000. **During this period 215 ships for the fighting fleet have been laid down or commissioned, practically seven times the number in the preceding seven-year period.** Of these 215 ships we have commissioned 12 cruisers; 63 destroyers; 26 submarines; 3 aircraft carriers; 2 gunboats; 7 auxiliaries; and many smaller craft. **Among the many ships now being built and paid for as we build them are 8 new battleships**…and speaking of airplanes, airplanes that work with the Navy, in 1933 we had 1,127 of them…and today we have 2,892 on hand and on order. Of course, nearly all of the old planes of 1933 have been replaced by new planes because they became obsolete and worn out. Yes, the Navy is far stronger today than in any peacetime period in the whole long history of our nation…The Army of the United States…In 1933, it consisted of 122,000 enlisted men. Now, in 1940, that number has practically doubled…and by the end of this year, every existing unit of the present regular Army will be equipped with its complete requirements of modern weapons…Since 1933, we have actually purchased 5,640 modern airplanes, including the most modern type of long-range bombers and fast pursuit planes, though, of course, many of these that were delivered four and five and six and seven years ago have worn out through use and have been scrapped…To go on. In 1933 we had only 355 antiaircraft guns. We now have more than 1,700 modern antiaircraft guns of all types on hand or on order…In 1933 we had only 48 modern tanks and armored cars; today we have on hand and on order 1,700…in 1933…we had 1,263 Army pilots. Today the Army alone has more than 3,200 of the best fighting fliers in the world…**Within the past year the productive capacity of the aviation industry to produce modern planes has been tremendously increased---in this past year more than doubled. But that capacity is still inadequate. This** government, working with industry, is determined to increase that capacity to meet our needs. **We intend to harness the efficient machinery of of these manufacturers to the government's program of being able to get 50,000 planes a year**…In line with my request, the Congress, this week, is voting the largest appropriations ever asked by the Army or the Navy in peacetime…The world situation may so change that it will be necessary to reappraise our program at any time…I will not hesitate at any moment to ask for additional funds when they are required…I know that private business cannot be expected to make all of the capital investments required for expansions of plants and factories and personnel this program calls for at once…**Therefore, the government of the United States stands ready to advance the necessary money to help provide for the enlargement of factories, the establishment of new plants, the employment of thousands of necessary workers, the development of new sources of supply for the hundreds of raw materials required, the development of quick mass transportation of supplies.** And the details of all this are now being worked out in Washington day and night. We are calling on men now engaged in private industry to help us in carrying out this program, and you will hear more of this in detail in the next few days…**It is our purpose not only to speed up production but to increase the total facilities of the nation in such a way**

		that they can be further enlarged to meet emergencies of the future…While our Navy and our airplanes and our guns and our ships may be our first lines of defense, it is clear that way down at the bottom, underlying them all, giving them their strength, sustenance, and power, are the spirit and the morale of a free people…As more orders come in and as more work has to be done, tens of thousands of people, who are now unemployed, will, I believe, receive employment…And, I can assure you that labor will be adequately represented in Washington in the carrying out of this program of defense…At this time, when the world---and the world includes our own American hemisphere---when the world is threatened by forces of destruction, it is my resolve and yours to build up our armed defenses. We shall build them to whatever heights the future may require. We shall rebuild them swiftly, as the methods of warfare swiftly change…Day and night I pray for the restoration of peace in this mad world of ours. It is not necessary that I, the President, ask the American people to pray in behalf of such a cause---for I know you are praying with me." [Emphasis Added]
May 26-27, 1940	**Prime Minister Winston Churchill and his Foreign Secretary, Lord Halifax (Edward Wood), square off against each other in a series of six War Cabinet Meetings on May 26th and 27th, over**	The two-week period after Churchill assumed office as Prime Minister has been called by some the Black Fortnight, so grim was the war news from both Norway and the Continent. Holland surrendered to Germany on May 15th, and Belgium sued for peace on May 27th. The British BEF and the French Army

whether or not to: (a) continue fighting Germany against seemingly hopeless odds (Churchill's position); or (b) to make a peace deal with a seemingly invincible Germany---recognizing its conquests on the Continent---which would spare England invasion, ruin, and occupation---and which would permit the rich aristocracy to keep its property, and would keep the British Empire largely intact. These crucial discussions, unknown to the British people at the time (and even to most of the government and the bureaucracy), were taking place amidst the dark backdrop of the complete rout of the British Expeditionary Force, and the Belgian and French Armies, on the Continent. Indeed, during the middle of this internal policy struggle, on May 26th, Churchill ordered the seaborne evacuation of the surrounded BEF (a quarter of a million men) from Dunkirk. Churchill himself, on May 26th, feared that only about

continued to retreat before a seemingly unstoppable German Army and Air Force; indeed, the German Army reached the English Channel in just 10 days of fighting, something they had been unable to accomplish in 4 years of conflict during World War I. The Wehrmacht made its biggest gains on May 17th and 18th, setting off a panic among the aristocracy back in the British Isles. (The average citizen did not yet know how badly the war in France was going, but the well-connected members of the upper class did.) King George VI and Chamberlain had both preferred Halifax over Churchill for Prime Minister earlier in May, and if Churchill could not stem the internal panic among the British elites, and restore confidence within his own Conservative Party (which had long distrusted his judgment), his Government might not long survive. Under this backdrop, the Foreign Secretary, Lord Halifax, commenced discussions with the Italian Ambassador to Great Britain on May 25th, ostensibly to attempt to persuade Mussolini not to enter the war against France (a dubious proposition at this point), but in reality, to see if Italy might be willing to discuss "the problems between England and Italy" in the context of a "general European settlement." (What Halifax and many in the aristocracy favored was offering Mussolini the British territories of Malta and Gibraltar in the Mediterranean, and offering Hitler some British colonial possessions in East Africa, in exchange for a no-invasion pledge, nominal

	50,000 men could be saved.	independence for Great Britain, and the ability to keep most of her Empire.) France, fearing total collapse of its Army, supported the concept of this approach (which amounted to continued appeasement), since it favored anything that would stop the fighting. As Halifax put his position on May 26th, *"We had to face the fact that it was not so much now a question of imposing a complete defeat upon Germany, but of safeguarding the independence of our Empire…We should naturally be prepared to consider any proposals which might lead to this, provided our liberty and independence were assured."* Churchill's position was that peace and security could not be achieved under a German domination of Europe: *"That we could never accept. We must assure our complete liberty and independence."* Churchill opined that in the event of a peace deal with Hitler, Britain's rearmament program would not be permitted to continue, and England would become a vassal state, or satellite nation of Nazi Germany. Halifax thought that *"if we got to the point of discussing the terms of a general settlement and found that we could obtain terms that did not postulate the destruction of our independence, we would be <u>foolish</u> if we did not accept them."* On May 27th, their disagreement became more pronounced during the cabinet meetings. Churchill said that he *"was increasingly oppressed with the futility of the suggested approach to Signor Mussolini, which the latter*

would certainly regard with contempt…the approach would ruin the integrity of the fighting position in this country…". Churchill continued, saying that at present Britain's prestige in Europe *"was very low."* The only way to restore it, he continued, *"was by showing the world that Germany had not beaten us. If, after two or three months, we could show Germany that we were still unbeaten, our prestige would return. Even if we were beaten, we would be no worse off than we should be if we were now to abandon the struggle. Let us therefore avoid being dragged down the slippery slope with France. The whole of this maneuver was to get us so deeply involved in negotiations that we should be unable to turn back."* Churchill also said on May 27th, *"If the worse came to the worst, it would not be a bad thing for this country to go down fighting for the other countries which had been overcome by Nazi tyranny."* Halifax, who considered himself a pragmatist, and who privately accused Churchill of talking *"the most frightful rot,"* had had enough, and requested that the Prime Minister accompany him for a private walk in the garden. (Neither man left a record of it in his writings.) Immediately before this development, Halifax had confided to Alexander Cadogan (the ranking permanent civil servant in the Foreign Office) that *"I can't work with Winston any longer."* It is possible that Halifax offered to resign during the walk in the garden, and that Churchill dissuaded him for the sake of national

		unity in a time of crisis. John Colville, the Prime Minister's Secretary, wrote in his diary for May 27th: "There are signs that Halifax is being defeatist. He says our aim can no longer be to crush Germany, but rather to preserve our integrity and independence."[46]
May 28, 1940	**Winston Churchill triumphs over Lord Halifax in the crucial internal debate over whether or not to make a peace deal with Nazi Germany.** Churchill had worn Halifax down over three days of intense discussions, and on May 28th, the day their differences came most sharply into the open within the War Cabinet, outmaneuvered him by enlisting the strong support of the members of the Outer Cabinet. After this day, while privately often still critical of Churchill, Halifax never again publicly challenged him on this issue. In December of 1940, Churchill solved his "Lord Halifax" problem by appointing him as the new Ambassador to the	This victory by Churchill over domestic defeatism is what historian John Lukacs has called a major turning point in the Second World War, for during the five days between May 24-28, 1940 (inclusive), when Hitler came closest to winning World War II (before the United States or the Soviet Union were even involved), <u>Churchill was the one man who refused to lose it</u>. As Lukacs points out, while the tide of battle against the Axis did not turn until late in 1942, and while it took the combined resources of the USSR and the U.S. to defeat Germany, these events were not foreordained: Hitler <u>could have won the Second World War in 1940</u> if Britain had cut a deal to avoid invasion and ruin, and had become a satellite nation of Germany. He would then ***not*** have broken his air weapon against the RAF (as he did in August and September), and furthermore, the United States would never have had an "unsinkable base" (the British Isles) from which to bomb Germany from 1942-45, and from which to spearhead an invasion of occupied France in 1944.[47] The story of how

---

[46] Lukacs, *Five Days in London,* 82-161; and *Finest Hour: The Battle of Britain* (PBS, 2003).

[47] As Lukacs so eloquently summarized in his 1999 masterpiece, *Five Days in London: May 1940,* "Churchill saw Hitler and the Reich as incarnating something evil and dangerous, some of the brutal sources of which may

	United States after the unexpected death (due to kidney failure) of Lord Lothian on December 11th ---thus removing a political thorn from his side, and a potential source of disloyalty from the British Isles, while the eventual outcome of the war was still very much in doubt. In spite of his unexpected (and to many, shocking) demotion and banishment from the British Isles, Halifax proved to be an able British Ambassador throughout the war, and even on into 1946. (Churchill, like Roosevelt, directly controlled all important matters pertaining to foreign relations with his	Churchill outmaneuvered Halifax on May 28th is a dramatic one. As the meeting minutes of May 28th for the War Cabinet reveal, "The Prime Minister said that ***the French*** [in suggesting to Halifax that Britain make certain concessions to Italy to bring about a negotiated general settlement] ***were trying to get us on to the slippery slope. The position would be entirely different when Germany had made an unsuccessful attempt to invade this country***…The Foreign Secretary said that we should not ignore the fact ***that we might get better terms before France went out of the war*** and our aircraft factories were bombed, ***than we might get in three month's time.***" The War Cabinet meeting notes continue: "The Prime Minister then read out a draft which expressed his views…***If we once got to the [conference] table, we should then find that the terms offered us touched our independence and integrity.***

have been very old, but some of which were also alarmingly new. And his vision was such that he turned out to be the savior not only of England but of much else besides---essentially all of Europe (p. 213)." He was not exaggerating when he stated early in his book (on p. 2), "…Britain could not [alone] win the war. In the end America and Russia did. But in May 1940 Churchill was the one who did not *lose it*. Then and there he saved Britain, and Europe, and Western civilization." He continued his summation on page 217: "Churchill understood something that not many people understand even now. The greatest threat to Western civilization was not Communism. It was National Socialism. The greatest and most dynamic power in the world was not Soviet Russia. It was the Third Reich of Germany. The greatest revolutionary of the twentieth century was not Lenin or Stalin. It was Hitler. Hitler not only succeeded in merging nationalism and socialism into one tremendous force; he was a new kind of ruler, representing a new kind of populist nationalism. What was more, the remnants of the old order (or disorder) were not capable of withstanding him…". Churchill alone in May of 1940---and soon assisted by the strong moral and materiel support of Franklin D. Roosevelt and the United States as that year progressed---kept Hitler from scoring an early knockout. As Lukacs appropriately puts it (p. 218), Churchill, like King Canute, tried to hold back the sea, but unlike Canute, he succeeded: "He was surely no saint, he was not a religious man, and he had many faults. But so it happened."

opposite number across the Atlantic himself; in America, Halifax was not in a position to make policy. His true intent in assigning Halifax---banishment---is confirmed by the fact that he first attempted to appoint <u>Lloyd George, a defeatist</u>. FDR expressed a polite concern about the old statesman's open admiration for Hitler during the mid 1930s, and Lloyd George himself turned down the opportunity, citing old age, prompting Churchill to substitute Halifax instead. Halifax may be viewed as an appeaser, but at least he was not an open admirer of Adolph Hitler, as Lloyd George was.)

In one of the supreme ironies of history, Neville Chamberlain, the "arch appeaser of Munich," ultimately supported Churchill's position to fight on rather than sue for peace and engage in more appeasement by giving away British colonies. In doing so, he provided Churchill a three-to-two majority on

When, at this point, we got up to leave the conference table, we should then find that all the forces of resolution which were now at our disposal would have vanished…***It was impossible to imagine that Herr Hitler would be so foolish as to let us continue our re-armament. In effect, his terms would completely put us at his mercy.*** We should get no worse terms if we went on fighting, even if we were beaten, than were open to us now…The Foreign Secretary said that ***he still did not see what there was in the French suggestion in trying out the possibilities of mediation*** [by Italy] ***which the Prime Minister felt so wrong.*** The Lord President [Chamberlain] said that, on a dispassionate survey, it was right to remember that ***the alternative to fighting on nevertheless involved a considerable gamble***…The Prime Minister said that <u>***the nations which went down fighting rose again, but those which surrendered tamely were finished***</u>…The Minister Without Portfolio [Greenwood] said that any course which we took was attended by great danger. The line of resistance was certainly a gamble, but ***he did not feel that this was a time for ultimate capitulation.*** The Foreign Secretary said that ***nothing in his suggestion could even remotely be described as ultimate capitulation.*** [Emphasis added]

It was now 5 PM on May 28th, and when the War Cabinet adjourned for two hours, **Churchill met with the Outer Cabinet (i.e., all except the five members of the War Cabinet)---about twenty five to**

this issue in the War Cabinet. Halifax, who had flipped his position in 1938 and had decided to oppose Prime Minister Chamberlain on appeasement just prior to the signing of the Munich agreement, had now become the appeaser; and Chamberlain, who had realized with stunning clarity his error at Munich when Germany seized the remainder of Czechoslovakia in March of 1939, now opposed further appeasement, or even negotiations with Hitler. Halifax, to be sure, considered himself a *pragmatist* and a realist (not an appeaser), and considered Churchill a visionary who was being *impractical.* History, with 20-20 hindsight, has clearly rendered its verdict here; but things were not nearly so clear in late May of 1940.

Chamberlain, who at this

thirty individuals---and solidified his position with a masterstroke. It took about one hour to accomplish this.

Historian John Lukacs summarized Churchill's political coup at the outer cabinet meeting first by quoting MP Hugh Dalton's memoirs and his diary (on pp. 4-5 of *Five Days in London*). Churchill said, ***"I have thought carefully in these last days whether it was part of my duty to consider entering negotiations with That Man."*** He then reportedly said, "It was idle to think that, if we tried to make peace now, we should get better terms from Germany than if we went on and fought it out. ***The Germans would demand our Fleet---that would be called 'disarmament'---our naval bases, and much else. We should become a slave state,*** though a British government which would be Hitler's puppet would be set up---'under Mosley or some such person.' And where should we be at the end of all that? On the other side, we had immense reserves and advantages. Therefore, he said, '*<u>If this long Island story of ours is to end at last, let it end only when each of us lies choking in his own blood upon the ground.</u>*'"[48] To this sentiment Dalton wrote that "there was a murmur of approval around the table."

---

[48] The original version of this sentence (in Dalton's memoirs) read: "We shall go on and we shall fight it out, here or elsewhere, and if at last the long story is to end, it were better it should end, not through surrender, but only when we are rolling senseless on the ground." The more dramatic (and more "Churchillian") version of this statement quoted above in the main text was found in Dalton's marginalia, apparently corrected after he showed the passage to someone with a better memory than he---presumably Churchill himself. (See Lukacs, *Five Days in London,* 4-5.)

time was gravely ill (but did not yet know it), was broken by the tragedy of his failed foreign policy of appeasement and the resulting war. He died in November of 1940. Churchill, his biggest critic before war began on September 3, 1939, was unswervingly loyal after he joined Chamberlain's Government as First Lord of the Admiralty. Chamberlain returned his loyalty by supporting Churchill's decision to fight on, no matter what, and not to negotiate a peace with Hitler. Chamberlain had learned the hard way that Hitler could not be relied upon to keep any formal diplomatic agreement, or abide by the written terms of any treaty, for the mere sake of complying with legalities. Hitler could only be relied upon to follow his own self interest. He was intent upon destroying the old world order, and substituting it with a new world order: one based on force, and survival of the fittest.

Churchill himself, while he did not mention the struggle with Halifax in volume II of his six-volume *History of the Second World War,* did mention (on pp. 99-100) the support he received when he met with the Outer Cabinet on May 28th: "Then I said quite casually, and not treating it as a point of special significance: *'Of course, whatever happens at Dunkirk, we shall fight on.'* There occurred a demonstration which, considering the character of the gathering---twenty-five experienced politicians and Parliament men, who represented all the different points of view, whether right or wrong, before the war---surprised me. Quite a number seemed to jump up from the table and came running to my chair, shouting and patting me on the back. *There was no doubt that had I at this juncture faltered at all in leading the nation, I should have been hurled out of office.* I was sure that every minister was ready to be killed quite soon, and have all his family and possessions destroyed, rather than give in." [Emphasis added]

Significant to me is Churchill's admission years later, even in the glow of victory, that his hold on office was precarious at this time. The intense pleasure that he obviously took in recalling his good feeling upon the congratulations he received at this meeting, in my view, supports the likelihood that Dalton's dramatic rendition of Churchill's resolve to go down fighting, if necessary, rather than to surrender, was accurate. Churchill,

		exercising the magnanimity in victory for which he was so famous, had chosen in his memoirs to avoid discussing the crucial struggle for the future of the nation between himself and his Foreign Secretary. As Lukacs summarized (on p. 2), **"…Churchill had won. He declared that England would go on fighting, no matter what happened.** *No matter what happened:* **there would be no negotiating with Hitler."** [Emphasis in original]
		When the War Cabinet met again at 7 PM on May 28th, Churchill reported the unanimous consent he had received from the Outer Cabinet to his decision not to negotiate, and that effectively killed the effort by Halifax to commence negotiations with Hitler, through Italy. Now that Churchill had achieved a strong consensus within the Government to fight on, even to the bitter end if necessary, he set about to strengthen the resolve of the British people to do just that. His speeches throughout that summer, and that autumn, were designed to build the same determination in all the Britons that he had stoked in his Cabinet, and to persuade the President of the United States, and the American people, that Great Britain would not quit (as France and Belgium had done), and was worthy of America's assistance.
May 26 through June 4, 1940	**The Dunkirk Evacuation takes place from France to England,** during which the bulk of the British Expeditionary	The British Navy, and a large, irregular fleet of merchant vessels and private craft (most British, but some French and Belgian), evacuates the trapped British Expeditionary Force and some elements

	Force in Northern France, and some elements of the French Army, are evacuated to Great Britain. A total of 338,226 allied soldiers were evacuated, of which 228,500 were British and nearly all of the remainder were French. Records indicate that 861 ships of all kinds participated in the evacuation; that 243 of them were sunk; about 2,000 soldiers died in the process. It was not possible to evacuate vehicles or artillery. **The successful evacuation of the bulk of the BEF made it possible for Churchill to fight on, as he had persuaded the Cabinet to do on May 28th.**	of the French Army, which had been encircled by the rapidly advancing German Armies in Belgium and France. The evacuation takes place under shellfire, and amidst a terrible air battle overhead in which the RAF battled the Luftwaffe, and in which the Luftwaffe severely punished the British Navy ships performing the evacuation. If the bulk of the B.E.F. encircled at Dunkirk had been captured, Britain would most likely have had to sue for peace, and Hitler would have dominated all of Western Europe. The evacuation of most of the trapped British Army allowed Great Britain---just barely---to stay in the war against Hitler, and to avoid defeat. (Tens of thousands of British soldiers remained elsewhere in France after the Dunkirk evacuation, but could not forestall the inevitable defeat of the demoralized and leaderless French Army. Most of them, along with a fair number of their French brothers-in-arms, were later evacuated between 15-25 June.)
June 4, 1940	**"We Shall Fight on the Beaches, We Shall Fight on the Landing Grounds…We Shall Never Surrender."** Churchill addressed the House of Commons about the just-completed Dunkirk evacuation, and prospects for the future, at a very dark time when most of the world	Only some of the most exemplary quotations from this incredibly stirring (and lengthy) address can be reproduced here, in this format: "When, a week ago today, I asked the House to fix this afternoon as the occasion for a statement, *I feared it would be my hard lot to announce the greatest military disaster in our long history*…the whole root and core and brain of the British Army…seemed about to perish on the field or to be led into an ignominious and starving captivity…*a miracle of*

expected that Great Britain would either have to surrender, or would soon suffer invasion, ignominious defeat, and occupation.[49]

In the United States, FDR and his administration had been pursuing guarantees from Great Britain (via the Canadian government) that should Britain be defeated in an invasion, that the British Fleet would not scuttle or surrender itself to Nazi Germany, but instead sail to the Western Hemisphere to keep it out of Hitler's hands, and to help defend the U.S. and Canada. This was an irritation to Churchill throughout May, June, July, and August, for FDR was insisting on such a written guarantee as a precondition for lending significant amounts of material aid to Britain. Churchill thought it would be fatally injurious to British morale to even discuss such eventualities as defeat, scuttling, or

deliverance, achieved by valour, by perseverance, by perfect discipline, by faultless service, by resource, by skill, by unconquerable fidelity, is manifest to us all. The Royal Air Force engaged the main strength of the German Air Force, and inflicted upon them losses of at least four to one; and the Navy, using nearly 1,100 ships of all kinds, carried over 335,000 men, French and British, out of the jaws of death and shame, to their native land and to the tasks which lie immediately ahead. **We must be very careful not to assign to this deliverance the attributes of a victory. Wars are not won by evacuations.** But there was a victory inside this deliverance, which should be noted. It was gained by the Air Force…We got the Army away…all our pilots have been vindicated as superior to what they have at present to face…May it not also be that the cause of civilization itself will be defended by the skill and devotion of a few thousand airmen? There never has been, I suppose, in all the world, in all of the history of war, such an opportunity for youth…But our losses in material are enormous….*Nevertheless, our thankfulness at the escape of our Army, and so many men…must not blind us to the fact that what has happened in France and Belgium is a colossal military disaster*…We are told that Herr Hitler has a plan for invading the British Isles. This had often been thought of before…We must never forget the solid

---

[49] Churchill, ed., *Never Give In!,* 210-218.

	surrender in a written agreement---but he indirectly addressed those American concerns at the end of his magnificent address on June 4th. In doing so, he also presented a golden, glowing confidence in the goodness and strength of America---obviously directed at those who were still sitting on the fence regarding the issue of whether or not to render significant material aid to Great Britain.	assurances of sea power and those which belong to air power if it can be locally exercised…we shall prove ourselves once again able to defend our Island home, to ride out the storm of war, and to outlive the menace of tyranny, *if necessary for years, if necessary alone.* At any rate, that is what we are going to try to do…*Even though large tracts of Europe have fallen or may fall into the grip of the Gestapo and all the odious apparatus of Nazi rule, we shall not flag or fail.* <u>We shall go on to the end; we shall fight in France, we shall fight on the seas and oceans, we shall fight with growing confidence and growing strength in the air, we shall defend our Island, whatever the cost may be; we shall fight on the beaches, we shall fight on the landing grounds, we shall fight in the fields and in the streets, we shall fight in the hills; we shall never surrender,</u> and *even if,* which I do not for a moment believe, *this Island or a large part of it were subjugated and starving,* then our Empire beyond the seas, *armed and guarded by the British Fleet,* would carry on the struggle, until, in God's good time, *the New World, with all its power and might, steps forth to the rescue and liberation of the old."* [Emphasis added]
June 6, 1940	**Aid for Great Britain:** In a letter to Treasury Secretary Henry Morgenthau, FDR indicates his approval of the efforts within the	Marshall and his squad of government attorneys had come up with the strategy of first declaring items the British (or French) could use as surplus U.S. war materiel; the Army could then sell the weaponry to private companies, who in turn could then legally resell them to the

government during the previous three weeks to balance the requests of Britain with the urgent needs of the American armed forces. Morgenthau, who was responsible to FDR for coordinating the American response to the requests of the British purchasing mission and Prime Minister Churchill, had leaned heavily upon Army Chief of Staff George C. Marshall to develop ways and means to provide Great Britain with critical items urgently needed in its defense. FDR wrote on June 6th: "I am delighted to have that list of surplus materiel which is ready to roll. Give it an extra push every morning and every night until it is onboard ship."[50]

British or the French. In considering the items requested in Churchill's cable to Roosevelt of May 15th, Marshall had vetoed the request for aircraft, since it would retard the training of our own pilots; and had also disapproved sending antiaircraft guns, since the U.S. had a severe shortage of such weapons and very little ammunition for them. However, Marshall was generous in assigning other aid to Great Britain, using as a formula in determining what could be declared "surplus" a hypothetical Army of 1.8 million men—six times the size of the regular Army in May of 1940. Based on this generous formula, Marshall agreed that the following items could be declared surplus and then sold to the British: 500,000 Enfield rifles; 35,000 machine guns; 500 75 mm field guns; 500 mortars with 50,000 shells; and 100 million rounds of rifle and machine gun ammunition. Stripping U.S. stockpiles to help the British was made feasible by the massive rearmament plans submitted to Congress by FDR on May 16th. The obsolescent but still serviceable equipment being sent to Great Britain would soon be replaced by new models. And since Great Britain had just left a considerable amount of artillery and field arms on the beaches at Dunkirk, these items were considered essential to helping them to prepare for a possible invasion of the British Isles by Hitler's Germany. In addition to the above

---

[50] *Shogan,* Hard Bargain, 83.

		equipment, on June 6th, the Navy disclosed it was sending 50 Hell Diver scout bombers, currently assigned to Naval reserve squadrons, back to the manufacturer, Curtiss-Wright, for resale to the British. This necessitated the subterfuge of declaring them "temporarily in excess of requirements" and as "aging," a white lie gleefully supported by Roosevelt with the press on June 8th.[51] This was all legal sleight-of-hand, and it was a poorly kept secret, but with German armies crushing France, no one in a position of power seriously objected.
June 10, 1940	**Italy declares war on France, attacking in the south when France is all but beaten.**	This cowardly and opportunistic action by Italy earned public scorn from Franklin D. Roosevelt in a commencement address he delivered at the University of Virginia in Charlottesville on the evening of the same day Italy invaded Southern France. In his toughest speech yet on the war in Europe, Roosevelt added this dramatic phrase over the objections of the State Department, his voice steely and laced with contempt: ***"On this tenth day of June 1940, the hand that held the dagger has struck it into the back of its neighbor."*** This elicited an audible gasp of surprise and whistles of astonishment from an audience of reporters listening to the speech on the radio at the National Press Club in Washington. "Calling for 'effort, courage, sacrifice, and devotion' in times of national peril, in words that

---

[51] Ibid., 80-83.

		were directed as much at Britons as at Americans, Roosevelt came closer than ever before to linking the security of the United States directly to England's fate. 'To the opponents of force,' he promised to extend 'the material resources of this nation,' at the same time as he vowed that the U.S. would speed up its own rearmament. 'All roads leading to the accomplishment of these objectives must be kept clear of obstructions,' he declared. 'We will not slow down or detour. Signs and signals call for speed---and full speed ahead.'"[52] President Franklin D. Roosevelt had placed the U.S. economy on a war footing---or at least had given the orders to do so---and he was announcing it to the world.
June 14, 1940	**The German Army occupies Paris, the French capital.**	This event, more than any other since Hitler came to power in 1933, signals to the world that the German Army and Air Force are invincible.
June 17, 1940	**The French government sues for peace.**	Germany informs the French to prepare to sign an armistice on June 22nd.
June 18, 1940	***"This* Was Their Finest Hour"** "Determined to quell suggestions---especially abroad---that Britain might soon succumb to the German onslaught like France, Churchill delivered this immortal	Like the speech on June 4th, this one can only be properly appreciated by reading it in its entirety. However, some of the best of this peroration is excerpted here: "The disastrous military events which have happened during the past fortnight have not come to me with any sense of surprise…I made it perfectly clear then that whatever happened in France would make no difference to the resolve of

---

[52] Ibid., 85.

	speech to a packed House of Commons."[53]	Britain and the British Empire to fight on, 'if necessary for years, if necessary alone.' During the last few days we have successfully brought off the great majority of the troops we had…in France, and seven-eighths of the troops we have sent to France since the beginning of the war---that is to say, about 350,000 out of 400,000 men---are safely back in this country…We have, therefore, in this Island today a very large and powerful military force…We have under arms at the present time in this Island over a million and a quarter men…We expect very large additions to our weapons in the near future…Thus, the invasion of Great Britain would at this time require the transportation across the sea of hostile armies on a very large scale, and after they had been so transported they would have to be continually maintained with all the masses of munitions and supplies which are required for continuous battle---as continuous battle it will surely be. Here is where we come to the Navy---and after all, we have a Navy. Some people seem to forget we have a Navy. We must remind them…Therefore, it seems to me that as far as seaborne invasion on a great scale is concerned, we are far more capable of meeting it today than we were at many periods in the last war and during the early months of this war…This brings me naturally, to the great question of invasion from the air, and of the impending struggle between

---

[53] Churchill, ed., *Never Give In!,* 219-229.

the British and German Air Forces…no invasion on a scale beyond the capacity of our land forces to crush speedily is likely to take place from the air until our Air Force has been definitely overpowered…Can we break Hitler's air weapon?...we have a very powerful Air Force which has proved itself far superior in quality, both in men and in many types of machine, to what we have met so far in the numerous and fierce air battles which have been fought with the Germans…There remains, of course, the danger of bombing attacks, which will certainly be made very soon upon us by bomber forces of the enemy. It is true that the German bomber force is superior in numbers to ours, but we have a very large bomber force also, which we shall use to strike at military targets in Germany without intermission. I do not at all underrate the severity of the ordeal which lies before us; but I believe our countrymen will show themselves capable of standing up to it…Much will depend upon this; every man and every woman will have the chance to show the finest qualities of their race, and render the highest service to their cause…If Hitler can bring under his despotic control the industries of the countries he has conquered, this will add greatly to his already vast armament output. On the other hand, this will not happen immediately, and we are now assured of immense, continuous, and increasing support in supplies and munitions of all kinds from the United States; and especially of aeroplanes and pilots from

		the Dominions and across the oceans coming from regions which are beyond the reach of enemy bombers…**What General Weygand called the Battle of France is over.** *I expect that the Battle of Britain is about to begin. Upon this battle depends the survival of Christian civilization.* **Upon it depends our own British life, and the long continuity of our institutions and our Empire.** *The whole fury and might of the enemy must very soon be turned on us. Hitler knows that he will have to break us in this Island or lose the war.* **If we can stand up to him, all Europe may be free and the life of the world may move forward into bright, sunlit uplands.** *But if we fail, then the whole world, including the United States, including all that we have known and cared for, will sink into the abyss of a new Dark Age made more sinister, and perhaps more protracted, by the lights of perverted science.* <u>Let us therefore brace ourselves to our duties, and so bear ourselves that if the British Empire and Commonwealth last for a thousand years, men will still say, '*This* was their finest hour.'"</u> [Emphasis added]
June 20, 1940	FDR appoints like-minded internationalists (who are prominent Republicans) to head the Army and Navy, in an attempt to build a	Accomplished lawyer and former public servant (who had once been Governor-General of the Philippines, and later Secretary of State under Herbert Hoover) **Henry L. Stimson** is appointed Secretary of War,[54] and newspaper

---

[54] Stimson was replacing Henry Woodring, who had used every means at his disposal to obstruct aid to Great Britain. In an unusual move (for FDR disliked confrontations very much), Roosevelt fired him.

		bipartisan foreign policy.	publisher **Frank Knox** is appointed Secretary of the Navy.[55] Both men are Republican internationalists (not isolationists)---some would even call them interventionists---and support giving all-out aid to Great Britain, as the best means for America to help stop Hitler without getting involved in the war immediately. This helps Roosevelt with the public, and sows disarray within the Republican Party establishment just prior to the Republican Presidential nominating convention. (At the time the three leading Republican candidates for that party's Presidential nomination were Robert Taft, Thomas Dewey, and Arthur Vandenberg---all isolationists.)
	June 22, 1940	An armistice is signed at Compiegne in France, between the French surrender government of the aged Marshal Phillipe Petain (a revered World War I hero) and Adolf Hitler and his Nazi power elite.	Hitler has the railroad car in which the World War I armistice was signed taken out of a museum to an outdoor memorial commemorating the defeat of Germany in World War I, and uses the exact same railroad coach as the site for the signing of the armistice celebrating his great victory. Afterwards, the monument is blown up. The war of revenge is over; Hitler has accomplished in 6 weeks, what the German Army could not accomplish in four years, during the First World War. Southern France, a nominally independent state which became known as "Vichy France," after its capital, was not occupied by Germany during 1940 because it declared itself neutral, was under the spell of Berlin, and had no

---

[55] Knox was replacing Charles Edison, for whom Roosevelt had secured a face-saving exit, securing for him the Democratic nomination as candidate for Governor of New Jersey.

		military forces, except for what remained of the French Fleet in North Africa. Vichy France, under octogenarian Field Marshall Phillipe Petain's leadership, remained passive and submissive to Germany.
June 21, 1940	The **Republican National Convention** meets, and in a major surprise later that week, will nominate (on the sixth ballot) a dark horse who was not a favorite of the party establishment, **Wendell Willkie,** as the Republican candidate for President. Willkie, an interventionist, believed (like Roosevelt) in providing all possible aid short of war to those nations fighting Hitler's Germany and Fascist Italy. His nomination was a Godsend to FDR, for it freed Roosevelt's hands to continue funneling all possible aid to Great Britain that summer and fall, when the British people---who were now fighting alone---desperately needed to know it was on the way for the sake of their morale. When the convention began it was believed by party professionals that either	Wendell Willkie's nomination was one of the most extraordinary political events in American political history. His candidacy, in hindsight, seems absurdly improbable (almost as if it had been contrived by the Democratic opposition to provide the candidate the least threatening to Roosevelt's foreign policy agenda, whether or not that was actually the case). In 1938 he was still a registered Democrat; had never run for any political office; and had not entered any of the primary races in 1940. Willkie was a delegate at the 1932 Democratic convention and supported Roosevelt at that convention. He only joined the Republican party when he became its Presidential candidate. He had made a fortune as President of a holding company that owned six utilities, and had clashed with the Tennessee Valley Authority and New Deal legislation. He had become popular on a radio program called *Town Meeting of the Air*. Willkie was a burly, disheveled figure with rumpled hair who was an attractive speaker---enthusiastic, witty, and with a reputation as a bit of a rebel. His candidacy was aggressively promoted by the following publications: the New York Herald-Tribune newspaper; the Saturday Evening Post; and Time magazine. He received the

	Senator Robert Taft, Thomas Dewey, or Senator Arthur Vandenberg would be nominated to run against Roosevelt; all three were staunch isolationists, and if one of them had been nominated as FDR's Republican opponent, his actions in aiding Great Britain would have been much more constrained throughout July, August, September, and October. In short, Willkie's nomination freed up FDR to pursue a means for accomplishing the "loan" of 50 vintage, overage destroyers to Great Britain, something that was very important to Churchill, and which looked increasingly vital in view of the accelerating sinkings of British ships by German U-boats, and the possibility of an imminent Nazi invasion of Great Britain.	open support of newspaper commentators Walter Lippmann and Dorothy Thompson. His polling numbers among Republicans went from 3% on May 8, to 17% on June 12, to 29% on June 20, on the eve of the convention in Philadelphia, which made him (at that time) second in popularity only to Thomas Dewey. All of the techniques of Madison Avenue were used to generate a grass roots movement for Willkie that succeeded, and eventually carried him to the nomination on the sixth ballot. The party professionals were stunned and dismayed. Most who have analyzed his candidacy and campaign have concluded that his nomination was not only the result of slick advertising and early and effective promotion by powerful backers in the Eastern media, but that it reflected the changing focus of the American public following the invasion of France by Nazi Germany on May 10th.[56] He ran a vigorous campaign against Roosevelt, campaigning primarily against "one man rule" and FDR's unprecedented try for a third term as President. Willkie closed to within a few percentage points of Roosevelt in the polls in October, and forced FDR out of the Oval Office and onto the campaign trail two weeks before the election. After the election was over, Willkie testified in favor of FDR's Lend-Lease policy of free aid to Great Britain before a Senate Committee.

---

[56] Moss, *19 Weeks,* 226-232.

| July 3, 1940 | "The Deadly Stroke" **The British Navy attacks the French Fleet at the naval base at Mers-el-Kebir near the port of Oran, in Algeria.** Winston Churchill addressed the House of Commons about the event on July 4, saying: "A large proportion of the French Fleet has…passed into our hands or been put out of action or otherwise withheld from Germany by yesterday's events…I leave the judgment of our action, with confidence, to Parliament. I leave it to the nation, and I leave it to the United States. I leave it to the world and history…Now I turn to the immediate future…We are making every preparation in our power to repel the assaults of the enemy…These preparations are constantly occupying our toil, from morn till night…I call upon all subjects of His Majesty, and upon our Allies, and well-wishers---and they are not a few---all over the world, on both sides | Negotiations between Great Britain and Vichy France throughout June, 1940---with both Prime Minister Reynaud prior to the surrender, and with Field Marshall Petain after the armistice between France and Germany---intended by Britain to prevent the Germans from acquiring the French Fleet (the second most powerful surface fleet in Europe, and the world's fourth largest Navy), were unsuccessful: Great Britain failed to gain satisfactory assurances from the French government that their ships would not be turned over to the enemy. Somewhat alarmingly, Vichy France had entered into a peace with Germany which required all French Naval vessels outside of France to return home, clearly signaling German intent to eventually acquire the French fleet, if possible. Some French ships had fled to British ports, and the seizure by Britain of two French battleships in the ports of Casablanca and Dakar in West Africa presented no problem. However, the powerful Atlantic Squadron, consisting of two older battleships, two powerful modern battlecruisers, and six destroyers, which had all fled to Algeria from Brest in June as the Germans ravaged France, presented a serious problem since it was correctly assumed that the French admiral there would neither transfer his ships to British ports with reduced crews for transfer; nor sail them to neutral ports in the West Indies to sit out the war; nor would he agree to sail with the Royal Navy and fight the Axis. Accordingly, late on the afternoon of July 3, after day-long unsuccessful negotiations between |

	of the Atlantic, to give us their utmost aid…This is no time for doubt or weakness. It is the supreme hour to which we have been called…***The action we have already taken should be sufficient to dispose once and for all of the lies and rumors which have been spread by German propaganda…that we have the slightest intention of entering into negotiations in any form and through any channel with the German and Italian governments.*** We shall, on the contrary, prosecute the war with the utmost vigour with all the means that are open to us until the righteous purposes for which we entered upon it have been fulfilled." [Emphasis added]	the British and French Naval commanders on scene, the Royal Navy reluctantly opened fire on the moored French vessels. One of the French battleships blew up, another ran aground, one of the modern battlecruisers was severely damaged and put out of action, and one destroyer was sunk. One modern battlecruiser and five destroyers escaped and found refuge in Toulon, but this battlecruiser (*Strasbourg*) was damaged by British aerial torpedo attack. In the first naval engagement between the British and French in 125 years, almost 1,300 French sailors were killed. The political ramifications were profound, for Britain demonstrated to the world that it possessed a ruthless Navy with fighting teeth, and was not afraid to use it---and furthermore, that Great Britain was absolutely determined to continue the war whatever the costs. The demonstration of resolve by Great Britain at Oran had a favorable effect upon American military opinion, and upon Franklin D. Roosevelt, in particular. Britain, after all, appeared worthy of American support and material aid. (And the successful attack on Oran made obvious the military and political weakness of Vichy France, which was duly noted by the Japanese.)
July 5, 1940	**FDR commences a series of symbolic economic sanctions against Japan which are designed to <u>deter Japanese aggression</u>. Great care is taken to send**	Vichy France presided over French colonial possessions in the West Indies, Africa, and Southeast Asia. The large overseas colony in French Indochina (what is now Vietnam and Cambodia) was a tempting target for Japan, both for its resources (rubber and rice) and as a

"warning signals" of diplomatic displeasure to Japan that would *not* serve as provocations, i.e., that would *not* incite Japan to go to war immediately in the Far East, but rather, (hopefully) restrain and moderate its behavior as the Japanese war machine's appetite for raw materials grew. On July 5, 1940 President Roosevelt invoked the Export Control Act against Japan by prohibiting exportation, without license, of strategic minerals and chemicals, aircraft engines, parts, and equipment. This was largely a symbolic moral statement, for the U.S. continued to knowingly export large quantities of **bunker oil** (fuel for ships) to Japan from the U.S. West Coast, in large quantities, until July of 1941. High-grade aviation gasoline, and high-grade scrap metal were added to the prohibited list on July 26th. (Japan was still

site for air bases which could help Japan attack China, and in the future, extend its reach into Southeast Asia. On July 25, encouraged by Henry Stimson's report to him that the Japanese were trying to corner the American market on aviation fuel (and that this might cause a shortage for the U.S. military for 6 to 9 months), Roosevelt, with Morgenthau's encouragement and concurrence, quickly signed a Treasury Department proclamation preventing the export of *all oil and scrap metal to Japan.* This hasty action caused a split within the administration, for an alarmed Sumner Welles cautioned that shutting off all oil would provoke Japan to move militarily against the Dutch East Indies; Roosevelt backed off. The very next day, on July 26, 1940, FDR disingenuously explained to reporters that he had not "embargoed" the sale of all oil and scrap metal to Japan, as they had been reporting, but had only extended the government's licensing system to specific items. **On July 26, 1940, therefore, *high-octane* aviation gasoline and lubricants, and *high grade* scrap iron, were added to the export control list.** [57] This action prevented a high-octane aviation gasoline shortage within the United States, satisfied some domestic demand (and FDR's personal desire) for stronger diplomatic actions against Japan, and allowed Roosevelt to do so without immediately provoking the Japanese into war. (The United States continued to sell

---

[57] Dallek, *Franklin D. Roosevelt and American Foreign Policy,* 239-240.

| | | permitted to purchase the medium-grade aviation fuel it needed.) With the European colonial powers distracted and weakened by the war in Europe, it was hoped these steps (diplomatic warnings which amounted to signals of America's moral displeasure, and which did not truly harm Japan) would restrain the Japanese leadership from immediately going to war to grab what it needed from European colonies in Asia. The U.S. State Department feared that stronger actions, which really and truly hurt the Japanese war economy, might inadvertently push Japan into immediately going to war in Southeast Asia to obtain the critical resources it needed. | medium-grade aviation gasoline to Japan, which was adequate for its military needs.) **FDR's goal with Japan was still deterrence, and not yet provocation.** Regardless of these restrictions, in August and September Japan "…intimidated the British into withdrawing troops from Shanghai, the Dutch into discussing Japan's economic demands on the Dutch East Indies, and the [Vichy] French into recognizing Japan's preponderant interest in Indochina."[58] Recognizing Japan's preponderant interest in Indochina meant that the Vichy French were pressured by the Japanese into ceding them <u>transit rights for troops, and permission to construct airfields,</u> in Northern Indochina (now North Vietnam). In response to this, in late September FDR expanded the prohibition of July 26th <u>and banned sales of *all* scrap metal to Japan.</u>[59] In September and October, when Japanese negotiators were pressing the Dutch East Indies government for a *sixfold increase* in annual oil shipments to Japan over the next five years, the State Department, with FDR's approval, endorsed a possible settlement satisfying 60 per cent of this demand, in an attempt to prevent the Japanese from immediately going to war against the Dutch East Indies. |

---

[58] Ibid., 240-241.

[59] Heinrichs, *Threshold of War,* 10; and Dallek, *Franklin D. Roosevelt and American Foreign Policy,* 241-243. Heinrichs writes that scrap iron and steel from the United States had previously satisfied 40 per cent of Japan's industrial needs for iron.

| July 8, 1940 | **Admiral Richardson meets with President Roosevelt and the highest levels of the U.S. defense and diplomatic establishment.**

<u>Richardson explained in his memoirs the reasons why he had requested a meeting with President Roosevelt and the military leadership in Washington:</u>

"The objective of my conversations was to develop as fully as possible the ideas or policy which underlay the retention of the fleet in Hawaii; **to put forth the view that its retention inevitably involved considerable risk of war,** and that, in my view, we were not taking, at the same time, the vital measures made necessary by the considerable risk involved." | Richardson's trip to Washington was only permitted after he requested it on three different occasions. He and his War Plans officer (CAPT Murphy) commenced their trip on July 5th incognito, under assumed names. In addition to the President, he met with Admiral Stark (CNO), Rear Admiral Nimitz (then the head of the Bureau of Naval Personnel), Secretary of the Navy Frank Knox, Secretary of State Hull and Under Secretary Welles, and General George Marshall.[60] Richardson said of his trip: "Both specifically and generally, I got the impression, from my various conversations, that the top flight of officials in Washington believed that Japanese aggression could be restrained by a strong attitude on the part of the United States; [and] that the retention of the fleet in Hawaii was a reflection of this strong attitude. <u>There was a considerable body of opinion in Washington that the Japanese could be 'bluffed.'</u> **I was told that the fleet would remain in Hawaii indefinitely---as long as required to support our diplomatic activity**---and that I should move out to Hawaii the necessary training services, and should proceed with intensified training activities to increase the readiness of the fleet… <u>**I came away with the impression that, despite his spoken word, the President was fully determined to put the United States into the war, if Great Britain**</u> |

---

[60] Richardson, *On the Treadmill to Pearl Harbor*, 383-395.

		could hold out until he was reelected."[61] [Emphasis added]
July 10, 1940	**The German Luftwaffe begins wide-scale combat with the Royal Air Force in an unsuccessful attempt to gain control of the air space over the English Channel.**	The Luftwaffe's attacks on convoys in the channel, and on some of the channel ports, achieve less than satisfactory results. During the month of July the British lose 110 planes, and the Germans lose 142. On July 16th, Hitler issued a formal directive to the Wehrmacht to begin preparing for an invasion of England. To this end, the German Army begins concentrating troops near the channel ports in France, Belgium, and Holland; and by assembling invasion barges and shipping in English Channel ports under Nazi control. By month's end the Germans are nowhere near ready to invade England---they have not gained air superiority over the English channel; are logistically unprepared to move the German Army across the Channel; and after losing so many destroyers and heavy cruisers in the Norway campaign in April and May, do not have a surface navy capable of forcing the invasion. Furthermore, to Hitler's great frustration, the British (more particularly, one person---Churchill) have adamantly refused to cut a deal with him granting Nazi Germany hegemony over Europe, and ceasing hostilities, in exchange for Great Britain getting to keep most of its Empire. The realities of geography, and the remarkable determination of a national war leader, have combined to help save the British from immediate

---

[61] Ibid., 385-7.

		doom, and the American public is increasingly impressed by Britain's plucky resistance to the armed might of The Third Reich. Great Britain works feverishly throughout the summer and early autumn to prepare for what is viewed as an imminent invasion, by stringing defenses and building fortifications along the southern and southeast coasts, while Churchill prepares his people psychologically to fight the invaders when and if they come.
July 13, 1940	Hitler indicates to his army leadership that Britain's unwillingness to make peace with Germany was because of the hope England placed in the Soviet Union eventually falling out with Germany.	Franz Halder, the Chief of the Army General Staff, made this diary entry on July 13th: "The Fuhrer is greatly puzzled by Britain's persisting unwillingness to make peace. He sees the answer (as we do) in Britain's hope on Russia, and therefore counts on having to compel her by main force to agree to peace."
July 19, 1940	The Konoye government is formed in Japan around the new Prime Minister, Prince Fumimaro Konoye (his second term as Prime Minister), which includes the fiery and erratic Yosuke Matsuoka as Foreign Minister (who coined the phrase "East Asian Co-Prosperity Sphere," signaling Japan's intention to dominate and economically exploit the entire East Asian region); and General Hideki Tojo	Simply put, the change in government in Tokyo signaled a major shift in policy in response to the startling success of Nazi Germany's Western European offensive: that shift can be summarized by the phrase "northern defense, southern advance" and the decision to forge much closer ties with Nazi Germany and Fascist Italy.

In May and June of 1940 Hitler's Western offensive quickly defeated the Netherlands, crushed France, and brought England almost to her knees. As summarized by historian Ian Kershaw, "It was in the wake of Hitler's astonishing military triumphs that Japan, |

(nicknamed "the razor," a man of few words and a leading spokesman of the uncompromisingly expansionist position of the Army) as War Minister.

The previous administration, led by its Prime Minister, Admiral Mitsumasa Yonai (in power since January 16, 1940), had opposed the Japanese Army's desires for closer ties with Hitler's Germany. Yonai's Foreign Minister, Hachiro Arita, had been keen to improve relations with the United States and Great Britain, which was opposed by the dominant groups within the Army.

The engineered resignation of Prime Minister Yonai on July 16, 1940 represented a new consensus just reached in June and July between the Army and Navy to achieve self-sufficiency for Japan by dominating---taking---the resources of Southeast Asia and the Dutch East Indies, even if it seeking to exploit the weakness of those countries, took the fateful decisions to expand into south-eastern Asia (where Britain, France, and the Netherlands held significant colonial possessions) and to forge a pact with the Axis powers, Germany and Italy. In so doing…Japan made choices which greatly increased the risk of her involvement in armed conflict not only with the European powers, but also with the United States…summer of 1940 was the time when the Japanese leadership took vital steps that would lead eventually to blending the two separate wars in Europe and in China into one huge global conflagration."[62]

Prince Konoye, a member of the most important and influential political family in Japan below the Imperial household itself, had first served as Prime Minister in 1937 and had presided over the beginning of the war with China. Konoye had always been in favor of correction of the "unfair" distribution of territories among nations, and the maldistribution of resources. He did not believe in the maintenance of peace if it upheld the *status quo* which supported these inequities, and believed that Japan, like Germany, would have no resort but to destroy the *status quo* in order to assure its survival. Japan's inability to force a conclusion to its war of aggression in China, or to extricate itself (simple withdrawal was unthinkable for a nation whose mythology taught that it

---

[62] Kershaw, *Fateful Choices,* 91-92.

	(regretfully) meant war with the United States. The only real question was timing---when should Japan go to war to obtain what it needed to expand and maintain its empire?	was a superior race destined to rule Asia), only exacerbated its shortages of food and raw materials. Kershaw describes Konoye at the time of the China incident as "a weak and ineffectual individual, unable to offer a clear lead to the Cabinet, given to helpless hand-wringing, resigned apathy and lamentations at his inability to shape events." It is no wonder that the Japanese Army championed him as Prime Minister once again in July of 1940, at a time when the Army was the driving force behind immediate Japanese expansion to take advantage of the collapse of the Western powers in Europe.
July 19, 1940	**FDR gives his acceptance speech to the Democratic National Convention by radio.** Excerpts follow: "It is with a very full heart that I speak tonight. I must confess that I do so with mixed feelings---because I find myself, as almost everyone does sooner or later in his lifetime, in a conflict between deep personal desire for retirement on one hand, and that quiet, invisible thing called "conscience" on the other…When the conflict [in Europe] first broke out last September, it was still my intention to	Franklin Roosevelt was of a mixed mind about running for an unprecedented third term, since the Presidency by tradition had always been limited to two terms (a tradition set by George Washington). He was mentally and physically weary after 8 years in the White House, and if there had been no war in Europe, he may well have retired to Hyde Park. But clearly, he felt he was indispensable to safely guiding America through the troubled state the world was in, with the Second World War having begun in Europe. He was deeply engaged in America's commitment to rearm, and to provide all aid short of war to those powers fighting Axis aggression; and with eight years of experience under his belt as Chief Executive, he had his hands firmly on the levers of government, and dared not relinquish control at such a crucial time in World history. His long program of

	announce…at an early date, that under no conditions would I accept reelection. This fact was well known to my friends, and I think was well understood by many citizens. It soon became evident, however, that such a public statement on my part would be unwise from the point of view of sheer public duty. As President…it was my clear duty, with the aid of the Congress, to preserve our neutrality, to shape our program of defense, to meet rapid changes, to keep our domestic affairs adjusted to shifting world conditions…Swiftly moving foreign events made necessary swift action at home and beyond the seas. Plans for national defense had to be expanded and adjusted to meet new forms of warfare…Today all private plans, all private lives, have been in a sense repealed by an overriding public danger. In the face of that public danger all those who can be of service to the	educating the American people about foreign affairs and instructing them as to their international responsibilities was well underway, and his strong sense of duty and responsibility would not let him quit. Knowing that by now he had many personal and political enemies, and that many would oppose anyone running for a third term on principle, Roosevelt publicly played "hard to get" by refusing to enter any primary contests and by refusing to reveal whether he would run for President again. He let it be known that while he would not actively seek the nomination again, he would not be able to refuse his party or his country if "drafted" at the Democratic convention. He raised the tension and the level of interest by not even attending the Democratic convention in Chicago. Privately, he engineered it so that he *would* be drafted, and would then be nominated by acclamation in Chicago; Chicago mayor Ed Kelley, and Harry Hopkins (now his closest advisor) carried this off without a hitch.[64]
		On this same date, July 19th, Hitler delivers a major address to the Reichstag in the Kroll Opera House (its new home, following the burning of the Reichstag in 1933), giving his summary of the war to date and *making a final peace offer to Great Britain* (his 'appeal to reason' to come to terms with Germany and avoid the destruction of the British Empire). The British government

---

[64] Moss, *19 Weeks,* 232-235.

	Republic have no choice but to offer themselves for service for those capacities for which they may be fitted…my conscience will not let me turn my back upon a call to service…Whatever its new trappings and new slogans, tyranny is the oldest and most discredited rule known to history…I do not regret my consistent endeavor to awaken this country to the menace for us and for all we hold dear…I felt it my duty…to arouse my countrymen to the danger of the new forces let loose in the world…all that I have done to maintain the peace of this country, and to prepare it morally, as well as physically, for whatever contingencies may be in store, I submit to the judgment of my countrymen."[63]	makes known, through the press within an hour of Hitler's speech, that his offer would be rejected. In a supreme irony, Churchill directs his Foreign Minister, Lord Halifax (who strongly favored making peace with Germany in late May), to deliver the British refusal, and Halifax does so in a short statement on July 22nd. Aware that the British will formally reject his "peace offer," ***on July 21st, the day before the Halifax rejection***, <u>Hitler first raises with his military commanders the possibility of invading the USSR that autumn</u> (!). Shortly thereafter, on July 31st, Hitler tells Admiral Raeder that eight days of intensive air attacks are about to begin against England in an attempt to destroy the British air force and its airfields. (Weather would delay the commencement of the assault until August 13th.) He confides to Raeder that if the short air campaign does not effectively destroy the Royal Air Force, he will postpone the invasion of England (Operation Sea Lion) until May of 1941. It seems his heart was never truly behind the risky invasion of England, and that he was already considering turning on his "ally," the Soviet Union, as forecast in *Mein Kampf*.
July 19, 1940	**Ben Cohen writes a legal brief titled "Sending Effective Material Aid to Great Britain With Particular References to**	Ben Cohen was an attorney working for Harold Ickes in the Department of the Interior; Cohen had previously written many defenses and justifications of New Deal programs in support of the

---

[63] Hunt, ed., *The Essential Franklin D. Roosevelt,* 181-189.

	the Sending of Destroyers." He concluded that FDR did *not* have to gain the assent of Congress to legally transfer the 50 destroyers Churchill wanted to Great Britain. [FDR had known since May 15th that he had two possible avenues through which to pursue the transfer: (1) speak directly to the public about the matter, persuade them that such a transfer would actually enhance U.S. security, and then go openly to the Congress and ask permission; or (2) circumvent the legal obstacles and go behind Congress's back to affect the transfer.]	Roosevelt administration. Journalist Joe Alsop (one of the unofficial liaisons between the British Embassy in Washington and the Roosevelt administration) encouraged Cohen to write the legal brief, knowing that Ickes, a Cabinet member who favored aid to the British, would forward it to the President. Ickes did so, but FDR was not swayed (yet) by this recommendation to go around Congress. In Roosevelt's view, Cohen's ingenious legal arguments lacked the force to override political reality. In his cover letter to the President, Cohen had written: "I appreciate that even if Congressional approval is not required, Congressional opinion would have to be taken into account." On July 22nd, FDR wrote a memo to Secretary of the Navy Frank Knox saying it was worth reading, but adding, "I fear Congress is in no mood at the present time to allow any form of sale." Going directly to the Congress would have required Roosevelt to risk his personal prestige over this issue, a risk he was not prepared to take at the time.[65]
July 27, 1940	In Japan, a key meeting of the **Liaison Conference** (a consensual decision-making body begun during the China war and reinstituted by Konoye in 1940) approves a policy document titled: **"Main Principles for Coping**	The day prior to this meeting, on July 26th, the Konoye government defined the framework of its foreign policy in a statement titled: **"Outline of a Basic National Policy"** (drafted by the Army Ministry) which dramatically declared the world was "at a major turning point," and envisaged Japan building "a new order in Great East Asia," and which

---

[65] Shogan, *Hard Bargain,* 177-183; and Lukacs, *The Duel,* 202.

With the Changing World Situation."

Since Japan was not a dictatorship, major decisions of war and peace did not spring from one man, as they did in Germany and Italy. A typical **Liaison Conference** included key Cabinet members (the Prime Minister, Foreign Minister, War Minister, and Navy Minister), as well as the Army and Navy chiefs of staff and their deputies from the Supreme Command.

Imperial Conferences often ratified major decisions reached at Liaison Conferences. The same Liaison Conference members attended, and Imperial Conferences were held in the presence of the Emperor (who usually did not speak), with the President of the Privy Council speaking for him and raising questions. Once the Emperor sanctioned a recommended course of action, thereby legitimating it, the decision was seen as

declared Japan was to be converted into a "national defense state" ready for war.

On July 27th, the principal decisions laid down in **"Main Principles for Coping With the Changing World Situation"** were those reached by consensus between the Army and the Navy earlier in the month: <u>namely, to pursue a southern advance (while not engaging in any hostilities with Russia), and to strengthen relations with the Axis powers</u>.

The Navy had successfully sought to prevent the Army from immediately attacking and seizing the Dutch East Indies, and the following compromise was reached: armed force against the Dutch East Indies would be used only if favorable circumstances arose, and for the present diplomatic means would be employed to attempt to greatly increase the amount of oil and other key resources from the East Indies.

The Navy fully recognized that an occupation of French Indochina would likely lead to an oil embargo by the United States, and that in this event the Empire would be faced with a life-or-death situation, and would be compelled to attack and seize the Dutch East Indies to obtain an alternate source of petroleum. Without oil from the U.S. or the East Indies, the Navy knew it could only fight for about 4 months; even with oil from the Dutch East Indies, the Navy estimated it could only fight effectively for about one year. No one was

	binding on all present.	optimistic about Japan's chances for success in any long war with the United States, and yet Japan stated its readiness to go to war with other powers if necessary to obtain the resources it needed. The fleet was placed into a condition of "preparatory mobilization," and the "southern advance" was now given priority over the "China Incident." The Navy concluded that operations against French Indochina (the jumping off point for the southern advance) should proceed no later than November.[66] The die was cast.
July 29, 1940	Hitler meets with army General Alfred Jodl (his operations officer at Supreme Headquarters) and informs him that Germany will invade the Soviet Union in May of 1941.	Once Hitler was informed that an invasion of the Soviet Union was logistically and operationally not possible in the autumn of 1940, he set May 1941 as the target date in a meeting with Alfred Jodl, and General Jodl promptly passed this decision on to his own planning staff. The implications are many: (1) Hitler's heart was really not in Operation Sea Lion, the proposed invasion by sea of Great Britain; (2) the real purpose of the forthcoming air assault on Britain (in Hitler's mind) may not have been to soften England up for invasion, but to force out the Churchill government after the destruction of its air force, and compel Britain to sue for peace, cease hostilities, and recognize the new German hegemony in Europe, instead of opposing it; (3) both ideology (the lure of lebensraum in the East, as

---

[66] Kershaw, *Fateful Choices,* 115-118.

		advocated in *Mein Kampf*), and his strategic fear of the dangers involved in risking his army at sea in a cross-channel gamble, were pulling him away from a knockout blow to Great Britain, and causing him to focus on the titanic struggle to come with the USSR, even at a time when the world thought he was solely focused on the contest with Britain; (4) by conquering the USSR in a quick campaign, Hitler thus planned to force the stubborn British to make peace (if Herman Goering could not do this with the Luftwaffe in the coming blitz), and get England out of the war, before America could become a belligerent.
July 31, 1940	**Hitler informs his military leadership, during a meeting at his Alpine retreat, the Berghof, in the mountains high above Berchtesgaden in Bavaria, <u>that Germany will invade the Soviet Union in May 1941</u>.** Although this would not become an operational order until December 18, 1940, he had clearly made his decision, and was imparting it to his highest commanders. He confides that the best way to defeat Great Britain may be without an invasion---by turning on the USSR and first defeating Russia, which	Hitler's exact words are recorded in Franz Halder's war diary: "With Russia smashed, Britain's last hope would be shattered. Germany then will be master of Europe and the Balkans. Decision: Russia's destruction must therefore be made a part of this struggle. Spring 1941…if we start in May 1941, we would have five months to finish the job." These astonishing sentences announced Hitler's most fateful choice in the Second World War. As Ian Kershaw dramatically frames this decision, "It ushered in the bloodiest conflict in history, a titanic struggle in eastern Europe that would cost the lives of over thirty million Soviet and German citizens and leave vast areas of unprecedented destruction, ending nearly four years later with the German dictator's suicide in the Berlin bunker and the Soviet Union dominant over half of the European continent for the following

	would then compel Britain to dump Churchill and acknowledge German hegemony in Europe. He informs his audience that he will wait and see how the coming air assault on Great Britain develops, and that he will launch the invasion of the Soviet Union even if Britain has not been knocked out yet, simply to remove any hope Britain has of staying in the war.	four and a half decades." At the time, neither Churchill nor Roosevelt had any inkling of this decision---nor did Japan. German preparations would begin to leak early in 1941, but at this juncture, in the summer of 1940, with the air assault on Great Britain imminent, and logistical preparations for a cross-channel invasion underway, no one in the West dreamed of such a breathtaking betrayal of the USSR, or of such an amazing strategic about face, when Germany seemingly had Great Britain on the ropes, totally isolated, waiting for the "knockout punch."
July 31, 1940	**FDR receives an urgent cable from Winston Churchill, refocusing on the still urgent need for "50 or 60" old U.S. destroyers.** Churchill knows that although initially rebuffed on this score back on May 17th, the issue has not died in Washington, and knows that it is time to weigh in again and make another plea, with all his force. (Churchill had raised the issue a second time on June 11th, and again three days later, and had been ignored. Now that FDR had received the Democratic party's nomination for President, Churchill believed the timing was much more	Churchill's telegram of July 31st was the first substantive message he had sent FDR in eight weeks: "It is some time since I ventured to cable personally to you, and many things both good and bad have happened in-between. It has now become most urgent for you to give us the destroyers, motorboats, and flying-boats for which we have asked. The Germans have the whole French coastline from which to launch U-boats and dive-bomber attacks upon our trade and food, and in addition we must be constantly prepared to repel by sea action threatened invasion…In the last ten days we have had the following destroyers sunk [he names four] and the following damaged [he names six more], total ten…Destroyers are frighteningly vulnerable to Air bombing, yet they must be held in the Air bombing area to prevent sea-borne invasion. We could not keep up the present rate of casualties for long, and if we cannot get a

	propitious than it had been earlier in July.)	substantial reinforcement, the whole fate of the war may be decided by this minor and easily remediable factor. **I cannot understand why, with the position as it is, you do not send us 50 or 60 of your oldest destroyers.** <u>**Mr. President, with great respect I must tell you that in the long history of the world this is a thing to do now.**</u>"[67] [Emphasis added]
August 1 and 2, 1940	In the wake of Churchill's cable, several events occur which combine to make FDR feel favorably disposed to the transfer of the 50 old destroyers for the first time. On August 1st, FDR meets with a delegation from the **Century Group** (members of the East Coast establishment elite, from both parties, who are interventionists <u>openly advocating that the U.S. enter the war against Germany</u>) and receives a report from them advising that he transfer **100 destroyers** to Great Britain; on the same day Lord Lothian, the British Ambassador, requests an urgent meeting with Navy Secretary Frank Knox and proposes the idea of exchanging the overage	**On August 2nd, Roosevelt chaired a Cabinet meeting at which was discussed the British request for 50 old U.S. Navy destroyers** which had first been made by Churchill on May 15th, and which had been repeated incessantly since that time by everyone from King George VI, to the members of the British purchasing mission, to the British Ambassador, and by pro-British American lobbyists. Roosevelt did not mention the new cable from Churchill received July 31st, nor did he mention his meeting with three members of the Century Group the day before, on August 1st. After Navy Secretary Frank Knox reported on the deal offered by Lord Lothian the previous evening, FDR noted that the Cabinet was unanimous in its agreement that the swap of destroyers for bases was definitely something that was in America's best interests, and that should be done. Roosevelt, uncharacteristically, then wrote a memo for file about the meeting which stated: **"At cabinet meeting, in afternoon, long discussion in regard to devising ways**

---

[67] Meacham, *Franklin and Winston*, 70-71.

	U.S. destroyers for some British bases in the Western Atlantic and Caribbean; and on August 2nd, FDR (through a cut-out) obtains the implied promise of Republican Presidential nominee Wendell Willkie that while he will not openly support such a transfer, or lobby for it with Republicans in Congress, he will not oppose it, either.[68]	**and means to sell directly or indirectly fifty or sixty World War I old destroyers to Great Britain. It was the general opinion, without any dissenting voice, that the survival of the British Isles under German attack might very possibly depend on their getting these destroyers. It was agreed that legislation to accomplish this is necessary. It was agreed that such legislation, if asked for by me without any preliminaries, would meet with defeat or interminable delay in reaching a vote."** The remainder of the memo was about FDR's intent to get Wendell Willkie to help gain support from Republicans in Congress, and about FDR's need to get a guarantee that the British Fleet would not be scuttled or surrendered if Britain was defeated.[69] The members of the Century Group with whom Roosevelt met on August 1st (many of its members were liberal Republicans) recommended that he attempt to get Wendell Willkie's support in enlisting Republican support for the destroyer transfer in Congress, and so after the cabinet meeting on August 2nd, FDR approached Willkie through newspaper magnate William Allen White, who was vacationing with Willkie in Colorado. In the end, Willkie was not willing to buck the Republican establishment on this issue, but since he also sincerely believed in aiding Great

---

[68] Lukacs, *The Duel,* 202-203, 207.

[69] Ibid., 203-204.

		Britain, he indicated he would not oppose such a transfer, either. This decision was a Godsend to Roosevelt.[70]
August 3, 1940	**FDR meets with the British Ambassador, Lord Lothian, and tells him he will need "molasses" to get Congress to swallow the transfer of the destroyers to Great Britain.**	The "molasses" Roosevelt referred to, in FDR's mind, had to be: (1) a written guarantee that if Great Britain succumbed to a German invasion, that the British Fleet would neither be scuttled nor surrender, but that instead it would sail to the New World and operate to defend Canada and the United States; and (2) naval bases on British possessions in the Atlantic and Caribbean, which would dramatically help the case that the transfer would be enhancing U.S. security. Roosevelt told Lothian that he could transfer the destroyers to Great Britain only with Congressional approval, and that without a deal that strongly favored the United States, a determined filibuster in the Senate by 15 or 20 determined isolationists could delay the transfer until *after* the Presidential election in November. It was for this reason that he said he needed the "molasses," to help Congress accept the proposal.[71]
August 4, 1940	The aging, but still revered **General John "Black Jack" Pershing** (who had commanded the American Expeditionary Force in France in World War I, and is now 80	This speech was FDR's idea: he proposed it to the Century Group on August 1st, and journalists Joe Alsop and Walter Lippmann (and others, who got to Pershing) made it happen; the arrangements for air time with the radio networks were facilitated by journalist

---

[70] Ibid., 207.

[71] Shogan, *Hard Bargain,* 193-207

	years old), **America's most celebrated living hero, makes a speech <u>suggesting the transfer of 50 U.S. destroyers to Great Britain</u>.** This brings the issue into the public eye for the first time.	Joe Alsop, and Pershing's speech was largely written by Republican columnist Walter Lippmann. Pershing said: **"I am telling you tonight before it is too late that the British Navy needs destroyers to convoy merchant ships, hunt submarines, and repel invasion."** He continued: "We have an immense reserve of destroyers left over from the other war, and in a few months the British will be completing a large number of destroyers of their own. The most critical time, therefore, is the next few weeks and months. If there is anything we can do to help save the British fleet during that time, we shall be failing in our duty to America if we do not do it. If a proper method can be found, America will safeguard her freedom and security by making available to the British or Canadian governments at least fifty of the overage destroyers which are left from the days of the World War." [Emphasis added][72] The next day an eloquent editorial titled: **"Destroyers for Britain"** was published in the *New York Herald Tribune,* and the *New York Times* led its Monday editions with a three-column headline that read: **"Pershing Would Let Britain Have 50 Old U.S. Destroyers to Guard Our Own Liberty."**
August 11, 1940	Dean Acheson, a pillar of the Washington legal establishment and a member of the Century	This public letter, appearing so soon after the popular Pershing speech, gave Roosevelt the political cover he needed to pursue a back-door deal with the

---

[72] Ibid., 154-156.

	Group---and destined to become a future Secretary of State---works with Ben Cohen to prepare a public letter supporting the legality of the destroyer transfer. It is signed by Acheson and three others, and published in the *New York Times on* Sunday, August 11, under a three column headline titled: **"No legal bar seen to transfer of destroyers. Ample authority for sale of overage Naval vessels to Great Britain exists in present laws, according to opinion by legal experts."**[73]	British ***without the consent of Congress.*** In addition, a rather sobering straw poll taken of opinion in the Senate in early August gave Roosevelt a push in this direction, since it revealed that 23 Senators opposed the idea; only 7 were probably in favor; and 63 were undecided. The public was way out ahead of the Senate on this issue, and Roosevelt, who had been personally managing how the issue was introduced to the public, sensed this. Ben Cohen's arguments had originally fallen on deaf ears when they first reached the President on July 19th, but by the time those rehashed and massaged legal arguments had been published in the *New York Times* three weeks later, the climate had improved: most of the public liked the idea, and Willkie would not oppose it. Roosevelt was seriously beginning to consider bypassing the Congress on the issue, when Adolph Hitler's Luftwaffe gave him an assist by launching a massive air attack on the Royal Air Force. The attack seemed to surely be an attempt to "soften up" England for the forthcoming invasion by the German Army (as indeed it was), and the intense air war over southeast England not only created a much greater sense of urgency in Washington, but increased the already growing public support for aid to Britain.
August 13, 1940	**"Eagle Day"** On August 1, 1940, Hitler had decided to see	**The main phase of what is commonly called "The Battle of Britain" begins on this day.** (Most historians declare

---

[73] Ibid., 187-192.

whether his air force could destroy the capacity and the will of the English to defend themselves. He issued Directive No. 17 on that date: "I have decided to carry on and intensify air and naval warfare against England in order to bring about her final defeat." The principal goal was the elimination of the Royal Air Force. ***"Terror bombing as reprisals is a matter to be decided by me."*** (Hitler underlined that sentence himself.)[74]

that it actually began on July 10, and ended on October 31, 1940.) Hitler has decided to allow Goering's Luftwaffe to attempt to put the Royal Air Force's fighter command out of action in an overwhelming, decisive 8-day assault. If British defensive air power can be destroyed or nullified, the German Navy has indicated that they could land an invasion force on <u>one beachhead in September 1940</u>, ***or on a wide front in several locations, in May of 1941.***[75] On August 1st, Hitler had ordered that all invasion plans and preparations should be completed by September 15th, in support of a possible invasion of England the following week.[76] (The Germans and the British both knew that the nasty weather in the English Channel would not permit landings on the English beaches much beyond mid-September.) By August 14th, only the second day of the intensified air attacks (which at this time were being levied exclusively on British airfields and radar installations in southeastern England), Hitler already sensed that it would not be decisive. He knew his Navy alone was unable to force an invasion if British air power was not destroyed, and that a failed invasion would mean a great psychological triumph for Great Britain. Despite his intuition that the Luftwaffe would not be able to knock out the Royal Air Force,

---

[74] Lukacs, *The Duel,* 204.

[75] Ibid., 195-210.

[76] Shogan, *Hard Bargain,* 184.

		Hitler ordered that invasion preparations be continued, even if the invasion should not occur in 1940, for the purpose of maintaining the *threat* of invasion.[77]
August 13, 1940	FDR meets with Frank Knox, Henry Stimson, Henry Morgenthau, and Sumner Welles in the afternoon to discuss the British need for the old destroyers. Although he makes no mention of the Acheson letter published in the New York Times on August 11th, he polls them, asking whether he should cut a deal with Great Britain and tell Congress afterwards, or vice-a-versa. Only Morgenthau favors going to Congress first (which had been FDR's openly expressed methodology as late as August 3rd); the other three men advise FDR to cut a deal with Great Britain first, and inform Congress later.[78]	For three months, Roosevelt has begun every discussion of the subject by discussing negatives---the difficulty of getting Congressional approval before acting. He began this discussion with the assumption that he was going to transfer the destroyers, and was only polling his confidants about the best strategy to employ in getting it done. **FDR cabled his proposals for approval of the deal to Churchill that evening;** they closely resembled the conditions he set forth to Lord Lothian on August 3rd. Churchill immediately discussed them with his War Cabinet, saying that the closing of the deal would mean that "the United States would have made a long step toward coming into the war on our side." Churchill pointed out to his Chiefs of Staff that this action by the United States "was certainly not a neutral action." Churchill stated that the ships would be very useful to the Admiralty, and the impact on Germany would be "immense." The official minutes of the War Cabinet meeting noted: "...the present proposal could not be looked at merely from the point of view of the exchange of motor torpedo boats, destroyers, and flying-boats for certain

---

[77] Lukacs, *The Duel,* 206.

[78] Shogan, *Hard Bargain,* 191-192.

		facilities by way of naval and air bases. ***It might well prove to be the first step in constituting an Anglo-Saxon block or indeed a decisive point in history.***"[79] On August 19th, Sumner Welles read the draft text of the agreement to FDR (who was at Hyde Park) on the telephone. Sweeteners had been added, at the request of the British: twenty motor torpedo boats, five PBY flying-boat patrol planes, five Army B-17 bombers, 250,000 Enfield rifles, and 5 million rounds of ammunition.[80]
August 15-31, 1940	<u>FDR's concerns about the safety of the British Fleet</u> in the event of disaster are assuaged by Churchill, **but the specific written guarantee so desired by Roosevelt does *not* go into the text of the destroyers-for-bases agreement.**	After FDR met with Lord Lothian on August 3rd and presented his terms for a deal, Churchill twice discussed Roosevelt's desire for a written guarantee with the War Cabinet, and then wrote with some bitterness to Halifax: "We have no intention of surrendering the British Fleet or sinking it voluntarily. Indeed such a fate is more likely to overtake the German fleet or what is left of it. The nation would not tolerate a discussion of what we should do if our island were overrun. Such a discussion, perhaps on the eve of invasion, would be injurious to public morale, now so high…We must refuse any declaration such as is suggested and confine the deal solely to the colonial bases."[81] On August 15th, Churchill cabled FDR the following: "We intend to fight this out

---

[79] Ibid., 204-207.

[80] Ibid., 210.

[81] Lukacs, *The Duel,* 208.

		here to the end, and none of us would ever buy peace by surrendering or scuttling the fleet. But in any use you may make of this repeated assurance you will please bear in mind the disastrous effect from our point of view, and perhaps also from yours, of allowing any impression to grow that we regard the conquest of the British Islands and its naval bases as any other than an impossible contingency. The spirit of our people is splendid."[82] Finally, on August 31st, Churchill provided his last word on the subject in a cable to Roosevelt: "You ask, Mr. President, if my statement in Parliament on June 4, 1940, about Great Britain never surrendering or scuttling her fleet 'represents the settled position of His Majesty's Government.' It certainly does. I must, however, observe that these hypothetical contingencies seem more likely to concern the German Fleet or what is left of it than our own."[83]
August 16-20, 1940	The possibility of a destroyers-for-bases "deal" reaches the press in an August 16th article in the *New York Times*.[84] FDR publicly denies any connection between	At a press conference the same day as the *New York Times* article, **Roosevelt dissembles---lies---saying, "This has got nothing to do with destroyers,"** and then announces that he is indeed negotiating for British sea and air bases in North American waters.[85] At this point in time, FDR does not want to tip

---

[82] Meacham, *Franklin and Winston*, 71.

[83] Ibid., 72.

[84] Shogan, *Hard Bargain*, 207.

[85] Ibid., 208.

destroyers and the acquisition of basing rights (to avoid upsetting an isolationist Congress), *all the while knowing that after the deal was announced, he would most definitely be bragging that there had indeed been a deal, and implying that the U.S. had gotten the better part of the bargain, thus improving upon its defense posture.*

Churchill, on August 20th, says the leasing of British bases is an altruistic act, and is hoping that the transfer of the 50 U.S. destroyers will later be presented in the same vein, as an act totally unconnected with the lease of British bases. His stubborn pride (and failure to recognize Roosevelt's domestic political needs when dealing with an isolationist Congress in an election year) will almost sink the deal in late August.

his hand about the fact that he is arranging for a giveaway of 50 U.S. Navy ships behind the back of the Congress, without first asking for its permission. His ultimate strategy now is to announce the destroyer-bases deal as a *fait accompli* once it is concluded, but not to admit that it is in the works until the documents are all signed. The last thing he wants is a furor in Congress that would delay the vital transfer of the badly needed ships until after the election---<u>so he lies</u>.

In his speech about the Battle of Britain in the House of Commons on August 20th (see more below), Churchill, perhaps feeling a bit battered by those "damn Yankees" and the hard bargain the Americans had driven over the summer, prepares the British people for the long-term lease of the British bases to America by presenting the leases of basing rights as if they were not connected to any *quid pro quo:* "Some months ago we came to the conclusion that the interests of the United States and the British Empire both required that the United States should have facilities for the naval and air defence of the Western Hemisphere against the attack of a Nazi power…**We had therefore decided spontaneously, and without being asked or offered any inducement,** to inform the Government of the United States that we would be glad to place such defence facilities at their disposal by leasing suitable sites in our Transatlantic possessions for their greater security against the unmeasured dangers of the future…[this was true enough on the surface; the British had offered base leases back in May but had been turned down by the U.S.]…Presently we learned that anxiety was also felt in the United States about the air and naval defence of their Atlantic seaboard, and President Roosevelt has recently made it clear that he would like to discuss with us, and with the Dominion of Canada and with Newfoundland, the development of American Naval and Air facilities in Newfoundland and in the West Indies. There is of course, no question of the transference of any sovereignty---that has never been suggested…but for our part, ***His Majesty's government are entirely willing to accord defence facilities to the United States on a 99 years' leasehold basis…***".[86] Churchill makes no mention in this speech of the destroyers, since he does not want the forthcoming deal to look like a trade---a trade in which a desperate British Government got the worst of the deal, and was forced to barter away part of its Empire's overseas possessions; in the short term, this fits nicely with FDR's dissimulation of August 16th at his press conference.

But Churchill's pride---his sudden insistence upon never admitting that the British were willing, in their desperation, to cut a deal in which they appeared to be the long-term loser---threatened in late August to sink the arrangement. Churchill let it be known on August 22nd

---

[86] Churchill, ed., *Never Give In!,* 247-248.

		that he wanted the U.S. to suddenly announce a "gift" of 50 destroyers to Great Britain, with no strings attached, once the secret deal was consummated. This Roosevelt found completely unacceptable, politically, for if he was to announce the "giveaway" of 50 destroyers, he absolutely had to present it as a way to <u>strengthen the security of the United States</u>, and he could only do this if he emphasized (*after* the deal was consummated) that there had <u>most definitely been a *quid pro quo*</u>, and that the securing of eight bases vital to hemispheric defense in exchange for 50 old destroyers (which were being scrapped for only 4,000 to 5,000 dollars each) had been a lopsided deal strongly in favor of the United States.
August 20, 1940	**"The Few"** **Winston Churchill addresses the House of Commons at the height of Germany's attempt to destroy the Royal Air Force, and praised the young fighter pilots of the RAF.** While most of the speech was aimed at a domestic audience in Great Britain, key sections of it were aimed at the American public, and at one American in particular: Franklin D. Roosevelt.	This is one of Churchill's very best speeches, and like his addresses of June 4th and June 18th, it is best appreciated when read in its entirety. Nevertheless, some excerpts will provide a sense of its brilliance. Churchill said that this war [as opposed to World War I, and its mass casualties] "is a conflict of strategy, of organization, of technical apparatus, of science, mechanics and morale…Since the Germans drove the Jews out and lowered their technical standards, our science is definitely ahead of theirs. Our geographical position, our command of the sea, and the friendship of the United States enable us to draw resources from the whole world and to manufacture weapons of war of every kind, but especially of the superfine kinds, on a scale hitherto practiced only by Nazi

Germany…The British nation and the British Empire, finding themselves alone, stood undismayed against disaster. No one flinched or wavered; nay, some who formerly thought of peace, now think only of war. Our people are united and resolved, as they have never been before. Death and ruin have become small things compared with the shame of defeat or failure in duty…We have rearmed and rebuilt our armies in a degree which would have been deemed impossible a few months ago. We have ferried across the Atlantic, in the month of July, thanks to our friends over there, an immense mass of munitions of all kinds: cannon, rifles, machine guns, cartridges and shell, all safely landed without the loss of a gun or a round…More than 2,000,000 determined men have rifles and bayonets in their hands tonight, and three-quarters of them are in regular military formations…The whole Island bristles against invaders, from the sea or from the air…Our Navy is far stronger than it was at the beginning of the war. The great flow of new construction set on foot at the outbreak is now beginning to come in. We hope our friends across the ocean will send us a timely reinforcement to bridge the gap between the peace flotillas of 1939 and the war flotillas of 1941…The great air battle which has been in progress over this Island for the last few weeks has recently attained a high intensity. It is too soon to attempt to assign limits either to its scale or to its duration. We must certainly expect that greater efforts will be made by the enemy than any he has so far put forth…It is quite plain that Herr Hitler could not admit defeat in his air attack on Great Britain without sustaining most serious injury…The enemy is, of course, far more numerous than we are. But our new production…largely exceeds his, and the American production is only now beginning to flow in…We believe that we shall be able to continue the air struggle indefinitely and as long as the enemy pleases…**The gratitude of every home in our Island, in our Empire, and indeed throughout the world…goes out to the British airmen who, undaunted by odds, unwearied in their constant challenge and mortal danger, are turning the tide of the World War by their prowess and by their devotion.** <u>**Never in the field of human conflict was so much owed by so many to so few**</u>. **All hearts go out to the fighter pilots, whose brilliant actions we see with our own eyes day after day;** but we must never forget that all the time, night after night, month after month, our bomber pilots and our bomber squadrons travel far into Germany, find their targets in the darkness by the highest navigational skill, and…inflict shattering blows upon the whole of the technical and warmaking structure of the Nazi power…" [Emphasis added]. After summarizing his intent to lease bases in the Western Atlantic and Caribbean to the United States for purposes of mutual benefit, he ended with this stirring peroration: "Undoubtedly this process

			means that these two great organisations of the English-speaking democracies, the British Empire and the United States, will have to be somewhat mixed up together in some of their affairs for mutual and general advantage. *For my own part, looking out upon the future, I do not view the process with any misgivings. I could not stop it if I wished; no one can stop it. <u>Like the Mississippi, it just keeps rolling along. Let it roll. Let it roll on full flood, inexorable, irresistible, benignant, to broader lands and better days</u>.*"[87] [Emphasis added]
	September 2, 1940	**The Destroyers-Bases Deal is signed at 7 PM, Eastern Standard time,** in an exchange of notes between Secretary of State Cordell Hull and the British Ambassador, Lord Lothian. The following day CNO Harold R. Stark formally gave his opinion that the transfer of the destroyers in exchange for the bases would enhance the security of the United States, a certification that was required to seal the deal and ensure its legality.[88]	It was made possible domestically by an August 17th legal opinion formulated by Attorney General Robert Jackson, who determined in his brief that **"…The Chief of Naval Operations may, and should, certify…that such destroyers are not essential to the defense of the United States if in his judgment the exchange of such destroyers for strategic naval and air bases will strengthen rather than impair the total defense of the United States."** CNO "Betty" Stark would go along, even though it caused him great discomfort professionally. He had lobbied Congress in November of 1939 to pay for the recommissioning of 108 old World War I destroyers---which had cost about 50 million dollars to accomplish---on the grounds that they were essential to

---

[87] Churchill, ed., *Never Give In!,* 237-248.

[88] Moss, *19 Weeks,* 298.

America's national defense; now he was being forced to formally certify that the U.S. could give away 50 of them because they were not essential to America's defense.[89] ***Tellingly, on this occasion, and on future occasions, Stark would do anything desired to please his boss, FDR.***

The late-August impasse between Churchill and FDR over whether linkage would be acknowledged between the transfer of the destroyers and the leasing of the bases was resolved by a compromise: the bases in Newfoundland and Bermuda would be announced as "gifts" to America, and the lease of six bases closer to the Panama Canal would be announced as in exchange for the transfer of the destroyers. This two way face-saver allowed Churchill to say to Britons that he had not lied in his August 20th speech about giving bases away as an altruistic act, and allowed Roosevelt to say at home that he had made a very wise trade that had enhanced U.S. strategic security interests. (In the final analysis, the motor torpedo boats were stricken from the list of American items to maintain the legality of the deal; this had to be done because earlier in the summer the Attorney General had declared transfer of the MTBs illegal, since they were not old, surplus property but were to have been modified specifically to British specifications.)

---

[89] Shogan, *Hard Bargain,* 213-239.

| Sept 3, 1940 | **FDR holds a news conference onboard his train (enroute Washington, D.C. from West Virginia), and announces the Destroyer-Bases Deal as a *fait accompli*.** He tells the reporters the associated documents (the exchange of notes between Hull and Lothian; Attorney General Jackson's legal opinion; and his message to Congress on the transaction) will be released in Washington, but are unavailable for the White House press corps with him on the train--- thus, his opinions, generalizations, and characterization of the deal at this carefully choreographed press event mold the way it is reported to the country. FDR has managed the transaction so well, and has finessed public opinion so carefully over the summer (by late August, 3 out of 5 Americans are in favor of selling destroyers to Great Britain), that with the | Long-term leases (99 years) for two of the bases, in Newfoundland and Bermuda, were offered "freely and without consideration" by His Majesty's Government; the other six facilities, located in The Bahamas, Jamaica, St. Lucia, Trinidad, Antigua, and British Guiana, were to be leased for 99 years "in exchange for naval and military equipment and material" which the U.S. would then transfer to Britain. [90]

Privately, Assistant Secretary of State Breckinridge Long and his boss, Cordell Hull, agreed in late August that the transfer of the 50 destroyers was a violation of international law, and that Germany might take umbrage at it, since it did away with all pretense of American neutrality over the European war. After the transfer of the destroyers was announced, the United States would only be giving lip-service to its purported neutrality.

Publicly, it was a triumph for Roosevelt. A *New York Times* headline on September 4th read: **"Roosevelt trades destroyers for sea bases; tells Congress he acted on his own authority; Britain pledges never to yield or sink fleet."** The newspaper ran six separate stories on the trade, and a map showing the eight new bases, titled: **"U.S. Acquires Defense Bastions."** The *New York Herald Tribune* called the bases a "stockade of steel" on America's eastern |

---

[90] Ibid., 232.

exception of the known isolationists in Congress (especially Senators Walsh and Vandenberg) and a few anti-Roosevelt newspapers (most notably the *St. Louis Post Dispatch* and *New York Daily News*), the deal went over quite well with the public. Wendell Willkie does not object to the deal, only to the way it was transacted, complaining that the President should have gone to Congress first for permission. His initial, mild objections to the way the deal was carried out were not strident enough to suit powerful isolationists in the House and Senate---in particular, Senator Vandenberg---and this disparity in views between Willkie and the old guard isolationists creates a wedge in the Republican party.

Historian Ian Kershaw, in *Fateful Choices,* wrote this about the Destroyers-Bases Deal: "Traditional isolationism was now

flank. *Time* magazine and the *Christian Science Monitor* were strongly supportive as well.

If Roosevelt had simply transferred 50 destroyers to Great Britain, he would have been vulnerable to the charges of isolationists that he was stripping America of its defenses to save the British Empire. But by acquiring the bases in exchange, FDR successfully claimed he was strengthening the defense of the United States in the Western Hemisphere (a major plank in the isolationist platform), something they could hardly complain about.

Shortly before the deal was sealed, FDR told his secretary, Grace Tully, "Congress is going to raise hell about this, but even another day's delay may mean the end of civilization. Cries of 'war monger' and 'dictator' will fill the air, but if Britain is to survive we must act."[91] FDR confided to his friend and advisor Bernard Baruch shortly before the announcement, that "he might get impeached for what he was about to do."[92] William J. Donovan (future head of the OSS for FDR), who had visited England in July to informally assess for Roosevelt whether or not Great Britain could hold out against Germany, wrote to MP Brendan Bracken (a close associate of Churchill) about one week prior to the consummation of the destroyers-bases

---

[91] Ibid., 241.

[92] Ibid., 235.

starting to run out of steam, even if fear of intervention was still strong. More important, as was widely recognized, the Americans had now effectively abandoned neutrality. For the British, this was the key point. The United States was no longer neutral in any conventional understanding of the term. The totemic aspect of the destroyer deal, privately as well as publicly emphasized by British leaders, was the outward display of American military support for Britain." While Kershaw criticized Roosevelt for taking three and a half months to bring the deal to fruition, at a time when it truly looked like a German invasion was imminent, I believe he misses the mark. It is remarkable to the author that Roosevelt proceeded to "find a way" to transfer the destroyers in the midst of a hotly contested Presidential election, in deal, "He [FDR] says…he will lose the election on the destroyers, but still feels that it should be done."[93] Roosevelt later told intimates that maneuvering his way through the minefield of isolationist opinion, and constitutional and legal obstacles, to find a way to transfer the 50 destroyers to Great Britain, had caused him more concern than any other political challenge he took on during his time in the White House. But rather than igniting a firestorm and imperiling his reelection, as he had originally feared it might, the transfer of 50 destroyers to Great Britain, and the associated acquisition of eight defensive bases in the Western hemisphere, "…heartened Americans at a moment when it appeared that only the Axis nations could act decisively. The destroyer deal elevated FDR above the status of a candidate and, more than any other event of his Presidency until then, established him as Commander-in-Chief."[94]

The first dozen of the fifty ships departed on September 5th for Halifax, where British crews were waiting to board them. The obsolete World War I "Town Class" destroyers were very poorly designed, top-heavy ships which could not maneuver well at high speeds, and experienced numerous steering failures. After three months only about 30 of the 50 ships had been delivered to British waters, and because more extensive

---

[93] Ibid., 241.

[94] Ibid., 242.

spite of the fact that he sincerely believed that bypassing Congress might cost him his job (that is, might get him impeached, or might cause him to lose the election by providing ammunition to his opponent). While it is true that the Destroyer Deal was pushed by public opinion, i.e., aided by lobbying groups that favored the deal, it is also true that Roosevelt was involved behind the scenes in orchestrating some of those lobbying activities. FDR himself was assisting in molding the public opinion that he ended up following, which is why the consummation of the deal took so long. All of his Machiavellian skills were displayed in the manner in which he finally pulled off the transfer, in the midst of an election campaign---without Congressional approval. So adroitly was this done, that there was barely a peep of protest nationwide. Such an accomplishment would

repairs and renovations were required than anticipated, of these only 9 (nine) of them were in operating condition by the end of 1940; and no more than 30 of the 50 ships were in an operational status by May 1st, 1941. However, six months after the deal, all of the ships had finally been delivered, and eventually were all put to use as minelayers or convoy escorts. By June of 1941 about one fifth of the 200 ships in the British Navy available for convoy escort duty were these Town Class destroyers, and of the 27 German U-boats sunk by surface ships of the British Navy, the U.S.-built destroyers accounted for five of them.[95] But by the time the deal was sealed and announced, its **symbolism** was more significant than the actual military value of the ships that were transferred, for the Destroyers-Bases deal signaled to the world, and most significantly to the British people (as well as to Hitler), that America's "neutrality" was in name only, and that the United States henceforth intended to provide all aid short of war to Great Britain, in ever increasing quantities. (And eventually, as we shall see, FDR would even **make war** against the German Navy in the Atlantic Ocean, **without declaring it.** The Destroyer-Bases deal was the first step down that road.)

---

[95] Shogan, *Hard Bargain,* 248-250; Lukacs, *The Duel,* 209; and Kershaw, *Fateful Choices,* 218.

	have been unthinkable back in mid-May when Churchill first proposed the idea.	
Sep 7, 1940	**"The Blitz" (i.e., the indiscriminate terror bombing of civilians in British cities) begins on this date.** Late in August the German Air Force had attempted to bomb industrial targets in Birmingham, Liverpool, Bristol, and the London docks. In July, 258 British civilians were killed; and in August, 1,075. More than half of these "collateral damage" casualties were women and children. Bombing London on September 7th was the "terror reprisal" prerogative that Hitler had reserved for himself back on August 1st when he issued Directive No. 17. London sprawled across 600 square miles and its population was 8.2 million people, the largest of any city in the world. London was the seat of the British government, the royal family, finance,	Hitler's Luftwaffe switched from its concentrated assault on RAF airbases and infrastructure to the terror-bombing of cities (with the focus on London, of course) on this date. Military historians universally, in hindsight, consider this to have been a major error, for at the time, the RAF was "on the ropes." Hitler, probably having (privately) decided by this time not to launch a seaborne invasion of England in 1940, decided to punish the British people psychologically for their failure to bring down Churchill's government and make a peace deal with Germany. It was not known at this time how Britons would stand up to terror bombing of London (the world's major commercial center and their capital), and Hitler was determined to find out, in the hope that it might just break British morale. Destroying London would allow him to claim a public, propaganda victory in the Battle of Britain; in reality, as he well knew, the air battle had already failed in its primary goal of knocking out RAF Fighter Command's ability to defend Great Britain. Some have speculated that Churchill cleverly provoked Hitler into shifting from attacks on aerodromes to civilian population centers, and that this successful strategy saved the RAF from continued attrition of its radar sites and airbase infrastructure, which was already severely stressed, and of pilots, the most

	commerce, and entertainment---and was the location of one seventh of Great Britain's population. The attack commenced 76 days and nights of terror bombing of civilian targets in London and other cities, in which about 43,000 civilians were killed. Rather than break British morale, London's ordeal united the British people as never before, and gained Great Britain much sympathy overseas, especially in the United States.	precious resource of all. (Britain was training 280 fighter pilots per month, but 348 fighter pilots had been either killed, or put out of action, in August.) In fact, after some Luftwaffe bombs from two errant aircraft (whose mission was to bomb the docks) fell harmlessly on central London the night of 24-25 August, Churchill twice ordered the RAF to launch night raids on Berlin (even though Berlin was five times farther away from England than London was from the German airbases in France). The raids on Berlin did little physical damage, but they provoked an angry speech by Hitler on September 4th at the Sportzpalast in Berlin before a mass meeting of thousands of women health workers, and soon thereafter, he abandoned his attacks on British fighter bases, and attempted to flatten London.[96]
Sept 11, 1940	**"These Cruel, Wanton, Indiscriminate Bombings of London"** Churchill broadcast a speech to the nation preparing his people psychologically for invasion, and expressing his outrage over the terror bombing of London. Millions in America listened to this powerful speech as well.	Excerpts follow: "The effort of the Germans to secure daylight mastery of the air over England is, of course, the crux of the whole war. So far it has failed conspicuously. It has cost them very dear…for him [Hitler] to try to invade this country without having secured mastery in the air would be a very hazardous undertaking. Nevertheless, all his preparations for an invasion on a great scale are steadily going forward…Behind these clusters of ships or barges, there stand very large numbers of German troops…We cannot tell when they will try to come; we

---

[96] Moss, *19 Weeks,* 293-297, 306.

cannot be sure that in fact they will try at all; but no one should blind himself to the fact that a heavy, full scale invasion of this Island is being prepared with all the usual German thoroughness and method…If this invasion is going to be tried at all, it does not seem that it can be long delayed. The weather may break at any time…Therefore, we must regard the next week or so as a very important period in our history. It ranks with the days when the Spanish Armada was approaching the Channel…or when Nelson stood between us and Napoleon's Grand Army at Boulogne. We have read all about this in the history books; but what is happening now is on a far greater scale and of far more consequence to the life and future of the world and its civilisation than these brave old days of the past. Every man and woman will therefore prepare himself to do his duty, whatever it may be, with special pride and care… **These cruel, wanton, indiscriminate bombings of London are, of course, a part of Hitler's invasion plans.** He hopes, by killing large numbers of civilians, and women and children, that he will terrorise and cow the people of this mighty imperial city, and make them a burden and an anxiety to the government and thus distract our attention unduly from the ferocious onslaught he is preparing. Little does he know the spirit of the British nation, or the tough fibre of the Londoners, whose forbears played a leading part in the establishment of Parliamentary institutions and who have

		been bred to value freedom far above their lives. **This wicked man, the repository and embodiment of many forms of soul-destroying hatred, this monstrous product of former wrongs and shame, has now resolved to try to break our famous island race by a process of indiscriminate slaughter and destruction.** <u>What he has done is to kindle a fire in British hearts, here and all over the world,</u> which will glow long after all traces of the conflagration he has caused in London have been removed. <u>**He has lighted a fire which will burn with a steady and consuming flame until the last vestiges of Nazi tyranny have been burnt out of Europe,**</u> and until the Old World---and the New---can join hands to rebuild the temples of man's freedom and man's honour, upon foundations which will not soon or easily be overthrown."[97] [Emphasis added]
September 12, 1940	U.S. Ambassador Joseph C. Grew in Japan sends a warning about Japan's intentions to Secretary of State Hull and President Roosevelt.	"On September 12, in a telegram that impressed FDR, Grew advised against further attempts to conciliate Japan or attempts to protect American interests merely by expressions of disapproval. Describing Japan as a predatory power temporarily without ethical or moral sense, Grew urged a policy of striving by every means to preserve the status quo in the Pacific."[98] (Background: Japan had just pressured Vichy France into granting transit rights for Japanese troops, and

---

[97] Churchill, ed., *Never Give In!*, 250-253.

[98] Dallek, *Franklin D. Roosevelt and American Foreign Policy*, 241.

		permission to construct airfields in northern French Indochina---clear intent that Japan was considering going to war in Southeast Asia, and using French Indochina (Vietnam) as a jumping off point.)
September 14, 1940	**The Selective Service and Training Act is passed by Congress.** For the first time in history, the United States has a peacetime draft. **President Roosevelt signed the Act on September 16, 1941.** The bill was introduced on June 20, and the debate was fierce, particularly in the U. S. Senate. Except for one brief statement of support in July, FDR stayed out of the fray; he was extremely pleased, of course, with the outcome. Only men 21 to 35 years of age were subject to the draft, not 18 to 45 as originally envisaged by the War Department. Army Chief of Staff George Marshall gave a nationwide radio address on September 16th explaining how much more serious the situation was than in 1917.	All males *between* the ages of 21 and 36 were required to register in October, the following month. Men who were to serve were selected by a lottery system, which picked the draft numbers of those who were registered at random. **The term of service enacted by this first peacetime draft law was only 12 months;** a maximum of 900,000 men were allowed to be in training at any one time. (Draftees were allowed to declare themselves conscientious objectors, and if these requests were approved by their local draft boards, objectors were to be assigned to non-combat roles.) **The Act required that the men drafted serve only in the Western Hemisphere, or in U.S. military establishments in U.S. territory or possessions overseas (i.e., not in "foreign wars");** this provision was essential to getting the legislation passed in isolationist and war-wary America. President Roosevelt issued a written message about the draft on September 19, 1940 which explained its provisions to the American people. Enacting universal conscription was essential to preparing the nation for the possibility of war, with World War II raging in Europe, and all of Western Europe subjugated except Great Britain.

| Sept 17, 1940 | **Hitler postpones "Operation Sea Lion," the invasion of England, indefinitely.** He knows he has not gained mastery of the air over southeast England, and the rough Channel weather will now make an invasion impossible until the following spring. Meanwhile, Hitler's attention and focus shifts to his forthcoming invasion of the Soviet Union. By his reasoning, if it succeeds, the Churchill government will then fall; a more realistic government will replace it---one which will recognize German hegemony over continental Europe; and he will never have to invade England. (Churchill and his government do not immediately know about the formal postponement of "Sea Lion," but eventually reconnaissance photos reveal that the German preparations for an imminent invasion have ceased.) | **On this same date, Churchill speaks to a Secret Session of the House of Commons.** The Battle of Britain reached its climax two days prior to this speech, when all of the RAF's reserves were thrown into the life-or-death struggle in the air with the Luftwaffe. Excerpts from Churchill's speech follow:

"These next few weeks are grave and anxious. I said just now in the Public Session that the employment of the enemy's invasion preparations and the assembly of his ships and barges are steadily proceeding, and that any moment a major assault may be launched upon this island. I say now in secret that upwards of seventeen hundred self-propelled barges and more than two hundred seagoing ships, some very large ships, are already gathering at the many invasion ports in German occupation. If this is all a pretence and stratagem to pin us down here, it has been executed with surprising thoroughness and on a gigantic scale...The shipping available and now assembled is sufficient to carry in one voyage nearly *half* a million men. [Emphasis in original] We should, of course, hope to drown a great many on the way over, and to destroy a large proportion of their vessels. But when you reflect upon the many points from which they could start...one must expect many lodgments or attempted lodgments to be made on our island simultaneously. These we shall hope to deal with as they occur...I am confident that we shall succeed in defeating and largely |

		destroying this most tremendous onslaught by which we are now threatened, and anyhow, whatever happens, we will all go down fighting to the end. I am sure as the sun will rise tomorrow that we shall be victorious."[99] Churchill and his countrymen do not know it, but the Royal Air Force had broken the will (if not the back) of the Luftwaffe on September 15th, two days prior to this speech, and Hitler---like Napoleon, fearing the water and unable to safely cross the English Channel---had postponed the invasion of England. Germany's nighttime bombing of British population centers would continue for some time (in fact, off and on until May 11, 1941), but history now reveals to us what Churchill and his colleagues could not then know, which is that commencing the day Churchill gave this speech in Secret Session, the threat of invasion was over.
September 19, 1940	FDR embargoes the sale of **all** iron and scrap metal to Japan, thus expanding upon a partial embargo on scrap metal imposed on July 26th; the effective date of the embargo was announced as October 16th.	This action was considered the mildest possible, least provocative response to Japan's successful pressuring of Vichy France to allow the construction of Japanese airfields in northern French Indochina, and transit rights for Japanese troops. It was obvious to all observers that these actions were preparatory steps to an aggressive southern advance into Southeast Asia. The Hawks in the Roosevelt administration---Henry Stimson, Frank

---

[99] Churchill. Ed., *Never Give In!*, 253-254.

			Knox, Henry Morgenthau, and Harold Ickes, all favored *a total embargo on sale of oil to Japan,* not just scrap metal. But their hard line was resisted by Cordell Hull and Sumner Welles at State, and Navy CNO Harold Stark and CINCUS James O. Richardson, who warned that an embargo of Japan's oil would incite Japan to go to war in Southeast Asia. Furthermore, the governing authorities in the Dutch East Indies (in a precarious position since Holland had been overrun by Germany in May) had already informed the State Department that they did not want American action taken that would expose them to the threat of Japanese invasion.
September 25, 1940	**The team of Army cryptanalysts** working under the general supervision of Army civilian William F. Friedman (the "Father of American Cryptography") **breaks the high-level Japanese diplomatic code** used between the Foreign Office in Tokyo and its various Embassies around the world, and a steady flow of decrypted diplomatic intercepts commences on this date. The team leader selected by Friedman whose working group actually performed this feat was **Frank B. Rowlett** of the Army's Signals		Navy Lieutenant Jack Holtwick, on a team working under the Navy's Commander Laurance F. Safford (within OP-20-G, the Navy Communications Security section in Washington, D.C.), had originally performed the feat of breaking the high-level Japanese diplomatic code (Type A) back in 1936, with a machine dubbed "Red" (after the name given by the Americans to the Type A coded transmissions), but the Japanese government changed its method of encrypting diplomatic messages in 1939, and the U.S. cryptologists had to start all over again. Commander Safford knew the Navy would need help with the new code and enlisted the aid of William Friedman of SIS, his counterpart within the Army Signal Corps. The Navy loaned Friedman's group one of the Red machines designed by Lieutenant Holtwick, some technicians, and largely

Intelligence Service (SIS). After a concentrated effort lasting about 18 months, his team (which included Leo Rosen and Genevieve Grotjan) deduced through a series of mathematical associations that the Japanese encoding machine (dubbed the "Type B encryption device") used a series of electrical switches, rather than rotors as in the previous model, to encode high level diplomatic messages. A Navy mechanic on his team invented a prototype device using similar stepping switches to mimic the mathematically deduced behavior of the Japanese Type B machine, and multiple copies of the American analog decoding device were then constructed by the Naval Code and Signals Laboratory in the Washington Navy Yard. The decoding machine, and the code it was deciphering, were both dubbed **"Purple,"** and the machine could decrypt Japanese diplomatic cables as fast as the

funded the joint effort, which was primarily an Army enterprise this time around. The information gleaned (dubbed **"MAGIC"**) was of the highest interest and importance to President Roosevelt, his Secretary of War Henry Stimson, and Secretary of State Cordell Hull, as well as Army Chief of Staff General George C. Marshall, and CNO Harold R. ("Betty") Stark, between late November 1940, and December 7, 1941 (and remained of vital importance to the American leadership throughout the Second World War). Between the months of March and December of 1941, of the 227 messages sent from Tokyo to the Japanese Embassy in Washington, 223 of them were intercepted and decrypted. As time went by, Army and Navy cryptologists and translators were often able to process messages from Tokyo to Washington so quickly that they were often in the hands of Secretary of State Hull before he met with the Japanese Ambassador to receive the latest Japanese proposal. <u>The raw intercepts were often viewed on a daily basis by the President and his inner Cabinet</u>, and by a very select group of others in Washington, D.C. (and later in Manila, as well). One particular reason for the high level of interest was the fact that the Japanese Ambassador in Berlin, Baron Hiroshi Oshima (who was a trusted confidant of the Nazi regime), was regularly reporting everything he learned from Hitler, Ribbentrop, Goering and others about the German conduct of the war and its future war plans. So not

| | Japanese could break them at the receiving end with their own Type B device; all the Americans had to do was then translate the decoded telegrams from phonetic Japanese, into English. The radio teletype cable traffic fed into the **Purple** machines was obtained primarily by radio intercept stations all over the Pacific (and in Washington), most of them run by the Navy. (Significant amounts of diplomatic cable traffic were also given to the U.S. government by commercial cable companies, at the government's request.) ***The intelligence obtained was given the rubric "MAGIC" throughout the war.*** | only could those reading the **MAGIC** intercepts learn what the Tokyo Foreign Minister's instructions were to his major Embassies (including the one in Washington, D.C.), but they could divine many of Hitler's plans ahead of time from Baron Oshima's faithful transmissions from Berlin back to Tokyo. (Publicly, in their news and propaganda broadcasts, the Nazis were the most outrageous liars, but they had developed such a profound trust for Oshima during the mid-1930s, that they were unusually frank with him about their future intentions, and even about the battle front.)[100] Historian John Prados, in *Combined Fleet Decoded* (pp. 163-4), notes that the combined Army-Navy effort that broke the **Purple** code was even more impressive than the British breaking of the German military's Enigma machine: "The break into **Purple** was especially remarkable because the B Machine was highly sophisticated---much more sophisticated than the Germans' Enigma ---and because the code was solved entirely by mathematical analysis. The B Machine used…stepping switches, of a type then common in telephone exchanges, where the Enigma utilized |

---

[100] Lee, *Marching Orders,* 4-18; Prados, *Combined Fleet Decoded,* 163-165; and Greaves, Jr., *Pearl Harbor,* 130-133. Prados corrects the historical oversimplification that usually credits William Friedman with breaking "Purple." He properly credits Frank B. Rowlett (appointed by Friedman), and cryptanalysts Genevieve Grotjan, Harry L. Clark, and numerous others with making the breakthrough necessary to decrypt the Japanese Type B machine transmissions, and credits Leo Rosen with designing and building the first, prototype "Purple" machine. The museum exhibit titled "The Magic of Purple," at the NSA's National Cryptologic Museum just outside the main gate at Fort Meade, contains more detail about the roles of Rowlett, Grotjan, and Rosen.

			rotors. The electrical principles upon which the Japanese relied were inherently more flexible than the mechanical ones in Enigma. Moreover, the British analysts who solved Enigma had the benefit of previous important breakthroughs by French and Polish experts and could even examine early versions of the machine, commercially available. Americans solved **Purple** all by themselves."
September 27, 1940		The <u>Tripartite Pact</u> is signed in Berlin between Italy, Germany and Japan. *It is a ten-year defensive alliance aimed solely at the United States;* the terms of the pact stipulate that if any members of the Pact are attacked by any country not presently involved in the European War or the Sino-Japanese war (excepting the Soviet Union), that the other members of the Pact will come to their aid. All of the Pact's signatories on September 27th are prominently aware of strong isolationist sentiment in America, and are counting on the Tripartite Pact to put a brake on FDR's strategic moves to	The aim of the Tripartite Pact was deterrence: to politically immobilize the United States, and induce caution, delay, and vacillation into American foreign policy vis-à-vis what actions it took against Germany. Hitler believed that the U.S. would be far less likely to declare war against Germany if America knew that this would mean war against Japan, as well. The nation that derived the greatest psychological comfort from the Pact was expansionist Japan. Japan's foreign policy was increasingly being driven by a "don't miss the bus" philosophy, as its warlords looked hungrily toward the rich resources in the Far East colonial possessions of the defeated Western European powers, France and Holland. Japan knew that Britain and the United States would be morally and strategically opposed to any Japanese move to conquer and occupy French Indochina and/or the Dutch East Indies; but Great Britain was seriously preoccupied and weakened by its fight to the death with Nazi Germany, and Japanese strategists believed the United States was far less likely to aggressively

aid Great Britain and oppose Hitler. The Pact's intention, in their minds, is to make it less likely that the United States would enter the European War, *or* that the U.S. would oppose southern expansion by Japan with military force.

This Pact formally identified the three major Axis Powers--- whom FDR had often (correctly) referred to as ***"the bandit nations"*---** and was soon signed by Germany's satellite states: Hungary, Romania, Slovakia, Bulgaria, Yugoslavia, and---after the dismemberment of Yugoslavia in April of 1941---by Croatia.

While the *intent* of the pact was *deterrence*---to make it less likely that the United States would become a belligerent---it seemed to have backfired, for it had the opposite effect on the United States. The Tripartite Pact confirmed the views of many in the U.S. that Japan was the equivalent of Nazi Germany in the Far East---a belligerent, oppose southward expansion by Japan if it meant war with Germany, as well.

Key provisions of the Tripartite Pact were:

Article 1: "Japan recognizes and respects the leadership of Germany and Italy in the establishment of a new order in Europe."

Article 2: "Germany and Italy recognize and respect the leadership of Japan in the establishment of a new order in Greater East Asia."

Article 3: "Japan, Germany, and Italy agree to cooperate in their efforts along these lines. They further undertake to assist one another with all political, economic, and military means if one of the Contracting Powers is attacked by a Power at present not involved in the European War or the Japanese-Chinese conflict." (It was expressly stated that the provisions of the Pact did not apply to the Soviet Union.)

The Tripartite Pact, in short, in addition to being a defensive alliance, was also a clear statement about the intent of these three nations to reestablish a new world order by conquest, and to loot the planet.

Hitler viewed world history as a Darwinian struggle to the death between stronger nations and weaker nations, with no apologies necessary by the victors. He therefore admired Japan, and engineered a major shift from Germany's traditional support of China, to support

	bullying, imperial force---and therefore had to be stopped.	instead for China's mortal enemy, expansionist-minded Japan, in 1936. While military coordination between Germany and Japan was minimal throughout World War II---indeed, almost non-existent---Hitler's admiration for Japan was sincere.
Late September, 1940	**The U.S. Navy's codebreakers in Washington, D.C. (at OP-20-G) fully decode and translate their first JN-25(a) message.**	Depending upon one's source, this happened either one week before, or one week after, **Purple** was broken by the Army's SIS. It had taken OP-20-G one year longer to break JN-25(a) than it had taken GCCS and its Far East Combined Bureau, because OP-20-G had fewer human resources to call on. CDR Laurance Safford's "ace" civilian cryptanalyst, the brilliant and enigmatic Agnes Meyer Driscoll (an Ohio State University graduate who had completely "broken" and "recovered" the Japanese Navy's two previous operational codes, the Red Book and the Blue Book), reportedly took the lead in this effort. She had trained numerous Navy linguists and cryptanalysts, including Laurance Safford, Joseph J. Rochefort, and Edwin T. Layton. By January 4, 1941, 2000 words in the basic 33,333 word code book had been recovered.[101]
October 4, 1940 [Note: One source, Robert Stinnett, author of *Day of Deceit*, in multiple references, lists the	**FDR speaks to an unidentified caller in the Oval Office** (as heard on his secret voice recordings made that day).	Roosevelt reads the text of the Scripps-Howard article written by Roy Howard in Tokyo (quoting a Japanese spokesman): **"A condition of staying out of war is that the United States will recognize a new era in the Far East, and that in token of that recognition,**

---

[101] Costello, *Days of Infamy,* 280; Rusbridger and Nave, *Betrayal At Pearl Harbor,* 166-169.

recording of this phone call as having been made on October 4th; however, two other sources---George Victor, in *The Pearl Harbor Myth,* and the A&E documentary *FDR: A Presidency Revealed*---both indicate the conversation took place on October 8th. In the documentary, the narrator even states that it took place at 4:20 PM, on October 8th. See citations below.]	Roosevelt's clandestine recording system recorded his side of a telephone call with an unidentified caller. The subject of discussion was a newspaper story written by press baron Roy Howard, head of the Scripps-Howard News Alliance, and distributed by UPI and Scripps-Howard to newspapers all over the world, and published on October 2nd. Howard had interviewed a Japanese official and quoted him as saying that the U.S., if it wished for peace in the Pacific, should take certain specified actions.	**the United States must abandon its bases, military or naval bases, in Guam, Midway, Pearl Harbor, and Wake---including Pearl Harbor, that's giving up Hawaii. [showing real astonishment] God! That's the first time that any damn Jap has told us to get out of Hawaii. And that has me more worried than any other thing in the world."**[102] [Emphasis in original] The voice recording continues: *"**This country is ready to pull the trigger if the Japs do anything**. I mean, we won't stand any nonsense, public opinion won't, from the Japs, if they do some fool thing…**And the time may be coming when the Germans and the Japs will do some fool thing. That would put us in**."*[103] This is not the language of someone who wishes to avoid war; rather, it is the language of someone who wishes to enter the war, and who is looking for a pretext to do so. The language here suggests that author Robert Stinnett may be wrong about the date of October 4th, and that George Victor and the History Channel may be correct in dating this conversation as having taken place on October 8th. *It may reflect FDR's attitude after reading Commander McCollum's ONI memo, written on October 7th (see entry below).*

---

[102] Stinnett, *Day of Deceit,* 28, 317-318; and the History Channel documentary, *FDR: A Presidency Revealed.* The first half of the conversation, in which Roosevelt reads from the article, and says **"God!…"**, can be heard in the History Channel documentary, in the subsection titled: "The Pacific Crisis."

[103] Victor, *The Pearl Harbor Myth,* 159; and Stinnett, *Day of Deceit,* 312. This portion of the same phone call is quoted in both books, but is not included in the History Channel documentary.

| October 7, 1940 | Commander Arthur H. McCollum, Head of the Far East Section of the Office of Naval Intelligence (ONI), submits a memo to the Director of Naval Intelligence, Rear Admiral Walter S. Anderson, titled: **"Estimate of the Situation in the Pacific and Recommendations for Action by the United States."** One stimulus for the memo was certainly the Tripartite Pact, for Japan was now a military ally of Germany and Italy. Another likely stimulus was the President's upcoming meeting with Admiral Richardson, CINCUS, scheduled for October 8th, the day after it was submitted. President Roosevelt knew he was meeting (again) with a rather troublesome and outspoken Fleet Commander, who had already expressed his serious reservations about keeping the major elements of the U.S. Fleet at Pearl Harbor, so it would have been natural for him to ask for a policy | The memo's author, Arthur McCollum, was one of a select group of Naval officers who had intimate knowledge of both the Japanese language, and the Japanese culture. He was born in Nagasaki, Japan in 1898 of Southern Baptist missionary parents. Stationed in Japan in 1923, he became acquainted with Crown Prince Hirohito (the future Emperor) and taught him the dance steps to the "Charleston;" later that year he helped coordinate the U.S. Navy's relief efforts following the great Tokyo earthquake. From 1928-1930 he returned to Tokyo as assistant Naval Attaché, and taught a Japanese language class to three U.S. Naval officers who all had prominent roles in Naval intelligence during World War II: Joseph J. Rochefort, Edwin T. Layton, and Ethelbert Watts. McCollum originally served in the Far East Section of ONI (the Japan Desk) from 1933-1935, and after two subsequent assignments, returned to head the Far East Section at ONI in 1939. Bright, confident, and dynamic, he inspired the respect and trust of his colleagues and superiors. Furthermore, he was one of only *twelve persons* who were **regular recipients** of the **MAGIC** decrypts of the Japanese **Purple** diplomatic code between late September of 1940, when the code was broken, and December 7, 1941 (the attack on Pearl Harbor), an indication that he was a member of an exalted circle in official Washington. (His specialty made him important, not his rank.) Even more significant, McCollum (helped by |

paper from Naval Intelligence regarding "what to do about Japan" just prior to his second meeting with Richardson in three months.

It is vital to understand the context in which this memo was written, and the environment in which it was circulated. The memo's low level of classification when it was written---Confidential---belies its importance. It was addressed to Rear Admiral Walter S. Anderson, USN, who was not only the Director of Naval Intelligence, but also a Naval confidant of the President, who had direct White House access to FDR. Since the only known written endorsement attached to the memo was written by Captain Dudley Knox (a naval strategist who was in charge of the ONI library), it would surely have been routed immediately to the Director (for whom it was written) by Captain Knox (immediately after his endorsement), and thence straight to FDR. My personal guess is that it his assistant, Lieutenant Commander Ethelbert Watts, who held down the Japan Desk at ONI) was responsible for routing ONI's military and diplomatic intelligence about Japan to President Roosevelt between February of 1940 until the Pearl Harbor attack. Sometimes he would deliver messages and reports to the President's Naval Aide, and sometimes he would deliver the items himself. For all of these reasons, it is safe to conclude that FDR was the ultimate recipient of McCollum's provocative memo, which is quoted in part immediately below.

The McCollum memo itself was a five page, single-spaced product, with a short one page endorsement written by Captain Dudley Knox, as mentioned earlier. **Its final paragraphs, nos. 9 and 10, read as follows:** [emphasis added by me]

"**It is not believed that in the present state of political opinion the United States Government is capable of declaring war against Japan without more ado**; and it is barely possible that **vigorous action on our part might lead the Japanese to modify their attitude. Therefore, the following course of action is suggested:**

   A. **Make an arrangement with Britain for the use of British bases in the Pacific, particularly Singapore.**

   B. **Make an arrangement with Holland for the use of base facilities and acquisition of**

was probably on FDR's desk the next day when he met with Admiral Richardson.[104] FDR was a "Navy President," and a hands-on operator, and many Naval officers had direct access to him at the White House. (Rear Admiral Anderson could have delivered it himself, or might have given it to the President's Naval Aide, Captain Dan Callaghan.)	supplies in the Dutch East Indies. C. Give all possible aid to the Chinese Government of Chiang Kai-Shek. D. Send a division of long range heavy cruisers to the Orient, Philippines, or Singapore. E. Send two divisions of submarines to the Orient. F. Keep the main strength of the U.S. Fleet now in the Pacific in the vicinity of the Hawaiian islands. G. Insist that the Dutch refuse to grant Japanese demands for undue economic concessions, particularly oil. H. Completely embargo all U.S. trade with Japan, in collaboration with a similar embargo imposed by the British Empire. **<u>If by these means Japan could be led to commit an overt act of war, so much</u>**

---

[104] Robert B. Stinnett, author of *Day of Deceit* (who discovered the memo in 1995 at the National Archives), has concluded (see note 10, on page 312) that at a minimum the following persons (and probably more) were almost certainly privy to the memo and its explosive recommendations: President Roosevelt; Admiral William Leahy (who was at FDR's meeting with Richardson on October 8th); CNO Harold Stark; Rear Admiral Anderson (Director, ONI, to whom it was addressed); Captain Knox (who endorsed it); General George C. Marshall (based on later events); and Admiral Richardson and Commander Murphy (his War Plans Officer). <u>I am not convinced that either Richardson or Murphy saw it, since Richardson does not mention it in his extremely frank and detailed memoir.</u> I ***am convinced*** that one other person who ***did*** see it was Rear Admiral Richmond Kelly Turner, Head of the Navy's War Plans Division (based upon his actions in October of 1941, and afterwards, which will be discussed later).

the better. **At all events we must be fully prepared to accept the threat of war.**

A. H. McCollum

In a final, summary page (the fifth page), McCollum states in recommendation no. 6 (of 7): **It is to [sic] the interest of the United States to eliminate Japan's threat in the Pacific at the earliest opportunity by taking prompt and aggressive action against Japan.**

In his book *Day of Deceit,* Stinnett makes a compelling point that by the time the Pearl Harbor attack took place, all of the actions in McCollum's memo had been taken by the United States Government, either substantially or in toto.[105] In his words, "Roosevelt's

---

[105] A facsimile of the McCollum memo can be found on pages 262-267 of *Day of Deceit.* Background information about McCollum can be found in Prange's *At Dawn We Slept* (pp. 32-33); in *Day of Deceit* (pp. 6-16); throughout *Combined Fleet Decoded,* by John Prados; and in an article penned by McCollum himself (and published posthumously long after the war), in Stillwell's *Air Raid: Pearl Harbor!* (pp. 79-87). McCollum was among the small, select group of those in Washington, D.C. on the permanent distribution list for **MAGIC** intercepts. The "twelve apostles" who were regularly routed the raw **MAGIC** intercepts between November of 1940 and December 7, 1941 were: President Franklin D. Roosevelt; Secretary of State Cordell Hull; Secretary of the Navy Frank Knox; Secretary of War Henry Stimson; Admiral Harold R. Stark (CNO); Rear Admiral Royal E. Ingersoll (Deputy CNO); Rear Admiral Richmond K. Turner (Navy War Plans); **Commander Arthur H. McCollum (Far East Section, ONI);** Lieutenant Commander Ethelbert Watts (Japan Desk, ONI); General George C. Marshall (Army Chief of Staff); Brigadier General Leonard T. Gerow (Army War Plans); and Brigadier General Sherman Miles (Army G-2, or Intelligence). Others who saw them obviously included the cryptanalysts and linguists themselves, notably Commander Laurance F. Safford, USN (in charge of the Navy codebreaking effort in Washington D.C.) and Lieutenant Commander Alwyn D. Kramer, USN (an excellent Japanese linguist who was on loan from the Far East Section of ONI to Safford's Communications Intelligence Division, OP-20-G, as a translator). Another who regularly saw the **MAGIC** intercepts was Army Colonel Rufus G. Bratton, U.S.A. (head of the Far East Section, Army G-2, or McCollum's counterpart---who was also a Japanese linguist and cultural expert). Safford, Kramer, and Bratton frequently served as the couriers for the **MAGIC** intercepts distributed throughout Washington, because so few people were cleared for access at this time. The resources available to the Army's SIS and the Navy's OP-20-G were extremely thin at this time---for example, the number of personnel working for SIS in Washington in 1941 increased *from a mere thirteen to only twenty-one people* in

		fingerprints can be found on each of McCollum's proposals."
		Analysis: The tone of paragraph nine's first sentence is almost apologetic in tone, saying that in the present political climate the U.S. Government was **"not capable"** of declaring war against Japan, ***as if this were an important goal to be met.*** McCollum then implies that **more "ado"** would be required before war against Japan could be declared by the U.S. In paragraph ten, at the close of the memo, after discussing the eight actions that should be applied to Japan, <u>the baldly stated goal of pressuring Japan into committing an</u> **"overt act of war"** is highly significant, for this concept---indeed, this exact phraseology---is used late in 1941 in official policy documents, and in discussions by the highest officials in the U.S. government (as will be cited below in this monograph).
October 8-10, 1940	**Ordered back to Washington, D.C. by Secretary of the Navy Frank Knox, <u>the Commander in Chief of the U.S. Fleet, Admiral J.O. Richardson, has a working lunch nearly</u>**	Richardson had insisted on meeting with the President prior to his first visit back in July; this time he did not want to go, but was ordered back.

During his long working luncheon with FDR and Leahy on October 8th, **Admiral Richardson frankly pressed the President to reconsider his previous** |

1941. Not only were resources thin, but the two organizations were also competitive: in 1941 it was agreed that the Army would handle the **MAGIC** decryptions on the even-numbered days of the month, and the Navy on the odd-numbered days; the Army was to distribute the material around official Washington on the odd-numbered months, and the Navy would distribute it during the even-numbered months. This bewildering state of affairs was compounded when the Army decided, during 1941, that there was a security breach at the White House, and stopped delivering **MAGIC** to the President. After this, the Navy took over responsibility for delivering all **MAGIC** intercepts to President Roosevelt. (*See* Lee, *Marching Orders,* p. 25.)

three hours long with President Roosevelt and retired Admiral William D. Leahy on October 8th, *the day after* **Commander McCollum generated his memo.** (A former CNO who was then serving as Governor of Puerto Rico, Leahy was a Roosevelt supporter and confidant, and would return to active duty after the Pearl Harbor attack to work for Roosevelt in the White House.) Richardson clashes sharply with the President over retaining the Pacific Fleet at Pearl Harbor, and openly questions FDR's leadership and judgment, to his face.

On October 10, 1941 Richardson meets with Secretary of the Navy Frank Knox and strongly opposes FDR's proposed plan to station two long picket lines of ships across the Pacific Ocean, as a "trip-wire" in concert with a proposal to cut off all trade with Japan, warning Knox that such action would lead to war.

Shortly after this disastrous visit to

decision (back in May) to move the U.S. Fleet's principal homeport from the West Coast to Pearl Harbor, using blunt language that neither Roosevelt, nor any Chief Executive, was accustomed to hearing.

Richardson made diary entries at the time, in which he recorded in detail the events surrounding his visits to President Roosevelt on July 8th and October 8th. In 1945, with the war then over, Congress scheduled Joint Hearings to investigate the Pearl Harbor disaster (they were conducted between November 15, 1945 and May 23, 1946). Fearing his diaries might be subpoenaed, Richardson, by his own admission, burned them. He provided an explanation for this to the co-author of his memoirs in 1958: "Since in the diary I expressed frank and sometimes offhand opinions (some of them highly critical) of various officers of the Navy, and of officials of the government for their actions or inactions during the 1939-1941 period, I thought it best that the diary be burned." While writing his memoirs from 1956-1958, he reconstructed his conversations with Roosevelt using the transcripts of his 1945 testimony at the Congressional Pearl Harbor inquiry, and his memory. His co-author wrote that he had "an inexhaustible memory for facts and figures and personalities." (*See* Richardson's memoir, *On the Treadmill to Pearl Harbor,* p. ix-x.)

The Navy was undergoing massive expansion in mid-1940, following the

| | Washington, FDR decides to replace Richardson as CINCUS with someone less argumentative. Richardson learns about his impending early relief in a report (based on a White House leak) published in the *Kiplinger Newsletter* in late October of 1940,[106] and this rumor of his early relief is confirmed by a Naval message transmitted on January 5, 1941.

In a major shakeup, FDR reorganized the Navy's leadership structure and on February 1, 1941, the position of CINCUS (with the unfortunate-sounding "sink us" acronym) was abolished; in its place was created the Commander in Chief, U.S. Pacific Fleet (CINCPAC); Commander in Chief, U.S. Atlantic Fleet (CINCLANT); and Commander in Chief, | Nazi conquest of France and the evacuation of the British Army from Dunkirk.[107] Admiral Richardson was obsessed with the present shortage of enlisted personnel in the Navy, and even more concerned that Roosevelt had not taken appropriate steps to recruit adequately to cover this rapid expansion. He pressed these points in his meeting with Roosevelt on October 8th.

<u>Richardson's reconstructed conversation with FDR on October 8, 1941---from his memoir---is excerpted below:</u>

"I took up [with the President] the question of returning to the Pacific coast all of the fleet except the Hawaiian detachment. The President stated that the fleet was retained in the Hawaiian area in order to exercise a restraining influence on the actions of Japan. I stated that in my opinion the presence of the fleet in Hawaii might influence a civilian political government, but that Japan had a military government which knew that the fleet was undermanned, unprepared for war, and had no train of auxiliary ships without which it could not undertake active |

---

[106] Stinnett, *Day of Deceit,* 10-11; Richardson, *On the Treadmill to Pearl Harbor,* 395-402; 423-436.

[107] On June 14th FDR signed the "11% Naval Expansion Act," increasing the carrier, cruiser, and submarine tonnage of the Navy by 167,000 tons; that of auxiliary ships by 75,000 tons; and Naval aviation strength from 3,500 aircraft to 4,500. On June 15th (the next day) he signed an act increasing Navy aeronautical strength to 10,000 planes; on July 19th that total was revised upward to 15,000 aircraft. On July 1, 1940 the Navy awarded contracts for the building of 44 new ships. On July 19, 1940 President Roosevelt signed the "Naval Expansion Act," providing for a "Two-Ocean Navy" and expanding the Fleet by 70 per cent. By September 9, 1940, the Navy had awarded contracts for the construction of 210 new ships, including 12 aircraft carriers and 7 battleships. This all presented the United States Navy with tremendous recruiting and training challenges.

Asiatic Fleet (CINCAF). Admiral Husband E. Kimmel---who had been Richardson's subordinate, serving as Commander, Cruisers Battle Force---relieved his former boss on this date (in Pearl Harbor, of course!) and became the first CINCPAC; Admiral Ernest J. King, who was already commanding the Atlantic Squadron, became the first CINCLANT; and Admiral Thomas C. Hart headed the small Asiatic Fleet, homeported in Manila, in the Philippines. All three Fleet Commanders would report, of course, to Chief of Naval Operations Harold R. ("Betty") Stark in Washington, who had held the post of CNO since August of 1939, when he had relieved Admiral Leahy. **This reorganization reflected the coming reality of a true two-ocean Navy** (which had been authorized by Congress in July of 1940), and was considered the opportune moment to replace the troublesome Richardson

operations. Therefore, the presence of the fleet in Hawaii could not exercise a restraining influence on Japanese action…The President said in effect, *'Despite what you believe, I know that the presence of the fleet in the Hawaiian area has had, and is now having, a restraining influence on the actions of Japan.'*

I said: *'Mr. President, <u>I still do not believe it</u>, and I know that our fleet is disadvantageously disposed for preparing or for initiating war operations.'* The President then said: 'I can be convinced of the desirability of returning the battleships to the west coast if I can be given a good statement which will convince the American people and the Japanese government that in bringing the battleships to the west coast we are not stepping backward.'

<u>Later I asked the President if we were going to enter the war.</u> *He replied that if the Japanese attacked Thailand, or the Kra Peninsula, or the Dutch East Indies, we would <u>not</u> enter the war, that if they even attacked the Philippines <u>he doubted whether we would enter the war</u>, but that they could not always avoid making mistakes and that as the war continued and the area of operations expanded <u>sooner or later they would make a mistake and we would enter the war.</u>"* [Emphasis added]

During the conversation with FDR Richardson also brought up his serious concerns about inadequate training in the

in Pearl Harbor.

As author George Victor points out in *The Pearl Harbor Myth* (p. 160-163), Richardson was *not* relieved simply because he hurt President Roosevelt's feelings: "Roosevelt…tolerated vehement argument from his subordinates remarkably well. He had been challenged by many…When arguing with Roosevelt, [Secretary of the Interior] Ickes often threatened to resign. [Secretary of War] Stimson and [Secretary of the Treasury] Morgenthau were also outspoken when opposing Roosevelt's position. None of them was relieved, nor is there evidence that Roosevelt considered doing so or had lingering bad feelings toward them over being challenged…Roosevelt's decision to relieve Richardson followed Richardson's letter [which he would write following his return to Hawaii] informing [CNO] Stark that, despite orders to the contrary, he was curtailing training in order

fleet, the present state of undermanning, and his concerns that recruiting was not at all keeping pace with the recently authorized new construction.

"He continued to maintain, as he had done on July 8, 1940 that men in mechanical trades in civil life could be quickly inducted and made adequate sailormen, if their services were suddenly required. I insisted that a seasick garage mechanic would be of little use at sea, and that it took time for most young men to get their sea legs. I said it was essential that the enlisted personnel of the fleet should be markedly increased immediately…The discussion waxed hot and heavy. I could not help but detect that reelection political considerations, rather than long-range military considerations, were the controlling factor in the President's thinking. It was less than a month before the 1940 Presidential election, and the President was reluctant to make any commitment to increase the number of men in the Navy…<u>Finally, when it became fully apparent that he had no intention of accepting my recommendations [to relocate the fleet to the west coast or to dramatically increase recruiting], I said to him very deliberately:</u>

'Mr. President, I feel that I must tell you that the senior officers of the Navy do not have the trust and confidence in the civilian leadership of this country that is essential for the successful prosecution of a war in the Pacific.'

to guard against an attack on the fleet. It was interference with Roosevelt's war strategy that was unacceptable."

In a letter to "Betty" Stark following his return to Pearl Harbor, Richardson had written that when he had returned from his July visit to see FDR, he had formed three impressions: "*First.* That the fleet was retained in the Hawaiian area solely to support diplomatic representations and as a deterrent to Japanese aggressive action; *Second.* That there was no intention of embarking on actual hostilities against Japan. *Third.* That the immediate mission of the Fleet was accelerated training and absorption of new personnel." He continued: *"...it now appears that more active, open steps aimed at Japan are in serious consideration and...may lead to active hostilities."* He closed this letter by stating that he must be kept better informed about national strategy. After receiving two replies from Stark that did

The President, with a look of pained surprise on his face, said: *'Joe, you just don't understand that this is an election year and that there are certain things that can't be done, no matter what, until the election is over and won.'*

I had prepared the above statement, which I made to the President after long thought and deliberation...prior to my departure of my flagship for Washington...I thought the President would be shocked into either changing his policies, or providing [for] adequate implementation of them. I thought that it was worth my own official neck to get this accomplished...I can state with complete accuracy that, when the President heard my statement, he looked and acted completely crushed. He was shocked. Unfortunately, the shock did not lead to a change in Presidential policies...I believe it did lead to my being relieved of my duties as Commander in Chief of the U.S. Fleet." [Emphasis added]

On October 10th, Navy Secretary Knox, in a strategy meeting with CNO Stark, Admiral Richardson, Commander Vincent Murphy (Richardson's War Plans Officer), and others, floated an idea of President Roosevelt's, in anticipation of the possibility of a hostile Japanese reaction to the impending reopening of the Burma Road (the main supply conduit to Chiang Kai-shek's armies in China) by the British on October 17th:

not address his concerns about the possibility the U.S. would be engaging in provocative actions, he wrote to Stark again on November 28th: "I feel that the fleet must operate on either of two assumptions, i.e., (a) that we are at peace and no security measures are required; or (b) that wartime measures of security must be carried out…Now, however…I have come to the conclusion that I must operate on the basis of (b) above." It was this letter which Victor believes was the last straw, and led directly to Richardson's relief.

"The Secretary stated that he had important information bearing on the employment of the fleet. He stated he had just talked to the President, and that…**In the event the Japanese took drastic action he, the President, was considering shutting off all trade between Japan and the Americas, and to this end** *was considering establishing a patrol of light ships in two lines [one] extending from Hawaii westward to the Philippines, and [the other extending] from Samoa toward the Dutch East Indies.* The question was raised [during the discussion with Knox]…as to whether this included stopping Japanese ships as well as others, **and the view was expressed that this [stopping Japanese ships] would be an act of war, and I asked whether the President was considering a declaration of war.** The Secretary stated that the President hadn't said, and that all he, Knox, knew was what he was told. I was amazed at the proposal and stated that the fleet was not prepared to put such a plan into effect, **nor for the war which would certainly result from such a course of action,** and that we would certainly lose many of the ships…The Secretary appeared displeased at the general reaction and mine in particular, and said: 'I am not a strategist; if you don't like the President's plan draw up one of your own to accomplish the purpose.' **Mr. Knox was really incensed with me when I spoke after he originally outlined the patrol line scheme. His feelings were not softened when I said

		the execution of such a plan would result in war." [Emphasis added]
October 8, 1940	Churchill Speech: **"We Can Take It,"** In the House of Commons.	Excerpts follow: "A month has passed since Hitler turned his rage and malice on to the civil population of our great cities and particularly of London…He declared in his speech of 4 September that he would raze our cities to the ground, and since then he has been trying to carry out his fell purpose…**Neither by material damage nor by slaughter will the people of the British Empire be turned from their solemn and inexorable purpose.** It is the practice and in some cases the duty of many of my colleagues and many Members of the House to visit the scenes of destruction as promptly as possible, and I go myself from time to time. In all my life, I have never been treated with so much kindness as by the people who have suffered most…**On every side, there is the cry, 'We can take it,'** but with it, there is also the cry, 'Give it 'em back.'… Meanwhile, what has happened to the invasion we have been promised every month and almost every week since the beginning of July? Do not let us be lured into supposing that the danger is past…Now that we are in October, however, the weather is very uncertain…**Do not let us lose the conviction that it is only by supreme and superb exertions, unwearying and indomitable, that we shall save our souls alive.** No one can predict, no one

		can even imagine, how this terrible war against German and Nazi aggression will run its course or how far it will spread or how long it will last. **Long, dark months of trials and tribulations lie before us.** Not only great dangers, but many more misfortunes, many shortcomings, many mistakes, many disappointments will surely be our lot…We must be united, we must be undaunted, we must be inflexible. Our qualities and deeds must burn and glow through the gloom of Europe until they become the veritable beacon of its salvation."[108] [Emphasis added]
October 16, 1940	A **MAGIC** intercept indicating that Japan had warlike designs upon the Dutch East Indies in order to obtain virtually unlimited future crude oil supplies was taken by CDR Arthur McCollum, Head of the Far East Section at ONI, to the President's Naval Aide, CAPT Callaghan. Since the Naval Aide to the President does not make foreign policy, this is considered proof that President Roosevelt saw the intercept.	The text of the intercept reads as follows: **"THE UNITED STATES IS INCAPABLE OF TAKING ACTION AT THE PRESENT TIME TO PREVENT JAPANESE SEIZURE OF THE DUTCH POSSESSIONS IN THE FAR EAST AND NO TIME SHOULD BE LOST IN EFFECTING SUCH A SEIZURE."[109] This message was sent back to Tokyo from an economic conference the Japanese delegation was attending in a resort near the isolated hamlet of Selabintanah, about 120 km southeast of Batavia. The conference was not going well, from Japan's point of view. The Japanese delegation wanted the Dutch to provide a minimum of 3,150,000 metric tons of petroleum annually, and to

---

[108] Churchill, ed., *Never Give In!,* 255-256.

[109] Stinnett, *Day of Deceipt,* 39-42, 321.

		guarantee this for a five-year period. Dutch economic minister H. J. Van Mook was not sympathetic, and stonewalled the Japanese. While Rusbridger and Nave, in *Betrayal at Pearl Harbor* (p. 81), wrote that President Roosevelt and Secretary of State Hull were not officially added to the access list for **MAGIC** message decrypts until January 23, 1941---a disturbing state of affairs, since supposedly the President and Secretary of State determine this nation's foreign policy under its Constitution---Robert Stinnett is quite positive that this particular message was taken by CDR McCollum to the President's Naval Aide. (Neither General Marshall nor Admiral Stark trusted many in Roosevelt's administration, considering them "long haired New Dealers.")
October 23, 1940	FDR makes a key campaign speech in Philadelphia, and promises **"No foreign wars, <u>except in case of attack</u>."** FDR's strategy had been not to campaign for President, except when necessary to counter false allegations by his opponent, Wendell Willkie, or Willkie's supporters. Rather, he hoped to remain in the Oval Office as much as	With his Republican opponent Wendell Willkie---who was an energetic campaigner---rapidly closing on Roosevelt in the polls, Democratic party officials persuaded FDR to come out swinging, and he did, scheduling five campaign speeches during the last two weeks of the Presidential campaign. The first of these five speeches was in Philadelphia, and during this speech Roosevelt responded to accusations by isolationists that he was a warmonger intent upon getting the United States into World War II: "I give to you and to the people of this country this most solemn assurance: There is no secret treaty, no secret obligation, no secret commitment,

	possible, claiming he was too busy acting as Commander-in-Chief to participate in a normal election campaign.	no secret understanding in any shape or form, direct or indirect, with any other Government, or any other nation in any part of the world, to involve this nation in any war or for any other purpose."[110] He closed with this assurance: "I repeat again that I stand on the platform of our party: **We will _not_ participate in Foreign Wars, and we will not send our Army, Naval, or Air Forces to fight in foreign lands outside of the Americas, _except in case of attack_.**"[111] [Emphasis in original] This precise wording had been included in the Democratic Party platform in July, but since then FDR had engineered the Destroyers for Bases deal, and Great Britain had been subjected to almost continuous attack from the German Air Force, with great loss of life and materiel. Roosevelt therefore felt he had to respond to charges that he was intentionally engineering America's entry into hostilities, by personally repeating this line from the Democratic Party Platform document.
October 30, 1940	**In a Boston campaign speech, FDR repeats his assertion that U.S. servicemen will not participate in foreign wars, but this time he drops the caveat,** _**"except in case of**_	In Boston, one week later---and only _one day_ after FDR presided over the public draft lottery in which draft numbers were pulled at random from a transparent container by a blind-folded Secretary of War, Henry Stimson---in response to continued allegations from isolationists that his actions and policies will drag the

---

[110] Burns, *Roosevelt: The Lion and the Fox*, 447.

[111] *FDR: Third Term to Pearl Harbor* (CBS Video Library of World War II, "Seeds of War," 1982).

	attack." FDR himself had insisted on the caveat "except in case of attack" being added to the Democratic Party Platform plank about "no foreign wars."[112]	United States into the Second World War, Roosevelt states: ***"While I'm talking to you fathers and mothers, I give you one more assurance. I have said this before, but I shall say it again, and again, and again ['agayne, and agayne, and agayne']: <u>Your boys are not going to be sent into any foreign wars.</u>"***[113] This time Roosevelt left off the caveat, "except in case of attack," and when his speechwriter Sam Rosenman challenged his reasons for this prior to the speech, FDR reminded him: ***"It's not necessary. If we're attacked it's no longer a foreign war."***[114] Leaving the caveat out of the speech made the promise sound more emphatic, to say the least (and helped soothe public nerves just one day after the draft lottery was enacted); it was Roosevelt's tacit admission that Willkie was making hay by accusing him of having secret designs for war.
November 5, 1940	**FDR is re-elected for a third term; he is the first President in U.S. history to be elected three times.**	Nearly 50,000,000 votes were cast in the Presidential election of 1940, the most in American history. Of these, Roosevelt received 27,243,466 (55%) and Willkie received 22,304,755 (45%). FDR's majority was the smallest any candidate for President had received since Woodrow Wilson's victory in 1916.

---

[112] Burns, *Roosevelt: The Lion and the Fox,* 449.

[113] *FDR: Third Term to Pearl Harbor* (CBS Video Library of World War II, "Seeds of War," 1982); the narrator of the documentary, Walter Cronkite, then intoned: "Listeners note that this time, FDR does not add 'except in case of attack' after 'no foreign war.' Critics try to pin him down; he replies: **'If somebody attacks us, then it is not a foreign war.'"** The author of the documentary is listed as Merriman Smith.

[114] Burns, *Roosevelt: The Lion and the Fox,* 448-449.

However, the Electoral College system, as always, magnified this into what seemed like a larger victory than it was: Roosevelt received 449 electoral votes by winning 38 states; Willkie received 82 electoral votes from the 10 states he won. Roosevelt won every city in the country with a population over 400,000, except Cincinnati; on the other hand, Willkie had gained five million more votes than the Republican candidate in 1936, Alf Landon. In the end, it was a decisive victory for Roosevelt, by American standards. **Afterwards, Churchill sent FDR the following telegram:** "I did not think it right for me as a foreigner to express my opinion upon American politics while the election was on, but now I feel you will not mind my saying that I prayed for your success and that I am truly thankful for it. This does not mean that I seek or wish for anything more than the full, fair, and free play of your mind upon the world issues now at stake in which our two nations have to discharge their respective duties. We are entering upon a sombre phase of what must evidently be a protracted and broadening war, and I look forward to being able to interchange my thoughts with you in all that confidence and goodwill which has grown up between us since I went to the Admiralty at the outbreak. Things are afoot which will be remembered as long as the English language is spoken in any quarter of the globe, and in expressing the comfort I feel that the people of the United States have once again cast these great burdens

		upon you, I must avow my sure faith that the lights by which we steer will bring us all safely to anchor."[115]
November 11-12, 1940	**British carrier-based torpedo planes** (only 24 planes, with only half of them carrying torpedoes), launched from one British carrier (HMS *Illustrious*), **successfully attack the moored Italian Mediterranean battle fleet at Taranto Harbor in southern Italy,** and put 3 of the 5 Italian battleships there out of commission for a considerable period of time (two of them for about half a year, and the third for the remainder of the war).	This attack, the first "all aircraft" naval attack in history, graphically demonstrated to the world the vulnerability of moored ships to air attack inside an exposed anchorage. It served as one of the inspirations for the Japanese Naval air attack on Pearl Harbor, just over one year later. Admiral Yamamoto, the Commander in Chief of the Imperial Japanese Navy's Combined Fleet, first mentioned the possibility of attacking Pearl Harbor to a high ranking subordinate in April or May of 1940,[116] and the plan gained conceptual momentum in December of 1940,[117] partially because of the success of the British attack on Taranto. (The British successfully torpedoed three Italian battleships using aerial torpedoes, even though they were moored in a shallow harbor.) Yamamoto first formally proposed crippling the American fleet at

---

[115] Meacham, *Franklin and Winston,* 76-77. In a strange and inexplicable footnote to history, Meacham records that Churchill received no reply to this warm, artfully phrased, and generous cable---and that after ten days, he inquired at the end of another cable whether FDR had received his congratulatory telegram. Roosevelt still did not answer, and decades later we can only wonder why, and speculate. Is this the "cold as ice" FDR of which Harry Truman and Harold Ickes later spoke? (In other words, was Roosevelt weary of Churchill's flattery and his begging for war aid? Did this reflect Roosevelt's disdain for the British Empire as an institution, and was he merely concerned about defeating the danger posed by Hitler and Nazi Germany, and rather uncaring about the future of the British Empire, and therefore <u>wary, as well as weary</u>, of Winston Churchill?) As Meacham states, "One thing is clear. Winston Churchill was still very much the suitor in the courtship of Franklin Roosevelt."

[116] Agawa, *The Reluctant Admiral,* 193; and Prange, *At Dawn We Slept,* 14.

[117] Prange, *At Dawn We Slept,* 15.

		Pearl Harbor with a massive surprise attack, using massed carrier air power, in early January of 1941, in a letter to the Navy minister.
November 12, 1940	**In a strategy memo to FDR, the CNO, Admiral Harold R. Stark, recommends a "Europe First" strategy for the United States.** This becomes known throughout the Navy as Stark's "Plan Dog" memo. This presages a future joint agreement to this effect made during combined staff conversations between the Americans and British, which would be held between late January and late March, 1941 in Washington.	Admiral Stark's strategy memo proposed four strategic alternatives for the United States, and endorsed the fourth, item "D," which became known within the Navy as "Plan Dog." ("Dog" was then the Navy's abbreviation for the letter "D.")

Plan Dog declared that the vital interests of the United States lay in defending Britain and the British Empire, requiring a concentration of effort toward Europe and an eventual invasion of the European continent to defeat Germany. This strategy of "Europe First" meant going on the defensive in the Pacific, strategically, and dictated avoidance of war with Japan, if possible. This strategy recognized that part of the Fleet in the Pacific might be needed in the Atlantic.

The U.S. Army supported Plan Dog, and while FDR did implicitly, he never formally endorsed it.[118] |
| December 1, 1940 | The Imperial Japanese Navy scuttles its first version of the 5-Num operational code [subsequently designated JN-25(a) by the U.S. Navy], and replaces it with a strengthened | Early in the new year of 1941, OP-20-G, overburdened by its **MAGIC** responsibilities, will direct Station "CAST" (in the Philippines) to join Station "NEGAT" (in Washington, D.C.) in the assault on JN-25(b). The cryptanalysts at COM-14 in Pearl Harbor (that is, Station "HYPO") protest, and |

---

[118] Heinrichs, *Threshold of War,* 38.

version, now dubbed JN-25 (b) by the U.S. Navy's codebreakers at OP-20-G in Washington, D.C. (Station "NEGAT"). In the new code book, 27,500 of the 33,333 code groups had two possible meanings, increasing the total number of words in the "dictionary" to over 50,000.[119] Both OP-20-G and FECB had to immediately begin anew the "recovery" of the basic code book.

But this recovery of the new "dictionary" or basic code book went surprisingly well, as revealed by Michael Smith, author of *The Emperor's Codes* (p. 79), who quotes one of the cryptographers working on JN-25 at the time: "The Japanese introduced a new codebook but, unfortunately for them, retained in use the current reciphering table and indicator system [i.e., the same additive tables and

ask to join the effort to break JN-25(b), but are instead ordered to remain focused on breaking the Flag Officer's Code (code AD), which OP-20-G (CDR Laurance Safford) considers more important. [The Flag Officer's Code stubbornly resisted all efforts at decryption, and was never broken. One reason was its complexity; another was the insufficient volume of traffic received by "HYPO" through its intercept site, Station "H" in Heeia---sometimes only 3 or 4 messages per day. The use of the Flag Officer's Code decreased markedly as the Imperial Japanese Navy's use of Code Book D (JN-25) markedly increased in late 1939 and throughout 1940, and appears to have been largely abandoned, for all practical purposes, after January of 1941.]

By January 4, 1941 OP-20-G had recovered 2,000 words from the old JN-25(a) code book or dictionary.[120] Two sets of these "recoveries" were provided to GCCS that same month along with two **Purple** machines as part of a high-level cryptologic information exchange between the U.S. and British governments.[121]

This new version of the basic code book, called JN-25(b), remained in use by the Japanese Navy from December 1, 1940 through the end of May, 1942. The

---

[119] Costello, *Days of Infamy,* 280-281.

[120] Rusbridger and Nave, *Betrayal at Pearl Harbor,* 167; Costello, *Days of Infamy,* 281.

[121] Rusbridger and Nave, *Betrayal at Pearl Harbor,* 108-110.

system of keys]. These had already been solved in some positions and new code groups [i.e., new words in the basic code book or dictionary] were discovered immediately. But for this mistake on the part of the Japanese the form of the book might have taken a matter of months to discover." His source for this is a British document from the Public Records Office.

Elliot Carlson, Joe Rochefort's biographer, wrote in *Joe Rochefort's War* (p. 120) that this window closed in late January of 1941 when the Japanese changed the additive tables again.

Smith cautions (p. 82) that while <u>the British at this point were well ahead of the Americans at Station CAST in breaking JN-25(b)</u>, that by April of 1941, FECB had recovered only 30 per cent of the new additive book, and that it was unclear how much of the new code book had been

normal practice was for the Japanese Navy to also change the additive tables once every six months. Each time this happened, it created a period of 3 to 4 weeks of confusion for American and British codebreakers, until they could make significant progress in breaking into the new additive tables. The high volume of JN-25 traffic assisted them in recovering the new additive tables relatively quickly each time they were changed out.

The degree to which JN-25(b) could be read during 1941 by the British and Americans is now uncertain, for the record is replete with contradictions. Two U.S. Navy codebreakers from Station CAST (in the Philippines) denied, long after the war, that CAST was breaking any JN-25(b) messages prior to the attack on Pearl Harbor. This was contradicted by CDR Laurance Safford himself, who on two occasions (in 1963 and in 1970) stated that by December 1941, OP-20-G had JN-25(b) solved "to a readable extent."[122] In a 1963 letter (to Percy Greaves), Safford made clear that what they were able to read at Station NEGAT by December 1941 was the <u>month-old traffic</u> received by ship and air mail from HYPO. In a May 1945 memo Safford wrote that JN-25(b) was "partially readable" in November 1941, and that Station CAST *was reading current messages* and was exchanging information with the British

---

[122] Carlson, *Joe Rochefort's War,* 204; Rusbridger and Nave, *Betrayal at Pearl Harbor,* 167

recovered by this time. Such descriptions are frustratingly vague and imprecise---almost useless---in indicating how many, and what types, of JN-25(b) messages could be broken and successfully read.

In this regard, Smith introduced a major caveat (p. 62) when he wrote this about the *earlier* decryption efforts on JN-25(a), before the code book was changed in December of 1940: "By May 1940 the penetration of the code book used as the basis for the main General Operational Code had progressed to the stage where stereotyped messages such as convoy schedules and individual ship movements could be decoded, although it was still not possible to read detailed operational orders." Smith's source note cites a Public Record Office (i.e., British) document.

at FECB prior to the Pearl Harbor attack.[123]

The U.S. government claims today that not one single *pre*-Pearl Harbor worksheet or decrypt or translation of a JN-25 message can be located in its archives,[124] and yet Safford's statements make it clear that **some** JN-25(b) messages were being broken by the United States in 1941. The U.S. Navy's official position in 1946 was that all of the JN-25(b) messages pertaining in any way to Pearl Harbor were decrypted and translated <u>only in 1945 and 1946, after the war ended</u>. A Top Secret ULTRA Navy report delivered to the CNO in early 1946---and intentionally withheld from the Joint Congressional Committee investigating the Pearl Harbor Attack---titled **Pre-Pearl Harbor Japanese Naval Dispatches,** was discovered at a records repository in Crane, Indiana 45 years later and declassified by the NSA on October 21, 1991.[125] The report states that between September and December of 1941, 26,581 Japanese Navy messages of all types were <u>intercepted</u> by the U.S. Navy; some 90 per cent of these messages were set aside by the Navy investigators as unimportant, based on their addressees---*leaving 2,413 (that were transmitted by the Japanese navy and intercepted by the U.S. Navy prior to*

---

[123] Rusbridger and Nave, *Betrayal at Pearl Harbor,* 169-170.

[124] Ibid., 170; Costello, *Days of Infamy,* 324.

[125] Costello, *Days of Infamy,* 279-283.

Carlson quotes a postwar U.S. Navy history (p. 204) that makes a similar statement about CAST's ability to break current messages in 1941: "The reading of the messages of the code before Pearl Harbor, however, must be read as a qualified success. Current messages were read on Corregidor but they were few in number and invariably were ship movement reports: arrivals and departures, together with some fragmentary schedules." In a related footnote (on page 501), Carlson writes: "Pacific War historian Robert Hanyock informed the author that the Japanese used a separate system to encode ship movements, not JN-25(b), a point that further weakens the case that messages encrypted in JN-25(b) were being routinely read."

The student of the "big question" in the Pearl Harbor historical debate, regarding how much of the Japanese Navy's JN-25(b) operational traffic could be read prior to the *December 7, 1941) that were deemed of sufficient importance to be decrypted and translated in late 1945 and early 1946. Of these, 188 were found after translation to contain vital intelligence clues about the forthcoming attack on Pearl Harbor.* The report states: **"All of the important dispatches were encrypted in JN-25B, the Japanese Fleet General Purpose System." [This means that <u>none of them</u> were encrypted in the Flag Officer's Code; the reader should keep in mind this vitally important fact when assessing crucial Japanese Navy messages from November 1941 which will be discussed later in this chronology.]**

John Costello, who discusses this find in great detail in chapter 13 of his 1994 book *Days of Infamy*---it was unknown to Rusbridger and Nave when they wrote *Betrayal at Pearl Harbor* in the late 1980s---writes (p. 283): "It is clear from the 1946 analysis" that if the U.S. Navy had dedicated enough manpower to decrypting JN-25 (instead of getting diverted by **MAGIC** and sidetracked into a dead end by the Japanese Navy's Flag Officer's Code), "it [the increased effort] would have revealed enough detail about the Japanese Hawaii Operation for the Americans to have a precise warning about the attack on Pearl Harbor." Fredrick Parker, the first NSA historian to study the 1946 report, concurred with Costello's opinion (p. 283): "The U.S. Navy's communications analysts in Corregidor, Hawaii, and Washington would have made that prediction if they

attack on Pearl Harbor, is most often confronted by very strong, categorical, and *contradictory* historical assessments.

On the one hand, historian Michael Smith writes in *The Emperor's Codes* (p. 84): "Although the British and American efforts against JN-25 *did not allow them to break detailed operational messages,* they were able to track the Imperial Japanese Navy and to build up a good picture of its activities through a combination of *those messages they could decode* [undefined! no specifics provided!] and traffic analysis." [Emphasis added; and the parenthetical comments are mine.] Smith's source note for this assertion is a British record in the Public Records Office.

Smith then writes somewhat vaguely (p. 100) about the inability of unspecified codebreakers to obtain foreknowledge of the Pearl Harbor attack: "The inability to decipher *any detailed operational orders* sent in had been able to read them at the time." Costello's conclusion is that the report was kept secret from the post-war Congressional Investigation because the U.S. Navy was guilty of the unpardonable administrative blunder of not focusing enough resources on the correct code prior to the Pearl Harbor attack. He opines (p. 282): "This explains why the Navy Department carried out a meticulous postwar 'housecleaning operation,' which removed from the official record all traces of the pre-Pearl Harbor JN-25 decrypts…".

John Costello clearly supports the U.S. Navy's position that it never decrypted *any* of the 188 Pearl Harbor-related messages prior to December 7, 1941---what he considers a bureaucratic blunder of cosmic proportions. But we don't really know if that is true or not, since the U.S. government claims not to be able to find *any* of the JN-25 decrypts and translations made before Pearl Harbor. Costello certainly admits to a cover-up, since he concludes that a "housecleaning operation" removed from the official record all traces of the pre-war decrypts. [But it is unclear to me whether this "housecleaning" took place in late 1941 and early 1942, or only in late 1945 after the war's end.] One must ask: "Was the cover-up simply concealing *action not taken,* or was it concealing *crucial information that may have been decrypted and translated---and known by high-level officials---prior to the attack on Pearl Harbor?"* Without

the JN-25 naval code had prevented *the codebreakers* [he does not specify which codebreakers, by nationality or location] from noting the existence of the 'northern force' that was to attack Pearl Harbor. Persistent references to training by the Japanese 1st Air Fleet in the use of torpedoes in shallow water were also intercepted *but not deciphered as a result of the difficulties with JN-25."* [Emphasis added; parenthetical comments are mine.]

Initially I thought that Smith was writing here specifically about British cryptanalysts at FECB, because that was the context of pages 99 and 100, but when I checked his source notes, it was revealed that the "codebreakers" he was referring to in the above passage were *U.S. Navy codebreakers,* for his source was none other than Frederick Parker (the

the pre-war decrypts we cannot know for sure.

As for the British government, although it finally released much **MAGIC** diplomatic material (its own **Purple** decrypts and translations) in 1993, its policy is still *not to release any* JN-25 decrypts from the period prior to the Pearl Harbor attack. The sparse British documentary record about JN-25 available to researchers (via two documents released inadvertently in May 1994) reveals the following:

A May 1942 memo reveals that **"intelligence from a wide field"** was produced from the JN-25(b) code book **"in November 1941;"** and another memo states that FECB did obtain **"besides routine intelligence…ample warning that Japan was going to war in 1941."** [126] [Emphasis added]

A third British report, titled: "Collaboration of British and U.S. Radio Intelligence," also states: "In May 1941 the policy of complete exchange of Radio Intelligence with the U.S. was decided on. An exchange of visits between the U.S. Unit at Corregidor and the British Unit at Singapore **showed that the British were well ahead with JN-25 results,** and the U.S. began a program of expansion."[127]

There is compelling anecdotal evidence

---

[126] Ibid., 321-322

[127] Ibid., 322-323.

NSA historian) and his two papers about *U.S. Navy* JN-25 codebreaking efforts. Smith thus used an American historian's conclusions---***about a U.S. Navy effort***---to apparently characterize the inability of *all codebreakers,* including those at FECB, to break JN-25 in the months prior to Pearl Harbor. His actions in doing so, to have any validity, must have assumed that the capabilities of FECB and Station CAST were the same (and they were manifestly not, as documented by Smith himself). With this realization, one tends to lose faith in Smith's book as any kind of definitive source regarding British abilities in decrypting JN-25(b) at FECB in the immediate run-up to Pearl Harbor.

On the other hand, in *Betrayal at Pearl Harbor,* co-authors Rusbridger and Nave make sweeping, declarative assertions on numerous occasions that FECB in Singapore could indeed break JN-25 messages throughout in *Betrayal At Pearl Harbor, Days of Infamy,* and other sources---which will be discussed in detail following the end of this chronology---that the British, at FECB in Singapore, achieved considerable success in breaking JN-25(b) in 1941, particularly in the run-up to the commencement of hostilities on December 7th in Hawaii (December 8th in the Far East). From my own reading of *Betrayal at Pearl Harbor,* it is clear that Eric Nave expressed his belief to co-author James Rusbridger that British penetration of JN-25 at FECB in Singapore---except for brief periods following additive table changes---was continuous and unbroken between December 1939 and December 1941; <u>but that is not proof, since Nave was no longer located at FECB in Singapore after February of 1940</u>. He maintained liaison with FECB from his new RAN signals intelligence organization in Melbourne, but he was not present at FECB from February 1940 through December 1941. A very strong statement of fact---perhaps too strong--- is asserted at the end of *Betrayal at Pearl Harbor* (p. 177), to wit: "Despite the deliberate policy of disinformation and censorship, [we conclude that] both British and American codebreakers were able to read the Japanese operational orders sent in JN-25 throughout the months leading up to Pearl Harbor…Churchill was able to read JN-25…during 1941 right up until the day of the attack. This is a fact that has never been publicly revealed before…". There is no doubt that

1940 and 1941.

For example (p. 137), in the context of a discussion about the many messages sent by Admiral Yamamoto (C-in-C, Japanese Combined Fleet) to the Pearl Harbor attack force in late November of 1941, they write: "…Nave is adamant that every message intercepted by the Americans would also have been intercepted by the British, *and because JN-25 had been broken by him since the autumn of 1939, all these intercepted messages would have been read without difficulty or delay by FECB and GCCS.*" [Emphasis added]

Another such sweeping assertion appears in the book's conclusion (p. 177), to wit: "…both British and American codebreakers were able to read the Japanese operational orders sent in JN-25 *throughout the months leading up to Pearl Harbor.*" [Emphasis added]

Nave's book with

Rusbridger and Nave both *believed* that FECB and Station CAST could *each* read current JN-25(b) traffic in 1941, but other records make it clear that FECB was *well ahead* of Station CAST in its ability to read JN-25 traffic in 1941, and the limited documentary record---and differing historians' assessments---about the *degree* to which JN-25 messages could be broken in 1941 is replete with qualifiers and contradictions.

One thing that *is* beyond dispute is Winston Churchill's rapacious appetite for raw codebreaking decrypts of all kinds throughout the war; he did not want to see watered-down staff summaries about intelligence---he demanded to see the raw intercepts, and did, several times a day. If JN-25(b) was being regularly broken by FECB in November of 1941, as seems likely, then there is no doubt that Churchill would have been a direct recipient of these important messages in raw form. His filter---the aide who decided what was worth his reading every day---was longtime associate Desmond Morton.

James Rusbridger wrote that when he requested permission in 1985 from the British Foreign Secretary (Sir Geoffrey Howe) to see the Japanese Ultra material from 1939-1941, he was refused access and told none of it would ever be released into the public domain. He wrote that he was twice informed by Howe that he could not see any pre-war Japanese intercepts and decrypts because it would endanger British "national

| | Rusbridger and his subsequent memoir of his own career were the first personal, anecdotal accounts yet written about Britain's effort to break the JN-25 fleet operational code. In the face of almost total official silence about this massive effort by the British government, and in view of the British government's policy that <u>no decrypts or translations</u> of *any* broken JN-25 messages ***will ever be released into the public domain,*** it is tempting at first blush to accept a personal account, by someone "who was there" and who has a sterling reputation, as gospel truth. The problem is that the retired CAPT Nave who was co-authoring a manuscript with James Rusbridger in the late 1980s was *NOT THERE* at FECB anymore *after February of 1940*, when | security."[128] Rusbridger was also denied permission to see *what he believed* was the suppressed telegram sent by Churchill to the American Embassy on November 26, 1941, to be transmitted to President Roosevelt; he wrote that it was being withheld from the Public Record Office "for the next seventy years," on the grounds of national security.[129] When Rusbridger published, he believed the purported Churchill telegram to FDR relayed evidence of the "Japanese intention to wage aggressive war on Great Britain and the United States"---quoting the 1944 Army Pearl Harbor Board investigation---and that it was in the file sealed "for the next seventy years."

Costello wrote that only 3 of the 6 boxes of ULTRA intelligence that Churchill received on November 25, 1941 had been released, and that the others were being withheld by the Foreign Office.[130] He further related that a whole section of Prime Minister Churchill's secret office file related to Japan was marked "closed for 75 years."[131]

Costello continued: there are two major gaps in the "BJ" serial numbers in the cover letters for material that "C" (the head of MI6, Stewart Menzies, who ran |

---

[128] Rusbridger and Nave, *Betrayal At Pearl Harbor,* 9 and 15.

[129] Ibid., 141.

[130] Costello, *Days of Infamy,* 311.

[131] Ibid., 313.

| | he transferred from FECB in Singapore to Australia, and set up his own signals intelligence organization in his home country. While he maintained liaison with FECB after relocating to Australia, it is unclear how detailed this liaison was, and therefore it is *also unclear* how reliable are his latter-year assertions about FECB's ability to freely break JN-25 messages in 1941.

Rusbridger died in 1992, and Nave passed away in 1993, so they cannot help us answer these questions.

This damnable state of affairs---not being able to trust the assertions or conclusions of any single author on the subject of JN-25 decryption---requires an extremely careful approach to the subject, calling on as many sources as possible in an attempt to ferret out the gist of the truth. I have attempted to do so, to some extent, here (at right). | GCCS) sent to Churchill on November 25, 1941, indicating that these two batches of SIGINT are still considered too sensitive by the British government to release. He further wrote: "Conspicuous by its complete absence from Churchill's most secret intelligence file is any report on Japanese Naval movements. This is a most surprising omission since the declassified files contain regular summary reports that he was receiving on German, Italian, and even Spanish naval intercepts…The absence of any report [on the Japanese Navy] gives reasonable grounds for suspecting that all traces of the Japanese naval intelligence summaries have been withheld because their release would reveal the extent to which the British codebreakers had succeeded---where the U.S. Navy had failed---in penetrating the Japanese navy ciphers." [132]

What is clear is that the British government has long considered raw decrypts of Japanese Naval message traffic too sensitive to release to the public, and to John Costello it seemed a safe assumption that the three boxes of Churchill's ULTRA material from November 25, 1941 (that Costello reported were still suppressed) included material of this nature.

Costello concluded his informed speculation and analysis by saying: "What is certain is that as long as the suspicious gaps remain in Churchill's |

[132] Ibid., 317.

files and Britain's SIGINT intelligence remains so glaringly incomplete, the 'missing' documentation will continue to suggest that the final secrets of Pearl Harbor are still being kept locked away by the British government in the closet of official secrecy."[133]

It will become clear later in this chronology that I believe I know *exactly* which two Japanese Naval messages---transmitted in the JN-25(b) code on November 25, 1941 in Japan (November 24th in Washington, D.C.) by Admiral Yamamoto, the Commander in Chief of the Combined Fleet---were decrypted and translated by FECB, sent to Churchill via "C" at GCCS on November 25th, and almost certainly became the subject of a highly classified warning that Prime Minister Churchill sent by telegram to President Roosevelt early on the morning of November 26, 1941.[134]

This ends the current digression about the controversy over how much of the Japanese Navy's JN-25(b) fleet operations code had been broken and

---

[133] Ibid., 329-330.

[134] Costello writes about the mysterious, *inferred* early AM November 26, 1941 Churchill cable in *Days of Infamy,* on pages 310-311. This is almost certainly the true cause of Roosevelt's dramatic, overnight "about-face" in his diplomacy toward Japan---from a "soft line" that was designed to buy time to beef up U.S. forces in the Far East, to a "hard line" that amounted to a *defacto* ultimatum that Roosevelt knew Japan could not accept---which will be written about in considerable detail later in this work. Costello writes with great drama and astute analysis about FDR's remarkable "about face" on the diplomatic front, on November 26, 1941, in chapters 4, 5, 6, and 14 of *Days of Infamy,* and thoroughly considers---and then convincingly discards---the feeble and unpersuasive speculations mainstream historians have offered up for why Roosevelt stopped "babying along" the Japanese on November 26, 1941, and instead presented them with a provocative, hard-nosed ultimatum. These 4 chapters are, in my opinion, the most valuable contribution made by his book.

		could be read by the Americans and the British in late 1941. (I will write more about this following the end of the chronology.) It will pay the reader to keep all of this in mind as the chronology you are reading marches inexorably toward the crucial period of late November, 1941.
December 5, 1940	Hitler directs Field Marshall von Brauchitsch and General Halder to prepare the army for an attack on Russia at the end of May 1941.	The feasibility studies for the attack on the Soviet Union begun immediately, following Hitler's July 31st conference at the Berghof, are now transformed into real operational plans.
December 9, 1940	FDR, vacationing with Secretary of Commerce Harry Hopkins (his most trusted confidant following the death of Louie Howe) onboard the heavy cruiser USS *Tuscaloosa* in the Caribbean, receives via seaplane, the **"very long letter" from Winston Churchill** (ten typewritten pages totaling some 4,000 words), which Churchill had warned Roosevelt he was working on more than three weeks previously, in a cable on November 16th.[135] The letter was as frank as it was long.	Historian Kenneth S. Davis quoted the most important passages from the letter in *FDR: The War President,* as follows: "The form which the war has taken and seems likely to hold does not enable us to match the immense armies of Germany in any theater where their main power can be brought to bear. We can however by the use of sea power and air power meet the German armies in the regions where only comparatively small forces can be brought into action." (Thus, Churchill admits that Britain can only engage in peripheral warfare by nipping at the flanks of the German Empire, and cannot defeat Germany alone.) Churchill then talked about the strengthening of the British Army since Dunkirk, and said that the "danger of Great Britain being destroyed by a swift overwhelming blow has for the time being greatly receded." He then said that

---

[135] Davis, *FDR: The War President: 1940-1943,* 62-73.

there was a "long, gradually maturing danger, less sudden [than the previous summer's threat of invasion] and less spectacular but equally deadly." Churchill warned of the "mortal danger" of German submarine, surface raider, and airplane attacks on merchant shipping. If unchecked, Churchill stated that the continued loss of merchant shipping could cause Britain to "fall by the way" before the United States had time to "complete her defensive preparations." In response to the German war of attrition on Britain's merchant Navy and import tonnage, <u>Churchill presented alternate courses of action by the United States</u>. One was **"the reassertion…of the doctrine of freedom of the seas…to trade with countries with which there is not an effective legal blockade"** <u>**and to protect such trade with "escorting battleships, cruisers, destroyers, and air flotillas.**"</u> Churchill acknowledged that this approach involved a risk that Germany would declare war on the United States, but thought the risk was small since Hitler "does not wish to be drawn into a war with the United States until he has gravely undermined the power of Great Britain. His maxim is 'one at a time.'" Churchill then stated that an alternative was **"the gift, loan, or supply of a large number of American vessels of war, above all destroyers,"** <u>**coupled with the extension of U.S. "sea control over the American side of the Atlantic**</u>, **so as to prevent molestation by enemy vessels of the approaches to the new line of naval and air bases** which the United States is establishing in British islands in the Western Hemisphere."** Regarding aircraft, the British Prime Minister said that his country would need many more airplanes than they could produce themselves in order to weaken the grip of Germany on Europe: **"…we shall need the greatest production of aircraft which the United States…are capable of sending us…May I invite you then, Mr. President, to give earnest consideration to an immediate order on joint account for a further 2,000 aircraft a month?** Of these…the possible highest proportion should be heavy bombers, the weapon on which above all others we depend to shatter the foundations of German military power." **In closing, Churchill turned to "the question of finance,"** stating the British case simply and with a bold frankness that is often lacking in diplomatic correspondence: ***"The more rapid and abundant the flow of munitions and ships which you are able to send us, the sooner will our dollar resources be exhausted…Indeed, as you know, the orders already placed or under negotiation…many times exceed the total exchange resources remaining to Great Britain…While we will do our utmost and shrink from no proper sacrifice…I believe you will agree that it would be wrong in principle and mutually disadvantageous in effect if, at the height of the struggle, Great Britain were to be divested of all saleable assets so that after victory was won with our*** *blood, civilization saved and time gained for the United States to be fully armed...we should stand stripped to the bone...<u>If, as I believe, you are convinced, Mr. President, that the defeat of the Nazi and Fascist tyranny is a matter of high consequence to the people of the United States and the Western Hemisphere, you will regard this letter not as an appeal for aid, but as a statement of the minimum action necessary to the achievement of our common purpose.</u>"* [Emphasis added] Churchill was asking for Roosevelt to send Great Britain everything it needed that it could not produce itself, and to send it free of charge; and furthermore, to consider convoying and protecting these goods upon the seas with American ships and airplanes. It was now up to Franklin Roosevelt to figure out how to respond to this desperate plea, at a time when he had already been in office for almost 8 years, and was mentally and physically exhausted.[136]

---

[136] In *FDR: The War President* (pp. 70-73), historian Kenneth S. Davis intuitively describes what went on in FDR's "forested mind" while he was attempting to respond to this challenge, while wrapped in a cocoon of isolation aboard USS *Tuscaloosa* in the Caribbean, away from the strife and continuous distractions of Washington, D.C.: "The letter had upon Roosevelt a chastening and stimulating effect...during the two days following the receipt of the Churchill letter he spent a more than usual number of quiet, solitary hours on the Tuscaloosa's deck, seated in a spot shielded from the wind. He had the Churchill letter always at hand, and sometimes he glanced at it or reread portions of it. But for the most part he simply sat there, his unseeing gaze sweeping the gently waved sea to the far horizon while his mind worked over his problem, or as one may say with equal accuracy, was worked on *by* his problem. For his mind did not move in straight logical lines; it was instead moved in feeling, brooding ways over a jumble of personal memories, past sensations, and ideas that had long lay dormant within him...as Hopkins later recalled, **'he suddenly came out with it---the whole program. He didn't seem to have any clear idea how it could be done legally. But there wasn't any doubt in his mind that he'd find a way to do it.'** Nor was it only this specific problem that he brooded over during these hours of rare quiet and solitude...If Great Britain and the British Commonwealth were destroyed by the Nazi-Fascists, the world would be dominated by the endlessly aggressive masters of Germany, Italy, and Japan.

December 17, 1940	**FDR Explains Lend-Lease at his most historically significant White House press conference,** using the now famous metaphor about *loaning* one's garden hose to a neighbor whose house is on fire, instead of charging him money for it during the	**Roosevelt had come up with the scheme for Lend-Lease on December 11th, about two days after receipt of the "very long letter" from Winston Churchill.** His working vacation in the Caribbean onboard USS *Tuscaloosa* had allowed him to relax, clear his mind, and focus upon the truly large issues at stake in the World War raging in Europe. He returned to Washington refreshed on December 16th, his post election physical

In such a world the American democracy and the human freedoms for which it stood could not long survive. Hence, the preservation of the American democracy, and of the very idea of human freedom, required the destruction of Adolph Hitler, of Nazi-Fascism, and, if less certainly, of Japan as an aggressive military power. **Very probably, indeed almost certainly, this would require the United States to enter the war as an ally of Britain within a year or two.** But such entry would lead to the kind of total victory that was necessary only if it were a full scale entry by a *united* United States---an America prepared, materially and psychologically, to wage total war and also, after military victory was won, to join with other nations in international organization where peace could be assured throughout the world. Roosevelt's great fear was that war would be forced upon an America that remained deeply divided ideologically…He must strive to make of himself the very personification of the kind of active American union that was vitally necessary, stressing the positive…while shunning, to the maximum possible degree, divisive words and deeds…**He must make upon the public's mind a personal impression that was, overall, self-contradictory, being that of a strong, bold leader who is pushed, forced by circumstances, into actions he is reluctant to take.** Above all, he must avoid like the plague what he saw as Woodrow Wilson's greatest mistake, especially in 1919, of going too far too fast in pursuit of his goals, outstripping his public support." [Emphasis added] While it is not certain that Roosevelt came to these conclusions during his December 1940 cruise onboard USS *Tuscaloosa,* it is a virtual certainty that this almost lyrical, literary summation is an accurate picture of how his thinking evolved during 1940, following the aggressive and overwhelmingly successful offensives launched by Hitler in April and May of 1940. Sometime after Hitler's invasion of France, and before the end of the year---probably before October--- FDR decided that he not only had to prepare America's industries for war, but that he also had to psychologically prepare the American people to enter the war on the side of Great Britain in order to jointly defeat Nazi Germany. There can be little doubt that he was convinced of the necessity for this. **But FDR was *also* determined to engineer America's entry in such a way that he led a *united populace into war against Germany,* and not a disunited nation.** Persuading the American people to fight Germany and the Axis proved much more difficult than Roosevelt ever dreamed it would---in fact, well-nigh impossible---and in the end, as it turned out, there was only one way to unite the divided American nation of 1940 and 1941 and get it to enthusiastically wage an unrelenting, total war against the Axis: FDR came to understand during 1941 that the enemy must be maneuvered into striking the first blow, in an unambiguous way. Always keeping the ultimate goal in sight---saving American democracy and Western civilization from barbarism---he set about to do just that.

	emergency---on the condition that it be returned after the fire is put out.[137]	and mental slump now over, ready to get on with the challenge of converting the American economy to expanded and more efficient war production; with

---

[137] Author Kenneth S. Davis, in *FDR: The War President* (pp. 74-77), provides the most noteworthy quotes from the White House press conference. Roosevelt explained that the British lack of money was not the real problem in America's attempt to defend herself against totalitarian aggression, but rather, it was the unpreparedness of America's industrial plant to support full-scale rearmament---saying that these "factories, shipbuilding ways, munitions plants, et cetera, and so on," needed to be vastly expanded, and that expansion had been and was being stimulated by British orders for war materiel. Lord Lothian, in a "calculated indiscretion" which angered FDR and earned Lothian a rebuke from Churchill, had freely admitted to the American press upon his return from Great Britain back on November 23rd that Great Britain was broke and needed America's money to fund its war purchases. Secretary of the Treasury Henry Morgenthau had confirmed this to FDR, explaining that based upon orders placed to date for war material, Great Britain's cash reserves were insufficient to cover the orders placed for delivery between November 1, 1940 and June 30, 1941, and that *the British dollar deficit for these purchases would be in excess of 2.1 billion dollars.* Roosevelt addressed this matter, which had been a hot topic in the United States ever since, by saying that one possible way for the United States to deal with this problem was "for the United States to take over British orders, and, because they are essentially the same kind of munitions that we use ourselves, turn them into American orders." Roosevelt told the reporters we could then "lease or lend" to the other side whatever portion of our total war production which would best serve our security interests "...on the general theory that...the best defense of Great Britain is the best defense of the United States, and therefore that these materials would be more useful to the defense of the United States if they were used by Great Britain, than if they were kept in storage here." FDR said that what he was trying to do was "eliminate the dollar sign...get rid of the silly, foolish old dollar sign." The President then sprung his inspired metaphor on his now attentive audience: **"Well, let me give you an illustration. Suppose my neighbor's home catches fire, and I have a length of garden hose four or five hundred feet away. If he can take my garden hose and connect it up with his hydrant, I may help him put out his fire. Now, what do I do? I don't say to him before that operation, 'Neighbor, my garden hose cost me fifteen dollars; you have to pay me fifteen dollars for it.' What is the transaction that goes on? I don't want fifteen dollars---I want my garden hose back after the fire is over."** [Emphasis added] Davis points out that Roosevelt's metaphor---inspired by a letter he received from Harold Ickes on August 2nd---required considerable revision to fit the facts: "What America must direct toward Britain was not a garden hose but a thick fire hose; this hose must be attached, not to a British, but to an American hydrant; and clearly the water pressure in the hydrant was at the moment much too low for the firefighting task at hand." But the metaphor about lending your own garden hose to help put out your neighbor's fire, <u>as the best way to protect your own house before it also caught fire</u>, worked with the public. Historian Robert Dallek characterized it in this way, in the PBS documentary *FDR*: "Lend-Lease was a way to give the British planes, tanks, guns, artillery, ammunition, without them really paying for it...Of course, it was patent nonsense..." [here referring to the point that items that had been expended or destroyed could certainly not be returned after the war] "...but Roosevelt's invocation of this homily about the neighbor and the garden hose is a wonderful way for him to sell it to the public. And that was his political genius. That was something

		providing unconditional and ever-increasing materiel support to Great Britain; and with the continuing education of the American electorate in the realities of the world geopolitical situation.
December 18, 1940	Hitler approves the operational military directive for the invasion of the Soviet Union in the spring of 1941.	**"Operation Barbarossa"** is the code name for the forthcoming German invasion of the USSR. Its goal is "to crush Soviet Russia in a rapid campaign," thus obtaining the coveted land for expansion in the East that is one of the principal themes of *Mein Kampf*. A secondary benefit hoped for by Hitler is that a quick defeat of the Soviet Union will take away Britain's only hope for continuing the war, thus causing the Churchill government to fall, and forcing Britain to sue for peace. As future directives issued by Hitler will make clear the following spring, this is to be a cruel, uncompromising, war to the death between two blood enemies, with no mercy whatsoever shown to any of the Russian population: it is to be a war of extermination.
December 29, 1940	**FDR Delivers the famous "Arsenal of Democracy" Fireside Chat.**[138]	**This remains perhaps the most important foreign policy address ever delivered by a U.S. President,** and will therefore be liberally quoted: "My

he had a kind of sixth sense for. You can't understand it, you can't define it, you can't put it under any scientific rubric, it simply was something that the man had."

[138] Buhite and Levy, ed., *FDR's Fireside Chats,* 163-173. The editors wrote: "This 'arsenal of democracy' fireside chat issued from the President's desire to prepare the American people for his Lend-Lease proposal. In its rhetoric of non-involvement, the speech also represented an extension, from the 1940 election campaign, of Roosevelt's disingenuous approach toward the question of American participation in the actual fighting. He continued to imply that the way to stay out of the war was to draw closer to it."

(I have quoted here the elements of this speech which focus on the need to put the American economy on a full time war footing, and to provide unlimited aid to Great Britain and other nations fighting the Axis powers. There were other, extensive sections of the speech about the need to unite all Americans in common thought about national defense, and to avoid civil strife and political discord. FDR expressed much concern about Axis "fifth column" activities inside the United States, and stated that Americans who disagreed with his policies, while not necessarily foreign agents, were becoming the dupes and victims of foreign agents. He also severely criticized the defeatists in high places who were certain that the Axis powers could not be beaten, and who were espousing the view that we should learn how to live with them, and accommodate their viewpoints and political systems, and perhaps

friends, this is not a fireside chat on war. It is a talk on national security; because the nub of the whole purpose of your President is to keep you now, and your children later, out of a last-ditch war for the preservation of American independence…<u>Never before since Jamestown and Plymouth Rock has our American civilization been in such danger as it is now</u>. **For on September 27, 1940, this year, by an agreement signed in Berlin, three powerful nations, two in Europe and one in Asia, joined themselves together in the threat that if the United States of America interfered with or blocked the expansion program of these three nations---a program aimed at world control---they would unite in ultimate action against the United States.** The Nazi masters of Germany have made it clear that they intend not only to dominate all life and thought in their own country, but also to enslave the whole of Europe, and then to use the resources of Europe to dominate the rest of the world…the Axis not merely admits, but the Axis *proclaims* that there can be no ultimate peace between their philosophy, their philosophy of government, and our philosophy of government. In view of the nature of this undeniable threat, it can be asserted, properly and categorically, that the United States has no right or reason to encourage talk of peace, until the day shall come when there is clear intention on the part of the aggressor nations to abandon all thought of dominating or conquering the world. At

even emulate some features of their governments and societies---and that we would have to learn to do business with them. This portion of his speech appears to have been written as a direct repudiation of the defeatist views of the recently dismissed U.S. ambassador to Great Britain, Joseph P. Kennedy, and of the isolationist views of the charismatic aviator-hero, Charles Lindbergh. Those readers who wish to learn more about those aspects of this famous fireside chat may consult the full text at their leisure.)

Joseph P. Kennedy was a personal friend of Neville Chamberlain and a supporter of the Munich pact, and a defeatist as well, following the beginning of Britain's war with Germany. As a result, he had been shunned and "cut out of the loop" by FDR during the summer and early fall of 1940, as Roosevelt moved to aid Great Britain. Kennedy, who

this moment, the forces of the states which are leagued against all peoples who live in freedom, are being held away from our shores. ***The Germans and the Italians are being blocked on the other side of the Atlantic by the British,*** and by the Greeks, and by thousands of soldiers and sailors who were able to escape from subjugated countries. ***In Asia, the Japanese are being engaged by the Chinese*** nation in another great defense. **In the Pacific Ocean is our Fleet.** Some of our people like to believe that wars in Europe and in Asia are of no concern to us. ***But it is a matter of the most vital concern to us that European and Asiatic war-makers should not gain control of the oceans which lead to this hemisphere***.

…***If Great Britain goes down, the Axis powers*** will control the continents of Europe, Asia, Africa, Australasia, and the high seas---and they ***will be in a position to bring enormous military and naval resources against this hemisphere.*** **It is no exaggeration to say that all of us, in the Americas, would be living at the point of a gun**---a gun loaded with explosive bullets, economic as well as military. We should [then] enter upon a new and terrible era in which the whole world, our hemisphere included, would be run by threats of brute force. And to survive in such a world, we would have to convert ourselves permanently into a militaristic power on the basis of war economy.

Some of us like to believe that if Britain

had contemplated resigning, returned to the U.S. for a vacation late in October in a foul mood, and FDR assuaged his feelings to prevent him from resigning, or from siding publicly with Willkie and possibly taking American Catholic voters with him, and throwing the election to Willkie. Roosevelt---in a great exercise of his ability to combine personal charm with political deal-making---in exchange for a promise to support Joe Kennedy Jr.'s possible candidacy for Governor of Massachusetts in 1942, persuaded Kennedy the father not to resign, and instead to openly support his own candidacy for President in an October 29th radio address. (FDR privately loathed Kennedy and thought him a very dangerous man.) Kennedy then revealed his true, innermost feelings to Assistant Secretary of State Breckinridge Long in a private interview the very next week, immediately after FDR won re-

falls, we are still safe, because of the broad expanse of the Atlantic and of the Pacific. But the width of those oceans is not what it was in the days of clipper ships. At one point between Africa and Brazil the distance is less than it is between Washington and Denver, Colorado---five hours for the latest type of bomber…Why even today we have planes that could fly from the British Isles to New England and back again without refueling. And remember that the range of the modern bomber is ever being increased.

…Frankly and definitely there is danger ahead---danger against which we must prepare. **But we well know that we cannot escape danger, or the fear of danger, by crawling into bed and pulling the covers over our heads**…And any South American country, in Nazi hands, would always constitute a jumping off place for German attack on any one of the other republics of this hemisphere…You and I think of Hawaii as an outpost of defense in the Pacific. And yet, the Azores are closer to our shores on the Atlantic than Hawaii is on the other side. There are those who say that the Axis powers would never have any desire to attack the Western hemisphere. That is the same dangerous form of wishful thinking which has destroyed the powers of resistance of so many conquered peoples. The plain facts are that the Nazis have proclaimed, again and again, that all other races are their inferiors, and therefore subject to their orders. And most important of all, the

election, the details of which Long recorded in his diary. Kennedy told Long that the British Empire was doomed, and that Hitler was and would remain the master of Europe, as Japan was becoming in the Far East. Kennedy told Long the U.S. government should "take some steps to implement a realistic policy and make some approach to Germany and Japan which would result in economic collaboration," and, as Long recorded, Kennedy "thinks that we will have to assume a Fascist form of government here or something similar if we are to survive in a world of concentrated and centralized power."[139] On November 10th, Kennedy proclaimed in a damaging newspaper interview, "Democracy is all finished in England. It may be here…it's the loss of our foreign trade that's going to change our form of government…". Kennedy expressed forceful views in favor of

vast resources and wealth of this American hemisphere constitute the most tempting loot in all the round world.

…<u>The experience of the past two years has proven beyond doubt that no nation can appease the Nazis</u>. *No man can tame a tiger into a kitten by stroking it.* There can be no appeasement with ruthlessness…We know now that a nation can have peace with the Nazis only at the price of total surrender.

…Thinking in terms of today and tomorrow, I make the direct statement to the American people that there is far less chance of the United States getting into war if we do all we can now to support the nations defending themselves against attack by the Axis than if we acquiesce in their defeat, submit tamely to an Axis victory, and wait our turn to be the object of attack in another war later on…we must admit that there is risk in any course we may take. But I deeply believe that the great majority of our people agree that the course that I advocate involves the least risk now and the greatest hope for world peace in the future. <u>The people of Europe who are defending themselves do not ask us to do their fighting</u>. **They ask us for the implements of war, the planes, the tanks, the guns, the freighters which will enable them to fight for their liberty and for our security.** *Emphatically we must get these weapons to them, get them to them in*

---

[139] Davis, *FDR: The War President,* 57-62.

appeasement and revealed himself to be a closet Fascist in many private settings, including with newspaper magnate William Randolph Hearst and Anna Boettinger, FDR's daughter. He finally submitted his resignation as ambassador to Great Britain on December 1, 1940. On January 19th Kennedy made a speech on a national radio network opposing Lend-Lease, and both he and Charles Lindbergh testified against Lend-Lease before a House Committee in late January of 1941.

In Lindbergh's testimony, he said he favored an American Air Force of about 10,000 planes, and other efforts to strengthen hemispheric defense, but remained adamantly against sending aid to Great Britain, since such aid, he said, merely prolonged the bloodshed abroad and reduced our strength at home. Lindbergh summarized his position by saying: "I do not believe we are strong enough to impose

sufficient volume and quickly enough, so that we and our children will be saved the agony and suffering of war which others have had to endure.

…Certain facts are self-evident. **In a military sense Great Britain and the British Empire are today the spearhead of resistance to world conquest. And they are putting up a fight which will live forever in the story of human gallantry.** There is no demand for sending an American Expeditionary Force outside our own borders. There is no intention by any member of your government to send such a force. You can therefore, nail, nail any talk about sending armies to Europe as deliberate untruth. Our national policy is not directed toward war. Its sole purpose is to keep war away from our country and away from our people.

Democracy's fight against world conquest is being greatly aided, and must be more greatly aided, by the rearmament of the United States and by sending every ounce and every ton of munitions and supplies that we can possibly spare to help the defenders who are in the front lines. And it is no more unneutral for us to do that than it is for Sweden, Russia, and the other nations near Germany, to send steel and ore and oil and other war materials into Germany every day of the week.

We are planning our own defense with the utmost urgency and in its vast scale we must integrate the war needs of our way of life on Europe and Asia." Like Kennedy, he was a closet Fascist.[140] (Lindbergh had accepted personal medals from Herman Goering in Germany, and had expressed great admiration for the German Air Force prior to the commencement of war between Britain and Germany. Back on August 4, 1940, in a nationwide radio address, Lindbergh had advocated "cooperation" with Germany if Hitler defeated Great Britain.)

The powerful **America First Movement,** for whom the already outspoken Lindbergh became the prime public advocate, was founded on September 3, 1940---the same day the Destroyer-Bases deal was announced by FDR. The four-point manifesto of the America First Committee insisted that America: (1) build an impregnable defense; (2) that no power dared attack a prepared

Britain and the other free nations which are resisting aggression. This is not a matter of sentiment or of controversial personal opinion. It is a matter of realistic, practical military policy, based on the advice of our military experts who are in close touch with existing warfare. These military and naval experts and the members of the Congress and the administration have a single-minded purpose---the defense of the United States.

…American industrial genius, unmatched throughout all the world in the solution of production problems, has been called upon to bring its resources and its talents into action…We must have more ships, more guns, more planes---more of everything. And this can be accomplished only if we discard the notion of 'business as usual'…**I want to make it clear that it is the purpose of this nation to build now with all possible speed every machine, every arsenal, every factory that we need to manufacture our defense material. We have the men, the skill, the wealth, and above all, the will…<u>We must be the great arsenal of democracy</u>. For us this is an emergency as serious as war itself.** We must apply ourselves to our task with the same resolution, the same sense of urgency, the same spirit of patriotism and sacrifice as we would show were we at war.

<u>**We have furnished the British great**</u>

---

[140] Ibid., 108-110.

America; (3) that American democracy could only be preserved by keeping out of a European war; and (4) that aid to other nations weakens national defense and threatens to involve America in war.[141] It became the principal anti-interventionist pressure group, the counterpart of the pro-interventionist lobbying group led by liberal Republican newspaper publisher William Allen White. The America First Committee refused to accept avowed Nazis or Communists as members, and would not accept their financial support. <u>It represented a strong core of isolationism, primarily in the American Midwest, that Roosevelt could never dislodge with all of his speeches and persuasion.</u> *Only the massive attack on Pearl Harbor by Japan was able to kill off isolationism, and it then happened overnight.*

<u>**material support and we will furnish far more in the future. There will be no bottlenecks in our determination to aid Great Britain.**</u> No dictator, no combination of dictators, will weaken that determination by threats of how they will construe that determination…I believe that the Axis powers are not going to win this war. I base that belief on the latest and best of information…I have the profound conviction that the American people are now determined to put forth a mightier effort than they have ever yet made to increase our production of all the implements of defense, to meet the threat to our democratic faith. As President of the United States I call for that national effort. I call for it in the name of this nation which we love and honor and which we are privileged and proud to serve. I call upon our people with absolute confidence that our common cause will greatly succeed." [Emphasis added]

Roosevelt had explained the clear need, and the intention, for the United States to shift to a war economy, but this proved extremely difficult to do. It was not possible to make such a total conversion using the spending stimulus of new war orders alone, as events in 1941 on the home front would prove; the American economy continued to produce large quantities of peacetime luxury goods (especially automobiles), and to lag behind in many of the production goals

---

[141] Moss, *19 Weeks,* 303-304.

		FDR had set for war materiel. Furthermore, 1941 was a year that was to see many strikes by organized labor which interrupted production. <u>Following the attack on Pearl Harbor</u> one year later, Roosevelt was authorized to create a command economy; and he brought labor and management together, ending strikes and work stoppages.
January 6, 1941	**FDR's Eighth Annual Message to Congress: "The Four Freedoms"**[142] This State of the Union Address---Roosevelt's Eighth---repeated all of the basic themes in his "Arsenal of Democracy" fireside chat of December 29th; he also provided four basic goals that in his view, all of humanity should strive to establish following the end of the current world crisis. Roosevelt was concerned in this speech both with the practical necessities required to safeguard America and beat the Axis, and also with the need to build a better, safer, and more stable world order following the end of the current World War. The "Four Freedoms" which FDR	**The first half of Roosevelt's speech was a clarion call, in the clearest and strongest possible terms, for converting America's economy to a war footing, and for doing so as soon as possible.** In the fireside chat of December 29th, he made this appeal directly to the American people, one-on-one, via radio---using the medium he had mastered more than any other politician. He *formalized* that challenge in this address to Congress (which after all, had to authorize the funds for these momentous plans) just eight days later, in the strongest possible and most authoritative way, speaking with all the confidence and assurance, and with the gravitas, of a recently re-elected Third Term President---the first one in American history---who had been retained in power by his nation for the express purpose of guiding it through the current world crisis. He was never more certain in his mind about what the nation had to do, and his words rang with his utter conviction and determination to succeed. Excerpts follow:

---

[142] Hunt, ed., *The Essential Franklin D. Roosevelt,* 194-201.

said the entire world must move toward in the future were: *freedom of speech and expression; freedom of religion; freedom from want; and freedom from fear.* (This concern with rectifying the underlying causes for the current World War would eventually lead to FDR's proposal for a United Nations organization in the postwar world.) FDR, both in this speech, as well as at the Argentia Conference eight months later with Churchill, was as concerned about the future structure of the post-war world, as he was with the problems of the present. He was not only physically preparing the American nation to wage war; he was also explaining what, in the long run, they were going to be fighting for: the very survival of democracy, and basic human rights.

" …I address you, the members of the Seventy-seventh Congress, at a moment unprecedented in the history of the Union. I use the word *unprecedented* because at no previous time has American security been as seriously threatened from without as it is today…Every realist knows that the democratic way of life is being at this moment directly assailed in every part of the world---assailed either by arms, or by secret spreading of poisonous propaganda by those who seek to destroy unity and promote discord in nations that are still at peace. During sixteen long months this assault has blotted out the whole pattern of democratic life in an appalling number of democratic nations, great and small. Therefore, as your President…I find it, unhappily, necessary to report that **the future and the safety of our country and of our democracy are overwhelmingly involved in events beyond our borders.** Armed defense of democratic existence is now being waged in four continents. If that defense fails, all the resources of Europe, Asia, Africa, and Australasia will be dominated by the conquerors…No realistic American can expect from a dictator's peace international generosity, or return of true independence, or world disarmament, or freedom of expression, or freedom of religion---or even good business…I have recently pointed out how quickly the tempo of modern warfare could bring into our very midst the physical attack which we must eventually expect if the dictator nations win this war…**Our** national policy is this:

First, *by an impressive expression of the public will and without regard to partisanship, we are committed to a strong national defense.*

Second…*we are committed to full support of all those resolute peoples, everywhere, who are resisting aggression and are thereby keeping war away from our hemisphere.* By this support, we express our determination that the democratic cause shall prevail; and we strengthen the defense and the security of our own nation.

Third…we are committed to the proposition that *principles of morality and considerations for our own security will never permit us to acquiesce in a peace dictated by aggressors and sponsored by appeasers…*

Therefore, the immediate need is a swift and driving increase in our armament production. Leaders of industry and labor have responded to our summons. Goals of speed have been set. In some cases these goals are being reached ahead of time; in some cases we are on schedule; in other cases there are slight but not serious delays; and in some cases---and I am sorry to say very important cases---we are all concerned by the slowness of the accomplishment of our plans…I am not satisfied with the progress thus far made. The men in charge of the program represent the best in training, in ability, and in patriotism. They are not satisfied with the progress thus far made. None of us will be satisfied until the job is done… **To change a whole nation from a basis of peacetime production of implements of peace to a basis of wartime production of implements of war is no small task.** And the greatest difficulty comes at the beginning of the program, when new tools, new plant facilities, new assembly lines, and new ship ways must first be constructed before the actual materiel begins to flow steadily and speedily from them…I shall ask this Congress for greatly increased new appropriations and authorizations to carry on what we have begun. <u>I also ask this Congress for authority and for funds sufficient to manufacture additional munitions and war supplies of many kinds, to be turned over to those nations which are now in actual war with aggressor nations.</u> **Our most useful and immediate role is to act as an arsenal for them as well as ourselves.** *They do not need manpower, but they do need billions of dollars worth of the weapons of defense.* <u>The time is near when they will not be ready to pay for them all in ready cash</u>. **<u>We cannot, and we will not, tell them that they must surrender, merely because of present inability to pay for the weapons which we know they must have.</u>**

I do not recommend that we make them a loan of dollars with which to pay for these weapons---a loan to be repaid in dollars…For what we send abroad, we shall be repaid within a reasonable time following the close of hostilities, in similar materials, or, at our option, in other goods of many kinds…

Let us say to the democracies: 'We Americans are vitally concerned in your defense of freedom. We are putting forth our energies, our resources, and our organizing powers to give you the strength to regain and maintain a free world. <u>We shall send you, in ever-increasing numbers, ships, planes, tanks, guns.</u> This is our purpose and our pledge.'

In fulfillment of this purpose we will not be intimidated by the threats of dictators that they will regard as a breach of international law or as an act of war our aid to the democracies which dare to resist their aggression. Such aid is not an act of war, even if a dictator should unilaterally proclaim it so to be…". [Emphasis added]

FDR then moved on to his grand statement of the principles which he hoped to see protected in a new, post-war world order:

"…In the future days…<u>we look forward to a world founded upon four essential human freedoms</u>.

The first is *freedom of speech and expression*---everywhere in the world.

The second is *freedom of every person to worship God in his own way*---everywhere in the world.

The third is *freedom from want*---which, translated into world terms, means economic understandings which will secure to every nation a healthy peacetime life for its inhabitants---everywhere in the world.

The fourth is *freedom from fear*---which, translated into world terms, means a worldwide reduction of armaments to such a point and in such a thorough fashion that no nation will be in a position to commit an act of physical aggression against any neighbor---anywhere in the world.

That is no vision of a distant millennium. It is a definite basis for a kind of world attainable in our own time and generation. That kind of world is the very antithesis of the so-called new order of tyranny which the dictators seek to create with the crash of a bomb. <u>To that new order we oppose the greater conception---the moral order</u>. A good society is able to face schemes of world domination and foreign revolutions alike without fear. Since the beginning of our American history, we have been engaged in change…without the concentration camp or the quick-lime in the ditch. The world order which we seek is the cooperation of free countries, working together in a friendly, civilized society." [Emphasis added]

The greatness of this speech lies in its combination of practical ways and means, and principle. It is sometimes now considered *chic* to smirkingly refer to Roosevelt as "the Great Man," as a supposedly sophisticated way of

		mocking his legions of sycophants, hagiographers, and even his own view of himself, as a "chosen" Man of Destiny. But who, after reading the text of "The Arsenal of Democracy" fireside chat, or this address to Congress, can deny that he *was* a great man? Franklin D. Roosevelt, like Winston S. Churchill, was the right man, in the right place, at the right time---uniquely placed by the forces of history (or God) at the pinnacle of power, at the precise moment he was needed, when no one else in American society was even remotely equipped to perform the tasks fate had assigned to him.
January 7, 1941	**Admiral Isoroku Yamamoto (Commander in Chief, Combined Fleet, Imperial Japanese Navy) formally proposes attacking the American Fleet at Pearl Harbor** in a letter to the Navy Minister, Admiral Koshiro Oikawa.[143] He asks to be placed in personal command of the carrier attack force---and does not expect to return alive. Yamamoto was violating protocol in a number of ways. Normally, the Japanese Navy's war	Yamamoto assumed the duties of Commander in Chief of the Combined Fleet in August of 1939. He had a brilliant mind, was a fervent advocate of air power (although not a pilot himself), and was a bold thinker and an inveterate gambler. He had lived and served in the United States on three occasions, had studied at Harvard, and had served as Naval Attaché in Washington, D.C. Yamamoto was also a fervent Japanese nationalist, a veteran of Japan's great victory over the Russian Fleet at the Battle of Tsushima Strait in May of 1905. While he very much disapproved of the Tripartite Pact with Germany and Italy, he felt that Japan's strategy of southern expansion (favored by the Navy) was not only inevitable, but necessary to sustain its Empire, and he

---

[143] Prange, *At Dawn We Slept,* 9-17.

plans were dictated by the Operations Section of the Naval General Staff, not by the Commander-in-Chief of the Combined Fleet. He pre-empted the Navy's General Staff because he wanted to command the task force himself, and going directly to the four-star Admiral who was the Navy Minister seemed the best way to accomplish this. Because of the force of his personality, and his prestige, he eventually prevailed in this unusual strategy (in October of 1941), although he eventually had to threaten to resign to obtain the approval of the Naval General Staff for his plan.

An advocate of Naval air power who is sometimes referred to as "The Father of Japanese Naval Aviation"---a great irony, since Yamamoto was not a pilot himself---he believed this initial attack on the American Fleet at Pearl Harbor should be carried out primarily by the Fleet Air Arm---by naval aircraft---and would most definitely not be a slugfest between

therefore had concluded, by December of 1940, that war with the United States was probably inevitable. **In that eventuality, he insisted that Japan take the war to the United States Fleet in a bold, surprise move and cripple the U.S. Navy at the outset, to permit Japan's southern expansion strategy to unfold without major opposition.** (In this he differed from the traditional thinking in the Japanese Navy---and the United States Navy as well---which had assumed for two decades that Japan would wait for the U.S. Fleet to fight its way across the Pacific, and then fight "the decisive battle," in the style of Trafalgar or Tsushima Strait, in home waters close to Japan.) Yamamoto, acutely aware that the U.S. Navy was expanding at a prodigious rate and that the American Congress had authorized a two-ocean navy in mid-1940, felt it absolutely essential, if war was inevitable, to disable the major elements of the U.S. Fleet at the outset before the American expansion program was completed. The hope was for Japan to expand rapidly into southeast Asia, and that a battered and demoralized America, <u>crippled in the Pacific at the war's outset, and preoccupied with events in Europe</u>, would sue for peace after a short war and allow Japan to keep its gains. Yamamoto was under no illusions, and knew Japan could not win a long war with the United States because of the industrial imbalance between the two nations. <u>In late September of 1940, he warned Prime Minister Konoye in a private meeting</u>:

battleships. This radical thinking is what made his concept so hard to sell to the Naval General Staff, but he eventually prevailed.

The goal, as he stated in his letter, was **"to decide the fate of the war on the very first day."** He proposed that the Japanese Navy should ***"fiercely attack and destroy the U.S. main fleet at the outset of the war, so that the morale of the U.S. Navy and her people"*** would ***"sink to the extent that it could not be recovered."***

The specific plan envisioned in his letter proposed attacking Pearl Harbor with a large number of carrier aircraft, augmented by submarines. If the U.S. Fleet was inport, he hoped to sink ships in the channel, blocking the harbor entrance; if the U.S. Fleet was not inport, he proposed hunting it down until it was destroyed. He emphasized: "In case the enemy main force comes out from Hawaii before

"If I am told to fight regardless of the consequences, I shall run wild for the first six months or a year, but I have utterly no confidence for the second or third year."

Ironically, because he had concluded by December of 1940 that war with the United States was probably inevitable (due to Japan's insistence upon expanding its Empire southward), the one Naval officer who best understand that Japan could not win a long war with America became the most fervent advocate for striking a massive, surprise blow at the outset. His powerful, relentless advocacy of this surprise blow actually increased the likelihood of the war that he was so pessimistic about Japan ultimately winning.

Yamamoto was imbued with both a sense of fatalism---and realism---about the coming war with the United States. On January 26, 1941---nineteen days *after* he wrote his letter to the Navy minister proposing the initial knockout blow at Pearl Harbor---Yamamoto bitterly wrote to an ultranationalist, and warned him as follows: "Should hostilities break out between Japan and the United States, it would not be enough that we take Guam and the Philippines, nor even Hawaii and San Francisco. ***To make victory certain, we would have to march into Washington and dictate the terms of peace in the White House.*** I wonder if our politicians, among whom armchair arguments about war are being glibly bandied about in the name of state

our attack and keeps coming at us," Yamamoto continued, the striking force must "encounter it with all our decisive force and destroy it in one stroke." <u>The key element was to be surprise, in a moonlight or dawn raid.</u>

Two adamantly opposed strategic overviews of the wisdom (or stupidity) of the Pearl Harbor attack---of its inception, planning, its goals, and execution---have been published; one is the long monograph titled *"The Hawaii Operation,"*[144] by former Rear Admiral Shigeru **Fukudome,** who was Yamamoto's Chief of Staff from November 1939-April 1941, and who then was promoted to become head of the First Bureau (Operations) on the Naval General Staff in Tokyo; the other is historian **Samuel Eliot Morison's** chapter V in Volume III of his monumental History of United States Naval Operations in World War II, *Rising Sun in the*

politics, have confidence as to the final outcome and are prepared to make the necessary sacrifices."

The question is often asked: "If Yamamoto was so certain Japan was unlikely to win a war with the United States, why did he so aggressively promote an attack on Pearl Harbor?" The answer is contained in his letter to Navy Minister Oikawa. He warned him that if the Navy felt the Pearl Harbor scheme was too risky, and disapproved it, preferring to wait for the American Fleet to fight its way toward them across the Pacific, "…<u>we cannot rule out the possibility that the enemy would dare to launch an attack upon our homeland to burn down our capital and other cities. If such a thing happens, our Navy will be subject to fierce attack by the public, even if we should be successful in the southern operation.</u>"

Yamamoto's request to personally lead the attack, therefore, was not an exercise in vanity---it was an expression of fatalism and of personal responsibility, for he expected the attacking task force to take heavy losses, and thought it only appropriate that he share those risks. As he explained in the closing passages of his letter of January 7th, "I sincerely desire to be appointed Commander in Chief of the air fleet to attack Pearl Harbor so that I may personally command that attack force." He urged Oikawa to approve his plan, **"…*so that I***

---

[144] Evans, *The Japanese Navy in World War II,* 1-38.

	Pacific, 1931-April 1942.[145] They are both highly recommended reading.	*may be able to devote myself exclusively to my last duty to our country."*
January 12, 1941	After FDR's Lend-Lease Bill was brought before Congress on January 10, 1941---empowering the President to "sell, transfer title to, exchange, lease, lend, or otherwise dispose of" any military resources he deemed in the ultimate interests of the United States---**Senator Burton K. Wheeler of Montana led the Congressional attacks on Lend-Lease in a speech in the U.S. Senate,** with extremely harsh language which epitomized the feelings of the isolationist movement in America at this time. Although Wheeler was a Democrat, and had supported Roosevelt for President in 1932, he had broken with FDR over his ambitious court-packing scheme in 1937, and more recently over Roosevelt's foreign policy. A Midwestern Progressive, Wheeler was afraid that	The most notable excerpts from Wheeler's January 12th Senate speech follow: "The Kaiser's blank check to Austria-Hungary in the First World War was a piker compared to the Roosevelt blank check of World War II. It warranted my worst fears for the future of America, **and it definitely stamps the President as war-minded.** **The lend-lease-give program is the New Deal's triple-A foreign policy; <u>it will plow under every fourth American boy</u>.** Never before have the American people been asked or compelled to give so bounteously and so completely of their tax dollars to any foreign nation. Never before has the Congress of the United States been asked by any President to violate international law. **Never before has this nation resorted to duplicity in the conduct of its foreign affairs.** Never before has the United States given to one man the power to strip this nation of its defenses. Never before has a Congress coldly and flatly been asked to abdicate. *If the American people want a dictatorship---if they want a totalitarian form of government and if they want war---this bill should be steam-rollered*

---

[145] Morison, *Rising Sun in the Pacific,* 80-146---especially the scathing comments on pages 125 and 132, which were rebutted by RADM Fukudome in his monograph.

Roosevelt wanted to do much more than simply provide aid to Great Britain; he sensed FDR's strong private desire to get the U.S. into the war. In early September of 1940, therefore---on the same day that Roosevelt announced the Destroyers for Bases Deal---Wheeler helped Charles A. Lindbergh and Norman Thomas found the "America First Committee," which soon became the most powerful and influential isolationist group in the United States. Within one year the AFC had over 800,000 members.

In his inflammatory Senate speech of January 12th (quoted here---at the right), Wheeler made a permanent enemy of FDR. The President felt Wheeler had "crossed the line," in speaking extremely harsh words that incited national passions unnecessarily, and had left political decency behind when he claimed that Lend-Lease would **"plow under every fourth American boy."** FDR said, in

through Congress, as is the want of President Roosevelt.

Approval of this legislation means war, open and complete warfare. I, therefore, ask the American people before they supinely accept it---Was the last World War worthwhile?" [Emphasis added]

In sharp contrast to Wheeler and the other isolationists, <u>Wendell Willkie, FDR's Republican opponent in the recent election the previous November, testified in support of Lend-Lease</u>: "Providing the aid we give to Britain is effective, it offers the best, the very best, clear chance for us to keep out of war. Hitler, in my judgment, will make war on us (or on our friends and allies in this hemisphere) when, as, and if he chooses." Wheeler was a prominent Democrat, and Willkie had been the Republican nominee for President. This illustrated how much the isolationist movement (as well as interventionist sentiment, like that shared by Republican Presidential nominee Wendell Willkie; the Republican Secretary of War, Henry Stimson; and the Republican Secretary of the Navy, Frank Knox) crossed party lines during 1940 and 1941.

Later, in November of 1941, Wheeler stated: *"If we go to war with Japan, the only reason will be to help England."*

After the attack on Pearl Harbor, however, Wheeler voted *for* the Congressional War Declaration, not against it. The day after the attack, even Wheeler, perhaps FDR's most ardent and

	heated response to this: "I regard it as the most untruthful, as the most dastardly, unpatriotic thing that has ever been said."[146]	outspoken Congressional foreign policy opponent up to that time, said that the only thing left to do was "to lick hell out of them."
January 24, 1941	**Navy Secretary Frank Knox sends a letter expressing concerns about Pearl Harbor's vulnerability to Secretary of War Henry Stimson.** The letter was drafted for Knox by the Navy's War Plans Division, headed by Rear Admiral Richmond K. Turner, and is ample evidence that the national leadership in Washington was not composed of incompetent or sleep-walking bureaucrats, and furthermore, that Rear Admiral Turner---the Chief of the War Plans Division---took the possibility of an attack on Pearl Harbor seriously.	The letter was quite prescient, voicing the concern in the Navy Department about the **"security of the U.S. Pacific Fleet while in Pearl Harbor, and of the Pearl Harbor Naval Base itself…If war eventuates with Japan, it is believed easily possible that hostilities would be initiated by a surprise attack upon the Fleet or Naval Base at Pearl Harbor."** [Emphasis added.] The letter asserted that the possibility of an "air bombing attack" and "air torpedo plane attack" were greater than the danger from enemy submarine operations or sabotage. The letter urged that priority be given to "location and engagement of enemy carriers and supporting vessels before air attack can be launched." Knox accepted that such protective measures were "largely a function of the fleet but, quite possibly, *might not be carried out in case of an air attack initiated without warning prior to a declaration of war.*"[147] [Emphasis added] CINCUS J.O. Richardson received the Knox letter

---

[146] Kershaw, *Fateful Choices*, 232.

[147] Costello, *Days of Infamy*, 45-46; and Stillwell, ed., *Air Raid, Pearl Harbor!*, 74-78. The individual who drafted the letter that Admiral Stark desired Knox send to Stimson (in an attempt to improve the Army's defensive posture in Hawaii) was Commander Walter Ansell, a member of the War Plans staff. The letter spent about one month in preparation, and regardless of who originally drafted it, it was seen and approved by Rear Admiral Richmond K. Turner, the Chief of War Plans. It came out of his shop, and bore his approval.

		as an enclosure to a letter from Admiral Stark just prior to his relief, and passed it on to his relief, Admiral Kimmel.
January 24, 1941	FDR, onboard the Presidential yacht *Potomac,* greets the new British ambassador to the United States, Lord Halifax, as he arrives onboard the new battleship *King George V,* off Annapolis, Maryland in Chesapeake Bay. This was an unprecedented gesture of solidarity between the United States and Great Britain, powerful in its symbolism---for it was unheard of for a Head of State to greet an arriving ambassador from another country by going to meet *him*---and was intentionally on display for all the country to hear about on the radio and see in newsreels at their local movie theaters.[148] By appointing Lord Halifax as Ambassador to the United States for the duration of the war, Churchill had neatly	Onboard HMS *King George V,* arriving in America for a highly classified conference that the public knew nothing about, were several high-ranking members of the British Army and Navy. On December 17, 1940, CNO Harold Stark had extended a formal invitation for them to come to America for secret staff talks---"discussions"---with members of the American military from the war plans divisions of the Army and Navy. (Roosevelt had given Stark permission to make the invitation on the same day he held his Lend-Lease press conference and employed the "garden hose" homily in the Oval Office). The purpose of the talks,[149] as stated in Admiral Stark's proposal, was threefold: (1) To determine the best methods by which the United States and Great Britain could defeat "Germany and the powers allied with her, should the United States decide [**FDR changed "decide" to "be compelled"**] to resort to war;" (2) To coordinate, in broad outline, plans for the employment of the two nations' armed forces; and (3) To reach agreements between the

---

[148] Davis, *FDR: The War President,* 139.

[149] Ibid., 77.

	disposed of his "Halifax problem"---he had removed from his presence a former rival for the office of Prime Minister, and the last holdover from the odious appeasement regime of former Prime Minister Neville Chamberlain. By all accounts, Halifax performed creditably and loyally as Great Britain's ambassador in Washington, D.C.	two regarding "areas of responsibility, the major lines of strategy to be pursued…the strength of the forces…and…common arrangements." **The staff talks between the military planners for the two English-speaking democracies came to be known as the American-British Conversations (ABC). They commenced on January 29th, and ended on March 29th. At that time, a joint report called ABC-1 was issued (more on this later).** <u>The fact that these staff talks were taking place for the reasons described above is the clearest indication that Franklin Roosevelt intended for the U.S. to enter the Second World War</u>---*when it was "compelled to" by the actions of others, of course.*
January 27, 1941	Secretary of State Cordell Hull receives a cable <u>from Ambassador Joseph C. Grew in Japan</u> warning that in the event of war with America, **Japan would attack the U.S. Naval Base at Pearl Harbor** with all of its military might.	Grew was reporting a warning that his Third Secretary had received from the Peruvian Ambassador to Japan.[150] The pertinent text reads as follows: *"My Peruvian colleague told a member of my staff that he had heard from many sources including a Japanese source that <u>the Japanese military forces planned in the event of trouble with the United States, to attempt a surprise attack on Pearl Harbor using all of their military facilities</u>. He added that although the project seemed fantastic the fact that he had heard it from many*

---

[150] Stinnett, *Day of Deceit*, 31.

		sources prompted him to pass the information." Yamamoto has already lost the element of surprise, and doesn't even know it. [Emphasis added]
January 30, 1941	A Gallup poll reveals that **88 per cent of the American people still oppose entering the war.**[151]	This high percentage of American citizens who were against the United States entering hostilities was constantly on the mind of Franklin Roosevelt, who was convinced the United States had to enter the war if Germany was to be defeated. Great Britain could never defeat Germany alone, even with unlimited materiel support from the United States; Great Britain could only 'hang on' and persevere, strengthen itself against a possible invasion, and peck at the periphery of the European Axis, *even with* huge quantities of American aid. Churchill knew that, and Roosevelt knew that. Roosevelt had to do one of three things: (1) change the mindset of the American people, through continuing education and persuasion, so that they would eventually come to understand that the U.S. must enter the war; *or* (2) hope that America's continuing aid would so anger Hitler that he would declare war on the United States and thereby solve FDR's problem for him; or (3) hope for an "incident"---a military clash---perpetrated by a member of the Axis upon the U.S. armed forces, that could serve as a *casus belli*.
February 1, 1941	Commander McCollum sends the **ONI analysis of the Pearl Harbor attack**	The ONI response drafted by McCollum told CINCPAC: "The Division of Naval Intelligence places no credence in these

---

[151] Ibid., 33.

	warning furnished by Ambassador Grew: **it is discounted as "rumor"** in a cable sent to the newly installed Commander in Chief, Pacific Fleet (CINCPAC), Admiral Husband E. Kimmel.[152]	rumors. Furthermore, **based on known data regarding the present disposition and employment** of Japanese Naval and Army forces, **no move against Pearl Harbor appears imminent or planned for in the foreseeable future."** [153] [Emphasis added] In hindsight, this analysis is so full of caveats, and is such a carefully phrased narrow denial, that it almost appears designed to lull its recipient to sleep. The author of this response is the same person who authored the crucial memo of October 7, 1940 proposing that the United States provoke Japan into committing "an overt act of war" against America. This almost cavalier dismissal of the possibility of an attack on Pearl Harbor---sent to Admiral Kimmel in Pearl Harbor---stands in stark contrast to the very serious concerns about the possibility expressed by the War Plans Division and Navy Secretary Knox on January 24th, *just eight days previously,* to the Secretary of War.
February 7, 1941	**A four-man team of U.S. cryptanalysts arrives in England in the first step of a wartime exchange of code-breaking intelligence between the two governments.**[154]	By most accounts the material transferred to the British at Bletchley Park during their six-week visit included the following: **Japanese Diplomatic Codes:**

---

[152] Ibid., 31-32.

[153] Ibid., 32.

[154] Slightly differing accounts of this remarkable, initial exchange of vital intelligence between two nations that were not yet formal allies (with one of them a belligerent and one still a non-belligerent) can be found in *Betrayal at Pearl Harbor* (p. 108-112); *The Ultra-Magic Deals* (p. 43-63); and *The Emperor's Codes* (73-77). The Americans received a "paper model" of the German Naval Enigma machine, but not one of the actual

They had travelled to Great Britain onboard HMS *King George V* when it returned to England after bringing the new British Ambassador, Lord Halifax, to America on January 24th. The four Americans who traveled abroad to share American intelligence with their British cousins were: Lieutenant Robert H. Weeks, USN and Ensign Prescott H. Currier, USN (both from OP-20-G); and from the Army's SIS, "Captain" Abraham Sinkov, and "Lieutenant" Leo Rosen. (Both civilian SIS cryptanalysts were given temporary ranks as Army junior officers, and were designated military attaches and given diplomatic passports, because at the time U.S. law forbade civilians from travelling on a belligerent vessel.) Cryptanalyst William Friedman, the dean of American code-breakers, was to have led the mission, but he could not travel because he had

Two **Purple** machines with current keys, plus the three-letter keying code, and techniques of solution;

Two Red machines (the previous diplomatic code superseded by **Purple** in major posts) with current keys and techniques of solution;

Two sets of Consular codes (J-17), and current keys with techniques of solution;

Two sets of minor diplomatic codes.

Japanese Naval Codes:

Two sets of JN-25 fleet codes with current keys (additive tables) and techniques of solution assembled by OP-20-G since its initial breakthrough in October of 1940;

Two sets of merchant ship codes with current keys;

Two sets of Naval Attache ciphers, but not the Coral cryptograph;

Two radio naval call-sign signal lists.

One historical account---*The Ultra-Magic Deals,* by Bradley F. Smith---claims that only one **Purple** machine was taken to England during this first exchange visit (not two). But Rusbridger and Nave, in *Betrayal at Pearl Harbor,* insist that the American team transported two **Purple** machines, and also stated that one of these two machines was

---

machines, leading to considerable acrimony on the part of OP-20-G (CDR Safford), who felt betrayed in this lopsided deal arranged initially by General George Marshall, and later concurred in by six major officials of the Army and Navy, without any prior consultation with Navy cryptanalysts.

	suffered a nervous collapse in early January as a result of the effort he had expended for 18 months on **MAGIC**. From the standpoint of this author's work, the key impact of this "most secret special relationship" is that it deprived Station HYPO in Pearl Harbor of its chance to receive a **Purple** machine---and thereby also deprived Admiral Kimmel of vital diplomatic intelligence throughout 1941, in the run-up to the attack on Pearl Harbor.	immediately sent out to FECB, to monitor the Japanese diplomatic traffic with Batavia in the Dutch East Indies. **Rusbridger and Nave state (p. 111) that _both_ Purple machines had originally been slated for Station HYPO at Pearl Harbor, and that a third Purple machine later earmarked for HYPO was also diverted to GCCS at Bletchley Park, later in 1941.** The British got the lion's share of the benefit from this initial exchange of signals intelligence; however, two days after the American team arrived at Bletchley Park, Admiral John Godfrey, British Director of Naval Intelligence, authorized the complete exchange of Japanese signals intelligence information between FECB in Singapore and Station CAST at Corregidor.
February 9, 1941	**"Give Us the Tools, and We Will Finish the Job"** In this radio broadcast (which not only went out to the British Empire, but also to America), Churchill did his best to overtly, yet skillfully interfere with American politics and assist with the passage of the Lend-Lease Bill, which was being interminably debated in Congress, and elsewhere. Wendell Willkie, FDR's opponent during the	Excerpts follow: "We stood our ground and faced the two dictators in the hour of what seemed their overwhelming triumph, and we have shown ourselves capable, so far, of standing up against them alone. After the heavy defeats of the German Air Force by our fighters in August and September, Herr Hitler did not dare attempt the invasion of this Island, although he had every need to do so and had made vast preparations. Baffled in this mighty project, he sought to break the spirit of the British nation by the bombing, first of London, and afterwards of our great cities. It has now been proved, to the admiration of the world, and of our friends in the United States, that this form of blackmail by

recent Presidential election, arrived in Great Britain in January and brought with him a letter of introduction from President Roosevelt, which contained the famous lines from a poem by Longfellow, which moved Churchill greatly and which he employed in this speech.[155]

The magnificent closing lines of Churchill's address, while great oratory, were absurd---for Great Britain had no hope of defeating Nazi Germany alone. But she desperately needed significant amounts of American aid simply to continue the war, and to prevent economic collapse and starvation. So Churchill made his grand statement at the close of his address, and it helped persuade America to pass the Lend-Lease Bill.

murder and terrorism, so far from weakening the spirit of the British nation, has only roused it to a more intense and universal flame than was ever seen before in any modern community…All through these dark winter months the enemy has had the power to drop three or four tons of bombs upon us for every ton we could send to Germany in return. We are arranging so that presently this will be rather the other way around; but, meanwhile, London and our big cities have had to stand their pounding. They remind me of the British squares at Waterloo. They are not squares of soldiers; they do not wear scarlet coats. They are just ordinary English, Scottish, and Welsh folk…standing steadfastly together. But their spirit is the same; their glory is the same; and, in the end, their victory will be greater than far-famed Waterloo…

In order to win the war Hitler must destroy Great Britain. He may carry havoc into the Balkan states; he may tear great provinces out of Russia, he may march to the Caspian [both of these predictions of imminent actions proved very astute]; he may march to the gates of India. All this will avail him nothing. It may spend his curse more widely throughout Europe and Asia, but it will not avert his doom. With every month that passes the many proud and once happy countries he is now holding down by brute force and vile intrigue are

---

[155] Churchill, ed., *Never Give In!,* 259-262.

learning to hate the Prussian yoke and the Nazi name as nothing has ever been hated so fiercely and so widely among men before. And all this time, masters of the sea and air, the British Empire---nay, in a sense the whole English-speaking world---will be on its track, bearing with them the swords of justice…

The other day, President Roosevelt gave his opponent in the late Presidential election a letter of introduction to me, and in it he wrote out a verse, in his own handwriting, from Longfellow, which he said, 'applies to you people as it does to us.' Here is the verse:

…Sail on, O Ship of State! Sail on, O Union, strong and great! Humanity with all its fears, With all the hopes of future years, Is hanging breathless on thy fate!

What is the answer that I shall give, in your name, to this great man, the thrice-chosen head of a nation of a hundred and thirty millions? Here is the answer I will give to President Roosevelt: Put your confidence in us. Give us your faith and your blessing, and, under Providence, all will be well. We shall not fail or falter; we shall not weaken or tire. Neither the sudden shock or battle, nor the long-drawn trials of vigilance and exertion will wear us down. <u>**Give us the tools, and we will finish the job**</u>." [Emphasis added]

March 5, 1941	**Admiral Thomas Hart, Commander in Chief, Asiatic Fleet, transmits**	The text of the message reads as follows [parenthetical comments are mine]:

	a Secret message to the CNO, Admiral Stark, about the commencement of the sharing of cryptologic material about JN-25(b) between Station CAST in the Philippines and FECB in Singapore. Hart's message states that 5-numeral code system values for the period December through February [that is, immediately following the introduction of the new JN-25(b) code book on December 1, 1940] had been received from the British, and that a secure method had been arranged for exchanging further recoveries by cable. In "gung ho" fashion, Hart declares that due to the combined abilities of CAST and FECB, CAST will assume the responsibility for breaking the 5-Num system *as its only assignment!* He is taking it upon himself to dictate SIGINT responsibilities of OP-20-G personnel within his AOR to Navy	"HAVE RECEIVED FROM BRITISH [the] FOLLOWING IN APPROXIMATE NUMBERS REFERRING TO FIVE-NUMERAL SYSTEM EFFECTIVE DECEMBER TO FEBRUARY X FIVE HUNDRED BOOK VALUE[s] X FOUR THOUSAND SUBTRACTOR GROUPS [presumably additive table values] X HALF THOUSAND WORKSHEETS WITH CIPHER [additive values] REMOVED X AND TWO HUNDRED NINETY INDICATOR SUBTRACTORS FOR SMS [meaning unclear] NUMBERS X HAVE ARRANGED SECURE METHOD OF EXCHANGING FURTHER RECOVERIES BY CABLE X BRITISH EMPLOY THREE OFFICERS [and] TWENTY CLERKS ON THIS SYSTEM ALONE X THEY ARE DELAYING ATTACK ON CURRENT CIPHER TABLE UNTIL MIDMARCH TO ACCUMULATE TRAFFIC AND OBTAIN FURTHER BOOK VALUES FROM PROCEEDING [sic] PERIOD X DUE COLLATERAL INFORMATION AVAILABLE HERE AND CAPABILITY RAPID EXCHANGE WITH ENGLISH CAVITE [Hart should have said "Corregidor" since CAST was no longer located at the Cavite Naval Yard] WILL ASSUME THIS SYSTEM AS ONLY NAVY ASSIGNMENT X REQUEST DEPT FORWARD RESULTS TO DATE AND

Communications in Washington, which prides itself in controlling all of the Navy's decryption efforts. Stinnett writes that this message was *not* made available to either the Congressional Committee investigating the Pearl Harbor attack in late 1945 and early 1946, or to the Pentagon in 1995 prior to issuance of the Dorn Report---nor was it shared with Admiral Kimmel in Hawaii in 1941.	TECHNIQUE ADVICE IF CONSIDERED HELPFUL"[156] <u>Comments</u>: someone in Communications in Washington, D.C. objected to Hart taking the bull by the horns, for the passage "<u>Cavite will assume this system as only Navy assignment</u>" has been *underlined* on the message. Stinnett offers several comments about the marginalia on the message (which is the Washington, D.C. receipt copy). He writes that a note in the right margin states that OP-20-A (CAPT Redman, assistant to Rear Admiral Leigh Noyes, who was OP-20) directs that the message be removed from Navy files and that a dummy message be inserted in its place. Stinnett further claims that a handwritten note elsewhere on the message states that **"both Singapore and Station US had obtained [together] at least 8200 recoveries in the 5-Num system and expected to obtain more."** The number **8200 recoveries** [meaning recovered words or 5-value groups from the basic code book] is significant, since the total number of recoveries in the basic book obtained by Station US (NEGAT) as of December 1, 1941---nine months later---*was only 3,800,* according to an official history written by OP-20-G. I find the marginalia on the facsimile copy of the message, on p. 300 of Stinnett's book, illegible for the most part. **If his reading of "8200 combined**

---

[156] A facsimile of the actual message and Stinnett's comments are to be found on pages 300 and 301 of *Day of Deceit;* his main text entry about this message is on page 80.

		recoveries" on the Archives copy of the message is correct, then this statistic indicates a **considerable British success in breaking JN-25(b) by the end of February 1941, just a short time after the new code book had been introduced on December 1, 1940.** In contrast, on October 1, 1941---seven months later---CAST's total recoveries in the JN-25(b) code book are listed *as only 2,400* in an OP-20-G official history.
March 5, 1941	OP-20-G in Washington, D.C. decides that the responsibility for assisting NEGAT with breaking JN-25(b) will be transferred from Station CAST in the Philippines to COM-14 in Pearl Harbor (Station HYPO), in July of 1941.[157] This decision is hard to understand, given the message received that day from Admiral Hart about the information sharing between CAST and FECB. One explanation that seems possible for the intended transfer of responsibility for JN-25(b)---from CAST to HYPO---is the fact that Safford had been personally negotiating the terms under which LCDR	One must ask, "Is it possible that CDR Safford---OP-20-G---intended to transfer responsibility for assisting Washington with JN-25(b) decryption from CAST to HYPO in a fit of pique, because of the temerity of Admiral Hart's message?" We will never know the answer to this question. However, from everything I have read about Laurance Safford, the "Father of Navy Cryptography," he would not have made such a decision for petty, personal reasons. Rear Admiral Leigh Noyes, however (the Director of Communications), and his assistant, CAPT Redman, both had parochial, combative, and even arrogant, self-assured personalities. And Safford, like everyone else, had to answer to his bosses to some degree. Station CAST protested vehemently after they were informed of this decision the following day, since they were sharing progress in decryption with the British Far East Combined Bureau (FECB) in Singapore, and because they believed

---

[157] Carlson, *Joe Rochefort's War,* 120.

		Joseph J. Rochefort "might" accept orders as OIC of Station HYPO in Pearl Harbor. Rochefort was initially very reluctant to accept the assignment, but Safford talked him into it by promising Rochefort he would get special equipment, and the best available linguists and cryptographers, according to Rochefort's biographer, Elliot Carlson.	their capability to receive Japanese Navy radio traffic was superior (geographically) to that in Hawaii, on the island of Oahu. In April, OP-20-G ordered the creation of three identical publications listing all "recovered" (i.e., broken) values from the master JN-25(b) code book. The original plan, at inception, was for the 3 publications to be distributed simultaneously to NEGAT, CAST, and HYPO in July of 1941.
	March 6, 1941	CNO replies negatively to CINCAF's desire of the previous day that CAST assume full-time responsibility for breaking JN-25(b).	This message, drafted by CDR Safford and released as OPNAV # 062134, stated in part that CAST lacked the "necessary statistical machinery" and manpower to take the lead in breaking JN-25(b). [HYPO in Pearl harbor had just been equipped with the latest IBM tabulating machinery to speed up the laborious process of decryption and book building.] Admiral Hart was therefore advised to forward the British JN-25 material to HYPO since "present plan [is] to transfer this attack to Pearl Harbor in July."[158]
	March 11, 1941	**The Lend-Lease Bill Passes in Congress.**	Three days earlier on March 8th, the bill had passed the Senate by a vote of 60-31 (with only 14 of 65 Democrats voting against the measure, and with 10 of 28 Republicans voting for it). On March 11th, the House passed the Senate's version of the bill by the overwhelming

---

[158] Costello, *Days of Infamy,* 298, 410.

margin of 317-71. Roosevelt signed the bill into law the same day. Churchill cabled a message: **"Our blessings from the whole of the British Empire go out to you and the American nation for this very present help in this time of trouble."** Churchill would later describe Lend-Lease to Parliament as **"the most unsordid act in the history of any nation."**[159] On March 12th, the very next day, FDR submitted a request to Congress for the 7 billion dollar appropriation which would fund the initial Lend-Lease material for Britain. Five days after Lend-Lease was passed, on March 16th, Roosevelt addressed the nation by radio, saying: "In this historic crisis, Britain is blessed with a brilliant and great leader." He then went on to describe the import of the great decision (which had taken much longer than he would have wished). Americans had just participated in a "great debate," one that had "not [been] limited to the halls of Congress," but "argued in every newspaper, on every wavelength, over every cracker barrel in the land" before being "finally settled and decided by the American people themselves. **Yes, the decisions of our democracy may be slowly arrived at. But when that decision is made, it is proclaimed not with the voice of one man but with the voice of one hundred and thirty millions. It is binding on us all."** FDR then discussed fast action, saying that five minutes after signing the bill on

---

[159] Davis, *FDR: The War President,* 135-136.

		March 11th, "I approved a list of articles for immediate shipment" to Britain and Greece, and "today---Saturday night---many of these are on their way."[160]
March 15, 1941	LCDR Joseph J. Rochefort, a talented Japanese linguist and one of the Navy's most gifted cryptanalysts, receives orders to transfer to shore duty at Station HYPO in Pearl Harbor, as its Officer in Charge.	Rochefort had learned Japanese while stationed in Japan in the 1920s, and had also filled in as OP-20-G for two years in the mid 1920s when Laurance Safford was posted to sea duty. During this period Rochefort benefitted from the tutelage of the legendary civilian cryptanalyst at OP-20-G, Agnes Meyer Driscoll.[161]
March 15, 1941	**FDR, at the annual dinner of White House correspondents, gave a bipartisan speech described as "one of the most powerful of his career."** Roosevelt warmly greeted Wendell Willkie (who had supported Lend-Lease during Senate hearings), and sought to move the minds of Americans from the "great debate" over Lend-Lease---now concluded---to increasing war production.	President Roosevelt called upon Americans to sacrifice, work harder, and increase the tempo of production. Upon this, he declared, depended "the survival of the vital bridge across the ocean---the bridge of ships that carry the arms and the food for those who are fighting the good fight." But he emphasized that speed, "speed now," must be the watchwords, "now, *now,*... NOW!"[162] And clearly, the principal concern of Roosevelt and his advisors now was that the Lend-Lease supplies get safely to Britain. (During March, 1941 Great Britain was losing merchant shipping at the rate of 500,000 tons per month.) On this same date, March 15th, "…orders went out to the Atlantic Fleet to return at once to homeports on the East Coast, to

---

[160] Ibid., 137.

[161] Costello, *Days of Infamy*, 297.

[162] Heinrichs, *Threshold of War,* 31.

		strip ship of flammables and peacetime conveniences, undergo overhaul, apply camouflage paint, and prepare for active duty."[163]
March 18, 1941	Churchill's Speech on the **"Battle of the Atlantic"** is given at a Pilgrim's Society Luncheon in London.[164] The German war of attrition against British merchant shipping with U-boats, surface raiders, and long-range aircraft was particularly effective during March, April, and May---imposing losses that could not be sustained over the long term, and creating a true sense of crisis in London and Washington.	Excerpts: "We are met here today under the strong impression and impact of the historic declaration made on Saturday last by the President of the United States, and where could there be a more fitting opportunity than at this gathering of the Pilgrims to greet the new American ambassador [John G. Winant, who was replacing the poisonous defeatist, Joseph P. Kennedy] for me to express on behalf of the British nation and Empire the sense of encouragement and fortification in our resolve which has come to us from across the ocean in those stirring, august, and fateful Presidential words?

…We welcome you here, Mr. Winant, at the moment when a great battle in which your Government and nation are deeply interested is developing its full scope and severity. **The Battle of the Atlantic** |

---

[163] Ibid., 31. Professor Waldo Heinrichs, in *Threshold of War,* brilliantly summarized FDR's position immediately after the passage of Lend-Lease (pp. 16-17): "Roosevelt was at a peak of skill and experience while retaining his buoyancy and strength…The 'great debate' was over, and the American people had chosen by decisive margins to intervene in the war at least to the point of supplying aid to Britain…Now, at last, he had some elbow room. He could not move too fast or too far, however. The nation was not ready for war as a matter of choice. Public opinion, as Roosevelt probably saw it, was touchy. It was moving in the right direction, passing the marker buoy of aid to Great Britain even at the risk of war. But a declaration of war was not even in sight. Decisive executive action might slow or shift it. Isolationism as it weakened became more bitter and vindictive. It would revive with attacks on Roosevelt as a warmonger and dictator. The result would be division and disunity when national consolidation was essential. He must avoid being the issue. He needed to dispel complacency, but opinion could not be forced: it must flow from the facts of international life themselves, from very real menaces. It required education, subtle reinforcement, nurturing---in short, time."

[164] Churchill, ed., *Never Give In!,* 262-264.

must be won in a decisive manner. It must be won beyond all doubt if the declared policies of the Government and people of the United States are not to be forcibly frustrated. *Not only German U-boats, but German battle cruisers have crossed to the American side of the Atlantic* and have already sunk some of our independently-routed ships not sailing in convoy…*Over here upon the approaches to our island an intense and unrelenting struggle is being waged to bring in the endless stream of munitions and food without which our war effort here and in the Middle East…cannot be maintained.* <u>Our losses have risen for the time being</u>, and we are applying our fullest strength and resource, and all the skill and science we can command, in order to meet this potentially mortal challenge…But our strength is growing every week. The American destroyers which reached us in the autumn and winter are increasingly coming into action. Our flotillas are growing in number. Our air power over the island and seas is growing fast. We are striking back with increasing effect…It is my rule, as you know, not to conceal the gravity of the danger from our people, and therefore I have a right to be believed when I also proclaim our confidence that we shall overcome them [the U-boats]. <u>But anyone can see how bitter is the need for Hitler and his gang to cut the sea roads between Great Britain and the United States, and, having divided these mighty Powers, to</u>

		destroy them one by one. **Therefore we must regard this Battle of the Atlantic as one of the most momentous ever fought in all the annals of war…".** [Emphasis added]
March 27, 1941	**President Roosevelt signs the 7 billion dollar Lend-Lease appropriation just approved by Congress,** by a vote of 336-55 in the House, and 67 to 9 in the Senate. Passage of the Lend-Lease Act on March 11th had approved the giveaway of materiel, but this funding was essential to implement the Act.	Earlier, on March 16th, Roosevelt had said: "This decision is the end of any attempts at appeasement in our land; the end of urging us to get along with the dictators; the end of compromise with tyranny and the forces of oppression. And the urgency is ***now***…The great task of this day, the deep duty that rests upon each and every one of us is to move products from the assembly lines of our factories to the battle lines of democracy ---***now!***" [Emphasis in original] Roosevelt seemed to be wishfully asserting that the passage of Lend-Lease marked the end of isolationism in America. Lord Halifax, Britain's new ambassador to the U.S., thought it was: "With the passage of the Bill, it can be said that except for a small number of irreconcilable isolationists the whole country is united in its support of the Allies against the totalitarian powers." But another British observer, T. North Whitehead---now serving in the Foreign Office after a professorship at Harvard---knew the American psyche better than Lord Halifax, who was a newcomer. *Americans, he wrote, are **"a mercurial people"** who could not be counted upon to eschew isolationism once and for all **"until they are finally committed to actual warfare.**"*[165] [Emphasis added]

---

[165] Davis, FDR: *The War President,* 138.

		These were prophetic words, for the desire of the vast majority of the American people <u>to stay out of the fighting in World War II</u> would remain very strong up until December 8, 1941---the morning after the Japanese attack on Pearl Harbor.
March 29, 1941	<u>The American-British Staff Conversations are concluded</u>, and what becomes known as **the ABC-1 Report** is issued. It is a Top Secret Joint Report, contingency planning at a high level concerning joint American and British war strategy and resource allocation, in the event America enters World War II; the public knows nothing about it. In the political atmosphere of the time, it was potential political dynamite, for while FDR had persuaded Americans to provide all material aid short of war to Great Britain, they still overwhelmingly ***did not*** want to go to war---and yet in secret, he was planning for war as if it were inevitable, while still speaking publicly about his intention to	**In ABC-1, the Americans and the British agreed that in the event both countries found themselves at war with the Axis powers, that a "Germany first" policy would be pursued,** *no matter what action Japan took in the Pacific.* The operative language to this effect was: "<u>Since Germany is the predominant member of the Axis Powers, the Atlantic and European area is considered to be the decisive theatre. The principal United States military effort will be expended in that theatre</u>, **and operations of United States forces in other theatres will be conducted in such a manner as to facilitate that effort.**"[166] During the discussions the American planners, aware of the tremendous industrial potential of the United States, favored a decisive frontal assault on German-occupied northern Europe as soon as practical; the British, remembering the horrors of four years of trench warfare, human slaughter, and stalemate in World War I, proposed pursuing a peripheral strategy (hitting the European Axis where it was weakest,

---

[166] Victor, *The Pearl Harbor Myth,* 171-172.

	keep the United States out of the conflict.	around the edges), and not launching a frontal assault against Germany in northern Europe until years of bombing and blockade had fatally weakened Nazi Germany. The British (and French) had lost a generation of young men by launching costly and futile frontal assaults in the First World War, whereas the Americans had only fought in Europe in the spring, summer, and fall of 1918, the fourth year of that war---when it had become a war of maneuver---and had not suffered nearly as many casualties as Great Britain. The differing strategies reflected the difference in economic strength between the two countries, as well as their different national experiences in the previous World War. Compromises were made, and the Americans agreed to a peripheral strategy until such time as it was safe and prudent to make a frontal assault on Germany. There had been sharp disagreement between the Americans and British over Singapore, with the British planners insisting that the Americans use the U.S. Navy to buttress this key British outpost in the Far East; <u>the American planners, not interested in propping up the British Empire, vowed they would not weaken the fleet at Pearl Harbor unless it was to send ships to the Atlantic to protect Lend-Lease shipments.</u>[167] This problem

---

[167] In April of 1941 Admiral Stark sent his Fleet Commanders a copy of ABC-1, and commented, "The basic idea of the United States-British plan is that the United States will draw forces from the Pacific Fleet to reinforce the Atlantic Fleet...". This happened immediately, even though ABC-1 had not been formally approved by the President, and even though the U.S. was not yet formally at war with any Axis power. <u>In April, Admiral Kimmel was ordered to send one aircraft carrier, three battleships, four cruisers, and eighteen destroyers---almost one fourth of the total strength of the Pacific Fleet---through the Panama Canal to join the Atlantic Fleet</u>. In May,

was a political one more than anything else, and so it was left unresolved, and deferred to higher authority (the national leadership of the two nations) for resolution at a later date.

The ABC-1 Report afterwards became the basis for the so-called Rainbow-5 American war plan; the Joint Army-Navy Board approved both Rainbow-5 and ABC-1 in mid-May of 1941, as did Secretaries Stimson and Knox. The plans were then sent on to President Roosevelt for consideration.

Fearing the public reaction if it became known that U.S. and British military planners had made joint contingency plans for how to beat Nazi Germany, FDR reviewed the plans carefully; did *not* disapprove them; but did not sign them, either, saying **he would have them returned to him for approval** in the event of war. General Marshall persuaded Secretaries Stimson and Knox, Admiral Stark, and to a lesser degree Cordell Hull at State, to proceed with defense preparations as though FDR had signed the planning documents.[168]

Kimmel was notified that additional ships would be sent to the Atlantic, prompting him to fly to Washington to protest directly to the CNO and the President. On June 2, 1941, Kimmel complained to Roosevelt: "Once the fleet was detained there, for the purpose of exerting a deterrent effect upon Japan, it was not maintaining a consistent policy thereafter to weaken the fleet, visibly and plainly, by diversion of powerful units to the Atlantic." **Admiral Kimmel pointed out to FDR that the Pacific Fleet was already dangerously weaker than the Japanese Combined Fleet; Roosevelt understood and accepted this.** (*See* Costello, *Days of Infamy*, pages 47-48.) This state of affairs was not only dictated by ABC-1 planning considerations, but in addition (and as Kimmel was surely unaware), by this time Roosevelt no longer considered the Pacific Fleet as a deterrent, but rather as a lure, to possibly provoke the Japanese into committing "an overt act of war."

[168] Davis, *FDR: The War President,* 138-144.

| April 6, 1941 | **Germany Invades Yugoslavia and Greece.** The prelude, and stimulus for this Balkan Campaign by Nazi Germany was Italy's ill-fated invasion of Greece (from Albania) on October 28, 1940; Mussolini foolishly thought the Greeks would be easy to knock off, and that Greece would greatly add to the luster of his "Mediterranean Empire." He was wrong. Within weeks the hapless Italian Army was driven out of Greece, and Greek forces pushed on to occupy much of southern Albania. The British began to send troops to Greece from North Africa in March of 1941, in accordance with treaty commitments. An Italian counteroffensive in March of 1941 failed, necessitating rescue of The Duce from his ill-fated adventure by Hitler. | Commencing with its occupation of the island of Crete in early November of 1940 (a response to Italy's invasion of Greece), Great Britain had decided to attempt to create a Balkan Front against Nazi Germany, comprised (hopefully) of Yugoslavia, Greece, and Turkey. Hitler responded by ordering, that same month, the invasion of Greece (primarily through its northern neighbor, Bulgaria, but also through southern Yugoslavia and Albania). Staff planning for the campaign went on for months, while the Wehrmacht waited for the spring to carry out Hitler's orders. Hitler's strategic goal was to drive the British from their Mediterranean bases. A Yugoslavian Crisis was precipitated for the Germans when, on March 27th, two days after Prince Paul (Regent of the Kingdom of Yugoslavia) signed the Tripartite Pact in Vienna on March 25th, a British-supported coup d'etat ousted Prince Paul and installed 17-year-old King Peter II, and his Prime Minister, General Dusan Simonvic. King Peter II and Simonvic attempted to renounce the Tripartite Pact, which enraged Hitler, who had planned to invade Greece partly through southern Yugoslavia. (The British had persuaded the new Yugoslav government to withdraw German permission to move troops through its country, and to oppose any German advance toward Greece and Albania.) **Accordingly, on April 6th, Nazi Germany simultaneously made war on both Greece and Yugoslavia.** The |

Luftwaffe bombed the Serbian capital of Belgrade (home base for the coup which had overthrown Prince Paul) for three successive days beginning April 6th, largely obliterating it; afterwards, the German Army quickly moved into Yugoslavia and the country capitulated on April 17th. The province of Croatia became a vassal state, willingly cooperating with Nazi Germany.

Unable to use southern Yugoslavia as a route to Greece because of the hostilities there, Germany invaded Greece solely through its northern neighbor, Bulgaria. The combined Greek and British forces fought back with great tenacity, but Athens fell on April 27th, and within 24 days, Germany's victory over Greece was complete. The British managed to evacuate about 50,000 of its troops and return them to Egypt. Germany attacked the large island of Crete on April 20th, using parachute troops in a massive airborne invasion, taking three key airfields. After 7 days of fighting, the British and Greek Allies began to withdraw, and by June 1, 1941, the evacuation of Crete was complete.

Probably the most consistently flawed (and persistently pushed) military-strategic concept of Churchill's during World War II was his obsession with creating a Balkan Front against Germany, which would chew at what Churchill mistakenly called "the soft underbelly of Europe." Great Britain, in 1941, did not have sufficient military resources in the Middle East to permit it

		to carry out simultaneous full-scale operations in both North Africa and the Balkans. Safeguarding Egypt (and the Suez Canal, Britain's lifeline to the petroleum in the Persian Gulf and its colonies in the Far East) took the higher priority, and so Great Britain's adventure in Greece ended in disaster for Churchill, and a complete German victory. Most historians agree, however, that Hitler's Balkan campaign caused a fatal delay in the commencement of his invasion of the Soviet Union, Operation Barbarossa.
April 7, 1941	**CNO Harold Stark informs CINCPAC (Admiral Kimmel) by letter that about one quarter of the Pacific Fleet will be transferred to the Atlantic, in concert with a recommendation made in the ABC-1 plan.** While the ABC-1 recommendation was to be carried out in the event that the U.S. went to war with Germany, Admiral Stark had recommended to President Roosevelt, in a meeting on April 3rd, that the transfer nevertheless take place now since the Battle of	Admiral King's Atlantic Fleet, with its three overage pre-World War I battleships (USS *Arkansas,* USS *Texas,* and USS *New York*), its five heavy cruisers, 4 light cruisers, two small aircraft carriers (USS *Ranger* and USS *Wasp*), and fifty-nine destroyers, urgently needed reinforcement, in order to carry out the Neutrality Patrols ordered by Roosevelt, and to prepare for future convoying---which many in the Navy favored immediately, but which Roosevelt was not yet ready to order. **CNO therefore obtained FDR's approval on April 3rd to transfer three battleships, one aircraft carrier, four light cruisers, and eighteen destroyers from Pearl Harbor to the Atlantic.**[169] The transfers actually took place in May of 1941.[170] This left nine battleships, twelve heavy

---

[169] Heinrichs, *Threshold of War,* 39-40; and Cressman, *That Gallant Ship: USS Yorktown,* 39-40.

[170] Wallin, *Pearl Harbor,* 52.

	the Atlantic was going Germany's way, and Roosevelt concurred. The Atlantic Fleet was insufficient in strength to carry out continuous patrols of Western Hemisphere waters, as desired by FDR.	cruisers, numerous light cruisers, three aircraft carriers, and fifty destroyers homeported in Pearl Harbor.[171]
April 9, 1941	**FDR extends the protection of the United States to Greenland,** per the request of the Danish Ambassador to the United States, in a move that pre-empts any possible use by Germany.	Greenland, a Danish possession, appeared to be of some interest to Germany during 1940 after Nazi Germany rolled into and occupied that small nation. The U.S. move prevented Germany from establishing weather stations or airfields on that continent, and also ensured that the U.S. had continued access to the rare mineral cryolite, essential to the smelting of aluminum from bauxite ore. America needed the cryolite to manufacture its planned 50,000 airplanes per year, as demanded by Roosevelt in May of 1940.
April 13, 1941	**Japanese Foreign Minister Matsuoka signs the <u>Japanese-Soviet Nonaggression Pact</u> in Moscow, on his way back to Japan from a visit to Germany.**	The signing of this neutrality pact provided that if either Japan or the USSR became involved in hostilities with a third power, that both signatories would remain neutral and not get involved. The pact lessened tensions following the undeclared border war between Japan and the Soviet Union in 1938 and 1939, in which the Japanese Army suffered serious defeats on the Manchurian border.

---

[171] Heinrichs, *Threshold of War,* 7 and 68.

		The pact recognized Japan's puppet state of Manchukuo, in Manchuria. By offering a degree of security on its northern frontier, the pact provided cover for a possible future Japanese advance into Southeast Asia.[172] The immediate impact of this neutrality agreement was to temporarily delay the transfers of several of the Pacific Fleet units to the Atlantic Fleet, since FDR did not (yet) want to embolden Japan by openly withdrawing major units from Pearl Harbor. The transfer of the three battleships was temporarily halted; however, the new aircraft carrier USS *Yorktown* quietly departed Hawaiian waters late in April (in the midst of regularly scheduled exercises), and along with the eighteen destroyers directed to leave by CNO Stark, transited the Panama Canal at night, entering the Atlantic Ocean on May 7th.[173]
April 15, 1941	President Roosevelt signs an unpublicized Executive Order that permits reserve officers and enlisted men to resign from the Army Air Corps, and from service in Naval and Marine Corps air units, to join retired Colonel **Clair Lee Chennault's <u>American Volunteer Group</u>, which**	FDR's authorization of this clandestine operation reflects how much influence the China Lobby (led by Ambassador T.V. Soong, Chiang Kai-Shek's brother in law) had in Washington, as well as how much public opinion supported the Nationalist Chinese in the ongoing war with the Japanese. One hundred P40B fighter planes procured under Lend-Lease were diverted from the British and assigned instead to AVG service; eventually a

---

[172] Ibid., 51-52.

[173] Cressman, *That Gallant Ship: USS Yorktown,* 39-41.

	became popularly known as "The Flying Tigers." Ostensibly the pilots and ground crew who volunteered for this duty were private American citizens employed by a company that had a contract with the Nationalist Chinese government. America was not at war with Japan, so the 100 pilots and several hundred ground crewmen in the first AVG had to resign from U.S. military service first, before going to work for a front company, the "Central Aircraft Manufacturing Company of China."	maximum of about 62 aircraft became operational in Burma, in squadrons of about 20 airplanes each. Training began in Burma in November of 1941, but "The Flying Tigers" (in reality, American mercenaries receiving three times their former military pay, flying American aircraft, with Chinese markings) did not go into combat until after the Pearl Harbor attack, on December 20, 1941. The unit was disbanded in July of 1942, when its functions were assumed by a U.S. Army Air Force unit. The AVG claimed that it lost only 14 pilots, compared to about 300 "enemy" (Japanese) aircraft shot down, in defense of the Burma Road supplying China with American and British military aid for use against the Japanese. Plans for a second and third AVG were nixed by the Japanese attack on Pearl Harbor, and U.S. entry into the Second World War.
April 23, 1941	William Bullitt, former U.S. ambassador to France, saw Roosevelt on this day and FDR told him "that the problem that was troubling him most was that of public opinion. He had just had an argument with Stimson on the subject. **Stimson thought we ought to go to war now. He, the President, felt that we must await an incident and was confident that the Germans would give**	**President Roosevelt sought to mold public opinion without outpacing it.** His greatest fear was of taking a divided nation into war---in hindsight, a well-founded concern, given America's Vietnam debacle in the late 1960s and early 1970s. He could ask for Congress to declare war against Germany, as many of his interventionist advisors wished, but the chances of persuading Congress to declare war were slim at this point; after all, Lend-Lease had just been sold to Congress and the American people as the best way to keep America *out* of the war. Even if FDR had prevailed and had been able to persuade Congress to declare war in the Spring of 1941, it

	us an incident."[174]	would have been by a slim margin, after protracted and bitter debate, and the President would have been taking a divided people into the storm. An "incident," on the other hand---a blatant and undeniable act of aggression by the Kriegsmarine against the U.S. Navy---might just provide the unity in the American people that an acrimonious debate in the Congress would not.
April 24, 1941	CDR Laurance Safford (OP-20-G) *changes his mind again* about which field activity shall take the lead in assisting NEGAT (Station US, in Washington D.C.) in breaking the Imperial Japanese Navy's JN-25(b) operational code. A message from CNO to CINCAF (Admiral Hart) reverses the negative decision of March 6, 1941 and grants Station CAST the lead responsibility in the Pacific for breaking JN-25(b).	In response to the vehement protestations of Station CAST, Safford agrees that CAST is better situated, geographically, to capture JN-25(b) transmissions, and he directs, "The project will not be transferred to COM-14 (HYPO) as previously planned."[175] CDR Safford drafted the message, which was released as an OPNAV message to CINCAF.[176] This decision was made more than one month prior to LCDR Rochefort reporting for duty as OIC of Station HYPO.
April 25, 1941	**President Roosevelt Dramatically Extends the U.S. "Neutrality Zone" Eastwards, into**	The announcement is cautiously worded, and Roosevelt has refused to publicly say whether this means the protection of shipping from attack, or what a U.S.

---

[174] Kershaw, *Fateful Choices,* 236.

[175] Carlson, *Joe Rochefort's War,* 120.

[176] Costello, *Days of Infamy,* 298, 410.

	the mid-Atlantic Ocean.	Naval patrol will do if it encounters an Axis vessel.[177] (At this point in time Roosevelt is adamantly **refusing** to protect merchant ship convoys with U.S. Navy escorts---that is, he will not yet authorize the "convoying" of British merchant ships by the U.S. Navy. However, by simply conducting these "neutrality patrols"---utilizing U.S. battleships, heavy cruisers, and destroyers---he hopes to discourage Axis vessels from entry into the waters specified to be within the zone, and thus to provide a safe area for British merchantmen in which they will not have to be heavily escorted by the overstretched British Navy before they reach the dangerous eastern half of the Atlantic Ocean.) **In the absence of specific written guidance from the President, Admiral Ernest J. King (Commander in Chief, Atlantic Fleet, or CINCLANT) directs U.S. vessels engaged in neutrality patrols to openly report, in the clear, the positions of all Axis vessels encountered (U-boats, surface raiders, and resupply ships) to the British Navy. King issues instructions to the Atlantic Fleet that say if the German Navy attacks any ships or territory under U.S. protection, these German units are to be captured or destroyed.**[178]
	FDR announces that the U.S. Navy will patrol much farther out in the Atlantic Ocean than it had formerly done, saying that this was necessary for the "protection of the American hemisphere." Earlier, FDR had secretly notified Churchill of this decision on April 11th, telling him that the U.S. "neutrality patrol" which had originally commenced on September 5, 1939 (out to 300 nautical miles beyond the coastline of all of the Americas south of Canada) would now be <u>dramatically expanded eastward</u>, from 60 degrees west longitude to 25 degrees west longitude, encompassing tens of thousands of square miles of additional ocean. (Twenty five degrees west longitude demarcated the midpoint between the west coast of Africa and the easternmost point of Brazil.)	
		During this period of apparent vacillation and shifting guidance from Roosevelt,

---

[177] Davis, *FDR: The War President,* 177.

[178] Buell, *Master of Sea Power,* 139-143.

		CNO Harold Stark wrote to a friend about his extreme frustration regarding the lack of specific instructions from the President about what to do in the event of specific situations that might develop between U.S. and German vessels on the high seas, knowing that with the war at sea raging between the British and German Navies, and with the U.S. "patrolling" an expanded "neutrality zone," <u>there were bound to be confrontations between American and German forces.</u> ***"To some of my very pointed questions"*** [to FDR], Stark wrote a friend in late July, ***"I get a smile or a <u>'Betty, please don't ask me that!'</u>"***[179]
April 27, 1941	**"Westward Look, The Land Is Bright"**[180] Churchill Radio Broadcast <u>There were so many negative developments in the war against Germany during the first several months of 1941 that this period became known as "Black Spring."</u> Not only did the Battle of the Atlantic take a decided turn for the worse against Great Britain, and not only did things go badly awry in Greece and Crete,	Churchill spent much of this speech talking about how he had just toured the many devastated areas of Great Britain, and reassuring his people that he understood their pain, and that his efforts would be worthy of their sacrifice. He then continued: **"During the last year we have gained, by our bearing and conduct a potent hold upon the sentiments of the people in the United States. Never, never in our history, have we been held in such admiration and regard across the Atlantic Ocean.** In that great Republic, now in much travail and stress of soul, it is customary to use all the many valid, solid arguments about American interests and American

---

[179] Ibid., 139.

[180] Churchill, ed., *Never Give In!,* 266-274.

but in North Africa, the major gains the British Army had made against the Italians in Libya between December 6, 1940 and February 7, 1941 had been reversed. Under General Irwin Rommel (who became known as "The Desert Fox"), a small German Panzer contingent (the Afrika Korps) originally inserted as a mere blocking move against the quick British advances over the Italian Army in Libya, went on the offensive, recaptured most of the 400 miles of coastal Libyan territory the British had taken from the Italians, and placed the British forces in the seaport of Tobruk under an extended siege. By the end of April, Rommel's six week offensive had pushed the British Army all the way back to the base from which its December offensive against the Italians had been launched, and was considered to be threatening the great British Naval base at Alexandria. Everywhere, Britain was on the

safety, which depend upon the destruction of Hitler and his foul gang and even fouler doctrines. ***But in the long run---believe me, for I know---the action of the United States will be dictated, not by methodical calculations of profit and loss, but by moral sentiment, and by that gleaming flash of resolve which lifts the hearts of men and nations, and springs from the spiritual foundations of human life itself…*** When I spoke to you last, early in February, many people believed the Nazi boastings that the invasion of Britain was about to begin. It has not begun yet, and with every week that passes, we grow stronger on the sea, in the air, and in the numbers, quality, training, and equipment of the great Armies that now guard our Island… **But how about our lifeline across the Atlantic? What is to happen if so many of our merchant ships are sunk that that we cannot bring in the food we need to nourish our brave people?** *What if the supplies of war materials and war weapons which the United States are seeking to send us in such enormous quantities should in large party be sunk on the way? What is to happen then?* In February, as you may remember, that Bad Man in one of his raving outbursts threatened us with a terrifying increase in the numbers and activities of his U-boats and in his air attack…upon our shipping far out into the Atlantic. We have taken and are taking all possible measures to meet this deadly attack, and we are now fighting against it with might and main.

	defensive in the spring of 1941.	That is what is called the Battle of the Atlantic, which in order to survive we have got to win on salt water just as decisively as we had to win the Battle of Britain last August and September in the air…
	In the Battle of the Atlantic, German U-boats had begun to use combined "wolf pack" tactics against convoys, and were taking advantage of a 1000-mile wide gap in the mid-Atlantic which the British could not defend adequately because of the Irish refusal to grant Great Britain the use of ports and airfields on its west coast. During the period February-April 1941, German U-boats sank 142 ships totaling 818,000 tons. The German battlecruisers *Scharnhorst* and *Gneisenau* sank or captured 22 ships totaling 122,000 tons; and the heavy cruiser *Hipper*, in the South Atlantic, sank 19 of 22 ships in one convoy bound for Sierra Leone.	**It was therefore with indescribable relief that I learned of the tremendous decisions lately taken by the President and people of the United States.** <u>The American Fleet and flying boats have been ordered to patrol the wide waters of the Western Hemisphere, and to warn the peaceful shipping of all nations outside the combat zone of the presence of lurking U-boats or raiding cruisers belonging to the two aggressor nations.</u> We British shall therefore be able to concentrate our protecting forces far more upon the routes nearer home, and to take a far heavier toll of the U-boats there. **I have felt for some time that something like this was bound to happen.** The President and Congress of the United States, having newly fortified themselves by contact with their electors, have solemnly pledged their aid to Great Britain in this war because they deem our cause just, and because they know their own interests and safety would be endangered if we were destroyed. They are taxing themselves heavily. They have passed great legislation. They have turned a large part of their gigantic industry to making the munitions which we need. They have even given us or lent us valuable weapons of our own. *I could not believe that they would allow the high purposes to which they have set*
	The Luftwaffe's night terror bombing of London and other cities continued when weather permitted, and the German Air Force began a frightening concentration upon the	

	port facilities in Portsmouth, Liverpool, Plymouth, Bristol, Hull, and the shipyards of the Clyde and the Mersey. In the Spring of 1941, the British were on the defensive everywhere, and were losing the war.[181]	***themselves be frustrated and the products of their skill and labour sunk to the bottom of the sea.*** U-boat warfare as conducted by Germany is entirely contrary to international agreements freely subscribed to by Germany only a few years ago…When I said ten weeks ago: 'Give us the tools and we will finish the job,' I meant, *give* them to us: put them within our reach, and that is what it now seems the Americans are going to do. And that is why I feel a very strong conviction that though the Battle of the Atlantic will be long and hard, and its issue is by no means yet determined, it has entered upon a more grim but at the same time a far more favourable phase. **When you come to think of it, the United States are very closely bound up with us now,** and have engaged themselves deeply in giving us moral,

---

[181] Davis, *FDR: The War President,* 147-152. As Davis wrote, Britain's "only hope of survival was a far more direct and energetic intervention in the struggle by the United States than had thus far obtained---at the very least, U.S. Naval vessels must provide escort for convoys---and the involvement must come very soon. **This meant that now as never before in history…the fate of Western democracy, indeed the very survival of Western civilization, depended upon the mental operations and decisive will of the President of the United States.** In part by pure accident, in part through the exercise of his own particular genius for locating and holding balance of power points, in part because Britain's increasingly desperate leaders insisted upon it, **Franklin Roosevelt had become the central pivotal figure of the whole free world.** Almost his every word, deed, gesture---his every act or refusal of action in response to a specific challenge---had worldwide consequence. Yet with the passage of Lend-Lease, which he himself has described as the death of isolationism, the birth of national unity, and the beginning of a redoubled national effort toward Nazi-fascism's destruction---an event that had therefore been expected to be followed by a burst of executive activity---there began instead what most knowledgeable observers saw as a strange, prolonged, exceedingly dangerous pause in Presidential leadership…". [Emphasis added] Davis expresses a strong opinion that FDR did fail to lead at this time, during "Black Spring," and that one of the causes was surely bad health: he suffered from a very serious, prolonged four-month respiratory ailment or "cold;" from a serious hemoglobin deficiency (his level was only one third of what it should have been); and diastolic hypertension. His Secretary, Missy LeHand, claimed his irritability and inactivity during this period sprang primarily from "sheer exasperation."

material, and, within the limits I have mentioned, Naval support...**No prudent and far-seeing man can doubt the eventual defeat of Hitler and Mussolini is certain, in view of the respective declared resolves of the British and American democracies.** There are less than seventy million malignant Huns...The peoples of the British Empire and the United States number nearly two hundred millions in their homelands and in the British Dominions alone. They possess the unchallengeable command of the oceans, and will soon obtain decisive superiority in the air. **They have more wealth, more technical resources, and they make more steel, than the whole rest of the world put together.** They are determined that the cause of freedom shall not be trampled down, nor the tide of world progress turned backwards, by the criminal Dictators.

While therefore we naturally view with sorrow and anxiety much that is happening in Europe and Africa, **and may happen in Asia,** we must not lose our sense of proportion and thus become discouraged or alarmed...Nothing that is happening now is comparable in gravity to the dangers through which we passed last year...**Nothing that can happen in the East is comparable with what is happening in the West.**

Last time I spoke to you I quoted the lines of Longfellow which President Roosevelt had written out for me in his own hand. I have some other lines which are less well known but which seem apt and appropriate to our fortunes tonight, and I believe they will be so judged wherever the English language is spoken or the flag of freedom flies:

For while the tired waves, vainly breaking, seem here no painful inch to gain, Far back, through creeks and inlets making, Comes silent, flooding in, the main. <u>And not by eastern windows only, When daylight comes, comes in the light; In front the sun climbs slow, how slowly! But westward, look, the land is bright</u>." [Emphasis added]

Churchill very much needed to give his people a pep-talk, and a sense of perspective, in the midst of the "Black Spring" of 1941. He did so primarily by focusing on the increasingly close ties with the President and people of the United States. (In retrospect, much of this speech appears to be a love poem aimed at an audience of one: Franklin Roosevelt.) His near exuberance at Roosevelt's decision, just two days prior, to extend U.S. military patrols far out into the mid-Atlantic was almost unseemly, for clearly (in his own mind) Churchill could now see the high likelihood that the United States would be dragged into the shooting war, and become a belligerent, and openly enter hostilities. He was still playing the role of the ardent suitor, and had reason to believe that he and his paramour would soon be united in common cause, but was soon to learn that the object of his desire ---Franklin D. Roosevelt---while responsive to his advances, was still

		playing "hard to get," for FDR was still bedeviled by a very strong isolationist movement which was extremely suspicious of what it correctly perceived were Roosevelt's intentions to move the United States closer and closer to belligerency. **Roosevelt was proceeding in the direction his suitor desired, but was doing so intuitively and incrementally, one step at a time, so as not to get out too far ahead of public opinion.**
May 13, 1941	**FDR orders the three battleships previously directed to depart Pearl Harbor in April, to physically move.**	USS *Idaho,* USS *New Mexico,* and USS *Mississippi* depart secretly without fanfare (in the midst of local exercises), and transit the Panama Canal at night. The four light cruisers directed to depart in April, and thirteen additional destroyers, move with them. The hope was that Japan would not immediately notice the transfer of the battleships, but its agents in the Canal Zone did. These three battleships had been extensively modernized with new turbines, gunfire control systems, and additional armor.[182]
May 27, 1941	*President Roosevelt declares an* **"Unlimited National Emergency"** **FDR delivers a fireside chat on the evening of the day that the British Navy sank the German battleship Bismarck---**	President Roosevelt spent much of the first half of this fireside chat giving the American people a heavy dose of bad news, telling them in graphic detail exactly how onerous an Axis victory in Europe would be. Excerpts follow: "…The first and fundamental fact is that what started as a European war has

---

[182] Heinrichs, *Threshold of War,* 40 and 73.

his first major foreign policy address since his "Arsenal of Democracy" speech on December 29, 1940---and declares an **"Unlimited National Emergency."** The speech had originally been scheduled for delivery on May 14th, but was postponed due to Roosevelt's bad health.

The backdrop for the speech was the bad war news that spring: British reverses in North Africa; the quick German conquest of both Yugoslavia and Greece; and most especially, the tremendous losses of British merchant ships in the Atlantic (including Lend-Lease material) to German U-boats, surface raiders, and aircraft.

Prior to the speech many of Roosevelt's inner circle---Frank Knox, Admiral Stark, Henry Stimson, Henry Morgenthau, and Harry Hopkins---had all favored aggressive American action against the German Navy in the Atlantic. <u>Stimson wrote a strong letter to FDR in late May</u>

developed, as the Nazis always intended it should develop, into a war for world domination…It is unmistakably apparent to all of us that, unless the advance of Hitlerism is forcibly checked now, the Western Hemisphere will be within range of the Nazi weapons of destruction. For our own defense we have accordingly undertaken certain obvious necessary measures…a year ago, we launched, and are successfully carrying out, the largest armament production program we have ever undertaken. We have added substantially to our splendid Navy, and we have mustered our manpower to build up a new Army, which is already worthy of the highest traditions of the military service. We instituted a policy of aid for the democracies---the nations which have fought for the continuation of human liberties…

In June 1940, Britain stood alone, faced by the same machine of terror that had overwhelmed her allies. Our government rushed arms to meet her desperate needs.

In September 1940, an agreement was completed with Great Britain for the trade of 50 destroyers for eight important offshore bases.

And in March 1941, this year, the Congress passed the Lend-Lease bill and an appropriation of $7 billion to implement it. This law realistically provided for material aid 'for the government of any country whose defense the President deems vital to the defense of the United States.'

recommending that the U.S. Navy convoy Lend-Lease materiel to Britain. Morgenthau had recommended that the President declare war on Germany.

The President's inner circle in Washington had for many weeks, ever since the passage of Lend-Lease, decried amongst themselves the apparent "malaise" he had exhibited in April and May as he struggled with the decision about whether or not to convoy British Lend-Lease goods with U.S. Navy warships. In April he seemed to approve of the Navy's plans to escort ships, then backed off. His view, according to Morgenthau, was "that public opinion was not yet ready for the United States to convoy ships." Despite pressure from Cabinet hawks---Stimson, Knox, Morgenthau, and Ickes---FDR continued to resist their advice to convoy. Instead, he only extended the boundaries of the U.S. security zone on April 25th. By mid-May, concern about his extreme

Our whole program of aid for the democracies has been based on hard-headed concern for our own security and for the kind of safe and civilized world in which we wish to live. Every dollar of material that we send helps keep the dictators away from our hemisphere, and every day that they are held off gives us time to build more guns and tanks and planes and ships…

…We have doubled and redoubled our vast production, increasing, month by month, our material supply of the tools of war for ourselves and for Britain and China---and eventually for all the democracies. The supply of these tools will not fail---it will increase...

Your government knows what terms Hitler, if victorious, would impose…And, under those terms, Germany would literally parcel out the world---hoisting the swastika itself over vast territories and populations, and setting up puppet governments of its own choosing, wholly subject to the will and the policy of a conqueror."

FDR then went on to describe in some detail the techniques that would be employed by a victorious Germany to subvert nations in the Western Hemisphere, and to strangle the American and Canadian economies. He then decried the moral values that would be dominant in a Nazi dominated hemisphere. Continuing, he said:

"…Today, the Nazis have taken military possession of the greater part of Europe.

caution with regard to the war amongst his inner circle was such that Stimson, Knox, and Attorney General Jackson met with Ickes and considered (but did not send) "some written representation to the President that we are experiencing a failure of leadership that bodes ill for the country," and further stating that "the country was tired of words and wanted deeds."

In retrospect it is clear that the country was more than happy at this juncture with just "words," and that it was the inner circle of avid interventionists who wanted "deeds."

Both senior officials in the administration, and the general public, assumed that FDR's declaration of an "unlimited national emergency," in the context of the strong closing to his speech, meant that the U.S. Navy would immediately commence convoying Lend-Lease goods to Britain; therefore, when

In Africa they have occupied Tripoli and Libya, and they are threatening Egypt, the Suez Canal, and the Near East…They also have the armed power at any moment to occupy Spain and Portugal; and that threat extends not only to French North Africa and the western end of the Mediterranean Sea, but it extends also to the Atlantic fortress of Dakar, and to the island outposts of the New World---the Azores and Cape Verde Islands. Yes, these Cape Verde Islands are only seven hours' distance from Brazil by bomber or troop-carrying planes. They dominate shipping routes to and from the South Atlantic.

The war is approaching the brink of the Western Hemisphere itself. It is coming very close to home. Control or occupation by Nazi forces of any of the islands of the Atlantic would jeopardize the immediate safety of portions of North and South America, and of the island possessions of the United States, and therefore, of the ultimate safety of the continental Unites States itself.

Hitler's plan of world domination would be near its accomplishment today, were it not for two factors. One is the epic resistance of Britain, her colonies, and the great dominions, fighting not only to maintain the existence of the Island of Britain, but also to hold the Near East and Africa. The other is the magnificent defense of China, which will, I have reason to believe, increase in strength. And all of these, together, are preventing the Axis from winning control of the seas

FDR appeared to "back off" this implied promise the very next day at a press conference, Americans were stunned: universally confused, and in many cases, disappointed.[183]

Part of the explanation for what FDR was doing lies in the public opinion polling at the time, and FDR's fervent desire *not* to lead a *sharply divided* (or unprepared) nation into war. **A public opinion poll taken the day after this fireside chat** revealed the following:

In favor of getting into the war "if no other way to win:" 75%

Believe we will eventually get in: 80%

Against getting into the war now: 82%

In addition, Army Chief of Staff General George C. Marshall provided FDR with the following **combat readiness report** immediately after the speech, effective June 1,

by ships and aircraft. **The Axis powers can never achieve their objective of world domination unless they first obtain control of the seas. That is their supreme purpose today; and to achieve it, they must capture Great Britain.**

They could then have the power to dictate to the Western Hemisphere. No spurious argument, no appeal to sentiment, no false pledges like those given by Hitler at Munich, can deceive the American people into believing that he and his Axis partners, would not, with Britain defeated, close in relentlessly on this hemisphere of ours.

But if the Axis powers fail to gain control of the seas, then they are certainly defeated. Their dreams of world domination will then go by the board; and the criminal leaders who started this war will suffer inevitable disaster. Both they and their people know this…That is why they are risking everything they have, conducting desperate attempts to break through to the command of the ocean…All freedom…depends on freedom of the seas…

The Battle of the Atlantic now extends from the icy waters of the North Pole to the frozen continent of the Antarctic. Throughout this huge area, there have been sinkings of merchant ships in alarming and increasing numbers by Nazi raiders or submarines…**The blunt truth**

---

[183] Buhite and Levy, ed., *FDR's Fireside Chats,* 174-187; and Davis, *FDR: The War President,* 183-193.

	1941:	seems to be this---and I reveal this with **the full knowledge of the British government: the present rate of Nazi sinkings of merchant ships is more than three times as high as the capacity of British shipyards to replace them; it is more than twice the combined British and American output of merchant ships today.**
	Readiness of Army ground forces: **13%**	
	Readiness of Army Air Corps: **0%**	
	In my view, the many historians who have criticized Roosevelt in the Spring of 1941 for "having no policy" or "refusing to lead," or who have claimed that his policy "was to have no policy," have unfairly criticized FDR, using "20-20 hindsight." <u>He did not request Congress to declare war on Germany</u>, *or initiate convoying,* in May of 1941 because an	<u>We can answer this peril by two simultaneous measures</u>: first, by speeding up and increasing our own great shipbuilding program; **and second, by helping to cut down the losses on the high seas.** Attacks on shipping off the very shores of land which we are determined to protect present an actual military danger to the Americas. And that danger has recently been heavily underlined *by the presence in Western Hemisphere waters of a Nazi battleship of great striking power.* [184]

---

[184] See *The Destruction of the Bismarck,* by Bercuson and Herwig. What was then the world's largest and most powerful battleship, the *Bismarck* (accompanied by heavy cruiser *Prinz Eugen*), had just days before FDR's speech escaped from a Norwegian fjord and broken out into the north Atlantic on a commerce-raiding mission. On the morning of May 24th, in a sharp engagement in the Denmark Strait (between Greenland and Iceland), *Bismarck* destroyed the revered British battlecruiser HMS *Hood* (the largest and most famous ship in the Royal Navy), whose aft *and* forward powder magazines dramatically blew up, killing all aboard save three souls---and damaged the new battleship HMS *Prince of Wales.* That same evening, the tiny and aged U.S. Coast Guard cutter *Modoc,* engaged in Neutrality Patrol duties, literally almost ran into *Bismarck,* sighting it at a distance of only 6 nautical miles. Shortly after this sighting occurred, obsolescent British Swordfish torpedo planes, launched from the carrier HMS *Victorious,* **formed up over USS *Modoc,* before flying on to attack the Bismarck.** (Whether *Modoc* actively assisted in helping to direct the British attackers, or simply served as a convenient assembly point, is unclear.) The crew of the *Modoc* then witnessed the display of pyrotechnics in the night sky as *Bismarck* fought off its attackers with antiaircraft fire. *Modoc* was fortunate; she had bravely challenged *Bismarck* by flashing light---and had surely reported its position to the British Navy as directed in Admiral King's standing orders---but the German battleship, being pursued by *Prince of Wales* and two cruisers at the time, chose to ignore the tiny American ship, rather than sink it. (FDR was thus almost presented with the *casus belli* he desired on May 24, 1941.) After escaping from the British Fleet, *Bismarck* was rediscovered

overwhelming majority of the country did not want to go to war---and also because the U.S. Army, hampered by rapid expansion, incomplete training, and materiel shortages, was still woefully unprepared for combat.

What he did was alert the nation to the danger posed by the dictator powers in more graphic terms than ever before; declare his intent not to relinquish control of the seas under any circumstances; *and psychologically prepare the nation for the high likelihood of future belligerency with the stirring closing to his peroration.* Given that FDR was trying to mold and unite public opinion, and not hopelessly fracture it, this is all he felt he could prudently do

You remember that most of the supplies for Britain go by a northerly route, which comes close to Greenland and the nearby island of Iceland. Germany's heaviest attack is on that route. Nazi occupation of Iceland or bases in Greenland would bring the war close to our own continental shores, because those places are stepping stones to Labrador, to Newfoundland, to Nova Scotia, yes, to the northern United States itself…

We have accordingly, extended our patrol in North and South Atlantic waters. We are steadily adding more and more ships and planes to that patrol. It is well known that the strength of the Atlantic Fleet has been greatly increased during the past year, and that it is constantly being built up. These ships and planes warn of the presence of attacking raiders, on the sea, under the sea, and above the sea. The dangers from these raiders is, of course, greatly lessened if their location is definitely known. And we are thus being forewarned…

Our national policy today, therefore is this:

First, we shall actively resist wherever necessary, and with all our resources,

---

on May 26th by an American-built PBY Catalina flying boat in the service of the RAF (with an American Naval officer serving as co-pilot of the aircraft). Subsequently, the Royal Navy---expending all of its available resources in a desperate chase---finally trapped *Bismarck* and sank her on May 27th, the very day of FDR's speech. The incident was a dramatic example of the very real dangers that Roosevelt was discussing, and the facts about *Modoc* and the PBY (which were then unknown to the American public) were illustrative of the very close working relationship that had grown up between the American and British Navies since the summer of 1940.

at the time.

<u>Another highly likely reason that FDR did not commence convoying Lend-Lease goods in the spring of 1941 is because he had advance, reliable intelligence that Hitler was going to invade the Soviet Union</u>. Roosevelt was surely loath to commence convoying in the spring, because if the convoying decision itself (or the inevitable hostile "incidents" which were bound to occur between U.S. Navy ships and U-boats) had triggered war between the United States and Germany, that may have delayed or even cancelled the planned German invasion of the USSR. Roosevelt knew that to a large extent, the outcome of Germany's forthcoming invasion of Russia would probably determine the outcome of the war. Aware that Hitler might be about to make his first big mistake of the war, and take on more than Germany could handle by invading the USSR, he was not about to take any major action that might delay or

every attempt by Hitler to extend his Nazi domination to the Western Hemisphere, or to threaten it. *We shall actively resist his every attempt to gain control of the seas…*

Secondly, from the point of view of strict military and naval necessity, we shall give every possible assistance to Britain and to all who, with Britain, are resisting Hitlerism or its equivalent with force of arms. *Our patrols are helping now to ensure delivery of the needed supplies to Britain.* **<u>All additional measures necessary to deliver the goods will be taken</u>…I say that the delivery of needed supplies to Britain is imperative. I say this can be done; it must be done; and it will be done…**

Today the whole world is divided, divided between human slavery and human freedom---between the pagan brutality and the Christian ideal. None of us can waver for a moment in his courage or his faith. We will not accept a Hitler-dominated world. And we will not accept a world, like the postwar world of the 1920s, in which the seeds of Hitlerism can again be planted and allowed to grow. We will only accept a world consecrated to freedom of speech and expression, freedom of every person to worship God in his own way, freedom from want, and freedom from terror…Our people and our government will not hesitate to meet that challenge.

<u>As President of a united and</u>

	change that key Hitler decision. Hence, in spite of his "unlimited national emergency" declaration, he would not yet commence convoying in the Atlantic. He could not share this thinking with the public, of course, anymore than he could share the true state of American unpreparedness for war. So the inevitable result of the "no convoying" clarification the day after his speech was confusion and disappointment in the minds of interventionists, and among the hawks in his Cabinet. Since Hitler went ahead and invaded the USSR on June 22, 1941, and since the Battle of the Atlantic was *not* lost, the verdict of history is clearly that FDR **did not err** by postponing the convoy decision until mid-September.	**determined people, I say solemnly:** *We reassert the ancient American doctrine of freedom of the seas.* *We reassert the solidarity of the twenty-one American Republics and the Dominion of Canada in the preservation of the independence of this hemisphere.* *We have pledged material support to the other democracies of the world---and we will fulfill that pledge.* *We in the Americas will decide for ourselves whether, and when, and where, our American interests are attacked or our security threatened.* *We are placing our armed forces in strategic military position.* *We will not hesitate to use our armed forces to repel attack.* **Therefore, with profound consciousness of my responsibilities to my countrymen and to my country's cause, I have tonight issued a proclamation that an unlimited national emergency exists and requires the strengthening of our defense to the extreme limit of our national power and authority."** [Emphasis added]
June 2, 1941	LCDR Joseph J. Rochefort reports to COM-14 (Commandant, Fourteenth Naval District) in Pearl Harbor, as	As part of a deal Rochefort made prior to his posting with CDR Laurance Safford (OP-20-G), who recruited him, the Navy's best available cryptanalysts and Japanese linguists were henceforth

Officer-in-Charge of what soon became known as the "Combat Intelligence Unit" (the public cover name for Pearl Harbor's highly classified Naval codebreaking unit), which was known only in high official circles as Station HYPO. He immediately begins transforming what had been a research establishment since it was founded in 1936, into an operational unit---whose goal was "to predict today what the Japanese Navy would do tomorrow." Rochefort had been passed-over (denied promotion) by a selection board in December of 1939, but was finally promoted to Commander on October 13, 1941---retroactive to April 1st.

By prior arrangement with OP-20-G, Rochefort's HYPO remained under the administrative control of COM-14 (ADM Bloch), and was technically under the operational control of OP-20-G (CDR Safford) in Washington; but Rochefort was granted *cart blanche* by Safford to report all radio routed to Station HYPO. Joe Rochefort, who loved sea duty and who initially resisted the assignment, filled the hybrid role of cryptanalyst-linguist-analyst. When he arrived as OIC at HYPO, the station's primary task had aleady been defined by Washington: break the Flag Officer's Code for the Imperial Japanese Navy. Numerous JN-25(b) intercepts in raw form came into HYPO on a daily basis from Station "H" in Heeia, near Kaneohe on the windward side of Oahu; but the "cryppies" and linguists at HYPO were not allowed to attempt decryption. After gathering the "externals" of those messages (headers and call signs) each day for radio traffic analysis, the raw, still coded Japanese messages were bundled up and sent on to Station NEGAT in Washington, D.C.---by either Pan Am clipper, or by ship. The intercepted but unbroken JN-25(b) traffic was sometimes one month old by the time it reached Station NEGAT. Although unable to break the Flag Officer's Code, Rochefort's staff, aided by its IBM collators and tabulating machines, became adept at radio traffic analysis, the revelation of call signs and naval organization, and occasionally of naval movements. While cryptanalysis was deductive and predictive, traffic analysis was inferential. Since the Flag Officer's Code could not be broken, HYPO's daily intelligence summary sent to CINCPAC (ADM Kimmel) was based almost entirely on radio traffic analysis, and at this time, was somewhat limited in the hard information it could provide.

	intelligence directly to CINCPAC (ADM Kimmel).	These reports were useful in reporting what had been happening to Japanese fleet organization, but were not good predictors of future events.
June 6, 1941	**MAGIC** intercept: Berlin to Tokyo, sent June 4th	The American leadership learns that Baron Oshima told the Foreign Minister in Tokyo on June 4th that the German Army was an "irresistible force" capable of an "annihilating movement against the Red Army." Ribbentrop had strongly hinted at the coming war between Germany and the USSR, saying that in terms of the war against Britain, it was "imperative that the Soviet Union be beaten down now." Oshima told Tokyo that both Hitler and Ribbentrop had told him, as a matter of "gravest secrecy," that in all probability war with the USSR could not be avoided.[185]
June 7, 1941	The government of the Dutch East Indies (in Batavia) terminates its protracted negotiations with Japan over Japan's demands for huge amounts of oil, politely but firmly refusing to grant the concessions Japan had been demanding.[186]	**This was action item G in the eight-point memo written on October 7, 1940 by Commander Arthur McCollum.** *With this refusal, Japan's only major source of oil (in a peacetime environment) remains the United States.*
June 10, 1941	FDR sends a Message to Congress on the Operations of the Lend-	Some key excerpts from this written message to Congress are provided below: "In June of 1940, the British government

---

[185] Heinrichs, *Threshold of War,* 93-94.

[186] Ibid., 98.

Lease Act. The language of the Lend-Lease Act required the President to report on his activities in relation to the Act to the Congress at least once every 90 days.	received from our surplus stocks rifles, machine guns, field artillery, ammunition, and aircraft in a value of more than $43 million. This was equipment that would have taken months and months to produce and which, with the exception of the aircraft, cost about $300 million to produce during the World War [One] period. Most of this material would not have been useable if we had kept it much longer. This equipment arrived in Britain after the retreat from Dunkirk, where the British had lost great quantities of guns and other military supplies… Since June 1940, this government has continued to supply war materiel from its surplus stocks, in addition to the material produced by private manufacturers. The fifty overage destroyers which Britain received in exchange for the defense bases were a part of the aid supplied by the government. By the turn of the year 1941, the British commitments in this country for defense articles had reached the limit of their future dollar resources…The will of our people, as expressed by the Congress, was to meet this problem, not only by the passage of the Lend-Lease Act but by the appropriation of $7 billion made on March 27 of this year to carry out this task. In the ninety days since the Lend-Lease Act was passed, and in the seventy-four days since the funds were appropriated, we have started in motion the vast supply program which is

essential to defeat of the Axis powers.

In these seventy-four days, more than $4.25 billion out of the $7 billion have been allocated to the War, Navy, Agriculture, and Treasury departments and to the Maritime Commission to procure the aid authorized. Contracts have been let for long-range bombers, ships, tanks, and the other sinews of war that will be needed for the defense of the democracies. The balance of less than $2.75 billion is being rapidly allocated.

To be effective, the aid rendered by us must be many-sided. Ships are necessary to carry the munitions and the food. We are immediately making available to Britain two million gross tons of cargo ships and oil tankers. But this is not enough…Since the Appropriation Act was passed, $550 million has been allocated for the construction of new ships under the Lend-Lease Act. Contracts have been let and the new ways required to build these ships are now nearing completion. Allied ships are being repaired by us…Naval vessels of Britain are being repaired by us so that they can return quickly to their naval tasks.

The training program of seven thousand British pilots in our schools in this country is underway…

With our national resources, our productive capacity, and the genius of our people for mass production we will help Britain to outstrip the Axis powers in munitions of war, and we will see to it

		that these munitions get to the places where they can be effectively used to weaken and defeat the aggressors…".[187] A detailed statistical report was appended.
June 14-16, 1941	**FDR freezes all German and Italian assets in the United States, and closes all German consulates.**	Roosevelt issued an Executive Order on June 14th freezing the American assets of Germany, Italy, occupied European countries, and even neutrals, including the Soviet Union (which at this time was still a silent partner of Germany).[188] On June 16th he ordered all German consulates and agencies in the United States closed. The symbolism was clear: the United States had done everything it could diplomatically to show its displeasure with Nazi Germany, short of declaring war.
June 16, 1941	**MAGIC** intercept: Berlin to Tokyo, sent June 14th	Baron Oshima points out that Hitler had given him advance warning of both the Norway and Western European offensives in 1940, and that therefore his word can be counted on regarding the "apparently imminent" German surprise attack on the Soviet Union. Oshima reported that all signs pointed to war: the Rumanian Army had mobilized; Hitler had returned to Berlin; and the Chief of Staff of the Armed Forces and the Commander in Chief of the Army had left for the eastern front.[189]

---

[187] Hunt, ed., *The Essential Franklin Delano Roosevelt,* 216-219

[188] Heinrichs, *Threshold of War,* 95.

[189] Ibid., 94.

June 17, 1941	**MAGIC** intercept: Tokyo to Vichy, sent June 16th	Tokyo informs its representative in Vichy France that Japan was seeking German help in forcing the Vichy government to grant it sea and air bases in southern Indochina. These included (according to a June 19th decrypt of another message sent on June 17th): Cam Ranh Bay, Hue, Nhatrang, Sactrang, Kompontrach, Siemriep, and Pnompenh.[190]
June 21, 1941	Hitler issues orders that all German naval vessels in the Atlantic *are forbidden to fire on American ships, <u>even in self-defense</u>.*	"Hitler knew what Roosevelt wanted: an incident in the Atlantic that would enable him to go to Congress with a message of war. He would not give Roosevelt that opportunity."[191] **What Hitler did not realize was that FDR had known since January 1941 of his plans to invade the Soviet Union (see below) and that Roosevelt, while definitely planning to enter the war against him after he could unite the American people (i.e., "when the moment seemed right"), <u>was not going to do this until AFTER the Nazi dictator had committed all of his forces to the attack on the USSR</u>. FDR and Hitler were both playing a waiting game with each other, and Roosevelt, the Fox, had won out.**
June 22, 1941	**Germany Invades the Soviet Union.** The most incredible thing about this event is that	The German Armed Forces launched the biggest offensive in world history across a front about 500 miles wide, extending from the Baltic Sea in the north, to the Carpathian Mountains in the south.

---

[190] Ibid., 98.

[191] Lukacs, *The Duel,* 216.

advance intelligence of it, from numerous sources, was both received and confirmed; Stalin, the Soviet dictator, was warned about it by both Roosevelt and Churchill (as well as by his own spy in Tokyo, Richard Sorge); and yet he chose not to believe the intelligence. Stalin was not only a butcher, therefore, but also a bungler.[192]

Advance intelligence was sent to the United States by the commercial attaché at the U.S. embassy in Berlin, Sam Woods, from a well-connected former German government official (Dr. Erwin Respondek) who was strongly anti-Nazi in orientation---who handed him two key analytical reports, on January 3rd, and February 19th, at a movie theater in Berlin! Both reports indicated that Hitler had two military goals in 1941: the invasion of Great Britain, and the conquest of the USSR. (The January report stated Britain

Three Army Groups ate into the vitals of the Soviet Union: Army Group North (which reached and encircled Leningrad, beginning a 900 day siege); Army Group Center (which penetrated close to Moscow's outer suburbs in December of 1941 before being halted by winter weather, Soviet reinforcements, and lack of supplies); and Army Group South (which later, in late 1942 and 1943, blunted itself at Stalingrad). But initially, Hitler and his generals were determined to avoid getting lost within the vast spaces of Russia and not to get bogged down in a war of attrition. Since most of the Red Army was massed at the USSR's western borders, the initial German plans were to drive armored wedges between the Soviet lines, and then encircle and crush the Soviet armies within about 300 miles of the border, within easy reach of the German supply system---classic Blitzkrieg warfare. (Like Yamamoto in Japan, Hitler hoped that massive initial defeats would cause his enemy to give up the fight, and break his will, so that there would be no spirit to continue a long war.) Summarizing, the initial goal of these Army groups was to destroy the Red Army as an effective fighting force and thereby force the collapse of the Soviet government. The original German timetable was to destroy or defeat the Red Army by August 15th, and complete the occupation of European Russia by September 30th. When the Soviet Union survived the initial political

---

[192] Davis, *The War President,* 214-216; and Heinrichs, *Threshold of War,* 23-25.

would come first in the spring, followed by the Soviet Union in the summer. The February report emphasized preparations in the East, but failed to reveal that Hitler had set aside the invasion of Great Britain until he had completed the land war in Europe.) Swedish diplomatic reports early in 1941 were more definitive: at the end of February the Swedish minister in Moscow told the American Ambassador to the USSR that if the German submarine campaign failed to subdue Great Britain by March or April, that Germany would turn on Russia. (None of these intelligence sources knew that Hitler had committed Germany to an invasion of the Soviet Union with the issuance of the final directive for "Operation Barbarossa" on December 18, 1940, thus formalizing his unconditional decision to invade Russia and the Ukraine in mid-May of 1941.) Subsequent intelligence reports from

and military shocks---and did not capitulate or disintegrate---Leningrad and Moscow became political objectives designed to break the morale of the Soviet people if and when they fell; and of course, the Caucasus oil fields in the south became an imperative logistical goal, if Hitler was to support an extended war of attrition in the USSR (for which he did not initially plan).[193]

The initial planning goal of the German General Staff was to ultimately absorb territory as far east as a line about 2,000 miles long, running from north to south: from Archangel on the White Sea, to the Caspian Sea east of the Volga river---a line <u>about 1,200 miles east of the starting point for the invasion</u>. By December of 1941, the high watermark of his invasion, <u>Hitler's armies had penetrated about 600 miles into the USSR</u>---halfway to its ultimate objective---before logistical difficulties, unusually harsh winter weather, and massive Soviet reinforcements from Siberia halted them. Leningrad was then nearly encircled and under siege in the north, and the German Army was near the outskirts of Moscow, the Soviet capital. The front, at this point, was nearly 1,200 miles long, from north to south.

In their planning beforehand, the German estimates were that they would be attacking the Soviet Union with about 149 divisions of their own, against an estimated 200 Soviet divisions; they

---

[193] Heinrichs, *Threshold of War,* 13-15.

all over Europe (and especially from Eastern Europe) confirmed the movement of large numbers of German troops to the Russian frontier, and the accumulation of huge stockpiles of war materiel near the border with the Soviet Union. Finally, London and Washington came to jointly believe in the inevitability of a German attack on the Soviet Union in the late spring or early summer of 1941. Accordingly, FDR directed the State Department to provide the USSR with advance warning, and Sumner Welles did so by briefing Soviet Ambassador to the United States, Constantine Oumansky, on March 20th. The British Ambassador to the USSR, Sir Stafford	knew their roughly 3,350 tanks would be opposed by as many as 10,000; and that the Soviet Union had many more airplanes than the Luftwaffe.[194] Normally, nations do not dare to attack when the strength of the defender is superior in numbers, since under most circumstances, an advantage of 4 (or 5) to 1 is necessary to overcome a good defense. However, the Red Army had put in a dismal performance against little Finland from November 30, 1939 until the end of its "Winter War" on March 13, 1940,[195] which made the German General Staff supremely confident about its chances against even the numerically superior Soviet forces. The German Army was counting on superior training, superior leadership, superior soldiers and machines, and the element of surprise to achieve a quick victory before the onset of winter. Stalin had most of the Red Army and Air Force massed on his western borders when Germany launched its invasion, which made it possible for the German Army to encircle and destroy entire Soviet armies at the outset, and which similarly allowed much of the numerically superior Red Air Force to be

---

[194] Historian Waldo Heinrichs writes in *Threshold of War* (p. 13) that Germany had gathered seventy-five per cent of its army, about 3.3 million men, in 142 divisions, on its eastern front when the invasion began.

[195] Stalin's bloody purge of the Red Army's officer corps in 1937, in which 30,000 officers were either imprisoned or shot, had a terrible effect upon Red Army performance in the Russo-Finnish war. As a result, Finland held out much longer than the world expected against overwhelming Soviet numerical superiority, and the USSR failed in its goal to completely occupy that country. Finland ceded 11% of its territory to the Soviet Union, and 30% of its economic resources. The reputation of the Red Army suffered terribly as a result.

Cripps, after an unconscionable delay of one week, finally delivered a terse three-sentence warning of the invasion (drafted personally by Churchill) to the Soviet Deputy Foreign Minister on April 19th. (He failed to deliver it personally to Stalin, as Churchill directed him to.)

Perhaps most remarkable was that Soviet spy Richard Sorge in Tokyo (because of his personal access to the German ambassador to Japan) had actually provided the Soviet government with the modified invasion date of June 22nd---and yet Stalin was still caught with his pants down around his ankles. (The Yugoslavian Crisis and Hitler's Balkan campaign had indeed postponed the invasion, from May 15th to June 22nd.)

What *is known* is that Stalin, immobilized by shock, suffered a nervous breakdown of sorts for eight days following the invasion, and retired incommunicado to his destroyed on the ground.

Roosevelt and Churchill were both aware, from a variety of sources, of the impending Nazi onslaught for many months; their attempts to warn Stalin were fruitless, possibly because he was planning his own pre-emptive assault on Nazi Germany's eastern possessions, and felt supremely confident due to the huge numbers of his own troops and aircraft massed on the USSR's western borders. In particular, Stalin may have viewed the Roosevelt and Churchill warnings as an all-too-obvious ploy by the informal Anglo-American alliance to save a desperate England from an imminent German invasion---***by fomenting war between Germany and the Soviet Union.*** Furthermore, Churchill's lifelong fervent opposition to Bolshevism may also have made it inevitable that a paranoid personality like Stalin would ignore, and indeed discount, any such warning delivered by either the old Conservative politician, or his American ally. Hitler's renewed night bombing of British cities, seaports, and centers of industry---commencing late in February and concluding only on May 10-11, 1941 with the biggest-ever night raid on London---may have convinced Stalin that defeating Great Britain was still Hitler's main priority, and that the British and American warnings of an imminent invasion of the USSR were simply a desperate (and transparent) attempt to prevent, instead, an imminent invasion of England, by starting a war between

villa in suburban Moscow while the Soviet Union remained rudderless throughout the first week of the invasion, and came close to total political collapse.

The USSR also came close to total *military* collapse. More than 3,000,000 superbly led German troops, armed with 3,350 tanks, about 2,770 airplanes, 7,200 artillery pieces, and supported by 600,000 motorized vehicles and 625,000 draft horses---thanks to the political and military incompetence of Joseph Stalin---initiated a massive, successful surprise attack against a numerically superior force, and were everywhere routing it. The Red Air Force lost over 2,000 planes in the first two days of the invasion. Aside from the strategic surprise which was improbably achieved, the Red Army was hampered by inept tactical and strategic leadership, as a result of Stalin's

Germany and the USSR.

Some historians have claimed that Hitler's invasion was a "pre-emptive" war that had to be launched because of Stalin's purported plans to invade Western Europe;[196] and yet the record reveals that Hitler directed the planning for his invasion of the USSR to begin as early as July 31, 1940. Whether or not Stalin was planning a major offensive in the West was immaterial in a way, for Hitler was extremely worried that if he became embroiled in a messy and problematic cross-channel invasion of England, that Stalin would then opportunistically seize Germany's only major source of oil---Ploesti, in Rumania---which in 1941 was only about 100 miles away from the Red Army. And in any case, Adolph Hitler had long planned a war of annihilation in European Russia and the Ukraine, in order to secure "lebensraum" for the German Reich. For this reason, starting a two-front war did most certainly *not* seem to Hitler to be the utter madness that it appeared to be to more conventionally-oriented Western military minds.

Most mainstream historians have concluded---incorrectly---that FDR had "no policy" or "a policy of drifting into war" in the Spring of 1941, and that for this reason he demonstrated vacillation, and even ambivalence, over the convoying issue in April and

---

[196] Most notably, Victor Suvorov, in *The Chief Culprit: Stalin's Grand Design to Start World War II.*

bloody purges of his officer corps in the late 1930s.

By the end of the war in 1945, the Russian people had suffered horribly, as no other people ever had, losing approximately 27 million killed overall, in Germany's ruthless war of extermination against the Slavs, whom Hitler and Nazi doctrine considered to be subhuman.

Of course, in the end, Hitler's invasion of the USSR proved to be his undoing at a time when he was clearly winning World War II. The Soviet Union proved to offer the same insurmountable obstacles to Hitler from 1941 to1944, that Russia did to Napoleon in 1812 and 1813. Germany, in the end, did not have enough soldiers to conquer the Soviet Union; and like Napoleon, could not adequately supply its army over the vast expanse of captured Russian territory. Additionally, Germany could not build enough tanks or airplanes to

May of 1941. I believe these critics have all missed the boat. FDR knew that the commencement of convoying might well prompt an immediate German declaration of war on the United States for policy reasons; or that a German declaration of war against America might well have been stimulated by the inevitable military "incidents" that were bound to occur between U.S. convoy escorts on the one hand, and German submarines and surface raiders on the other, as soon as convoying began. <u>**It was very much in the self-interest of the United States, FDR clearly concluded, NOT to precipitate war with Germany prematurely, before Hitler's planned invasion of the Soviet Union commenced.**</u> The best hope the British and Americans had of Hitler breaking his Army, and hopelessly depleting his Air Force, was for him to attack the numerically superior forces of the USSR. **This simple and basic calculation, I am convinced, lay behind Roosevelt's decision** *not to commit the U.S. Navy to convoying after his May 27th declaration of an "unlimited national emergency."*

FDR did not want to take any major action which would have caused Hitler to reconsider his decision to strike the USSR; he wanted Hitler to commit his forces to the gigantic gamble in the east, and like Napoleon before him, dare to invade this enormous country (with its incredibly harsh winters and intractable wastes), which had successfully resisted invasion by Napoleon's Grand Army in

counter the USSR's heavy industry, which built many more tanks and airplanes than Germany during the war. Furthermore, Hitler misjudged his enemy, for the USSR (once it righted itself politically and regained its poise) not only did *not* capitulate or sue for peace as it had during World War I, but proved to have a comparatively inexhaustible manpower pool, whereas Germany's manpower resources were finite, and could not adequately replace the heavy losses suffered in late 1942 and early 1943 on the eastern front.

1812. **Hence, the convoying decision was delayed, not only because the American people were still opposed to war and the American military was unready for war---but for the overriding strategic reason that <u>Roosevelt did not want to provide Hitler with any reason to postpone or cancel his invasion of the Soviet Union</u>.** FDR made masterful use of intelligence in this regard, and proved himself the superior opponent on the geopolitical chess board.

The world now knows that Hitler's one big mistake, from the standpoint of purely military strategy, was to invade the USSR. But that is hindsight. At the time, throughout the summer and early fall of 1941, the three German Army Groups inside the USSR were winning huge victories in a war of maneuver, and were destroying or capturing entire Soviet armies. **<u>For four months, Hitler appeared to be close to winning the quick victory over the Soviet Union that he had anticipated.</u>** The USSR was forced to trade space (and lives) for time, in a war of attrition, in which Stalin hoped he could outlast Germany, a country with a *qualitatively superior* military initially, but with a <u>resource base</u> *inferior* to that of the USSR. **Between June 22, 1941 and until the end of the year---while the USSR tottered on the brink of annihilation---the combined strategy of Roosevelt and Churchill was to do everything possible to keep the Soviet Union in the war, fighting (and weakening) Nazi Germany. This**

		political and military strategic imperative took precedence over all other concerns. Italy, by this time, was largely neutered, and Japan---while viewed as an irrational and aggressive opponent (and therefore considered dangerous)---was known to have an inferior industrial base, and could be "handled" in due time, no matter what reverses might occur initially in the Far East, should Japan chose to launch an expansionist war (to grab European and American colonies in the Far East). *Therefore, after June 22nd, any and all actions that would keep the USSR in the war, fighting Germans and weakening the Third Reich's military machine, were considered of paramount importance by Franklin Roosevelt.* <u>Two such actions proved to be promising Lend-Lease aid to the USSR in large quantities, and doing everything possible to ensure that Japan did not go to war with its traditional enemy, Russia.</u>
June 22, 1941	**Churchill Broadcasts His Unqualified Support of the Soviet Union in its battle to defeat Hitler's Germany.** Churchill moved with alacrity to declare his strong support for the USSR in a well-publicized radio broadcast,[197] knowing full	Excerpts from this vitally important and well-phrased address follow: "I have taken this occasion to speak to you tonight because we have reached one of the climacterics of the war. The first of these intense turning-points was a year ago when France fell prostrate under the German hammer, and when we had to face the storm alone. The second was when the Royal Air Force beat the Hun raiders out of the daylight air, and thus

---

[197] Churchill, ed., *Never Give In!*, 289-293.

well that he was not trusted by the Communist regime because of his long and ardent opposition to Bolshevism.

Shortly after Churchill learned of the invasion and declared that he would offer all moral support to Joseph Stalin in his fight against Hitler, he was mildly baited by his personal secretary, John Colville, who asked him if his lifelong opposition to Communism would not cause him some discomfort in these new circumstances. Colville recorded in his diary Churchill's response, the now historically famous rejoinder that he now ***"had only one single purpose---the destruction of Hitler---and his life was much simplified thereby; <u>if Hitler invaded Hell he would at least make a favorable reference to the Devil in the House of Commons</u>."***[198]

Prior to giving the speech, Churchill had obtained warded off the Nazi invasion of our island while we were still ill-armed and ill-prepared. The third turning-point was when the President and Congress of the United States passed the Lend-and-Lease enactment, devoting nearly 2,000 millions sterling of wealth of the New World to help us to defend our liberties and their own. Those were the three climacterics. The fourth is now upon us.

At four o'clock this morning Hitler attacked and invaded Russia…Thus was repeated on a far larger scale the same kind of outrage against every form of signed compact and international faith which we have witnessed in Norway, Denmark, Holland and Belgium, and which Hitler's accomplice, the jackal Mussolini, so faithfully imitated in the case of Greece.

All this was no surprise to me. In fact I gave clear and precise warnings to Stalin of what was coming…All we know at present is that the Russian people are defending their native soil and that their leaders have called upon them to resist to the utmost.

Hitler is a monster of wickedness, insatiable in his lust for blood and plunder. Not content with having all of Europe under his heel, or else terrorized into various forms of abject submission, he must now carry his work of butchery and desolation among the vast multitudes of Russia and Asia. The terrible military

---

[198] Davis, *FDR: The War President,* 219-220.

	the assurance of U.S. Ambassador Winant that the United States would also consider the Soviet Union an ally and support it in its fight against Nazi Germany.	machine, which we and the rest of the civilised world so foolishly, so supinely, so insenately allowed the Nazi gangsters to build up year by year from almost nothing, cannot stand idle lest it rust or fall to pieces. It must be in continual motion, grinding up human lives and trampling down the homes and the rights of hundreds of millions of men. Moreover, it must be fed, not only with men but with oil. **So now this bloodthirsty guttersnipe must launch his mechanised Armies upon new fields of slaughter, pillage, and devastation**…That is enough to make us hold our breath. But presently I shall show you something else that lies behind, and something that touches very nearly the life of Britain and of the United States. <u>The Nazi regime is indistinguishable from the worst features of Communism. It is devoid of all theme and principle except appetite and racial domination. It excels all forms of human wickedness in the efficiency of its cruelty and ferocious aggression.</u> **No one has been a more consistent opponent of Communism than I have for the last twenty-five years. I will unsay no word that I have spoken about it.** ***<u>But all this fades away before the spectacle which is now unfolding</u>.*** The past with its crimes, its follies and its tragedies, flashes away…I see the ten thousand villages of Russia, where the means of existence was wrung so hardly from the soil, but where are still primordial human joys, where

maidens laugh and children play. <u>I see advancing upon all this in hideous onslaught the Nazi war machine, with its clanking, heel-clicking, dandified Prussian officers, its craft expert agents fresh from cowing and tying-down of a dozen countries.</u> **I see also the dull, drilled, docile, brutish masses of Hun soldiery <u>plodding on like a swarm of crawling locusts</u>.** I see the German bombers and fighters in the sky, still smarting from many a British whipping, delighted to find what they believe is an easier and a safer prey.

Behind all this glare, behind all this storm, I see that small group of villainous men who plan, organize and launch this cataract of horrors upon mankind…now I have to declare the decision of His Majesty's Government---and I feel sure it is a decision in which the great Dominions will, in due course, concur---for we must speak out now at once, without a day's delay. I have to make the declaration, but can you doubt what the policy will be?

<u>We have but one aim and one single, irrevocable purpose</u>. **We are resolved to destroy Hitler and every vestige of the Nazi regime. <u>From this nothing will turn us---nothing. We will never parley, we will never negotiate with Hitler or any of his gang.</u> We shall fight him by land, we shall fight him by sea, we shall fight him in the air,** *until with God's help we have rid the earth of his shadow* **and liberated its peoples from his yoke.** <u>Any man or</u>

<u>state who fights on against Nazism will have our aid. Any man or state who marches with Hitler is our foe.</u> This applies not only to organised states but to all representatives of that vile race of quislings who make themselves the tools and agents of the Nazi regime against their fellow-countrymen…That is our policy and that is our declaration. **It follows, therefore, that we shall give whatever help we can to Russia and the Russian people.** We shall appeal to all our friends and allies in every part of the world to take the same course and pursue it, as we shall, faithfully and steadfastly to the end.

We have offered the Government of Soviet Russia any technical or economic assistance which is in our power, and which is likely to be of service to them. We shall bomb Germany by day as well as by night in ever-increasing measure, casting upon them month by month a heavier discharge of bombs, and making the German people taste and gulp each month a sharper dose of the miseries they have showered upon mankind…

This is no class war, but a war in which the whole British Empire and Commonwealth of Nations is engaged without distinction of race, creed, or party. It is not for me to speak of the action of the United States, but this I will say: if Hitler imagines that his attack on Soviet Russia will cause the slightest divisions of aims or slackening of effort in the great Democracies who are resolved upon his doom, he is woefully mistaken. On the contrary, we shall be fortified and encouraged in our efforts to rescue mankind from his tyranny. We shall be strengthened and not weakened in determination and resources.

This is no time to moralise on the follies of countries and governments which have allowed themselves to be struck down one by one, when by united action they could have saved themselves and saved the world from this catastrophe. But when I spoke a few minutes ago of Hitler's blood-lust and the hateful appetites which have impelled or lured him on his Russian adventure, I said there was one deeper motive behind his outrage. **He wishes to destroy the Russian power because he hopes that if he succeeds in this, he will be able to bring the main strength of his army and air force from the east and hurl it upon this Island, which he knows he must conquer or suffer the penalty of his crimes. His invasion of Russia is no more than a prelude to an attempted invasion of the British Isles.** He hopes, no doubt, that all this may be accomplished before the winter comes, *and that he can overwhelm Great Britain before the fleet and air power of the United States may intervene.* He hopes that he may once again repeat, upon a greater scale than ever before, that process of destroying his enemies one by one, by which he has so long thrived and prospered, and that then the scene will be clear for the final act, without which all his conquests would be in vain---namely, the subjugation of the

		Western Hemisphere to his will and to his system. <u>The Russian danger is therefore our danger, and the danger of the United States</u>, just as the cause of any Russian fighting for his hearth and home is the cause of free men and free peoples in every quarter of the globe. Let us learn the lessons already taught by such cruel experience. Let us redouble our exertions, and strike, with united strength while life and power remain." [Emphasis added]
June 23, 1941	**Harold Ickes,** whom FDR had appointed Petroleum Coordinator late in May (and charged with developing preservation measures, in response to the shortage of gasoline in the United States), *recommends an oil embargo be imposed on Japan as a way of getting into World War II through the back door.*	Ickes made the following recommendation to President Roosevelt: **"There might develop from the embargoing of oil to Japan such a situation as would make it not only possible but easy to get into the war in an effective way.** *And if we should thus be indirectly brought in,* we would avoid the criticism that we had gone in as an ally of communistic Russia…*it may be difficult to get into this war the right way,* but if we do not do it now, we will be, when our turn comes, without an ally anywhere in this world."[199] [Emphasis added] Roosevelt responded angrily to Ickes' presumption at recommending foreign policy to the President, and at this time declared that he would not embargo oil to Japan, but about a month later, late in July, FDR would institute a sharp policy reversal on this score---<u>contrary to the</u>

---

[199] Victor, *The Pearl Harbor Myth,* 189.

		advice he was receiving from the State Department and the Navy, who both warned him that such a move would likely precipitate war with Japan. Perhaps it took a while for Ickes' recommendation to percolate within FDR's "forested mind."
July 1, 1941	FDR writes to Interior Secretary Harold Ickes, and while he indicates he is not willing to impose the full embargo on sales of oil to Japan that Ickes pushed for in June, he does indicate knowledge of the serious internal Japanese strategy debate (obtained by **MAGIC** intercepts), and of his intention to manage how that debate was proceeding.	FDR to Ickes: "I think it will interest you to know that **the Japs are having a real drag-down and knock-out fight among themselves, and have been for the past week---trying to decide which way they are going to jump---attack Russia, attack the South Seas…or…sit on the fence and be more friendly with us.** No one knows what the decision will be." FDR later explained to Ickes that he had no intention at this time of choking off Japan's oil supplies; instead, he said he wanted to **"slip a noose around Japan's neck and give it a jerk now and then."**[200] [Emphasis added]
July 1, 1941	**Eight Japanese merchant vessels are ordered to depart East Coast U.S. ports immediately.** Since the U.S. Navy could read 99% of the merchant ship code, it was easy for the Americans to decipher this message.	To meet the deadline, officials of NYK Line and other Japanese shipping firms directed American longshoremen working the docks in Boston, New York City, Philadelphia, and Boston to "rush load" the holds of their ships. The Japanese government ordered the captains of these merchant ships to leave port immediately, clear the Panama canal, and be in the Pacific Ocean by July 22nd. (The Japanese timetable was to occupy southern French Indochina on July 24th.) U.S. Navy cryptologists had

---

[200] Costello, *Days of Infamy,* 57; and Victor, *The Pearl Harbor Myth,* 190.

		decoded the July 1st orders by July 3rd.
July 2, 1941	An **Imperial Conference** is held by key members of the Japanese Cabinet before Emperor Hirohito, in which the Army, Navy, and the nominal civilian head of the government (Prime Minister Konoye) <u>**declared their readiness to prepare for war in both the north (with Russia) and the south (against the British, Dutch, and Americans), while awaiting developments in Germany's war with the USSR.**</u> As summarized by Waldo Heinrichs, "The German-Soviet war had intensified Japan's expansionism, its opportunism, and also its unpredictability."[201] Foreign Minister Matsuoka had taken the unusual step of meeting with Emperor Hirohito immediately after Germany invaded the Soviet Union---without first meeting with Prime Minister Konoye and developing a consensus with the Cabinet---and	The results of the Imperial Conference reflected the ambivalence of the Army about the direction in which Japan's expansion should proceed. The Navy was adamantly opposed to war with Japan's traditional enemy, Russia, since this would divert to the Army a preponderant share of the nation's resources; the Navy favored southern expansion, to break what was viewed as encirclement by the British, Dutch, and Americans, and to grab the resources of Southeast Asia and the Dutch East Indies. Opinion within the Army was split, with some members of the Army now favoring war with Russia, and others still determined to move southward. The consensus of opinion at the conference was to proceed with the occupation of French Indochina. It was hoped that this could be accomplished without force, by exerting diplomatic pressure on the government of Vichy France; if persuasion failed, however, force was to be used to occupy all of Indochina, even if this meant war with Britain and America. It was agreed to wait fifty to sixty days, to see whether German progress in its war with the USSR would justify the risk of war with the Soviet Union in Siberia. Japan's indecision about how to continue its expansion was reflected by the results of the Imperial Conference, in a document which afterwards was signed by Prime Minister

---

[201] Heinrichs, *Threshold of War,* 145.

had rashly urged that Japan wage immediate war on Russia in Siberia, while delaying its long-planned-for push to the south to grab the rice, rubber, tin, and oil of Southeast Asia. He was directed to consult with the Prime Minister, and dismissed from the presence of the Emperor; and for the next ten days, from June 22nd through July 2nd, key members of the Japanese Cabinet and military (the Prime Minister, Foreign Minister, War Minister, Navy Minister, and the Army and Navy Chiefs and Vice Chiefs of Staff) met informally in Prime Minister Konoye's residence in daily "Liaison Conferences" to attempt to arrive at a consensus that would accommodate the changing circumstances of the titanic clash between Germany and the USSR.

During one of these Liaison Conferences, Konoye and the Army and Navy Chiefs of Staff, and affixed with the Imperial Seal.[202] The national policy arrived at on July 2nd is quoted in part:

"…In case the diplomatic negotiations break down [with the United States] preparations for a war with England and America will also be carried forward…In carrying out the plans [to occupy southern Indochina and Thailand] we will not be deterred by the possibility of being involved in a war with England and America…Our attitude with reference to the German-Soviet war will be based on the spirit of the Tripartite Pact. **However, we will not enter the conflict for some time but will steadily proceed with military preparations against the Soviet and decide our final attitude independently…<u>In case the German-Soviet war should develop to our advantage, we will make use of our military strength, settle the Soviet question and guarantee the safety of our northern borders</u>**…all plans…will be carried out in such a way as to place no serious obstacles in the path of our basic military preparations for a war with England and America…We will immediately turn our attention to placing the nation on a war basis and will take special measures to strengthen the defenses of the nation."[203] [Emphasis added]

A summary of the policy was sent by the

---

[202] Toland, *The Rising Sun*, 78-83.

[203] Victor, *The Pearl Harbor Myth,* 200.

| | Foreign Minister Matsuoka made the following revealing statement: "When Germany wipes out the Soviet Union, we can't simply share in the spoils of victory unless we've done something. We must either shed our blood or embark on diplomacy. And it's better to shed blood."

Without telling Matsuoka or the Navy, the Army had secret plans to attack the Soviet Union in Siberia if Moscow fell to the German advance before the end of August. There was a consensus between the Army and the Navy, however, that Japan could not proceed with military expansion in both the north and the south simultaneously. | Foreign Ministry in Tokyo to its Ambassadors in Moscow, Berlin, and Rome, as revealed in this **MAGIC** decrypt:

"As regards the Russo-German war, although the spirit of the three-power Axis shall be maintained, every preparation shall be made at the present and the situation shall be dealt with in our own way. In the meantime diplomatic negotiations shall be carried on with extreme care. Although every means available shall be resorted to in order to prevent the United States from joining the war…Japan shall decide when and how force will be employed."[204]

George Victor summarized what this meant quite succinctly in *The Pearl Harbor Myth* (p. 201): **"As discussed in Japanese policy deliberations [on July 2nd], this meant that Japan would prepare for war against the Soviet Union and the United States, but would only fight one of them. If peace with the United States were negotiated, she would invade the Soviet Union."** Victor should have added, ***"…contingent upon the continued rapid success of Hitler's offensive inside the USSR."***

Foreign Minister Matsuoka continued to press for war with the Soviet Union in Siberia, until he was dismissed on July 16th and a new government, without the erratic firebrand, was formed. The |

---

[204] Ibid., 200-201.

Japanese Army in Manchuria was greatly outnumbered at this time by the Soviet forces in Siberia, but the Army leaders had independently commenced serious reinforcement of their forces in Manchuria after Germany invaded the Soviet Union, so as to be ready for possible hostilities with Russia in the event that Stalin pulled out significant numbers of troops to help fight the invading German armies. Initially, the predominant opinion in Washington, and indeed, internationally, was that Japan would attack a weakened and preoccupied Soviet Union in response to Hitler's invasion. By the end of July, however, Hitler's offensive had begun to bog down, as a result of three factors: (1) lengthened lines of supply which could not keep up with the Army's advances inside the vast Soviet Union; (2) the serious attrition and maintenance problems with Germany's armored vehicles; and (3) the Red Army was proving to be much larger than the Germans had estimated, and the resistance of the Soviet soldiers was, in many cases, quite stubborn. While the German armed forces had won tremendous victories inside the Soviet Union, and had killed or captured large numbers of troops, and destroyed or captured masses of equipment, Hitler's *political failure* to achieve a quick knockout blow in the USSR (that is, his failure to cause the fall of Stalin's government, and its replacement with one that would sue for peace, similar to what had happened in World War I)---

		and the gradual slowing of his offensive within the vast spaces of the Soviet Union---was becoming more and more apparent throughout the month of July, as Japan carried out her planned aggressive moves against southern French Indochina. The acquisition of bases, and the stationing of troops there, was essential to its southern strategy as the "jumping off point" for possible future attacks against Singapore, the Dutch East Indies, and the Philippines.[205]
July 3, 1941	**The CNO (Admiral Stark) issues a war warning message to the major fleet commands, on the same day that Japan's orders to its merchant ships on the East Coast were decrypted in Washington.**	Stark's message was addressed from CNO to CINCPAC, CINCAF, CINCLANT, COM 15, and SPENAVO (the Special Naval Observer in London, with direct access to the highest levels of the British Military and to Prime Minister Churchill). It read in part: **"Japan's policy probably involves war in the near future.** <u>They have ordered all Jap vessels in the Atlantic ports to be west of the Panama canal by August 1st</u>."[206] [Emphasis added]
July 5, 1941	**FDR closes the Panama Canal to Japanese shipping.**	President Roosevelt received the decrypted orders for Japanese ships to leave East Coast ports (and be in the Pacific on July 22nd) at his home in Hyde Park on July 4th. He acted the very next day. Robert Stinnett writes in *Day of Deceit* (p. 130) that a cover story was employed so that FDR's actions would not appear to be a warlike act (or compromise the Navy's codebreaking

---

[205] Heinrichs, *Threshold of War,* 118-145.

[206] Stinnett, *Day of Deceit,* 130 and 346.

		ability): "A cover story was concocted. Major General Daniel van Voorhis of the Panama Canal Zone Command issued a press release claiming that the emergency closure was caused by water leaks in the transit locks of the canal. Japan had no choice. Denied the Panama Canal transit, the vessels were routed back to Japan the long way---via the Straits of Magellan at the southern tip of South America."
July 8, 1941	**A brigade of 4,400 U.S. Marines, transported by 25 ships, begins the occupation of Iceland, which lies athwart the great circle convoy routes from North America to the British Isles.** The deployment took place at the request of Winston Churchill, and its announced purpose was to replace the 20,000 British and Canadian troops there so they could be redeployed to combat zones. Churchill had pre-emptively occupied Iceland in May of 1940 to prevent the Germans from doing so, and it had become a vital center supporting air reconnaissance against German U-boats in the Battle of the Atlantic, and	The takeover had been planned since mid-June, but Roosevelt did not act until he received the long-awaited formal request from the government of Iceland on July 1st. FDR announced the action publicly on July 7th, the day before the task force's arrival. President Roosevelt used Marines for the occupation of Iceland to bypass the restrictions of the Selective Service Act of 1940, which prevented Army draftees from serving outside the Western Hemisphere. U.S. Marines were all volunteers, and thus were not affected by the restrictions of the draft law. Eight days after the Marines landed, Iceland was designated by the United States to be part of the Western Hemisphere (even though geographically, it was not). "The prospects of 'incidents' involving German submarines and the U.S. Navy, now engaged in the defence of Iceland as well as escort duties of American convoys as far as the island, were now far greater than they had been. But the

	also became the pickup point at which British Navy escorts would rendezvous with convoys bound for Great Britain. ABC deliberations in Washington early in 1941 had determined that in the event of war between the U.S. and Germany, responsibility for Iceland would fall to the United States.	occupation of Iceland was approved by 61 per cent of Americans questioned in an opinion survey, with only 20 per cent opposed…Though the opportunity appeared to present itself to introduce the escort of non-American convoys, Roosevelt did not seize it."[207] Both Churchill and Lord Halifax (now ambassador to the U.S.) both agreed that the primary significance of the event was that it accelerated the American intervention in the war alongside Britain.
July 22, 1941	**The Navy sends a policy memo to the State Department warning that the imposition of an oil embargo on Japan would likely lead to an immediate invasion of the Dutch East Indies by Japan. <u>The Navy recommended not imposing an oil embargo.</u>** The Navy's memo reinforced the longstanding position of the State Department that imposing a total embargo on the sale of oil to Japan *would result in war, rather than preventing it.* President Roosevelt also read the memo.	The Navy position paper sent to Cordell Hull by Admiral Stark was drafted by the Navy's Chief of War Plans, Rear Admiral Richmond K. Turner (who also believed that a Japanese invasion of Siberia was imminent): **"It is generally believed that shutting off the American supply of petroleum will lead to an invasion of the Netherlands East Indies**…[It] will have [sic] an immediate severe psychological reaction in Japan against the United States. It is almost certain to intensify the determination…to continue their present course. Furthermore, it seems certain that, if Japan should take military measures against the British and the Dutch, **she would also include military action against the Philippines, which would immediately involve us in a Pacific war**…RECOMMENDATION:

---

[207] Kershaw, *Fateful Choices,* 313.

		Japan's internal estimates were that in spite of the fact that it had been stockpiling oil and aviation gasoline at a record pace during 1940 and 1941, in the event of an oil embargo by the United States, its oil would be gone after two years if there was no war, and after 18 months if she did go to war.	**That Japan not be embargoed at this time."**[208] [Emphasis added] During 1940, President Roosevelt had indicated in private conversations with both his son Elliot, and with his wife Eleanor, that embargoes of crucial materials to Japan would likely result in war. That summer he responded to Elliot's suggested of an embargo of scrap iron by saying: "If we were suddenly to stop our sales of scrap iron to Japan, she would be within her rights in considering [it] an unfriendly act, that we were cutting off and starving her commercially. Even more, she'd be entitled to consider such…sufficient cause to break off diplomatic relations with us. I'll go even further. *If she thought we were sufficiently unprepared…she might even use it as an excuse to declare war."*[209] [Emphasis added] In September of 1940, when the First Lady **suggested an oil embargo** against Japan, FDR replied: "If we forbid oil shipments to Japan, *Japan…may be driven by actual necessity to a descent on the Dutch East Indies*…we all regard such action on our part as an encouragement to the spread of war in the Far East."[210] [Emphasis added]

---

[208] Victor, *The Pearl Harbor Myth*, 192.

[209] Ibid., 188-189.

[210] Ibid., 189.

July 23, 1941	Secretary of State Cordell Hull informs the Japanese Ambassador to the United States, retired Admiral Kichisaburo Nomura, that he is terminating the deliberations that had been underway for months in an attempt to improve U.S.-Japanese relations.	Hull and Roosevelt were well-aware, through **MAGIC,** of Japan's bullying efforts against Vichy France over gaining military access to the southern half of French Indochina; Hull and FDR knew that if Japan could not intimidate Vichy France into acquiescence, that Japan would invade Southern Indochina. (July 23rd in the U.S. was July 24th in the Far East, the same day the Japanese occupied Southern Indochina, thus *immediately* indicating American displeasure.)
July 24, 1941	**Japanese troops occupy southern French Indochina to secure vital bases after the Japanese government completed a successful policy of intimidation against Vichy France.** The following sites for air bases were secured in what is now Cambodia: Phompenh, Kompong Trach, and Siem Reap. In what is now southern Vietnam, sites for air bases were secured at Da Nang, Soc Trang, Nha Trang, and Bienhoa; and Cam Ranh Bay and Saigon were secured for use as seaports by the Japanese Navy.	Historian Waldo Heinrichs summarized this series of events in *Threshold of War* (pp. 121-123): "…British and American officials had no doubt about Japanese intentions toward southern Indochina. **MAGIC** provided a full account from Toyko's messages seeking Vichy's consent: that an expeditionary force of 40,000 troops was being sent, that Japan would use force if Vichy refused, that Vichy must respond by July 20, that the French did indeed bow to Japanese demands that day, that an agreement was worked out on July 23, and that Japanese troops were prepared to disembark July 24---which they did."
July 25, 1941	**The Navy transmitted a joint message from the Chief of Naval**	The Naval message was drafted by the Chief of the War Plans Division, Rear Admiral Richmond K. Turner, and read

	Operations and the Army Chief of Staff to all principal Navy commands, and to the principal Army commands overseas, notifying them of the imminent embargo of all trade with Japan (which would be imposed the next day).	as follows: "Addressed to CINCPAC[Admiral Kimmel], CINCAF[Admiral Hart], CINCLANT[Admiral King], COM 15, SPENAVO [the Special Naval Observer in London, Vice Admiral Ghormley]. Appropriate addressee, please deliver copies to the Commanding Generals of Philippines, Hawaii, and Caribbean Defense Command, and also to General [James E.] Chaney in London. **You are herewith advised that on July the 26th at 1400 GCT [Greenwich Civil Time] the United States will impose economic sanctions against Japan. It is expected that these sanctions will embargo all trade between Japan and the United States subject to modification through the medium of a license system for certain materials.** Import licenses may be granted for raw silk. It is expected that export licenses will be granted for certain grades of petroleum products, cotton, and possibly some other material. **Japanese funds and assets in the United States will be frozen except that they may be moved if export licenses are granted for such movement.** It is not expected that the Japanese merchant ships in ports of the United States will be seized at this time. U.S.-flag merchant vessels will at present be ordered to depart from or not to enter ports controlled by the Japanese. **CNO and Chief of Staff [Army] do not anticipate immediate hostile action by Japan through the use of military means, but you are furnished this information in order that you may**

		take appropriate precautionary measures against any possible eventuality. Action is being initiated by the United States Army to call the Philippine Army into active service at an early date. Except for immediate Army and Navy subordinates, the contents of this message are to be kept secret. SPENAVO London inform [British] Chief of Naval Staff but warn him against disclosure."[211] [Emphasis added] Gordon Prange tellingly wrote: "Thus, Washington warned Hawaii of possible trouble with Japan, yet at the same time discounted the danger of military action. This established a pattern which Washington was to follow almost to the eve of the Pearl Harbor attack."[212]
July 26, 1941	**FDR freezes all Japanese financial assets in the United States** and implements a complicated and restrictive two-tier licensing system (the only way to "unfreeze funds")--- designed to permit the U.S. a maximum in flexibility, and also impose upon the Japanese government a maximum of uncertainty about future oil supplies.	This action was in response to Japan's military occupation of southern Indochina, which was properly viewed as the acquisition of a "jumping off point" for future aggressive expansion toward the south---Singapore, the Dutch East Indies, and probably the Philippines. The decision was made at a July 24th Cabinet meeting and the freezing order was announced on July 26th. This action was taken by Roosevelt in spite of the dire warnings given to him repeatedly by the Navy and the State Department that doing so would likely provoke war with Japan, rather than deterring any future aggression. The

---

[211] Stillwell, ed., *Air Raid: Pearl Harbor!*, 83.

[212] Prange, *At Dawn We Slept,* 167.

	Although not publicly portrayed as an oil embargo, this system imposes a *de facto* embargo on the shipment of all oil to Japan.[213]	British (correctly) feared that this action would not be enough to stop Japan's expansion, but instead might cause the Japanese to initiate war against the United States; nevertheless, in a show of solidarity, Great Britain followed suit and likewise froze all Japanese financial

---

[213] Heinrichs, *Threshold of War,* 133-136 and 176-178; Davis, *FDR: The War President,* 261-263; and Dallek, *Franklin D. Roosevelt and American Foreign Policy,* 274-276. I reject Dallek's conclusion that FDR did not know the bureaucrats in his government had imposed a *de facto* oil embargo on Japan **until September**---and that he then let it stay in place so as to avoid the appearance of backing down. FDR was much smarter than that, and also much better informed; furthermore, the press release announcing the freezing order was issued on July 25th, the ***same day*** a seriously concerned Navy (Rear Admiral Turner, the Chief of War Plans) drafted and sent out its July 25th warning of an embargo of all trade between the U.S. and Japan, and the freezing of all Japanese funds and assets, one day in advance of the action. The press release and the Navy warning were clearly coordinated. The Navy had strongly opposed an oil embargo throughout 1940 and again on July 22, 1941, and knew that the Japanese might react suddenly and dramatically to Roosevelt's action; and the Navy knew the funds freeze meant an oil embargo, or it would not have sent out its warning message on July 25th. FDR also knew full well he was imposing a *de facto* embargo, because the officials controlling the licenses were aligned with those in government who had been advocating for an oil embargo since September of 1940. Stimson, Morgenthau, and Ickes had all pressed Roosevelt to impose a total trade embargo (including oil) during August and September of 1940, to halt Japan's designs on northern French Indochina. On September 26, 1940, following Japan's movement of troops into that region, FDR---after some vacillation--- had opted ***not*** to impose a full embargo. Instead, he only embargoed the sale of high-grade scrap iron and high-octane aviation gasoline. But with the Soviet Union now desperately trying to withstand a German invasion, FDR took the provocative action of ***shutting off all U.S. exports to Japan*** (including oil) by calling it a **"funds freeze,"** as a way of cloaking this very serious move in public ambiguity. Waldo Heinrichs writes: "The decision on an oil embargo was closely held and deviously managed. Action proceeded not in the formal realm of peacetime quotas and proclamations restricting export…but in the shadowy world of inaction, circumvention, and red tape…The United States had imposed an embargo without saying so." (The architect of its implementation was Dean Acheson, who was now working for the State Department.) By not publicly calling it an "oil embargo," and by instead labeling his economic action a "funds freeze," FDR could maintain the high ground, morally, and proclaim that he was not provoking the Japanese---while knowing full well that it would probably force Tokyo to move south to grab the Dutch East Indies. This was acceptable to him now, since his overriding priority in July of 1941 was to keep the USSR from collapsing; a war with Japan in Siberia (had Japan pursued its northern option) might have weakened the Red Army enough to permit a German victory in 1941, something FDR was determined to help prevent at all costs. Besides, since Hitler's U-boats in the Atlantic were continuing to avoid confrontations with the United States, and were therefore unlikely to provide a *casus belli* in the near future, a Japanese move south might provide FDR with the "overt act of war" he needed to finally enter the World War so he could actively take up arms against Nazi Germany. And this is exactly what happened on December 7th, since the attacks on Pearl Harbor and the Philippines were conducted for the express purpose of providing at least 6 months of cover for the safe and unhindered execution of Japan's

| | With the imposition of this action, <u>**FDR has implemented item H in the eight-point action memo written by Commander McCollum on October 7, 1940.**</u> **President Roosevelt was fully aware that this embargo was likely to result in the initiation of war by Japan in Southeast Asia.** | assets.

When Roosevelt froze Japanese funds (thus imposing a total oil embargo), he simultaneously broke off the ongoing negotiations with Japan, and commenced arming the Philippines in a very public way which was sure to be noticed by Japan---in spite of the fact that the United States Army had traditionally considered the Philippines indefensible.

I agree with authors Robert Stinnett and George Victor that FDR's oil embargo, and the arming of the Philippines, were clearly intended as provocations by Roosevelt, and not as deterrence. He knew that cutting off Japan's oil was likely to force Japan to move south to grab the oil fields in the Dutch East Indies, and that arming the Philippines (no matter how feeble and half-hearted the effort was in reality) would be perceived by Japan as a threat to its now-essential southern expansion. This provocative action was taken by FDR in the context of an influx of intelligence reports throughout July that pointed toward an imminent Japanese attack on the Soviet Union in Siberia. <u>**Roosevelt's goal in imposing the oil embargo was clearly to keep Japan**</u> |

southern strategy. Robert Dallek is unable to conceive of FDR intentionally doing anything to provoke the Japanese into attacking the United States. I have no such conceptual handicap. America's two-ocean Navy was funded and its construction was now well underway, and the United States was secretly planning for armed forces that would be 10-million-men-strong following full expansion; war with Japan would pose a serious irritant in the beginning, but would not threaten America's existence. The ABC-1 conversations and the resulting Rainbow-5 war plan both assumed the U.S. would be at war concurrently with both Germany and Japan. FDR was fully capable of thinking globally, taking the long view, and of sacrificing a knight or a rook, in order to checkmate his opponent.

		from going to war with the Soviet Union, by forcing Japanese leaders to choose the "southern option" to obtain the oil needed by its war machine, and thereby **abandon the "northern option."** FDR's primary foreign policy goal at this time <u>was to keep the Soviet Union in the war</u>, fighting Germany and weakening Hitler. He strove to channel the Japanese expansionist drive toward the south (instead of north), by starving Japan of oil. This was his strategy.[214] *Of course, if this provocation also caused Japan to make war on the United States, then---paraphrasing Commander McCollum's memo of October 7, 1940---"so much the better."*
July 26, 1941	President Roosevelt calls the Philippine Army (the "Philippine Scouts") into service and places it in a new combined command, along with the U.S. Army forces in the Philippines. On the same day the retired General Douglas MacArthur (the former U.S. Army Chief of Staff, who had been serving as the principal military advisor to the Philippine government) is recalled to active duty and placed in	On June 20th, in reply to a question from MacArthur, Marshall told him that there was no intention to arm the Philippines or to give him a command there, unless a crisis arose in the Pacific. (The Army had always considered the Philippines indefensible.) <u>An official Army history, writing about the late July decision after the war, said that it was adopted without consultation with the War Department.</u>[215]

There was no immediate substantive alteration in the military weakness of the Philippines as a result of the reorganization, since the Philippine units had little in the way of officers, weapons, |

---

[214] Historian Waldo Heinrichs, in *Threshold of War* (p. 179), summarizes Roosevelt's foreign policy after June 22, 1941: **"The central dynamic of his policies was the conviction that the survival of the Soviet Union was essential for the defeat of Germany and that the defeat of Germany was essential for American security."**

[215] Victor, *The Pearl Harbor Myth,* 195.

		command.	or training. Washington had no intention of reinforcing the Philippines by so much as one infantry division; Europe remained the top priority.[216] Between August and December, only a trickle of supplies reached the Philippines, with the exception of some long range B-17 bombers, and early model P-40 Army pursuit planes, which will be discussed below. Washington still had no intention of conducting anything but a token defense of the Philippines, but was telling MacArthur otherwise. In my view the high-profile, low-action "arming of the Philippines" was a provocative action designed to alarm the Japanese into viewing it as a threat to their southern expansion policy, thus stimulating a Japanese attack on U.S. forces there when the Japanese Empire did move south. The so-called "arming of the Philippines"---including the B-17 bombers that arrived late in 1941---was in reality a "lure" intended by FDR himself (possibly supported in private by Army Chief of Staff General George C. Marshall) to stimulate a pre-emptive attack by Japan, and thus provide a "back door" for American entry into the war in Europe. (See entries below for November 15th and December 5th.)
July 31, 1941		In the third and most provocative of three "pop-up" cruises, U.S. Navy warships appeared without warning in the	The formal diplomatic protest read in part: **"On the night of July 31, 1941, Japanese fleet units at anchor in Sukumo Bay [in the Bungo Strait, off the island of Shikoku] picked up the**

---

[216] Heinrichs, *Theshold of War,* 131.

Bungo Strait---located in between the Japanese islands of Kyushu and Shikoku---the Imperial Japanese Navy's access to its key bases in the Inland Sea. This generated alarm within the Japanese Navy, and a formal diplomatic protest was filed by Japan's Navy ministry in August with Ambassador Grew in Tokyo.

Two other "pop-up cruises" were conducted: one between March 15-21, 1941, in the Central and South Pacific adjacent to Japanese mandates, and another during July and August that was similar in nature. Both involved U.S. Navy heavy cruisers.[217]

sound of propellers approaching Bungo Channel from the eastward. Duty destroyers of the Japanese Navy investigated <u>and sighted two darkened cruisers that disappeared in a southerly direction behind a smoke screen when they were challenged</u>." The protest concluded: "<u>Japanese Naval officers believe the vessels were United States cruisers.</u>"[218] This was undoubtedly a provocation engineered by President Roosevelt, who was well aware that it could have resulted in great loss of life, as well as war with Japan, if the American heavy cruisers had been attacked and either damaged, or sunk. In discussions with "Betty" Stark earlier in the year (in February), FDR had called such evolutions "pop-up cruises," saying: **"I just want them to keep popping up here and there and keep the Japs guessing. <u>I don't mind losing one or two cruisers, but do not take a chance on losing five or six</u>."** [Emphasis added] When Kimmel was informed of Roosevelt's idea to conduct such "pop-up cruises," he had written to Stark on February 18th and objected, saying: ***"It is ill-advised and will result in war if we make this move."*** Stark told FDR that the cruises **"will precipitate hostilities."**[219] Of course, that was the idea---to try to engineer an "incident" with the Japanese Navy which might

---

[217] Stinnett, *Day of Deceit,* 313.

[218] Ibid., 10.

[219] Ibid., 9, 312-313.

		precipitate war with Japan, and get the U.S. into the war against Germany through the "back door," as recommended by Commander McCollum's eight point memo written on October 7, 1940, especially item D in paragraph 9 of that memo, to wit: "<u>Send a division of long range heavy cruisers to the Orient…</u>". As paragraph 10 of McCollum's memo stated: **"If by these means Japan could be led to commit an overt act of war, so much the better."**
August 1, 1941	The Imperial Japanese Navy changes the ciphers for JN-25(b)---the additive book---but not the basic 50,000 word code book. This was the 7th such change for the JN-25 additive tables.	OP-20-G and FECB were both greatly relieved when it was realized that "recoveries" of the basic code book could continue, and that the codebreakers did not have to start from scratch in deciphering the basic values of the 5-Num code. The additive tables were changed about every six months.
August 4, 1941	Emperor Hirohito of Japan approves the plan hatched by Prime Minister Konoye to meet with President Roosevelt somewhere in the Pacific, in an attempt to avert war with the United States through personal diplomacy in a high-level Pacific Summit. Cordell Hull was the initial recipient of the offer, and told the Japanese Ambassador that the U.S. could begin	The reaction of the Japanese Cabinet to the U.S. oil embargo was near-panic. Although the consensus in the Army and Navy following the oil embargo by FDR was that war with the U.S. now seemed inevitable, three people who still wished to avoid a U.S. war, if possible---while still guaranteeing the "Imperial Way" policy of expansion of the Empire in Asia---were Emperor Hirohito, Prime Minister Konoye, and Foreign Minister Toyoda. The Army and Navy Ministers in the Cabinet gave only lukewarm approval to Konoye's summit idea, and did so primarily because if it failed---which they expected it to---it would legitimate war. The High Commands

consultations only when Japan stopped using force in East Asia. Kershaw writes that "Hull was mistrustful of a summit without a precise, pre-formed agenda. 'It seemed to us that Japan was striving to push us into a conference from which general statements would issue,' he wrote later, 'and Japan could then interpret and apply these statements to suit her own purposes,' even citing the President's endorsement."[220]

Underlying this desperate attempt by Konoye to set up a summit with Roosevelt that would facilitate free-form, unscripted negotiations which might stave off war with the U.S., was a basic incompatibility between the U.S. and Japanese positions that no last-ditch summit would ever be able to bridge. The basic U.S. position had been set out by Secretary of State Cordell Hull with Ambassador Nomura in April, and was called the

and operational staffs of the Army and Navy vociferously opposed Konoye's attempt at summit diplomacy, and indeed, Konoye's gambit was personally dangerous, for multiple assassination plots against him were uncovered after August 4th. Konoye preferred to meet FDR in Honolulu, or even at-sea, if necessary. Nomura, Japan's Ambassador in Washington, was instructed on August 7th to try to arrange such a summit; Cordell Hull was never enthusiastic about the idea, and more than once discouraged it with FDR, believing it to be a diplomatic trap. FDR twice (on August 17th and 28th) expressed interest in the summit idea with Nomura, each time countering the idea of a Honolulu summit with one in Juneau, Alaska. And yet FDR never proposed a date for the summit, nor did he ever firmly say, "yes." The summit between himself and FDR that Konoye desired in Hawaii never came to fruition, and the idea died when Konoye resigned as Prime Minister on October 16, 1941. FDR and Hull were effectively playing "good cop, bad cop" with the Japanese Ambassador, Nomura. Each time Roosevelt met with Nomura and expressed interest in a summit with Konoye, Hull would shortly thereafter, in private conversations with Nomura, immediately throw cold water on the idea. Churchill prompted FDR at the Argentia Conference from August 9-12 (see the lengthy discussion later in this chronology) to take a tough line with

---

[220] Kershaw, *Fateful Choices,* 335-338.

	"four principles:" 1. Respect for the territorial integrity and sovereignty of each and all nations. 2. Support for the principle of non-interference in the internal affairs of other countries. 3. Support for the principle of equality, including the equality of commercial opportunity. 4. Non-disturbance of the *status quo* in the Pacific except by peaceful means. In opposition to the basic U.S. negotiating position was the deeply held view among the power elite in Japan that East Asia was none of the United States' business.	Japan, warning that only threats of war with the United States would prevent further Japanese aggression in Southeast Asia. Instead, Roosevelt---for three full months after Argentia---decided to "baby them along" (his exact words to Churchill)[221]---that is, to pursue a middle course, and avoid aggressive provocations, and thereby buy time (as his military chiefs were requesting throughout the autumn of 1941) for British and American reinforcements to reach Singapore and the Philippines. As Roosevelt said to Churchill at Argentia, he felt "very strongly that every effort should be made to prevent the outbreak of war with Japan."[222] When FDR told Churchill "I think I can baby them along for three months," his *primary strategy* was still to get into the war against Germany by waging an undeclared shooting war against Hitler's U-boats in the Atlantic, thus provoking "incidents" that would serve as a *casus belli*. For this reason, he did not (yet) take the strong stance against Japan that Churchill desired; that decision would come in late November, once the sought-after "incidents" in the Atlantic had failed to provoke a war fever in the United States.
August 9, 1941	The Japanese government formally **decides against operations in Siberia in**	One factor that contributed to the decision was the realization in late July that the German offensive in the Soviet

---

[221] Toland, *The Rising Sun,* 91.

[222] Ibid., 91.

1941. President Roosevelt does not yet know it, but he has achieved his goal of helping to prevent a Japanese invasion of the USSR. **The consensus within the Japanese government is now to expand southward,** ensuring that the Dutch East Indies, with its abundant supplies of crude oil, becomes the spigot supplying Japan's future expansion, and supporting her military hegemony over East Asia. Convinced of the righteousness of its manifest destiny to dominate East Asia, and at the same time impoverished by its four year old war in China, and huge military budgets, the Japanese Empire could only survive by expanding--- by looting and plundering other nations. There was a crisis atmosphere in Tokyo, driven by a paranoid fear of encirclement by the British, Dutch, the Americans, and China. The U.S. continued to insist on Japan's Union had stalled, and that Hitler was not going to win the quick two-month victory he had hoped for. Furthermore, Stalin had not yet withdrawn troops from Siberia to reinforce the Red Army facing the Nazi onslaught, so the Soviet forces in Siberia still substantially outnumbered the Japanese Army forces in that region. Finally, the tipping point was almost certainly FDR's freezing of Japanese funds and financial assets in the United States, and the unannounced but sharply felt oil embargo against Japan. On June 7th the government of the Dutch East Indies had rebuffed Japan's demands to purchase huge quantities of oil for the next several years; this had left Japan dependent almost solely upon the United States for bunker oil for ships, and aviation gasoline for its military airplanes. With the imposition of FDR's "silent embargo," the clock was ticking, counting down toward the day when there would no longer be enough oil or aviation gasoline to fight an offensive war. (In two years or less, Japan's large stockpiles would be gone, even with the imposition of economy measures.) The leaders of the Japanese Imperial Navy were all too aware of the rapid Naval construction program now taking place within the United States (since May of 1940). From the Imperial Navy's standpoint, therefore, there was a strong incentive to move southward and take the Dutch East Indies soon, before fuel stocks ran low, and before America's new naval construction could impact the coming war. (The U.S. was building

	withdrawal from China, and would not budge from this position. Japan was no more willing to abandon its war in China, or its new acquisition of French Indochina, than the United States was willing to abandon Hawaii, or return the southwest United States to Mexico. For this reason---Japan's insistence upon gaining an Empire by conquest---war with the United States and Great Britain was inevitable, and was only a matter of time.	three times the number of ships that Japan was, at this time---and building them faster.) And now, with all thought of going to war against Russia in Siberia set aside for the remainder of 1941, the Japanese Army was of one mind about the necessity to expand southward to acquire the resources demanded by the Japanese war machine---including war with the United States, if that proved unavoidable. Even former proponents within the Army of a northern move against Russia were now onboard with the need <u>to first strike south</u> to secure adequate resources for the future.[223]
August 9-12, 1941	**The "Argentia Conference" between Roosevelt and Churchill and their military staffs is conducted at sea in Placentia Bay, Newfoundland.[224]** In great secrecy, a British Naval Flotilla (which had transited the north Atlantic in U-boat infested waters) bearing Winston Churchill and his military chiefs; and an	It was imperative to Roosevelt that he and Churchill meet and begin to get to know each other---to attempt to take each other's measure in person, and to establish at least some little intimacy---and this could not be accomplished by mere letters, cables, nor even by transatlantic telephone calls. They each brought with them their military chiefs, as follows: on the American side, FDR brought with him the Chief of Naval Operations, Admiral Harold R. Stark; Army Chief of Staff George C. Marshall; Admiral Ernest J.

---

[223] Heinrichs, *Threshold of War,* 180-183.

[224] See Buell, *Master of Sea Power,* 142-146; Davis, *FDR: The War President,* 256-275; and Meacham, *Franklin and Winston,* 111-124.

American Naval flotilla bearing Franklin D. Roosevelt and his military chiefs, anchored in Ship Harbor at Placentia Bay---in Argentia, Newfoundland.

One author has described the Canadian wilderness at this location as "a barren, remote, windswept anchorage." And yet FDR wrote that it was "a really beautiful harbor," with "high mountains, deep water, and fjord-like arms of the sea."

The primary purpose of the conference was to hold a get-acquainted session between the American President and British Prime Minister; at the same time there were two other conferences going on---one, between Assistant Secretary of State Sumner Welles and Alexander Cadogan of the Foreign Office; and the other, a series of working sessions between the military chiefs of Great Britain and the United States. An exhausted Harry Hopkins, who was returning from an

King (CINCLANT); Rear Admiral Richmond K. Turner (War Plans); General Henry H. ("Hap") Arnold (Head of the U.S. Army Air Corps); Army Colonel Charles Bundy; and Navy Commander Forrest P. Sherman. The British military contingent sent to the staff discussions included: General Sir John Dill (CIGS); Admiral Sir Dudley Pound (First Sea Lord); and Air Chief Marshall Sir Wilford Freeman.

The British military contingent came well-prepared (with a fixed agenda), and displaying a well-scripted unanimity of purpose; the American military contingent came unprepared, and occasionally expressed internal disagreements before their British cousins. The major players in each of the two military establishments became acquainted, and gained a sense of each other's minds and motives, personalities, strengths and weaknesses, and differing points of view. Alarmed by the daring German airborne invasion and conquest of Crete, the British requested additional rifles on an urgent basis, and the Americans agreed to provide 130,000 of these. **More importantly, the British requested that the Americans begin convoying British and neutral merchant ships from Canada (the assembly point for the transatlantic convoys) as far as Iceland, and the Americans agreed to do so in the near future, on or about September 1st.** Other discussions were held regarding how to apportion war material manufactured in the United States

emergency visit to Dictator Joseph Stalin and his Foreign Minister, Molotov, in the embattled USSR (to personally assess their chances for survival and learn about Russia's most urgent materiel needs), had traveled to Argentia onboard HMS *Prince of Wales* with Winston Churchill. [Hopkins carried with him a personal message from Stalin to FDR saying that Britain and the USSR, *without the help of the United States,* would find it difficult to crush the German military machine; Stalin believed it inevitable that Germany and the United States would eventually fight each other, and urged FDR to enter the war against Hitler now. He had assured Hopkins that the Red Army would hold on in its fight against the Wehrmacht. His major requests for immediate aid were for anti-aircraft guns, machine guns, and rifles; his long-term requests were primarily for high-octane aviation gasoline and aluminum

between America, Great Britain, and the Soviet Union. (During the conference FDR promised Churchill he would request another $5 billion in Lend-Lease appropriations.)

The British military contingent brought with it a staff study titled: "Review of General Strategy," which emphasized peripheral warfare against the Third Reich (not massive frontal assaults), and primarily bombing Germany into submission, so much so that when an invasion of Europe did occur, it would only be a mopping-up exercise, that would not require large numbers of American troops. (This was a legacy of the fact that Great Britain had lost an entire generation of youth in World War I and was unwilling to see this happen again unless it was absolutely necessary.) General George C. Marshall, who was in the process of building a large American Army, was of the opinion that the efficacy of bombing was overrated, and that the Allies (once America was in the war, which was assumed to be only a matter of time) would be required to meet and defeat the German Army head-on, in Europe, in order to win the war. Without attempting to, Marshall established himself as the dominant personality among the attendees.

Harry Hopkins (who had just returned from visiting Stalin in the embattled Soviet Union) persuaded the reluctant and still-skeptical military chiefs of both nations that from now on, all-out military aid to the USSR would have to be a firm

for airplane construction. Stalin told Hopkins, "Give us anti-aircraft guns and the aluminum and we can fight for three or four years."[225]]

Roosevelt insisted on, and got, a joint statement on Anglo-American foreign policy or "peace aims" (that is, a statement of general principles for guidance in war-and-peacemaking) which would be used to both justify the conference to the world, and for propaganda effect against the Axis. **This document came to be called "The Atlantic Charter."** It was signed on August 12th, and publicly released by both sides two days later. The document espoused the basic principles of free trade and self-determination for all peoples (two concepts viewed as anti-colonialist, and inimical to the very structure of the British Empire, by many of the attendees, especially Lord Beaverbrook, who threw a temper tantrum when he

Anglo-American policy. With Stalin's concurrence, he laid the groundwork with the Anglo-American military chiefs for holding an international conference to discuss aid to the Soviet Union in Moscow in October, and Roosevelt and Churchill drafted a short message to Stalin proposing this.

Churchill pressed Roosevelt to send a stern warning to Japan---a joint communiqué to be sent by the U.S., Great Britain, and the Dutch government-in-exile---warning that future expansion in southeast Asia might mean war with the United States, and that if Japan went to war with any third party [i.e., Russia], that the United States would be compelled to assist that third party. Roosevelt agreed in principle with what such future Japanese conquests might mean, but did not approve the text of the joint message that Churchill had proposed, and none was issued. Churchill argued that only such a strong and direct message would deter Japan from further expansion by conquest. Roosevelt was concerned that such a direct approach might actually instigate an immediate sharp reaction by Japan, rather than restrain that nation. **At this time, he still preferred to get into the war with Germany by provoking incidents at sea in the Atlantic, and so demurred on Churchill's request for a strong joint communiqué, which might have provoked Japan into immediate**

---

[225] Kershaw, *Fateful Choices*, 304-308.

saw the draft on August 12th). The document also contained the seeds underlying the basis and rationale for the future United Nations organization (even if a bit watered down by FDR and Sumner Welles). [More on the Atlantic Charter below.]

Perhaps the most significant policy decision that came out of the conference was FDR's oral promise to wage an undeclared war against Germany at sea in the Atlantic, in the hopes of provoking an incident that would serve as a *casus belli,* and propel America to a formal declaration of war. Narrator David McCullough explained in the PBS documentary *FDR:* "They talked for 4 days; two titanic egos taking each other's measure. Churchill was determined to bind the Americans ever more firmly to the British cause. Roosevelt was wary; he was unwilling to ask Congress for a declaration of war without rock-solid support of the American people. But he

rash action. **His funds freeze and oil embargo was designed to stop Japan in its tracks and make it abandon a move north against the USSR, and plan instead for an eventual move south to grab the oil it could no longer purchase from the United States. FDR would be much more willing to exert a full court press on Japan in November, after the forthcoming Naval 'incidents' with Germany in the North Atlantic---in September and October---had failed to incite a war fever in the United States.**

The emotional high point of the conference was the Church Parade held onboard the fantail of HMS *Prince of Wales* on Sunday, August 10th, the second day of the Conference. It was attended by 300 American sailors from USS *Augusta,* the majority of the crew of *Prince of Wales,* and all of the visiting dignitaries and military staffs. Churchill had carefully orchestrated the entire service by personally selecting the three hymns, as well as the Bible verses and subjects of the various sermons. It was a profound emotional experience for all who attended, and Churchill openly wept at one point as the combined crews sang "Onward Christian Soldiers." The service not only *created the appearance* of unity in photographs taken that day for the historical record; it actually did help unite the leadership of the two English speaking nations informally allied against Nazi Germany. The emotional and cultural bonds between the two nations were irrevocably cemented by the

was searching for some way to support Great Britain before it was too late…**When Churchill returned to England he told his Cabinet that Roosevelt had made a secret promise: <u>that he would wage war against Nazi Germany, but not declare it. Everything was to be done to force an incident.</u>"**

events of August 10th. In spite of their disagreements over some policy and strategy issues, they had much more in common---namely, defeating Hitler's Germany---than they did dividing them, and the religious service drove that point home.[226] The service worked a kind of magic, forging an informal spiritual alliance between the two nations, even though one was a belligerent, and the other was officially still a neutral, which had not yet formally declared war. And this was one of the major goals, perhaps *the* major goal, of the whole conference, really: to announce to the world that the American and British governments had met, <u>on their ships of war</u>, ***to discuss strategies for defeating Nazi Germany.***

And while President Roosevelt did not promise Churchill that the United States would formally declare war on Germany, the working assumption throughout the conference, noted by Admiral King, was that the two nations were already allies

---

[226] In *FDR: The War President,* Kenneth Davis wrote the following (p. 260): "It was a service in whose planning Churchill had been personally much involved, to ensure that is was 'fully choral and fully photographic,' as he said. He had selected the hymns 'O God Our Help in Ages Past,' 'Onward Christian Soldiers,' and 'Eternal Father Strong to Save.' He had approved the…Bible lesson…He had even vetted the prayers, having them read to him, as he lay naked in his bath, by his private secretary, John Martin---prayers for the President, for the King and his ministers and his armed services, for the millions who suffered from war-injury and Nazi-Fascist oppression, and a closing prayer that 'we may be preserved from hatred, bitterness and all the spirit of revenge.' The event fully justified its careful preparation. The fine weather of the day before, rare in Newfoundland even at the height of the summer, continued. 'None who took part in it will forget the spectacle presented that sunlit morning on the crowded quarterdeck,' wrote Churchill in a later year, '---the symbolism of the Union Jack and the Stars and Stripes draped side by side on the pulpit; the American and British chaplains sharing in the reading of the prayers; the highest military, naval, and air officers of Britain and the United States grouped in one body behind the President and me; the close-packed ranks of British and American sailors…sharing the same books and joining fervently in the prayers and hymns familiar to both…Every word seemed to stir the heart. It was a great hour to live.'"

		and in the war together, for all practical purposes. Churchill's private secretary, John Martin, told Jock Colville (official secretary to the Prime Minister) that he had heard Roosevelt say: **"I do not intend to declare war; I intend to wage it."**[227]
August 12, 1941	The **Draft Extension Act** passes the House of Representatives *by only one vote.* President Roosevelt signs the Act on August 18, 1941. The vote was: **For: 203** (182 Dem.; 21 Rep.) **Against: 202** (133 Rep.; 65 Dem.) To ensure its passage, Speaker of the House Sam Rayburn had summarily gaveled the vote 'closed' just as several House members were about to change their votes. News of the narrow vote arrived at Argentia on the final day of the conference between Churchill and Roosevelt. It gave Churchill and his	**The Act *extended the term of service* for draftees beyond the short time span of 12 months originally enacted in the 1940 legislation, *by an additional 18 months* (2.5 years total, vice 1), thus preventing a mass exodus after the end of September and the "disintegration" of the expanding American Army.** This action was absolutely essential to maintaining a standing army and building upon the training of the draftees that had begun a year earlier, as the United States moved ever closer to entering the Second World War. The narrow margin of victory was indicative of how much the American people were still against entering the fighting in World War II, and was emblematic of the problem faced by FDR as he pushed the nation to provide ever-increasing aid to Great Britain and the USSR, while he endeavored to prepare the American people, psychologically, for the need to confront the Axis on the battlefield. The very narrow margin of the legislative victory in this battle *over simply extending the amount of time a draftee would serve,* highlighted to Roosevelt the need to manufacture an "incident" which

---

[227] Meacham, *Franklin and Winston,* 121.

	military heads, who were anxious to have the United States formally declare war on Germany, a better appreciation of the domestic political minefield in which FDR was operating, and of the constraints upon him. **(Immediately before the Argentia Conference, 75% of the American people <u>opposed entering the war</u>; shortly after the conference, this number had dropped only one point, to 74%).** Senator Burton K. Wheeler, a leading isolationist in Congress, said that the closeness of the vote to renew the draft demonstrated **"that the Administration could not get a resolution through the Congress for a declaration of war."**[228]	would unite America and propel it into World War II as a belligerent---for it was clear to him that no amount of speechmaking or persuasion by him was ever going to unite the nation and fill a reluctant citizenry with the will and desire necessary to fight the Axis powers. At this time Nazi Germany was clearly winning the war: the Soviet Union was "on the ropes," and Great Britain had suffered serious reverses during the spring of 1941 in Greece and Crete, and in Egypt---and was simply "hanging on" by virtue of the fact that Hitler was preoccupied by his invasion of the Soviet Union. **The American people, while willing to prepare for self defense in case of attack, and willing to support material aid to Great Britain and the USSR,** <u>were in no mood to fight the vaunted German war machine</u>. "Lord Beaverbrook, Churchill's Minister of Supply, had traveled on to Washington from Placentia Bay and had reported back that **there was no chance of the United States entering the war until a direct attack on its own territory forced it to do so."**[229] This was not only a profoundly accurate assessment of the mood of America in August of 1941, but it was eerily prophetic, as well.
August 14, 1941	The CNO (Stark) sends a Naval message to the Navy's Pacific commands	The message read in part: **"Japanese rapidly completing withdrawal from worldwide shipping routes. Scheduled**

---

[228] Kershaw, *Fateful Choices,* 315.

[229] Ibid., 318.

	advising the Fleet's commanders and other senior officers (the Naval District Commanders in San Diego, San Francisco, and Seattle) of Japan's withdrawal from worldwide trade.	**sailings cancelled and the majority of ships other than [those in] China and Japan sea areas are homeward bound.**" (When nations go to war, they not only want to avoid having their merchant ships interned---confiscated---in enemy ports, but they usually need them for war-related logistical purposes closer to home.)
August 15, 1941	**Hitler promises the Japanese Ambassador to Germany, Baron Hiroshi Oshima, that if Japan finds itself at war with the United States, he will commence hostilities against America.** This crucial information is revealed through a **MAGIC** intercept, which was read by both FDR and Churchill after the Argentia Conference. The significance of this Hitler statement is that whereas the <u>Tripartite Pact</u> was *formally only a defensive alliance*---in which the parties had agreed to aid each other if attacked by the U.S.---the German dictator, as an inducement for Japan to make war upon the United States, was in effect promising to make war on America even if	I quote here the operative paragraph from the book *The Emperor's Codes,* by Michael Smith (p. 90): "The **Purple** decrypts of Oshima's reports to Tokyo were now providing the Allies with a good deal of useful intelligence on the war in Europe. The Japanese Ambassador had unique access to the thinking of the High Command and even of the Fuhrer himself. As Hitler sought to draw the Japanese into the war with the Soviet Union, he had Oshima flown to his Eastern Front field headquarters in Rastenburg, East Prussia, for private briefings on the progress of Operation Barbarossa. By August, the Japanese Ambassador's telegrams to Tokyo were speaking of staggering Soviet losses 'estimated at between five and six million.' The **Purple** decrypts also revealed the extent of the pressure exerted by Hitler and his lieutenants to get Japan to declare war on the Allies. Oshima reported that 'the Fuhrer was not at all satisfied with Tokyo's attitude, particularly with regard to the continuation of Japanese-U.S. negotiations.' **This campaign culminated, in mid-August, in Hitler promising that 'in the event of a**

	Japan (and not America) initiated the hostilities.	**collision between Japan and the United States, Germany would at once open hostilities with America.'"**[230] Smith, on pages 97-98, also describes how, during the week prior to the Pearl Harbor attack, Baron Oshima sought to *reconfirm* that Germany would make war on America if hostilities commenced between Japan and the U.S.: "The **Purple** messages from Tokyo to Berlin also revealed the Japanese anxiety to ensure that Germany would support it in any confrontation with America. Oshima's problems in confirming this beyond a shadow of a doubt were exacerbated by Hitler's absence at Rastenberg…The Japanese Ambassador managed, however, to secure a firm promise from Ribbentrop. *'Should Japan become engaged in a war against the United States, Germany, of course, would join the war immediately.'* And

---

[230] The date of transmission of this **MAGIC** dispatch from Berlin is identified as August 15, 1941 in the book *Marching Orders,* by Bruce Lee (see pp. 5 and 6 of the main text, and footnote no. 5 at the bottom of page 6). The British had received **Purple** machines from the United States, at the unilateral direction of General George C. Marshall, and Churchill wrote in marginalia on the **MAGIC** intercept on August 23rd, the date he received his translated decryption: "In view of the fact that the Americans themselves gave us the key to the Japanese messages it seems probable the President [has seen this] already." Menzies, his intelligence chief, replied in his own hand on August 24th, the next day: **"The Americans have had this message."** This information is all confirmed in John Costello's *Days of Infamy* (p. 306-307, 412), in which Costello explains that Stewart Menzies ("C," the head of MI6) obtained his confirmation that the American President had seen the message via a special, secure telegraphic and cipher channel MI6 maintained with its Rockefeller Plaza headquarters at the British Security Coordination office (BSC) in New York City, using the British TYPEX cipher machine. Churchill had written a note to Menzies on August 23rd stating it was "desirable" that President Roosevelt be made aware of Hitler's promise, writing "Propose me action, please" on his copy of the diplomatic decrypt. Menzies could only have provided the assurance he did to Churchill the next day after consulting with either the U.S. Army or U.S. Navy (jointly in charge of **MAGIC**) via the TYPEX circuit established at BSC headquarters in Rockefeller Plaza before the war began. (*See* also Rusbridger and Nave, p. 274-5, footnote 44, for further confirmation of the secure underwater cable link between MI6 and BSC in New York City.)

		on page 99 Smith writes: "Meanwhile, Oshima was making frantic efforts to confirm Hitler's promise of support against America. <u>The Japanese Ambassador told Tokyo that he had negotiated a 'secret agreement' with Germany and Italy, adding that</u> *'should a state of war arise between Japan and the United States, Germany and Italy for their part will consider themselves at war with the United States.'*"[231] [Emphasis added] These early December assurances from the German government to the Japanese Ambassador, confirming Hitler's personal promise made in mid-August, were no doubt very much on Roosevelt's mind late on December 7th, and on the morning of December 8th, the day after the Pearl Harbor attack, when---after trying unsuccessfully to engineer a *casus belli* "incident" with Germany in the Atlantic since early September---**he only requested that the Congress declare war on Japan**. He knew that Hitler would soon solve his "Germany" problem for him. And on December 11th, as predicted by **MAGIC**, Hitler and Mussolini both declared war on the United States.
August 16, 1941	FDR Discusses the Argentia Conference with the press onboard the Presidential yacht *Potomac*, at Rockland,	FDR downplayed the true importance of the conference (by not discussing his commitment to begin convoying on or about September 1st, and his even more significant decision to wage an undeclared war at sea against Germany),

---

[231] Germany's definitive promise to make war on America should Japan do so is further confirmed in Bruce Lee's book *Marching Orders,* which is the definitive work published to date on the Allied use of the **MAGIC** intercepts. This is incontrovertibly confirmed on pages 24 and 33.

	Maine.	and emphasized its symbolic importance. (The Atlantic Charter had been released on August 12th, and this was the only firm knowledge of the conference that the press had.) When one reporter asked FDR <u>if the U.S. was any closer to entering the war</u>, FDR replied, **"I should say, no."** When asked if a bigger Lend-Lease appropriation would be needed to provide aid to both Russia and England, he gave a deflective answer: **"We are still studying it."**[232]
August 17, 1941	FDR meets with Japanese Ambassador Nomura; he delivers a stern warning to Japan against any further expansion in Southeast Asia, and then discusses with Nomura (without making any commitment) the concept of a possible summit meeting, first proposed by Prime Minister Konoye earlier in the month.	The warning note delivered by FDR to Ambassador Nomura was a watered down version of what Churchill had originally proposed sending to Japan, as parallel U.S. and British communiqués, during the Argentia Conference. (FDR had declined to send the two parallel communiqués, but had promised to consider some of the hard language Churchill proposed, and use it in his own message to Japan.) Churchill had wanted the key wording in Roosevelt's warning to read: "Any further encroachment by Japan in the South West Pacific would produce a situation in which the United States Government would be compelled to take counter measures ***even though these might lead to war between the United States and Japan.*** " *[Emphasis added]* The softened note Roosevelt passed to Nomura read: "…this Government now finds it necessary to say to the

---

[232] Davis, *FDR: The War President,* 274.

Government of Japan that if the Japanese Government takes any further steps in pursuance of a policy or program of military domination by force or threat of force of neighboring countries, the Government of the United States will be compelled to take immediately any and all steps which it may deem necessary toward safeguarding the legitimate rights and interests of the United States and American nationals and toward insuring the safety and security of the United States."[233]

The original draft language in Washington on August 15th had ended with these words: *"…notwithstanding the possibility that such further steps on its part [Japan's] may result in conflict between the two countries."*

The statement FDR delivered did not mention the word "war" as desired by Churchill, nor did it use the word "conflict" contained in the original draft by Sumner Welles.

As FDR expressed to Churchill at Argentia, he merely hoped that his warning would make the Japanese pause in whatever they were planning, and buy the U.S. and Britain an additional 30 days to reinforce their garrisons in the Far East.

FDR then adopted a conciliatory tone with Nomura at the meeting by responding in somewhat receptive, but

---

[233] Beard, *President Roosevelt and the Coming of War, 1941*, 486-496; and Greaves, Jr., *Pearl Harbor*, 100-101.

			non-specific terms to Konoye's summit proposal. (FDR proposed Alaska instead of Hawaii as a possible site, but made no firm commitment.) This more friendly tone was clearly part of his strategy (announced to Churchill at Argentia) to "baby them along" for about 3 months or so, to buy time in the Far East, and attempt to delay what seemed the likelihood of hostilities between Japan and the Western Powers.
August 19, 1941	**Churchill discusses the Argentia Conference with his Cabinet.** The Argentia Conference ended for the British, as historian Kenneth Davis writes, with "a glow of good feeling and renewed hope," in spite of the fact that there was some disagreement with the Americans over a number of policy issues. After all, they had come away from a glorified "get acquainted session" with confidential assurances from the U.S. President <u>**that he would soon commence convoying of merchant ships more than halfway to Great Britain, and that he would wage undeclared war against the German Navy in the Atlantic.**</u>		In his book *FDR: The War President*, Kenneth Davis (p. 274) <u>records the actual language used by Churchill to his Cabinet to describe the most significant oral conversations held between him and Roosevelt at Placentia Bay:</u> "He had 'got on intimate terms with the President'…Roosevelt personally ***'was obviously determined that they [the Americans] should come in'*** to the war, and despite the fact that he ***'was skating on pretty thin ice in his relations with Congress which, however, he did not regard as truly representative of the country,'*** had told Churchill <u>***'he would wage war, but not declare it,'***</u> that he <u>***'would become more and more provocative,'***</u> and that the Germans, if they did not like it, ***'could attack American forces!'*** Churchill had warned the President that if, say, next spring, Russia 'was compelled to sue for peace,' and 'hope died in Britain that the United States were coming into the war,' he, the Prime Minister, 'would not answer for the consequences.' Roosevelt in reply had <u>***'made it clear that he would look for an incident which would justify him***</u>

in opening hostilities' within the next few months." [Emphasis added]

In his book *Franklin D. Roosevelt and American Foreign Policy* (pp. 285-286), historian Robert Dallek discusses additional details of what Churchill told his War Cabinet about FDR's promises at Argentia. The Prime Minister told his cabinet that he told Roosevelt in private that "I would rather have an American declaration of war now and no supplies for six months than double the supplies and no declaration." In response to this, **Roosevelt complained to Churchill that if he asked Congress for a declaration of war under the current circumstances, a debate would ensue that would last for three months;** this underlay his decision to force an incident. Churchill also provided his Cabinet with the good news that FDR had promised to start convoying merchantmen bound for the United Kingdom with U.S. Navy ships between North America and Iceland, saying: "The American Navy would have their convoy system in full operation between their country and Iceland by September 1st...The President's orders to these escorts were to attack any U-boat which showed itself, even if it were 200 or 300 miles away from the convoy. Everything was to be done to force an 'incident.' This would put the enemy in the dilemma that either he could attack the convoys, in which case his U-boats would be attacked by American Naval forces, or, if he refrained from attack, this would be tantamount to giving us

		victory in the Battle of the Atlantic."
August 21, 1941	FDR sends a <u>written message to Congress</u> on the **Atlantic Charter**.[234]	The message is quoted here in its entirety: Over a week ago I held several important conferences at sea with the British Prime Minister. Because of the factor of safety to British, Canadian, and American ships and their personnel no prior announcement of these meetings could properly be made. At the close, a public statement by the Prime Minister and the President was made. I quote it for the information of the Congress and for the record: "The President of the United States and the Prime Minister, Mr. Churchill, representing his Majesty's Government in the United Kingdom, have met at sea. They have been accompanied by officials of their two governments, including high ranking officers of their military, naval, and air services. The whole problem of the supply of munitions of war, as provided by the Lend-Lease Act, for the armed forces of the United States and for those countries actively engaged in resisting aggression has been further examined. Lord Beaverbrook, the minister of supply of the British government, has joined in these conferences. He is going to proceed to Washington to discuss further details with appropriate officials of the United States government. These conferences

---

[234] Hunt, ed., *The Essential Franklin D. Roosevelt*, 222-224.

will also cover the supply problems of the Soviet Union. The President and the Prime Minister have had several conferences. They have considered the dangers to world civilization arising from the policies of military domination by conquest upon which the Hitlerite government of Germany and other governments associated therewith have embarked, and have made clear the steps which their countries are respectively taking for their safety in the face of these dangers. They have agreed upon the following joint declaration:

'The President of the United States of America and the Prime Minister, Mr. Churchill, representing His Majesty's Government in the United Kingdom, being met together, deem it right to make known certain common principles in the national policies of their respective countries on which they base their hopes for a better future for the world.

First, their countries seek no aggrandizement, territorial or other;

Second, they desire to see no territorial changes that do not accord with the freely expressed wishes of the peoples concerned;

Third, they respect the right of all peoples to choose the form of government under which they will live; and they wish to see sovereign rights and self-government restored to those who have been forcibly deprived of them;

Fourth, they will endeavor, with the

respect of their existing obligations, to further the enjoyment by all states, great and small, victor or vanquished, of access, on equal terms, to the trade and to the raw materials of the world which are needed for their economic prosperity;

Fifth, they desire to bring about the fullest collaboration between all nations in the economic field, with the object of securing, for all, improved labor standards, economic advancement, and social security;

Sixth, after the final destruction of Nazi tyranny, they hope to see established a peace which will afford to all nations the means of dwelling in safety within their own boundaries, and which will afford assurance that all the men in all the lands may live out their lives in freedom from fear and want;

Seventh, such a peace should enable all men to traverse the high seas and oceans without hindrance;

Eighth, they believe that all of the nations of the world, for realistic as well as spiritual reasons must come to the abandonment of the use of force. Since no future peace can be maintained if land, sea, or air armaments continue to be employed by nations which threaten, or may threaten, aggression outside of their frontiers, they believe, pending the establishment of a wider and permanent system of general security, that the disarmament of such nations is essential. They will likewise aid and encourage all other practicable measures which will lighten for peace-loving peoples the crushing burden of armaments.'

The Congress and the President having heretofore determined through the Lend-Lease Act on the national policy on American aid to the democracies which East and West are waging war against dictatorships, the military and naval conversations at these meetings made clear gains in furthering the effectiveness of this aid. Furthermore, the Prime Minister and I are arranging for conferences with the Soviet Union to aid in its defense against the attack made by the principal aggressor of the modern world---Germany.

Finally, the declaration of principles at this time presents a goal which at this time is worthwhile for our type of civilization to seek. It is so clear-cut that it is difficult to oppose in any major particular without automatically admitting a willingness to accept compromise with Nazism; or to agree to a world peace which would give to Nazism domination over large numbers of conquered nations. Inevitably such a peace would be a gift to Nazism to take breath---armed breath---for a second war to extend the control over Europe and Asia to the American hemisphere itself.

It is perhaps unnecessary for me to call attention once more to the utter lack of validity of the spoken or written word of the Nazi government.

It is also unnecessary for me to point out that that the declaration of principles

		includes of necessity the world need for freedom of religion and freedom of information. No society of the world organized under the announced principles could survive without these freedoms which are a part of the whole freedom for which we strive."
August 24, 1941	**Churchill Makes a radio broadcast about the Atlantic Charter.**[235]	Here are but a few representative excerpts from this very warm (and very long) speech: "I thought you might like me to tell you something about the voyage which I made across the ocean to meet our great friend, the President of the United States…In a spacious, landlocked bay which reminded me of the West Coast of Scotland, powerful American warships protected by strong flotillas and far-ranging aircraft awaited our arrival, and, as it were, stretched out a hand to help us in. Our party arrived in the newest, or almost the newest, British battleship, the *Prince of Wales,* with a modern escort of British and Canadian destroyers, and there for three days I spent my time in company, and I think I may say in comradeship, with Mr. Roosevelt; while all the time the chiefs of the staff and the naval and military commanders both of the British Empire and of the United States sat together in continual council. President Roosevelt is the thrice-chosen head of the most powerful state and community in the world. I am the servant of the King and Parliament at

---

[235] Churchill, ed., *Never Give In!,* 297-305.

present charged with the principal direction of our affairs in these fateful times…Therefore this meeting was bound to be important, because of the enormous forces at present only partially mobilised but steadily mobilising which are at the disposal of these two major groupings of the human family: the British Empire and the United States, who, fortunately for the progress of mankind, speak the same language, and very largely think the same thoughts, or anyhow think a lot of the same thoughts.

The meeting was therefore symbolic. That is its prime importance…Would it be presumptuous for me to say that it symbolizes something even more majestic---namely, <u>the marshalling of the good forces of the world against the evil forces</u> which are now so formidable and triumphant and which have cast their cruel spell over the whole of Europe and a large part of Asia?...*This is the highest honour and the most glorious opportunity which could ever have come to any branch of the human race…even the most skeptical person must have the feeling that we all have the chance to play our part and do our duty in some great design, the end of which no mortal can foresee…*

[Churchill then discussed at length the history of the war in Europe, the Nazi attack on the Soviet Union, the brave Russian resistance, and shifted to the depredations of Japan in the Far East.]

…For five long years the Japanese

military factions, seeking to emulate the style of Hitler and Mussolini…have been invading and harrying the 500,000,000 inhabitants of China. Japanese armies have been wandering about that vast land in futile excursions, carrying with them carnage, ruin, and corruption and calling it the 'Chinese Incident.' Now they stretch a grasping hand into the southern seas of China; they snatch Indo-China from the wretched Vichy French; they menace by their movements Siam; menace Singapore, the British link with Australia; and menace the Philippine Islands under the protection of the United States. **It is certain that this has got to stop.** Every effort will be made to secure a peaceful settlement. The United States are labouring with infinite patience to arrive at a fair and amicable settlement which will give Japan the utmost reassurance for her legitimate interests. We earnestly hope these negotiations will succeed. **But this I must say: that if these hopes should fail we shall of course range ourselves unhesitatingly at the side of the United States.**

And thus we come back to the quiet bay somewhere in the Atlantic where misty sunshine plays on great ships which carry the White Ensign, or the Stars and Stripes. We had the idea, when we met there---the President and I---that without attempting to draw up final and formal peace aims, or war aims, it was necessary to give all peoples, especially the oppressed and conquered peoples, a simple, rough-and-ready wartime statement of the goal towards which the

British Commonwealth and the United States mean to make their way, and thus make a way for others to march with them upon a road which will certainly be painful, and may be long!

…The ordeals…of the conquered peoples will be hard. We must give them hope; we must give them the conviction that their sufferings and their resistances will not be in vain. The tunnel may be dark and long, but at the end there is light…Keep your souls clean from all contact with the Nazis; make them feel even in their fleeting hour of brutish triumph that they are the moral outcasts of mankind. Help is coming; mighty forces are arming on your behalf. Have faith. Have hope. Deliverance is sure. This is the signal we have flashed across the water…You will perhaps have noticed that the President of the United States and the British representative, in what is aptly called the 'Atlantic Charter,' have jointly pledged their countries to the final destruction of the Nazi tyranny. *That is a solemn and grave undertaking. It must be made good; it will be made good.* **And, of course, many practical arrangements to fulfill that purpose have been and are being organised and set in motion.**

The question has been asked: How near is the United States to War? There is certainly one man who knows the answer to that question. If Hitler has not yet declared war on the United States, it is surely not out of love for American institutions; it is certainly not because he could not find a pretext. He has murdered half a dozen countries for far less. ***Fear of immediately redoubling the tremendous energies now being employed against him is no doubt a restraining influence.*** But the real reason is, I am sure, to be found in the method which he has so faithfully adhered and by which he has gained so much. What is that method? It is a very simple method. One by one: that is his plan; that is his guiding rule; that is the trick by which he has enslaved so large a portion of the world…

<u>Now Hitler is striking at Russia with all his might</u>, well knowing the difficulties of geography which stand between Russia and the aid which the Western Democracies are trying to bring. <u>We shall strive our utmost to overcome all obstacles and bring this aid</u>. **We have arranged for a conference in Moscow between the United States, British and Russian authorities to settle the whole plan. No barrier must stand in the way.** But why is Hitler striking at Russia…It is with the declared object of turning his whole force upon the British Islands, and if he could succeed in beating the life and strength out of us, which is not so easy, then is the moment when he would settle his account, and it is already a long one, with the people of the United States and generally with the Western Hemisphere. One by one, there is the process…I rejoiced to find that the President saw in their true light and proportion the extreme dangers by which the American people as well as the

British people are now beset. **It was indeed by the mercy of God that he began eight years ago that revival of the strength of the American Navy**[236] *without which* the New World today would have to take its orders from the European dictators, but *with which* <u>the United States still retains the power to marshal her gigantic strength, and in saving herself to render an incomparable service to mankind</u>.

We had a church parade on Sunday in our Atlantic bay. The President came on to the quarterdeck of the *Prince of Wales*, where there were mingled together many hundreds of American and British sailors and marines. The sun shone bright and warm while we all sang the old hymns which are our common inheritance and which we learned as children in our homes…**We sang the sailor's hymn 'For Those in Peril'---and there are very many---'on the sea.' We sang 'Onward Christian Soldiers.'** And indeed I felt that this was no vain presumption, but that *we had the right to feel that were serving a cause for the*

---

[236] In *That Gallant Ship: USS Yorktown,* author Robert Cressman documents the underfunding of Naval construction between the end of World War I and 1933, and the resulting atrophy of the American shipbuilding industry, especially with the onset of the Great Depression in 1929. In 1933 the U.S. Navy was well below the "treaty strength" authorized by the 1930 London Naval Treaty. He explains that President Roosevelt, "an avowed navalist," used the National Industrial Recovery Act (NIRA) of June 16, 1933 to fund new construction and Naval modernization. The NIRA's language provided for "the construction of Naval vessels within the terms and/or limits established by the London Naval Treaty of 1930." Roosevelt used the NIRA to fund 32 new ships during the early and mid 1930s, including two new aircraft carriers, *Yorktown* and *Enterprise*. This wise use of NIRA funds not only provided an effective jobs program, and helped revive the American shipbuilding industry, but it was the pilots and aircraft of *Yorktown* and *Enterprise* that won the critical Battle of Midway for the United States in June of 1942. It was this use of NIRA finds---to modernize and expand the U.S. Navy during FDR's first two terms---to which Churchill alluded in his speech.

		sake of which a trumpet has sounded from on high. <u>When I looked upon that densely packed congregation of fighting men of the same language, of the same faith, of the same fundamental laws and the same ideals, and now to a large extent of the same interests, and certainly in different degrees facing the same dangers,</u> **it swept across me that here was the only hope, but also the sure hope, of saving the world from measureless degradation."** [Emphasis added]
September 3, 1941	**In a crucial Japanese <u>Liaison Conference</u> lasting 7 hours, <u>a consensus is arrived at to ardently prepare for war</u> against Southeast Asia (including the Dutch East Indies, Britain, and America) <u>while simultaneously pursuing peace through diplomacy.</u>** The war preparations had a clear primacy over diplomacy. (The Navy's recommendation for concluding war preparations was October 15th, and this was also the Navy's recommendation for the diplomacy deadline.) Acutely aware that the "oil clock" was ticking---that delay was anathema, and would continue to sap Japan's	During the second half of August Army and Navy planners had assembled a document titled: "Essentials for Carrying Out the Empire's Policies." It resolved to go to war with the three Western powers in Southeast Asia if diplomacy was unsuccessful by early October. ("Diplomacy" meant getting the U.S. and Britain to cease providing aid to China; that they stop military buildups in the Far East; and that the U.S. reinstate Japan's access to oil. In exchange, Japan would withdraw from Indochina once it had won its war with China, and would guarantee the neutrality of the Philippines.) The Navy was not at all optimistic about its chances in a protracted war with the United States; the mood of the military leadership was one of fatalism, preferring defeat in war to shameful acquiescence to Western demands, which would have meant rejection of the "Imperial Way" and Empire, and withdrawal from China, both unthinkable concepts for the Army and Navy---and indeed, for the civilian

	strength---the consensus was that if there was to be war against Great Britain and America, it must begin soon while there was still a chance of winning the war. John Toland has summarized on page 100 of *Rising Sun:* "The decision to start war preparations at once while attempting to negotiate was much more than that. It meant, in fact, that hostilities would commence unless the negotiations were successfully concluded by October 10."	elites at this time. Optimists believed that quick victories against the Western Powers in Southeast Asia *might, if all went well,* result in the Western powers suing for peace. The only chance for a victory in war was to strike soon, while Japan was still strong, and while the West was still relatively weak. This vital document, advocating a policy committing Japan to war (and placing preparations for war well ahead of the importance of negotiations), was prepared even while Prime Minister Konoye was planning a peace summit with Roosevelt, and demonstrates the primacy of the military in formulating Japanese policy at this time, underneath what was only a thin veneer of civilian government. The decision of the Liaison Conference was rubber-stamped by the Cabinet the next day.[237]
September 4, 1941	**The *Greer* Incident in the North Atlantic becomes the first known instance in World War II of a German U-boat firing a torpedo at an American warship.** The incident occurred about 165 miles south of Iceland. Ian Kershaw's account of the incident differs in a few details from the long passage in which I have quoted (to the right of this column)	Historian Kenneth S. Davis described the Greer incident as follows in *FDR: The War President* (page 277): "On Thursday, September 4, 1941, in that wide area of the North Atlantic where the Hitler-proclaimed German war zone and the Roosevelt-proclaimed Western Hemispheric defense zone overlapped, an American destroyer, the USS *Greer,* was speeding toward Iceland, bearing mail for U.S. troops, when told by a British patrol plane that a German submarine lurked beneath the waves about ten miles ahead of it. The submarine, we now know, was U-652. The destroyer's

---

[237] Kershaw, *Fateful Choices,* 339-343.

historian Kenneth Davis. Kershaw points out that since *Greer* was not escorting American shipping, she had no authority to attack---and was only required to report the U-boat's position. Kershaw writes that after the first British bomber had departed the scene, *Greer* had kept the U-boat submerged for about an hour-and-a-half with aggressive sonar searches, and had given the U-boat's position to a second British bomber, which had arrived on-scene and continued the hunt. After about 4 hours of evasion, the U-boat's skipper turned the tables and fired two torpedoes at *USS Greer,* missing. Following this, Kershaw writes that Greer dropped 8 depth charges on U-652, causing minor damage. About ten hours after the hunt began, after a British destroyer had arrived on-scene, USS *Greer* (after dropping 11 more depth charges) abandoned the hunt and proceeded to

commander at once sounded general quarters and began a zigzag course at increased speed while seeking sonar contact with the submerged vessel. Such contact was soon made. Thereafter, the destroyer trailed the U-boat and continuously reported its location to the British, this in accord with the policy the President had announced, if publicly in rather vague terms, last May. After an hour or so the British plane was in position to drop depth charges in the U-boat's close vicinity and dropped four of them, with no evident effect, before turning back to Iceland to refuel. For two hours more the *Greer* tracked the submarine and reported to the British. Finally the harassed U-boat, its desperate commander probably believing that the destroyer had made the depth charge attack actually made by the British plane, suddenly fired a torpedo at the destroyer, then a second one, perhaps a third. The *Greer* dodged them and began to circle, dropping depth charges but losing contact with the submarine as it did so. When the resumed sonar search found the submarine after another two hours or so, the *Greer* again dropped depth charges, no fewer than eleven of them, before breaking off an engagement in which neither side had inflicted casualties or material damage on the other."

	Iceland with its passengers and mail.[238]	
September 5, 1941	**FDR discusses the Greer incident at a press conference.** He emphasizes the deliberate nature of the U-boat's attack: conducted in daylight, on a ship with an identification number painted on the hull, flying the American flag, and operating within the U.S. Security Zone.	Ian Kershaw provides this commentary in *Fateful Choices:* "At this point, the President may not have been in full cognizance of the facts. No mention, of course, was made of the harassing role of the *Greer*. In the circumstances, the U-652 could be said to have fired its torpedoes in self-defence. She had been under attack by British warplanes, within the German combat zone, and had merely chanced to gain a periscope glimpse of a four-funnel destroyer similar to those transferred to Britain the previous autumn. But no such considerations were likely to deter Roosevelt, now given an opportunity of the kind he had awaited."
September 5, 1941	**FDR meets with the CNO (Admiral Stark) and CINCLANT (Admiral King) and orders that convoying of British and neutral merchant ships begin on September 16th.** Following the Argentia Conference, Admiral King embarked upon hurried and determined preparations to commence convoying. The Fleet "support train" (oilers, tenders, and other supply	Admiral King (CINCLANT) had received an order from the CNO to commence convoying back on July 19th, but a vacillating FDR had then rescinded the order. Meeting with Churchill at Argentia had apparently strengthened the President's resolve to not only start convoying, but to attempt, by doing so, to force an incident between American ships and German submarines which would either: (a) cause Hitler to declare war on the United States; or (b) would so enrage the American people that it would serve as a *casus belli,* and stimulate a Congressional declaration of war on Germany. In the PBS documentary *FDR,* narrator David McCullough

---

[238] Ibid., 319-320.

	vessels) positioned themselves in Maine, Canada, and Iceland. By mid-September, King had established a destroyer pool of 33 ships at Casco Bay, Maine, and the Support Force Commander had established himself at Argentia. Another sixteen would be available by the end of October, and six more by year's end. The remainder of the Atlantic Fleet's destroyers were needed to escort the capital ships of America's Neutrality Patrol.[239]	summed up Roosevelt's approach following the Argentia conference in August: **"Without telling the American people, Roosevelt issued secret orders to the Navy to escort British convoys and, if necessary, sink Nazi submarines. The President was willing to risk war with Germany."** <u>It would have been more accurate to state:</u> *"Having now adequately educated the American people about the necessity of fighting Nazi Germany, Roosevelt was now willing to <u>precipitate</u> war with Germany, by taking action which virtually guaranteed that there would be shooting incidents at sea between vessels of the U.S. Navy and the Kriegsmarine."* The Cabinet minutes from August 19th of Churchill's account of his meetings with Roosevelt, cited above, support this conclusion.
September 6, 1941	At an <u>Imperial Conference</u>, **the Japanese Government formalized its consensus to complete its preparations to go to war with Britain and America in late October if the Empire's demands in the Far East are not met through negotiations with the United States and Great Britain by the beginning**	The text of the policy decisions made at the Imperial Conference was provided by the former Japanese Ambassador to the United States, Kichisaburo Nomura, in an article published in editor Paul Stillwell's *Air Raid: Pearl Harbor!* (pp. 37-42), which was a reprint of an article originally published in 1951: "1. The Empire of Japan should perfect the preparation for war by the latter part of October, with determination not to shrink from a war with the United States (as well as the United Kingdom and the

---

[239] Heinrichs, *Threshold of War,* 165.

	of October (i.e., October 10th). Paul Stillwell, editor of the excellent anthology *Air Raid: Pearl Harbor!*, quoted historian Samuel Eliot Morison's description of what "peace" meant to the Japanese at this time, when they were intent upon acquiring hegemony over East Asia: "complete control---military, political and economic---of all Oriental countries by a Japanese ruling class, a control imposed by force and terror if not abjectly accepted by other orientals." Japan's elites, and her general public, were ready to go to war to defend this concept of her manifest destiny in Asia.	Netherlands) in order to ensure the self-existence and self-defense of the Empire. 2. Parallel with the above, the Empire of Japan should try to obtain the demands of the Empire through negotiations with the United States and Great Britain, exhausting all diplomatic means for the purpose. 3. The Empire of Japan should determine to commence war at once on the United States (as well as on the United Kingdom and the Netherlands) in case by the beginning of October the negotiations should not have produced any prospect of obtaining the demands of the Empire." The Emperor had severe misgivings about the danger of a war with the United States, yet in spite of his misgivings (expressed at the conference) and his preference for diplomacy over war, and his support of the Konoye plan for a summit, <u>he assented to the policy</u>.[240]
September 11, 1941	**FDR delivers his "Shoot On Sight" fireside chat about the *Greer* Incident.** Although FDR did not specifically use the phrase "shoot on sight" in his speech, this was indeed the policy he initiated, and the very next day the	On Sunday, September 7th, FDR was at his mother's side at Hyde Park when she died. A few minutes later, the largest tree on the estate, a huge ancient oak tree, toppled over with an enormous crash, even though there was no storm, no wind, and no lightning. In the midst of grief, he then received a phone call from Harry Hopkins in Washington which informed him that the State Department's draft of his speech on the

---

[240] Kershaw, *Fateful Choices*, 343-347.

headline in the *New York Times* read: "Roosevelt Orders Navy to Shoot First." Public opinion favored "shoot on sight" with 62 per cent approving of the policy and only 28 per cent against it.[241]

Roosevelt knew that the "Greer Incident" <u>alone</u> would not serve as the *casus belli* that he was looking for. However, his address was successful in persuading Americans that it was necessary to "shoot on sight"---***that is, engage in an undeclared war against Germany in the Atlantic Ocean.***

In the PBS documentary *FDR,* historian Robert Dallek said this of Roosevelt's explanation of the incident in his speech: "What he hides from the American public is the fact that the *Greer* had been tracking the German submarine to help a British seaplane which was going to try to sink it with depth charges." And the narrator, David

Greer incident was completely unsatisfactory---too timid. FDR's address to the nation about the incident was postponed until September 11th, to accommodate his mother's funeral at Hyde Park on September 10th. (Earlier, in June, his confidential assistant and secretary, Missy LeHand, with whom he had shared work and play for two decades, had suffered two strokes, and an accompanying nervous or emotional breakdown---her third. She was incapacitated for the remainder of her short life, and institutionalized. With the exception of Harry Hopkins, the person whom FDR came closest to completely confiding in about matters of state at this point in his life, he was now very much alone.)

<u>FDR's speech was truculent in tone, and some of its most truculent phrases were penned by Roosevelt himself</u>: "The Navy Department of the United States has reported to me that on the morning of September 4, the United States destroyer *Greer,* proceeding in full daylight toward Iceland, had reached a point southeast of Greenland. She was carrying American mail to Iceland. She was flying the American flag. Her identity as an American ship was unmistakable. She was then and there attacked by a submarine. Germany admits that it was a German submarine. The submarine deliberately fired a torpedo at the *Greer,* followed later by another torpedo

---

[241] Kershaw, *Fateful Choices,* 322.

McCullough, intoned: "Roosevelt knew that the *Greer* had deliberately stalked the Nazi U-boat and that the British plane had fired first…Roosevelt did not ask Congress for a declaration of war, but he used the *Greer* incident to justify an undeclared war in the Atlantic, where he was sure that the real war would soon begin."

While Roosevelt ***did not specifically mention his agreement at Argentia to commence the convoying of British merchant ships by the U.S. Navy*** (or his order to the Navy on September 5th to commence doing so on September 16th), he employed strong language in his speech which would justify the escorting of convoys, saying the U.S. would keep the lines of commerce open in its defensive zone "no matter what it costs, no matter what it takes." **The themes of his speech used to justify "shooting on sight" were twofold:** the need to maintain freedom of the seas as a matter of principle, and

attack…**I tell you the blunt fact that the German submarine fired first upon this American destroyer *Greer* without warning, and with deliberate design to sink her.**

Our destroyer, at the time, was in waters which the government of the United States had declared to be waters of self-defense…The United States destroyer, when attacked, was proceeding on a legitimate mission…It would be unworthy of a great nation to exaggerate an isolated incident, or become inflamed by…one act of violence. But it would be inexcusable folly to minimize such incidents [FDR had just cited four other recent incidents between ships at sea and the German armed forces] in the face of evidence which makes it clear that the incident is not isolated, but is part of a general plan. The important truth is that these acts of international lawlessness are a manifestation of a design, a design that has been made clear to the American people for a long time. **It is the Nazi design to abolish freedom of the seas, and to acquire absolute control and domination of these seas for themselves.** For with control of the seas in their own hands, the way can obviously become clear for their next step---domination of the United States, domination of the Western Hemisphere by force of arms. **Under Nazi control of the seas, no merchant ship of the United States or of any other American republic would be free to carry on any peaceful commerce, except by the condescending grace of**

the need to keep war material flowing to Great Britain.

Finally, Roosevelt's statement that U.S. ships and planes would **"protect all merchant ships engaged in commerce within our defensive waters"** was a way of telegraphing that he was now going to convoy merchant ships to Iceland, *without specifically saying so.* If convoying was ever challenged in the future, he could point to this line in his speech and say, *"Oh, but I did tell you about it---I made it quite clear."*

Thus, the *Greer* incident allowed Roosevelt---if he was ever challenged about why he commenced convoying in mid-September---to justify the convoy decision without ever admitting that it was a secret promise his military chiefs made to Churchill's military chiefs at the Argentia Conference.

Ian Kershaw has summarized nicely FDR's

this foreign and tyrannical power…To be ultimately successful in world mastery, Hitler knows that he must get control of the seas. He must first destroy the bridge of ships which we are building across the Atlantic and over which we will continue to roll the implements of war to help destroy him, to destroy all his works in the end. He must wipe out our patrol on sea and in the air to do it. He must silence the British Navy. I think it must be explained over and over again to people who like to think of the United States Navy as an invincible protection, that this can only be true if the British Navy survives. And that, my friends, is simple arithmetic. For if the world outside the Americas falls under Axis domination, the shipbuilding facilities which the Axis powers would then possess in all of Europe, in the British Isles, and in the Far East would be much greater than all of the shipbuilding facilities and potentialities of all the Americas---not only greater, but two or three times greater---enough to win. Even if the United States threw all its resources into such a situation, seeking to double and even redouble the size of our Navy, the Axis powers, in control of the rest of the world, would have the manpower and physical resources to outbuild us several times over. *It is time for all Americans…to stop being deluded by the romantic notion that the Americas can go on living happily and peacefully in a Nazi-dominated world…*

Unrestricted submarine warfare in 1941 constitutes a defiance---and act of

victory over isolationism through his use of the *Greer* incident: "Two days before it happened, only a bare majority of 52 per cent had favoured the U.S. Navy 'convoying' war materials to Britain. The American people had been brought behind a policy [now 62 percent in favor to 28 against] practically guaranteed to draw the United States into future armed clashes with German vessels in the Atlantic. Open warfare was around the corner. The President had outmaneuvered his opponents. The isolationists were isolated. The escorting of convoys had been introduced."[242]

But this was the most FDR could get out of the *Greer* incident. Speaking to Lord Halifax after his speech, Roosevelt reportedly said that "if he asked for a declaration of war he wouldn't get it, and opinion would swing against him."[243]

aggression---against that historic American policy [of freedom of the seas]. It is now clear that Hitler has begun his campaign to control the seas by ruthless force and by wiping out every vestige of international law, every vestige of humanity. His intention has been made clear. The American people can have no further illusions about it. ***No tender whisperings of appeasers*** [in clear reference here to Joseph Kennedy and Charles Lindbergh] ***that Hitler is not interested in the Western Hemisphere, no soporific lullabies that a wide ocean protects us from him*** [a clear reference to the American First Committee and its principal spokesman Charles Lindbergh], ***can long have any effect on the hard-headed, farsighted, and realistic American people***…we Americans are now face to face not with abstract theories, but with cruel, relentless facts. This attack on the *Greer* was no localized military operation in the North Atlantic. This was no mere episode in the struggle between two nations. This was one determined step toward creating a permanent world system based on force, on terror, and on murder. **And I am sure that even now the Nazis are waiting, waiting to see whether the United States will by silence give them the green light to go ahead on this path of destruction…**

Normal practices of diplomacy---note

---

[242] Ibid., 321-322.

[243] Ibid., 326.

| | | writing---are of no possible use in dealing with international outlaws who sink our ships and kill our citizens. One peaceful nation after another has met disaster because each refused to look the Nazi danger squarely in the eye until it actually had them by the throat. The United States will not make that fatal mistake. No act of violence, no act of intimidation will keep us from maintaining intact two bulwarks of American defense: first, our line of supply of material to the enemies of Hitler; and second, the freedom of our shipping on the high seas. **No matter what it takes, no matter what it costs, we will keep open the line of legitimate commerce in these defensive waters of ours…**

I assume that the German leaders are not deeply concerned, tonight or at any other time, by what we Americans or the American government says or publishes about them. We cannot bring about the fall of Nazism by the use of long-range invective. **But when you see a rattlesnake poised to strike, you do not wait until he has struck before you crush him.**

These Nazi submarines and raiders are the rattlesnakes of the Atlantic. They are a menace to the free pathways of the high seas. They are a challenge to our own sovereignty…**Do not let us be hair-splitters.** Let us not ask ourselves whether the Americas should begin to defend themselves after the first attack, or the fifth attack, or the tenth attack, or |

the twentieth attack. *The time for active defense is now.*

Do not let us split hairs. Let us not say: "We will only defend ourselves if the torpedo succeeds in getting home, or if the crew and the passengers are drowned." This is the time for prevention of attack…

In the waters we deem necessary for our defense, <u>American naval vessels and American planes will no longer wait until Axis submarines lurking under the water, or Axis raiders on the surface of the sea, strike their deadly blow---first.</u>

Upon our naval and air patrol---now operating in large number over a vast expanse of the Atlantic Ocean---falls the duty of maintaining the American policy of freedom of the seas---now. **That means, very simply, very clearly, that <u>our patrolling vessels and planes will protect all merchant ships---not only American ships but ships of any flag---engaged in commerce in our defensive waters.</u>** They will protect them from submarines, they will protect them from surface raiders…

My obligation as President is historic; it is clear. Yes, it is inescapable. It is no act of war on our part when we decide to protect the seas that are vital to American defense. The aggression is not ours. Ours is solely defense.

But let this warning be clear. *From now on, if German or Italian vessels of* *war enter the waters, the protection of which is necessary for American defense, <u>they do so at their own peril</u>.*

<u>The orders which I have given as Commander-in-Chief of the United States Army and Navy</u> **are to carry out that policy---at once...**

I have no illusions about the gravity of this step. I have not taken it hurriedly or lightly. It is the result of months and months of constant thought and anxiety and prayer. In the protection of your nation and mine it cannot be avoided...". [Emphasis added]

Roosevelt had spoken to a small audience of family members, some of his key advisors, and many photographers, while wearing a black armband of mourning, only four days after his mother's death. As he concluded his address announcing a "shoot on sight" policy against Nazi Germany in the Atlantic, the playing of the National Anthem brought all those present emotionally to their feet.[244]

President Roosevelt was wise enough not to try to pin a declaration of war on one incident between two ships, in which no one had been killed---but he did succeed in justifying an undeclared war in the Atlantic, and in setting the stage for a *possible* declaration of war, in the event of continued, more serious shooting incidents in the future. His sin was one

---

[244] Buhite and Levy, ed., *FDR's Fireside Chats,* 188-196.

		of omission, in intentionally not revealing that the *Greer* was, on this occasion, the vessel on the offensive, participating in a joint seek-and-destroy mission to help a British airplane sink the German U-boat. Narrator David McCullough summed up FDR's approach to the *Greer* incident, and to his attempts in the fall of 1941 to get the United States into the war against Germany, in the 1994 PBS documentary *FDR*: ***"'You know, I am a juggler,' he [FDR] would tell a friend, 'and I never let my right hand know what my left hand does...<u>I am perfectly willing to mislead, and tell untruths, if it will help win the war.</u>'"***[245]
September 16, 1941	**The U.S. Navy, at long last, commences the convoying of British merchant ships (enroute the United Kingdom from the New World)---from their departure points in Canada, to the waters near Iceland---where the British Navy will then take over the job. (No public announcement is made of the implementation of**	When the first American convoy escort group joined up with fast convoy HX 150 out of Halifax on this date, "the United States Navy was in a state of full belligerency in the Atlantic."[246] This step had long been urged upon the President by his closest advisors (Stimson, Knox, Morgenthau, Hopkins, and Admiral Stark). It carried with it, of course, the risk (or the hope, rather) that it would bring an immediate declaration of war by Hitler upon the United States, once the German Navy became aware of the change in policy. ***This did not happen,*** so FDR's best hope of entering

---

[245] This is only a partial quote of a statement made by FDR on **March 15, 1942** (after the U.S. had formally entered WW II) to a Cabinet member, but it nevertheless served nicely to illustrate FDR's mindset when he used the *Greer* incident to justify undeclared war against Hitler in the Atlantic Ocean in the autumn of 1941, and the commencement of convoying---two decisions he had secretly made about one month previously.

[246] Heinrichs, *Threshold of War,* 167.

	this crucial decision.)	the war then became another shooting incident between American ships and German U-boats---one that would be more clear-cut and demonstrative than the *Greer* incident had been.
October 1, 1941	U.S. Navy records reveal the limited success of Station CAST's efforts to break the JN-25(b) code.	About 2,400 words of the 50,000 word code book had been recovered by October 1st. [247]

October 9, 1941	**An American Army cryptanalyst in Washington, D.C. decodes what came to be known as the "bomb plot" message, in which the Japanese Foreign Ministry---on behalf of Japanese Naval Intelligence---asked its Consulate in Honolulu, Hawaii to send <u>regular intelligence reports</u> of the specific ship types present at the Pearl Harbor naval base---<u>and their detailed locations within Pearl Harbor</u>---to Tokyo.**
	
	The message had been transmitted on September 24, 1941 in what was called the J-19 Consular code, and was not immediately decrypted because it was current
		<u>The "bomb plot" message reads as follows</u>: **"Strictly Secret. Henceforth, we would like to have you make reports concerning vessels along the following lines insofar as possible:**
		
		1. **The waters (of Pearl Harbor) are to be divided roughly into five sub-areas. (We have no objections to your abbreviating as much as you like.)**
		
		   Area A. Waters between Ford Island and the Arsenal.
		
		   Area B. Waters adjacent to the Island south and west of Ford Island. (This area is on the opposite side of the Island from Area A.)
		
		   Area C. East Loch.
		
		   Area D. Middle Loch.
		
		   Area E. West Loch and the communicating water routes.
		
		2. **With regard to warships and**

---

[247] Carlson, *Joe Rochefort's War*, 122.

practice to have "lower level" Consular traffic processed only in Washington, D.C. The "bomb plot" message was intercepted by the Army's intercept station (called station "MS") at Fort Shafter on Oahu (which did not have decryption capability), and while it would normally have been sent to Washington via the Pan Am Clipper, on this occasion the Clipper flight two days later was cancelled by bad weather, so the intercepted message was sent to the West Coast by ship, and thence to the nation's capital by air. It arrived in Washington on October 6th, and was decrypted by the Army's S.I.S. three days later, on October 9th.[248] The three Navy Communication Intelligence Stations in Washington (Station US), Pearl Harbor (Station HYPO), and Manila (Station CAST) were all theoretically capable of decoding J-19 message traffic, providing they possessed the current

aircraft carriers, we would like to have you report on those at anchor (these are not so important), tied up at wharves, buoys, and in docks. (Designate types and classes briefly. If possible we would like to have you make mention of the fact when there are two or more vessels alongside the same wharf.)"

The many replies sent to this message between September 29th and December 6th were extremely provocative, and revealed in various ways (well documented by Prange, Stinnett, and others) that the Japanese were planning an attack on Pearl Harbor. The first reply was sent by the Japanese Consulate on September 29th via Mackay Radio (with an informational copy to the Japanese Embassy in Washington). The Mackay office manager in Washington, D.C. allowed this telegram to be photographed by the U.S. Navy, and it was decoded by the Navy on October 10th, the day after the original "bomb plot" request from Tokyo. (This rapid coordination with MacKay and the immediate decryption of the first reply sent from Honolulu, all **within twenty-four hours** of the decryption of the "bomb plot" instructions by the Army on October 9th, indicates that Navy's OP-20-G was staffed with professionals who immediately understood the import of the

---

[248] Toland, *Infamy*, 60-61.

"keys," but were not tasked with doing so.

The individual responsible for gathering the necessary intelligence and drafting the replies to Tokyo (also in the J-19 code) was Ensign Takeo Yoshikawa, of the Imperial Japanese Navy, who had been assigned undercover as a consulate official ("Mr. Morimura") at the Honolulu Consulate. He carried out his assignment faithfully and regularly up through December 6, 1941. He had sent his first "bomb plot" of the locations of ships in Pearl Harbor to Japan's Embassy in Washington via RCA commercial telegram (encoded, of course) on August 21, 1941---long before the now infamous message of September 24th was transmitted to Honolulu by the Foreign Ministry in Tokyo. Altogether, the Japanese Consulate in Honolulu sent 69 intelligence reports to Tokyo between January 1, 1941 and December 6, 1941; and Yoshikawa himself sent 36 spy reports between

"bomb plot" message.) Four days later President Roosevelt lunched with David Sarnoff (of RCA) at the White House, and requested that he personally arrange for the U.S. government to receive copies of all communications sent by the Japanese Consulate in Honolulu, via RCA.

Colonel Rufus Bratton, USA, Head of the Far East Section of Army G-2 in Washington, told the Joint Congressional Committee after the war **that in no other instance did the Japanese set up what amounted to a grid system for reporting the presence and position of ships in any harbor; he testified that the Japanese were showing "an unusual interest in the port at Honolulu [sic]."**

The original "bomb plot" message was routed by Colonel Bratton to the Secretary of War (Henry Stimson), Army Chief of Staff (General Marshall), and Head of Army War Plans (Brigadier General Leonard Gerow). Troubled by the apparent sinister import of the message, Colonel Bratton (who was an extremely intelligent and alert analyst) discussed it several times with his counterparts in Naval Intelligence. Bratton told the Joint Congressional Committee after the war that during these discussions, they had jointly concluded that the subdivision of Pearl Harbor into several areas might indicate "…a plan for sabotage…a plan for a submarine attack…*or it might be a plan for an air*

August 21st and December 6th. These messages were all sent out from Honolulu by the Japanese using either Mackay (a British cable company) or RCA commercial radio transmissions---as telegrams containing encoded five-character alphabetic groups. Of the former category, 84% were intercepted by U.S. radio listening stations throughout the Pacific; of the latter category, fully 94% were successfully intercepted.

The FBI knew Yoshikawa was a spy, and had requested that the Hawaiian managers of Mackay Radio, RCA, Globe Wireless, and Commercial Pacific Cable provide copies of the Japanese Consulate's traffic to the U.S. government. They had all refused. President Roosevelt, aware that the Japanese Consulate in Honolulu was gathering intelligence on the U.S. Fleet (through

attack."[249] [Emphasis added]

Lieutenant Commander Kramer (on loan from ONI's Far East Section to OP-20-G) routed it to <u>the Director of Naval Intelligence (Captain Alan G. Kirk), the Chief of Navy War Plans (Rear Admiral Richmond K. Turner), the CNO (Admiral Stark), Navy Secretary Knox,</u> *and the White House.* Kramer prepared a cover sheet synopsis that read: "Tokyo directs special reports on ships with [sic] Pearl Harbor which is divided into five areas for the purpose of showing exact locations."

The Army and Navy Commanders in Hawaii, General Short (whose responsibility it was to protect the Naval Base), and Admiral Kimmel, <u>were never notified of the "bomb plot" message</u>, and the reasons for this have never been satisfactorily explained, to this day.

According to Layton in *And I Was There* (p. 166), and to Toland in *Infamy* (p. 60), the Director of Naval Intelligence (Captain Alan G. Kirk), ONI's head of Foreign Intelligence (Captain Howard D. Bode), and Kramer's boss, Commander Safford (OP-20-G), all wanted to share the bomb plot cable with Pearl Harbor; and Safford even drafted a message that would have instructed the Pacific Fleet radio unit (Station Hypo) to begin decrypting the Japanese Consular traffic from Honolulu. <u>Layton writes that Rear

---

[249] Layton, *And I Was There*, 165.

information regularly provided to Assistant Secretary Adolph Berle at the State Department by J. Edgar Hoover), on October 14th asked RCA's founder and President, David Sarnoff, to provide copies to the U.S. government of all outgoing RCA telegrams sent by the Honolulu Consulate (thus emulating the arrangement the British government had with Mackay). On November 13th, after spending nine days in Hawaii coordinating with the highest level U.S. officials (Admiral Kimmel, General Short, and Commander Joseph J. Rochefort, the head of Station HYPO), Sarnoff cabled FDR that the arrangement was in place. The Japanese sent their November messages via Mackay, **and their December messages via RCA.**

All of the Japanese intelligence reports prior to December 3rd were sent in the J-19 code. On December 3rd the Foreign Ministry in Tokyo directed its Honolulu

Admiral Leigh Noyes, Head of Navy Communications, killed Safford's message---refused to release it. **Toland wrote that Rear Admiral Turner (Chief of War Plans) refused to allow Kirk or Bode to relay the "bomb plot" decryption to Admiral Kimmel.**

Edward L. Beach writes in *Scapegoats* (pp. 34-37) that the "high-handed" Rear Admiral Richmond Kelly Turner (known throughout the Navy at this time and throughout World War II as "Terrible Turner"), the Chief of Navy War Plans, "angrily objected" when Captain Alan Kirk, and Captain Howard Bode, the two senior officers at ONI, wanted to share the "bomb plot" message with Admiral Kimmel. Beach writes: "Both were senior captains, experienced in intelligence, but they evidently pressed their case too strongly to suit 'Terrible' Turner, who saw to it that both were summarily reassigned to posts far from ONI. Strangely, although this incident was part of the lore of Pearl Harbor and was frequently called the 'battle of the second deck (of the Navy department)'--- or the 'October revolution,' a reference to the date of [decipherment of] the 'bomb plot message' that was its cause--- not one of the nine investigations of the disaster (from 1941-1946) called Kirk or Bode as a witness. Bode died in 1943 [a suicide], but Kirk had a distinguished career, including postwar ambassadorship to the USSR and three other countries, attained the rank of full Admiral, and must have carried some unusual memories to the grave with him

Consulate to destroy all code books except the relatively low-level PA code; therefore, the final messages from Yoshikawa, from December 3rd through December 6th, were sent in the PA code, which was easier to break than the J-19 code.

The FBI's Director, J. Edgar Hoover, repeatedly pressed FDR during the fall of 1941 to allow him to arrest, or for the United States to expel, "Mr. Morimura" from the Japanese Consulate in Hawaii. Roosevelt refused, even though he was fully aware of Yoshikawa's role. Assistant Secretary of State Adolph Berle wrote in his diary that he explained to Hoover, "No expulsion is possible as any charge leading to ouster would reveal American cryptographic success to Japan." (See Stinett, Day of Deceit, pages 83-118.)

My conclusion: **Since FDR's "Plan B" was to enter the war against Germany via the "back**

twenty years later." Beach continued, saying of the 1946 report of the Joint Congressional Committee, that "<u>the majority of the JCC wished to explain the message away [as not being proof of a forthcoming attack on Pearl harbor], which it could not do</u>." Beach concludes: "The message alone stands as proof of crucially important dereliction in the nation's capital. The message(s) were received and were read by everyone in the chain of distribution (although some of them denied it under oath). An obligation devolved on every one of them to ensure that Admiral Kimmel and General Short were solidly and completely aware of precisely what had been sent…The 'bomb plot' message was definitely shown to the President and other officials on the **MAGIC** distribution list…None of our other bases received comparable scrutiny. Yet extraordinarily, Admiral Turner personally and viciously prevented any information about it from being sent to the Hawaiian commanders, whose primary base had actually been named in the message. Turner furthermore caused the two senior intelligence officers who had dared to propose sending such a message to be summarily relieved of their duties."

Beach, in *Scapegoats,* describes Turner as arrogant, self-directed, and aggrandizing. Beach freely quotes Edwin T. Layton, former intelligence officer for the Pacific Fleet, and the frank and brutal assessment of Turner's personality and role in the Pearl Harbor

	door," that is, by pressuring Japan to commit an overt act of war against the U.S., no actions could be permitted that might risk Japanese cancellation (or delay) of any such plans.	debacle found in Layton's posthumously-published memoir, *And I Was There: Pearl Harbor and Midway---Breaking the Secrets.* Layton described Turner as "abrasive," and vividly portrayed his "stormy temper, overbearing ego, and celebrated bouts with the bottle." Layton explained that Turner was the dominant personality in a triumvirate that consisted of himself (Chief of War Plans), the Deputy CNO (Rear Admiral Royal Ingersoll), and the CNO (Admiral Harold Stark),[250] and Beach wrote that many in the Navy felt that Admiral Stark, although officially CNO, frequently acted under Turner's strong influence, and that Turner expected to be the next CNO. Layton wrote: "He had arrogated to himself many of the traditional functions of the office of Naval Intelligence…As in all triumvirates, one member exerted a dominating influence. In this case it was Richmond Kelly Turner, who aggressively promoted his own intelligence evaluations and made arbitrary decisions on their dissemination, knowing that he could

---

[250] This was confirmed by Arthur H. McCollum, a man on-the-scene, in the article "Unheeded Warnings" posthumously prepared for the book *Air Raid: Pearl Harbor!* (pp. 79-87) by editor Paul Stillwell [from the 1971 oral history interview McCollum gave to the Navy prior to his death in 1976]. McCollum claimed that Turner kept ONI in the dark about many of the U.S. government's plans and actions, and that War Plans promulgated conclusions about intelligence matters without consulting ONI.

count on Stark to rubber-stamp them."[251]

Beach writes (pp. 77-80) that Turner lied loudly and often throughout the war about Admiral Kimmel, assigning to him unwarranted blame for the Pearl Harbor attack, by saying that Admiral Kimmel had been privy to all of the Japanese messages [i.e., **MAGIC** intercepts and the "bomb plot" messages] seen in Washington, *which was most definitely not true.* In 1945 Turner told the Congressional investigators that Rear Admiral Leigh Noyes, head of Naval Communications in 1941, had assured him of this, and yet Admiral Noyes testified to the JCC: **"I would never have made the statement that all**

---

[251] Captain Alan G. Kirk, who had relieved Rear Admiral Walter Anderson as Director of Naval Intelligence, had previously been Naval Attaché in London, and was personally selected for the post at ONI by Navy Secretary Frank Knox. Commencing in February 1941 Rear Admiral Turner began his usurpation of the normal function of ONI---established in writing in the ONI manual---which was to provide estimates of enemy intentions to the Fleet. It became Turner's normal practice throughout 1941 to make such determinations himself, *without consulting ONI.* Turner preferred to treat ONI as a mere collector of information, and to interpret the information himself, and disseminate estimates of enemy intentions himself (again, without telling ONI). When ONI complained about this, Stark and Ingersoll supported Turner's informal assumption of this responsibility by allowing him to continue what they euphemistically referred to as "coordination." Kirk, on his own authority, sent several **MAGIC** decrypts to CINCPAC (Kimmel) during the first half of 1941, which enraged Turner. In mid-July, after Turner complained about this to Stark, the CNO ordered Kirk to stop this practice. Kirk, who had the courage to go toe-to-toe with Turner on a number of occasions, had lost out to a more forceful personality and to someone who outranked him. He threw in the towel and petitioned the Assistant Secretary of the Navy for a transfer to sea duty about three weeks before the "bomb plot" message was decrypted; after this he was a lame-duck ONI Director. After the October 9th row over whether or not to transmit the decrypted "bomb plot" message to CINCPAC, both Kirk and Bode found themselves suddenly transferred. Percy L. Greaves, Jr., in *Pearl Harbor: The Seeds and Fruits of Infamy* (p. 107-110), wrote: "The shift in ONI leadership took place on October 10, the day after the "berthing plan" message...became available in Washington. Rear Admiral Theodore S. Wilkinson, who had been serving as Commanding Officer aboard the battleship USS *Mississippi,* took over as chief of ONI on October 15." Wilkinson, who had no previous experience with Naval Intelligence, was personally selected by the CNO (Stark), and never challenged the existing arrangement in which the Chief of War Plans (Turner) dominated ONI. "Ping" Wilkinson was the third Director appointed to head the embattled Office of Naval Intelligence within a one year period.

[Japanese] ciphers could be translated in Pearl Harbor." (*See* Prange, p. 251.) Beach insinuates that Turner lied about this intentionally, since it was he---Richmond K. Turner---who had been instrumental in diverting the **Purple** machine originally intended for Pearl Harbor (Station HYPO) to the British at Bletchley Park. And since Turner is the individual who forbade Captains Alan Kirk and Howard Bode from forwarding the "bomb plot" message to Admiral Kimmel and General Short, **it is hard not to conclude that he intentionally withheld vital intelligence about enemy interests and intentions from the Hawaii establishment.** Beach sums up his suspicions of Turner by saying: "Throughout the thousands of pages of Pearl Harbor testimony the reader will see continual reference to Admiral Turner, and almost every time the context is in reference to his refusal to send warning messages to the Pacific."[252]

---

[252] In his posthumous memoir, *And I Was There: Pearl Harbor and Midway---Breaking the Secrets*, Edwin T. Layton, Admiral Kimmel's intelligence officer, wrote (p. 165) that both Stark (CNO) and Turner (War Plans) **denied under oath** to the Joint Congressional Committee investigating Pearl Harbor that they had ever seen the "bomb plot" message. (This was perjury---they did see it.) Stark and Turner also lied to the Congressional Committee about **MAGIC,** testifying in 1945 that they were of the belief that CINCPAC (Admiral Kimmel) had been a recipient of **MAGIC.** Layton (pp. 141-144) quoted Stark's testimony about this: "I inquired on two or three occasions as to whether or not Kimmel could read certain dispatches when they came up and which we were interpreting...and I was told [by the Chief of War Plans] that he could." Layton then quoted Turner as confirming to the Congressional investigators that Kimmel could read **MAGIC** because he had been assured by Noyes (Head of Naval Communications) in "March or April" of 1941 that Kimmel was not only "getting as much as we were" but "he was getting it sooner than we were." As Layton indicates, at the Naval Court of Inquiry in 1944, Noyes had testified that Turner had been apprised of who was getting what in "almost daily" meetings that "continuously discussed" the status of decrypting, and that Turner "should have understood." When cross-examined in 1945 by the Congressional Committee, Noyes testified that when the Chief of War Plans "asked what was our setup in regard to intercepted messages," it was "fully explained to him." When the Congressional investigators recalled Turner in December of 1945, four months after his original testimony,

Since Layton has written that Rear Admiral Leigh Noyes (Director of Navy Communications) **similarly forbade Commander Laurance Safford from warning Pearl Harbor of the bomb plot message, and from directing Station HYPO to decrypt Consular traffic from Honolulu, <u>one has to wonder whether Turner and Noyes were privy to FDR's strategy to provoke Japan into committing an overt act of war, and whether they were actively supporting that strategy with their actions.</u>** Otherwise, their actions make no logical sense, and appear worse than dumb-headed, or simply obtuse.

Likewise, Robert Stinnett, in *Day of Deceit* (pp. 107-118), is suspicious of why a revered national hero, Commander Joseph J. Rochefort (the OIC of Station HYPO, and the codebreaker who later divined the Japanese attack on Midway and who made possible America's improbable, brilliant victory in June of 1942), failed to break the many intercepted Japanese Consular messages

and he was confronted with the glaring conflict between his testimony and that of Noyes, he retreated and admitted that he "was entirely in error as regards the diplomatic codes." Layton caustically wrote: "Like a cuttlefish ejecting ink to escape danger, he blew a bombastic smokescreen that enabled him to dart for cover behind the failures of the intelligence specialists whose function he had so tenaciously usurped in 1941." As Edwin Layton points out, by 1945 Turner was a decorated full (four star) Admiral, and had successfully led America's amphibious landings throughout the Pacific War; he was politically untouchable at this point. Layton summarized: **"Turner's deceptive and evasive responses in December 1945 betrayed an ignorance that was highly unlikely, or a deception that was highly obvious.** But since none of his former colleagues was going to "spill the beans," he confused the Congressional investigators…Turner, by omission or commission, therefore played a leading part in shutting off Pearl Harbor from the best source of intelligence [both **MAGIC** and the Consular intercepts]…**In 1961 Turner died with his lies caught in his throat."** [Emphasis added]

which clearly pointed toward a forthcoming attack on Pearl Harbor, when he had "full capability" (according to Stinnett) to decrypt the J-19 and PA codes, and was receiving that traffic all along during the fall of 1941. The Consular intercepts were forwarded by hand from Station H near Kaneohe, on the northeast side of Oahu, where they were intercepted, to Station HYPO---Rochefort's codebreaking outfit in the basement of the 14th Naval District headquarters building inside the Pearl Harbor Naval Shipyard---and then packaged and sent either by air, or ship, to Washington, where they were decrypted. The official story is that Rochefort's personnel at Station HYPO were too busy attempting to break the Japanese Flag Officer's code to bother with Consular intercepts. Edwin Layton confirms in his book *And I Was There* (p. 144) that the Consular intercepts "were forwarded on to Washington unread by Pearl Harbor because of Rochefort's instruction to leave the diplomatic ciphers to Washington." Stinnett claims that HYPO had the capability to break them, with ease, using publications provided by Station US in Washington. Stinnett suggests (but cannot prove) a possible effort to suppress foreknowledge of the Pearl Harbor attack that may have been coordinated between: (1) Rear Admiral Anderson, Commander of the Pacific Fleet's battleships (someone who had been a confidant of FDR when he was Director of ONI, and who had also been McCollum's direct superior when Arthur McCollum wrote his crucial policy memo in October 1940); (2) McCollum himself in Washington, still Head of ONI's Far East Section; and (3) Rochefort, who---like McCollum---was a fellow Japanese linguist and intelligence officer whose specialty was the Japanese Navy and culture, and who was also the Officer-in-Charge of Station HYPO, the Navy codebreaking unit at Pearl Harbor. The suggestion is not *totally* absurd, since David Sarnoff, President of RCA, had discussed the importance of the Japanese Consular traffic with Rochefort (and indeed, had promised to make RCA's outgoing Japanese telegrams available to him) when he was in Hawaii the first two weeks in November 1941, and because Rochefort and McCollum had been personally very close, since 1928. Tantalizingly, Stinnett (p. 203) quotes Rochefort as saying during his oral history interview after the war, in 1970: **"It** [the damage occurred in the attack on Pearl Harbor] **was a pretty cheap price to pay for unifying the country."** Stinnett wrote (p. 117): "His unity observation parallels that of his close friend Arthur McCollum and suggests that Rochefort was aware of or approved of McCollum's eight-action plan that called for America to create 'ado' and provoke Japan into committing an overt act of war against the United States." Furthermore, McCollum himself (in his oral history interview with the Navy)[253]

---

[253] Stinnett, ed., *Air Raid: Pearl Harbor!,* 79-81.

admitted to an extremely close personal and professional relationship with Rear Admiral Anderson---his boss as Director of Naval Intelligence, and who, when transferred to Pearl Harbor in mid-December 1940 to become Commander, Battleships Battle Force, wanted to take McCollum with him as his operations officer (but was refused this request by Royal Ingersoll). Given the closeness between McCollum and Anderson---and between McCollum and Rochefort---Rear Admiral Anderson may well have communicated to Joseph J. Rochefort the McCollum-inspired FDR plan to provoke the Japanese into committing an overt act of war.

There is *some* smoke here, *implying* a source of combustion, but great caution is warranted. Rochefort's biographer, Elliott Carlson, in his 2011 book *Joe Rochefort's War: The Odyssey of the Codebreaker Who Outwitted Yamamoto at Midway,* makes it clear (p. 172-177) that Joe Rochefort simply was not interested in the Japanese Consular diplomatic traffic for Honolulu. Not only was he not assigned to tackle it, he did not consider it important---his mission was to break the Japanese Navy's Flag Officer's Code, and predict the movements of the Japanese Navy. His staff had some familiarity with the J-19 diplomatic code used by the Honolulu Consulate, but lacked the daily keys necessary to quickly break any messages. When some lower level "dip traffic" was finally broken by HYPO in early December just prior to the Pearl Harbor attack (after the Consulate stopped using J-19), it was revealed (as Rochefort predicted) to be "junk." In my estimation Stinnett's conspiracy theory about Rochefort does not hold water; Joe Rochefort was not working on *either* JN-25(b) *or* the J-19 Consular code, simply because he was ordered to work on the Flag Officer's Code (instead of JN-25), and was told to leave the "dip traffic" for Washington. Rochefort was dutifully carrying out Safford's directives.

But in my view the smoke in Washington, D.C. surrounding the "Bomb Plot" message controversy does indeed reveal a fire---serious skullduggery in Washington, D.C. Mainstream historians (and I include here Wohlstetter and Prange) preferred for decades to assume that Washington's failure to inform the Hawaiian commands of the "bomb plot" message was a simple oversight by very busy and preoccupied officials---that it was simply one more signal, lost in the noise of an overwhelming amount of incoming information. In view of what we know today of the provocative McCollum action memo (which was unknown to historians prior to the publication of Stinnett's book in the year 2000); of the contradictory and otherwise inexplicable behavior of Rear Admiral Richmond K. Turner (whose Division was very concerned about an attack on Pearl Harbor in January of 1941 when his shop prepared Knox's letter to the Army, but who <u>adamantly refused</u> to allow the "bomb plot" message to be shared with

Pearl Harbor nine months later); and the fact that FDR not only definitely saw the message, but understood its importance enough that he took steps immediately after seeing it to ensure that the Navy receive a guaranteed pipeline (from RCA) of outgoing radio traffic from the Japanese Consulate in Honolulu---in view of these factors, the ignorance in which Kimmel and Short were operating appears to have been intentionally imposed from above, and not to have been "an accident of history," or the result of incompetence, or mere inattention, at high levels. Keeping Kimmel and Short in the dark required <u>willful and otherwise inexplicable acts of commission</u>, acts which were taken by military professionals who in all other respects were intelligent and patriotic individuals. The Chief of War Plans (Rear Admiral Richmond K. Turner) was one of the coterie of Naval officers who had regular access to the President, and who therefore, by October of 1941, must surely have known that FDR was now intent on provoking Japan to commit an overt act of war.[254] In short, he had

---

[254] On page 18 of *Threshold of War,* professor Heinrich writes: "The President rarely saw Secretary of the Navy Frank Knox alone. **He not only dealt directly with Admiral Stark,** his Vice-Chief of Operations [Rear Admiral Ingersoll], **and his War Plans Director [Rear Admiral Turner],** but also individually with the dour and driving Commander-in-Chief of the Atlantic Fleet, Admiral Ernest J. King." On page 21, Heinrichs writes: "The President read **MAGIC** or heard the gist of it from regular briefings by Army and Navy intelligence officers, usually in the late afternoon after callers." The Navy intelligence officers who had personal access to the President were the various Directors of Naval Intelligence during 1940 and 1941 [Anderson, Kirk, and Wilkinson]; the Head of the Far East Section of ONI, Commander McCollum, and his assistant, Lieutenant Commander Watts---most often as couriers of intelligence estimates and messages; and Commander Safford (OP-20-G) and his assistant, Lieutenant Commander Kramer (both men were Japanese linguists and translators of **MAGIC** intercepts, and also served as couriers of **MAGIC** material to the White House). [Emphasis added]

		probably not been "read in" on FDR's "back door" strategy in January of 1941, shortly after he assumed his duties as Chief of War Plans; but by October of 1941, he surely had been.
October 9, 1941	**FDR requests that Congress amend the Neutrality Act <u>to permit the arming of American merchant vessels</u>.** (At this point in time, American ships were still prohibited from carrying war goods to Great Britain, and all Lend-Lease materials had to be transported by British ships, or the ships of her dominions.) FDR was "testing the waters" here by initially only pursuing the repeal of Section VI of the Neutrality Act. A bitter debate ensued, and only the crisis atmosphere resulting from of the torpedoing of USS *Kearney* on October 16th permitted easy passage of this amendment.	Such a revision was consistent with the stated purpose of Lend-Lease, and was necessary for its effective implementation.[255] As FDR stated in his message to Congress: "I earnestly trust that the Congress will carry out the true intent of the Lend-Lease Act by making it possible for the United States to help deliver the [war] articles to those who are in a position to effectively use them. In other words, I ask for Congressional action to help implement Congressional policy." Roosevelt continued, "Until 1937 [arming merchant ships for civilian defense of those vessels]…"had never been prohibited by any statute in the United States. Through our whole history American merchant vessels have been armed whenever it was considered necessary for their own defense." He ended his message with these bold assertions: "We will not let Hitler prescribe the waters of the world on which our ships may travel…We intend to maintain…the freedom of the seas against the domination by any foreign power which has become crazed with a desire to control the world. We shall do so with all our strength and all our heart and all our mind."

---

[255] Davis, *FDR: The War President,* 322.

October 16, 1941	Prime Minister Konoye of Japan submits his resignation to Emperor Hirohito.	Konoye's resignation was submitted because his government had failed to meet the new deadline of October 15th for successfully concluding negotiations with the U.S.; that deadline had been set by the Army and Navy Chiefs of Staff at a Liaison Conference on September 25th, modifying the original deadline of "early October." The crux of the failure to reach an accommodation with the U.S. was Japan's war with China: the U.S. insisted on an end to the war and withdrawal of Japanese troops, and Japan refused to consider such a loss of face after more than four costly years of war; *or* the abandonment of her Empire.
October 16, 1941	**USS *Kearney* is torpedoed by a German submarine.** A slow convoy of 40 merchantmen, guarded only by four tiny Royal Navy corvettes, loses ten of its ships to a German "wolf pack" of submarines about 400 miles south of Iceland, before five U.S. destroyers, dispatched from Reykjavik, can arrive to assist. That evening one torpedo stuck USS *Kearney,* causing her to lose power, and nearly sinking the vessel. Eleven members of her crew were killed, twenty-	As historian Kenneth Davis wrote, the torpedoing of USS *Kearney* was "an episode in the North Atlantic of the kind for which Roosevelt had long been waiting, since it had all the earmarks of a truly galvanizing incident (the *Greer* episode had served as a poor substitute)…The immediate effect of this in Congress was gratifying to the President: On the morrow of the fatal action the House approved 259-138 the arming of merchant vessels and immediately sent the Neutrality Act provision (repeal of Section VI) to the Senate, which was considerably more inclined toward the further revising amendments that Roosevelt wanted than the House was. <u>This, however, was the limit of an effect Roosevelt had hoped would be much greater.</u> **There was no huge outpouring of popular outrage and wrath.** He tried hard to overcome the lethargy, the apathy, or whatever it

	four were injured, and the ship barely made it back to Iceland safely.[256]	was that had America in its grip, when he delivered a nationally broadcast speech on Navy Day, October 27th." [Emphasis added]
October 18, 1941	**General Hideki Tojo, long an ardent and unapologetic expansionist, is selected by the Emperor as Japan's new Prime Minister, and forms his government on this date.**	Emperor Hirohito directs Tojo to "go back to blank paper"---that is, to re-examine the issue of war versus peace without being shackled by the Imperial Conference decision of September 6th. Never before had an Emperor ordered a decision made in his own presence to be bypassed. While extremely loyal to the Emperor, Tojo was, as Ian Kershaw describes him, "a man of limited vision," and his lifetime of parochial dedication to the Army accounted for his absolute refusal to budge on the issue of China; he adamantly refused to consider any withdrawal of troops from China, not even 25 years hence. He was hardly the most auspicious choice for Prime Minister. The man Tojo selected for his new Foreign Minister, Shigenori Togo, was an experienced career diplomat but did not have the confidence of the Army or the Navy. While the Emperor had directed Tojo to find a way to prevent war, "he had been ultra-hawkish in policy direction for too long to change course convincingly at the eleventh hour…he was no match for the military forces that he himself had helped to unleash."[257]

Tojo was the ultimate fatalist, who was |

---

[256] Ibid., 323-324.

[257] Kershaw, *Fateful Choices,* 356.

		prepared to support national hara-kiri in support of the Imperial Way, primarily because of his parochial obsession about not withdrawing *any* Japanese troops from China. One incident that occurred in August of 1941 is illustrative of this. A Colonel Hideo Iwakuro, who had been part of the Japanese negotiating team in the U.S. until he left at the end of July 1941, spent much of August lobbying against war with the United States after he returned to Japan. As John Toland recounts, "During the last week in August he attended a Liaison Conference where he contrasted the alarming differences between Japanese and American war potential. In steel, he said, the ratio was 20 to 1; oil more than 100 to 1; coal 10 to 1; planes 5 to 1; shipping 2 to 1; labor force 5 to 1. The overall potential was 10 to 1. At such odds, Japan could not possibly win…For once his listeners were impressed, and Tojo [who was then Army Minister] ordered Iwakuro to make a written report of everything he had just said. The following day Iwakuro arrived at the War Minister's office to discuss the report but was summarily told by Tojo that he was being transferred to a unit in Cambodia. 'You need not submit the notes in writing I requested yesterday.'"[258] Even in August, Hideki Tojo had his mind made up and did not want to be confused or distracted by contrary facts.
October 27, 1941	**FDR makes a stirring**	As Kenneth Davis points out below in

---

[258]Toland, *The Rising Sun,* 94.

Navy Day speech on nationwide radio and attempts to incite a war fever over the torpedoing of the USS Kearney.[259]

Some of the more noteworthy passages follow: "We have wished to avoid shooting. But the shooting has started. And history records who fired the first shot...America has been attacked."

"Hitler's torpedo was directed at every American."

"I say that we do not propose to take this lying down. *That determination of ours not to take this lying down has been expressed in orders to the United States Navy to shoot on sight.* Those orders stand."

"We stand ready in the defense of our Nation and in the faith of our fathers to do what God has given

excerpts of some of the most emotional phrases in the speech, FDR attempted to exploit the full wrath-producing potential of the attack on USS *Kearney*:

"The shooting has started, and history has recorded who fired the first shot...America has been attacked! The USS *Kearney* belongs to every man, woman, and child in this country...we Americans have cleared our decks and taken our battle stations."

Davis sardonically wrote, "But if they had, they waited there---disturbingly quiet, disturbingly passive---for orders their commander-in-chief refrained from issuing. They had heard from his lips that Hitler was the enemy of mankind and of all that America stood for. They had been told by him again and again in fervent words that American survival required Hitler's defeat. But the Executive action logically required by Executive words had not been taken."

Sensing his attempt had fallen short of the mark, FDR did not send a request for a declaration of war to Congress following his speech.

It is clear to me that Roosevelt refused to ask Congress for a declaration of war against Germany---as his Secretary of War, Henry Stimson, had repeatedly

---

[259] Davis, *FDR: The War President*, 324.

	us the power to see as our full duty."[260]	urged him to do---because not even the torpedoing of USS *Kearney* had produced the unified call for war he had hoped for, and he understood all too well the danger of taking a disunited nation into a world war. **He would not ask for such a declaration until an act had occurred which would unquestionably unite the country behind the ensuing war effort.**
October 30, 1941	**President Roosevelt notifies Joseph Stalin that the United States was immediately extending to the USSR a Lend-Lease credit of up to one billion dollars,** for which repayment did not have to begin until 5 years after the end of the Second World War. Of the total of 32 billion dollars in American Lend-Lease aid in World War II provided to Allied nations, the USSR received approximately 11 billion dollars' worth of that aid. Principal aid consisted of trucks, jeeps, tanks, anti-aircraft guns, aluminum, and some aircraft.	Confronted by only lukewarm support (at best) for Lend-Lease aid to the Soviet Union by the American people and Congress, FDR waited until the new six billion dollar Lend-Lease authorization had been approved by Congress on October 24, 1941 to act. By late September, Russian international finances were in complete disarray, and when Roosevelt was informed in late October that the USSR could no longer pay for war materiel from America, he acted swiftly, in spite of disingenuous assurances given to Congress during consideration of the Lend-Lease appropriation that he had no immediate plans to provide Lend-Lease to the USSR. FDR understood what the American people did not: that the success or failure of the Russian people against Hitler's armies would, more than any other single factor, determine the winning side in World War II.[261]

---

[260] Kershaw, *Fateful Choices,* 325.

[261] Wallin, *Pearl Harbor,* 35; and Dallek, *Franklin D. Roosevelt and American Foreign Policy, 1932-1945,* 292-299.

October 31, 1941	**USS *Reuben James* is sunk by a German submarine.** In this incident, the worst of the three incidents between U.S. destroyers and German U-boats, a single torpedo blew up the ammunition magazine, which caused the ship to sink within 5 minutes, with great loss of life. Ian Kershaw writes: "Given the inflammatory way Roosevelt had spoken following earlier attacks, where there had been less damage caused and fewer casualties, his restraint on this occasion was striking."[262]	This old 4-stack World War I vintage destroyer, escorting a British convoy that had sailed from Halifax, was torpedoed 600 miles off the west coast of Ireland. It was the first U.S. warship lost in World War II, and 115 of its crew, including all of the officers, were killed. **After the failure of the German U-boat attack on USS *Kearney* (and of Roosevelt's October 27th Navy Day speech about that incident) to galvanize the nation, FDR issued no public statement,** having already said everything he could about such occurrences, short of asking Congress to declare war. *Roosevelt was loath to sound the war tocsin too many times about the attacks on individual U.S. ships by individual German U-boats, especially when he had a better strategy in mind now: provoking the Japanese to commit an unmistakable, premeditated, and overwhelming act of war against the United States.*
November 1, 1941	The Imperial Japanese Navy changes the radio call signs for all operational units.	This type of change normally occurred about every six months, and each time presented an immediate challenge to all radio traffic analysts in the U.S. Navy.
November 1-2, 1941	At a **Liaison Conference** lasting 17 hours, the sixty-sixth such meeting since the conferences had been established in 1937, war with the United States becomes a virtual	As Ian Kershaw summarizes (p. 364), when this conference, which began at 8:30 AM on November 1st, concluded at 1:30 AM on November 2nd, "it had determined *'in order to resolve the present critical situation, to assure [Japan's] self-preservation and self-defence, and to establish a New Order*

---

[262] Kershaw, *Fateful Choices,* 326.

	certainty.	*in Greater East Asia…to go to war against the United States, Britain, and Holland,'* with a deadline for initiating military action in early December. Only if negotiations proved successful by *'zero hour on 1 December'* would military action be suspended."
November 4, 1941	The United States intercepts, decodes (via the **Purple** machine), and translates a sober message from Foreign Minister Togo to Ambassador Nomura sent earlier the same day. [Author's note: Keep in mind that all of the key members of the U.S. Government in Washington, D.C. are reading this, and all of the other key **MAGIC** decrypts, throughout November and December.]	The text read: "Well, relations between Japan and the United States have reached the edge, and our people are losing confidence in the possibility of ever adjusting them…Conditions…are so tense that no longer is procrastination possible, yet in any sincerity to maintain pacific relationships between the Empire of Japan and the United States of America, *we have decided…to gamble once more on the continuance of parleys, but this is our last effort…If through it we do not reach a quick accord, I am sorry to say the talks will certainly be ruptured. Then, indeed, will relations between our two nations be on the brink of chaos. I mean that the success or failure of the pending discussions will have an immense effect on the destiny of the Empire of Japan. <u>In fact, we gambled the fate of our land on the throw of this die</u>.*"[263] [Emphasis added]
November 5, 1941	An **Imperial Conference** before the Emperor confirms a decision reached the previous day in a Cabinet Meeting, **to go to war in early**	The Liaison Conference decision (discussed above) was confirmed at a cabinet meeting on November 4th, and was then formalized (or rather, "sanctified") at the Imperial Conference on November 5th. As summarized by

---

[263] Greaves, Jr., *Pearl Harbor,* 117-118.

		December against Great Britain, the United States, and the Netherlands. Barring a diplomatic breakthrough, i.e., reaching a last-minute settlement with the United States before the end of November 30th---a settlement that would acknowledge Japan's special place in East Asia and would not cause Japan to lose face---war was now a virtual certainty.	Kershaw (pp. 365-366), the alternatives were peace with austerity (and accompanied by shame) in a world dominated by America, or war with probable defeat, but upholding the national honor: "War was seen as preferable. As the American Ambassador in Tokyo, Joseph Grew, put it, Japan would risk 'national hara-kiri' rather than 'yield to foreign pressure,' adding cryptically that 'Japanese sanity cannot be measured by American standards of logic.' The fateful Imperial Conference ended. The decision was that, short of a diplomatic miracle, Japan would go to war. No objections were raised. The Emperor's seal of approval was given."
	November 5, 1941	**The Chief of Staff for the Imperial Japanese Navy** (ADM Osami **Nagano**) sends a message to the **Commander-in-Chief, Combined Fleet** (ADM Isoroku **Yamamoto**), which was titled: "**Imperial Japanese Navy Headquarters (Naval General Staff) Order 1.**" *It formally warned of impending war between Imperial Japan and the United States, Great Britain, and the Netherlands, and directed Yamamoto to carry out the necessary operational preparations*	The text read as follows: "5 November 1941 From: Chief, Naval General Staff To: CinC, Combined Fleet 1. In view of the fact that it is feared war has become unavoidable with the United States, Great Britain, and the Netherlands, and for the self-preservation and future existence of the Empire, the various preparations for war operations will be completed by the first part of December. 2. The CinC of the Combined Fleet will effect the required preparations for war

	by early December.	operations.
	This Naval Order (and another one very similar to it addressed that same day to the CinC of the China Area Fleet)---and a series of additional Orders and Directives from the Naval General Staff through the period of December 2, 1941---relayed a series of *general* orders and directives about the impending war and the attack on Pearl Harbor to the CinC, Combined Fleet (ADM Isoroku **Yamamoto**), who in turn, subsequently issued	3. **Execution of details will be as directed by Chief of the Naval General Staff."**[264] [Emphasis added] This message, and the string of operational orders which followed it up through December 2nd, came as no surprise to the recipients. After all, it was ADM Yamamoto (CinC, Combined Fleet) who had first proposed the Pearl Harbor attack in January of 1941; who began planning for it in earnest in September of 1941; and it was Yamamoto who literally forced acceptance of his plan by an initially reluctant and skeptical Naval General Staff. What the string of Naval General Staff Orders and Directives, and subsequent CinC Combined Fleet orders

---

[264] This precise version of the text was published in English in a 1946 report prepared by the Naval Analysis Division of the Strategic Bombing Survey (Pacific), titled: *Campaigns of the Pacific War;* it was later repeated verbatim in the 1968 Naval History Division book titled: *Pearl Harbor: Why, How, Fleet Salvage, and Final Appraisal,* by Vice Admiral Homer C. Wallin. A paraphrased version---a less polished translation---can be found in the July 1946 JCC PHA *Hearings,* volume 13, p. 415. (The JCC *Hearings* reveal the specific Order or Directive numbers on many of the "kickoff" messages from the Naval General Staff (which are not included in the text in *Campaigns of the Pacific War,* or in Wallin's book.) Since the Japanese Navy burned its operational files at the end of the war, this specific telegram and all of the other operational directives found in the JCC PHA *Hearings,* volume 13 (p. 415-418), and in *Campaigns of the Pacific War* (p. 49-51)---with one exception which will be noted later---had to be reconstructed from memory by surviving Japanese Naval Officers in the fall of 1945. But the IJN officers doing the reconstructing *were those who literally drafted and received the messages,* and they all reconstructed the text of each message by consensus, in October of 1945: former CAPT Sadatoshi **Tomioka** (Chief of the Operations Section, Naval General Staff); former CAPT Kameto **Kuroshima** (the Senior Staff Officer and operations wizard on Yamamoto's Combined Fleet staff); and former Commander Mitsuo **Fuchida** (the aviator who led the attack on Pearl Harbor). When compared, the two English versions of the texts of this string of crucial operational orders (from November 5 through December 2, 1941) are virtually identical in content, and the only differences in the two versions published in 1946 are minor variations in style. Because of the source, there can be little doubt that the <u>content</u> of these late 1941 messages *was as reconstructed in late 1945* (only 4 years later), and that they were transmitted *on the dates indicated.*

tactical directives to the Pearl Harbor Striking Force (*Kido Butai*)---the First Air Fleet, commanded by Vice Admiral Chuichi **Nagumo.**

As revealed in the 1946 U.S. government publication *The Campaigns of the Pacific War* (p. 15), Admiral Nagano and Admiral Yamamoto had together decided (in private), on November 3, 1941, to attack Pearl Harbor providing diplomatic negotiations with the United States failed. That this final decision was made privately between the two men who ran the Imperial Japanese Navy, and not in council (the normal Japanese mode of decision-making), was confirmed in the JCC PHA *Hearings,* volume 13 (p. 400).

In a sense, this message, and all those that followed it up through December 2nd, were an elaborate form of to the First Air Fleet (the Pearl Harbor Striking Force, or *Kido Butai*) did, was **formalize** planning that had long been in the works. This string of messages (from November 5, 1941 through December 2, 1941) captures the Japanese love of detail and formality. From the standpoint of operational security (OPSEC), they also constituted a terrific risk, in the detail that they conveyed to any foreign powers eavesdropping and intercepting the messages. At this point, however--- late in 1941 and before the commencement of hostilities---the Japanese displayed a supreme confidence (which translated as reckless arrogance) that due to the complexities of their language, their Naval Code Book D (the operational code, called JN-25 by the Americans) could not be decrypted by any foreign power. What the Japanese Navy high command failed to appreciate was that because of the pragmatic realities of radio telegraphy by Morse Code, their complex language (of many thousands of Chinese ideographs or characters, combined with two phonetic "alphabets," which were really composed of syllables---vowels or consonants--- and not individual letters), in order to be transmitted by radio, had to be reduced to a mere 73 versions of their *kana* phonetic alphabet (which had English "romajii" equivalents). This made their Code Book D (the 5-numeral or Five-Num code) much more susceptible to decryption

	"window dressing" that satisfied the Japanese love of formality, and vertical chains-of-command and decision-making.	than they ever dreamed possible, in their worst nightmares.[265] And because their JN-25 encrypted messages were transmitted in Morse Code, *any* radio operator from *any nation* could **intercept** the transmissions, for later decryption and translation by cryptanalysts and linguists. And this is exactly what happened: between September and December of 1941, specially trained U.S. Navy radio operators (who necessarily had limited training in the Japanese language---enough to understand the phonetic kana "alphabet," and how to render the unique Japanese Morse Code radio telegraphy into Latin-alphabet "romajii" equivalents of the spoken Japanese language on specially modified Underwood typewriters called the RIP-5 ---but none of whom were trained as cryptanalysts) intercepted and copied down 25,581 Japanese Navy messages of all types,[266] and about 16,000 of the Japanese Navy messages intercepted by the USN in calendar year 1941 were encrypted and transmitted in JN-25(b).[267]
	Those directives from the Naval General Staff transmitted by radio (and not sent in sealed envelopes---more at right) also provided a tremendous opportunity for foreign powers (especially the British and the Americans) to learn of the supposedly secret Japanese war plans prior to the commencement of hostilities.	
	ADM Yamamoto's Chief of Staff, RADM Matome **Ugaki,** implies in his diary, published posthumously as *Fading Victory* (p. 21-22), that this message was transmitted by radio, when he writes on November 7th that it was **"sent [by Nagano] and received by us [onboard** *Nagato*] **just before we**	It is virtually certain, based on the contents of a Top Secret ULTRA 1946 U.S. Navy report that was only declassified in 1991 (see chapter 13 of John Costello's *Days of Infamy*---page 283, in particular) that ***this message,*** and

---

[265] Costello, *Days of Infamy,* 284; Rusbridger and Nave, *Betrayal at Pearl Harbor,* 60-61, and Appendix 1; Stinnett, *Day of Deceit,* 56.

[266] Costello, *Days of Infamy,* 282.

[267] Rusbridger and Nave, *Betrayal at Pearl Harbor,* 6.

| | **left the ship yesterday;"** Ugaki's diary reveals he left the flagship *Nagato* at **0800 on November 6th**. *The delay involved in sending and then receiving a message dated November 5th strongly implies the need to encode it in JN-25(b) by IJN communications personnel in Tokyo; transmit it by radio; and for communications personnel onboard the flagship to decode it upon receipt.* Subsequent events involving General George C. Marshall on November 15th, discussed in detail later in this chronology, imply that this message was not only transmitted in JN-25(b) by radio telegraphy, but that is was intercepted and decrypted by either the Americans or the British. | all others in the string of operational directives between November 5 and December 2, 1941 that were transmitted by radio or telegraphed by secure cable, were encrypted in the JN-25(b) operational code by the Japanese Navy. What is not known with certainty is exactly how many of the **Imperial Naval Headquarters** (i.e., Naval General Staff) **Orders and Directives** during this period **were transmitted by radio,** and how many of them (such as messages to the CinC, Combined Fleet onboard his battleship *Nagato* moored in the Inland Sea) **were possibly sent as encoded telegrams by secure cable lines.** Messages to ships inport were sometimes sent by secure cable, rather than being transmitted by radio. We do know that **two (2)** of the "kickoff" messages *from the Chief of the Naval General Staff (ADM Nagano)* in this string of pre-war orders and directives were hand-delivered to the CinC, Combined Fleet (ADM Yamamoto) in sealed envelopes ahead of time, and were later ordered to be opened, via wireless telegram transmissions (on December 1st and 2nd).[268] |

---

[268] These were the formal and final Imperial decision to go to war on December 1st, and the order of the next day, December 2nd, to commence hostilities on December 8, 1941 (Tokyo time). This is revealed in the diary of RADM Matome Ugaki, Yamamoto's Chief of Staff, on pages 32-34, in the diary entries for December 1, 1941 and December 2, 1941. **Those two messages from ADM Nagano to Yamamoto, at least---*but perhaps only those two messages* (the formal Imperial decisions to actually go to war, and to commence hostilities on December 8, 1941)**---were brought to Yamamoto's staff by courier in sealed envelopes, with instructions to open when so ordered, and therefore were almost certainly **not** encrypted in JN-25(b), since they were not transmitted electronically. Ugaki reveals in his diary that he personally opened both sealed envelopes when directed to do so by radio telegrams received on December 1st and 2nd, respectively (since his chief, Yamamoto, was absent in Tokyo). **But he does not speak of the use of sealed envelopes, or of telegrams**

| | As the chronology continues and events accelerate during the month of November 1941, it is important for the reader to understand the differences between Tokyo Time, Eastern Standard Time in Washington, D.C., and the corresponding time in Pearl Harbor, Hawaii.

As Prange explains in *At Dawn We Slept* (p. 372), "Tokyo time was nineteen and a half hours ahead of the special U.S. military time zone for Hawaii, and fourteen hours ahead of Washington, D.C. Eastern Standard Time." (And London was five hours ahead of Washington, D.C.)

Thus, an event that occurred at 6 A.M. on November 26th in Japan (e.g., the time the Pearl Harbor Striking Force got underway from Hitokappu Bay to attack the U.S. Pacific Fleet in | [This uncertainty about whether those "kickoff" messages from the Naval General Staff that were encoded in JN-25(b) were transmitted by radio, or telegraphed by secure cable, does ***not*** apply to any orders sent <u>by the CinC, Combined Fleet to ships of the First Air Fleet</u> commencing **on or after** November 22nd, for commencing on that date, all 33 vessels of the Pearl Harbor Striking Force had rendezvoused and assembled in the remote Hitokappu Bay anchorage (on the western coast of Etorofu Island north of Hokkaido) for provisioning, fueling, and for last-minute pre-sail briefings about the upcoming operation. No less an authority than Gordon Prange has confirmed, in *At Dawn We Slept* (p. 350), that <u>there was no telephone or telegraph communications capability with Hitokappu Bay</u> when the Striking Force arrived there to reprovision and refuel in late November 1941. The co-authors of *Betrayal at Pearl Harbor*, Rusbridger and Nave (p. 133-134), agree. **Thus, two key operational messages in this well-documented string of "kickoff" war messages, which were sent from ADM Yamamoto (CinC, Combined Fleet) to all units (ships) of the First Air Fleet on November 25, 1941 <u>were definitely transmitted by radio, and in the JN-25(b) Fleet</u>** |

<u>ordering the opening of sealed envelopes, in connection with any of the other high-level "kickoff" messages.</u> Apparently [this is my own interpretation after carefully reading and re-reading his diary entries from November 5th until the outbreak of hostilities on December 8th], this caution <u>involving the delivery of high-level orders in sealed envelopes</u> only applied to **the actual, formal declaration of war, and to the formal decision relaying the day hostilities would commence.**

	Hawaii) was occurring at 10:30 A.M. on November 25th in Pearl Harbor; at 4 P.M. on November 25th in Washington, D.C.; and at 9 P.M. on November 25th in London. In general terms, a message transmitted from Tokyo on November 25th local (Japan) time, can be safely thought of as having gone out during November 24th in London, Washington and Pearl Harbor.	**General Purpose Operations Code.** Much will be written about these two key messages later in this work---see the two entries in the chronology below about ADM Yamamoto's "grand execute" order, and the "get underway" message or "sailing order," both confidently reported during interrogations in October 1945, as having been transmitted to the Pearl Harbor Striking Force, the First Air Fleet. The "grand execute" order was transmitted on either November 22nd or 25th, Tokyo time, depending upon which source one relies on; and all agreed that the "sailing order" was transmitted on November 25th, Tokyo time.]
November 5, 1941	**ADM Yamamoto issues COMBINED FLEET TOP SECRET OPERATION ORDER 1,** the grand plan for war to be followed by the entire Japanese Navy, in accordance with the instructions in Navy Order No. 1, transmitted by the Naval General Staff on that same date. That message instructed Yamamoto to "effect the required preparations for war operations," and Yamamoto was complying by issuing his grand overview of the forthcoming war to his fleet on the same day. The OPORDER had been in preparation by	When one studies the text and the detail in this **Combined Fleet OPORDER 1** (it is reproduced in its entirety in English translation, in JCC PHA *Hearings,* volume 13, p. 431-484), it is abundantly clear that it was NOT reproduced solely from memory in October 1945, as were the brief operational directives issued by the Naval General Staff and CinC, Combined Fleet.

As reproduced in the JCC PHS *Hearings,* the OPORDER specifically mentions that *the American Fleet will be destroyed "in the east,"* that British Malaya will be invaded and occupied, that the Philippines will be invaded and occupied, and that strategic areas--- Thailand, and the Netherlands East Indies (specifically, the Celebes, Borneo, Sumatra, the Moluccas, Timor, and Java) will subsequently be occupied, or invaded and conquered. Thailand |

	Yamamoto's staff for months, and the Naval General Staff printed it, using labor (Naval yeomen) from the Combined Fleet staff. A remarkable 700 copies were run off, and it was distributed to the fleet and its commanders as a bound, printed document before ships and their commanders sailed off to war. (It was too long, and much too complex, to be transmitted as a radio message.) One copy of this complex document survived the destruction of the Naval General Staff's files at the end of the war; this copy of what Prange characterizes as a 100 page OPORDER (the English translation published by the U.S. Congress runs to 54 pages) was reportedly found aboard the wrecked Japanese heavy cruiser *Nachi* in 1944.[269] According to the 1946 U.S. government publication *The*	opened its doors to the Japanese and endured a 'friendly occupation' rather than an invasion, and of course the Japanese had to take by force the Netherlands East Indies. The OPORDER specifically states that all enemy forces in the Orient will be destroyed; that all lines of communication and supply between the U.S. and the Orient, and Britain and the Orient, will be severed; and that victories will be ***"exploited to break the enemy will to fight."*** Areas with natural resources would be occupied; strategic areas would be seized and developed; and defenses would be strengthened to establish a durable basis for operations. The OPORDER specifies the order of battle of the Japanese forces, and contains much guidance about future submarine operations and about fleet communications. The OPORDER, writes Prange (p. 331), "…was more than a directive for the tactical employment of Japan's naval forces; it presented a long-range strategic plan." Prange explains in *At Dawn We Slept* (p. 332) that detailed information about the Pearl Harbor attack was originally included in the OPORDER but later deleted from all other copies for security reasons. Prange records, however, that RADM **Kusaka** (ADM

---

[269] Rusbridger and Nave, *Betrayal at Pearl Harbor,* 133 and 271; and PCC PHA *Hearings,* volume 13, p. 430 both confirm that the OPORDER published by the Congressional Committee was a captured source document (and therefore was not reconstructed from memory). The captured copy was retrieved from the wrecked Japanese Navy heavy crusier *Nachi,* according to Rusbridger and Nave.

	Campaigns of the Pacific War (p. 47), the outline of operations pursued by the IJN against the United States, Great Britain, and the Netherlands at the commencement of hostilities was designed to: -continue control over the China coast and Yangtze River; -quickly destroy enemy fleet and air power in East Asia; -occupy and hold strategic points in the Southern Area; -destroy the enemy fleet in Hawaii; -consolidate defensive strength to hold out for a long time; and -destroy the enemy will to fight. All of these points were incorporated into OPORDER 1.	Nagumo's deputy) made a private copy of the excised portion, which read as follows: 1. **The Task Force will launch a surprise attack at the outset of war upon the U.S. Pacific Fleet supposed to be in Hawaiian waters, and destroy it.** 2. **The Task Force will reach the designated stand-by point for the operation in advance.** 3. **The date of starting the operation is tentatively set forth as December 8, 1941.** In the portions of the OPORDER published by the JCC PHA *Hearings,* it states: "When the decision is made to complete over-all preparations for operations, orders will be issued establishing **the approximate date (Y Day)** for commencement of operations…" and subsequently the OPORDER also states: "The time for **the outbreak of war (X Day)** will be given in an Imperial General Headquarters order. *The order will be given several days in advance."* [Emphasis added] So upon receipt of **Y Day**, <u>the fleet was to "get ready;"</u> and upon receipt of **X Day**, <u>the fleet was to consider itself at war as of 0000 hours that day, and actually commence the attack on that day.</u>
November 5, 1941	**The Purple machine decrypts Tokyo's deadline for successfully concluding negotiations**	<u>The alarming text read</u>: "Because of various circumstances, **it is absolutely necessary that all arrangements for the signing of this agreement be completed**

	with the United States. (As in the **MAGIC** decrypt of November 4th, this message is from Foreign Minister Togo in Tokyo to Ambassador Nomura in Washington.)	**by the 25th of this month.** I realize that this is a difficult order, but under the circumstances it is an unavoidable one. Please understand this thoroughly and tackle the problem of saving the Japanese-U.S. relations from falling into a chaotic condition. Do so with great determination and with unstinted effort, I beg you."[270] [Emphasis added]
November 5, 1941	General Marshall and Admiral Stark send FDR a joint appraisal about the current strength of the U.S. Pacific Fleet and about the **military readiness** of the U.S. for war with Japan in the Pacific. Everything written in this report was correct from a purely military standpoint, but FDR was responsible for juggling many competing concerns at once, **including the psychology of the American people as the United States moved closer to war, and his primary concern: the defeat of Nazi Germany.** No doubt Roosevelt was conscious of the old football adage: *"You can't win the game without getting on the*	Principal excerpts from the report are quoted below from Prange (p. 336): "**At the present time the United States Fleet in the Pacific is inferior to the Japanese Fleet** and cannot undertake an unlimited strategic offensive in the Western Pacific…If Japan be defeated and Germany remain[s] undefeated, decision will still not have been reached…*War between the United States and Japan should be avoided while building up defensive forces in the Far East,* until such time as Japan attacks or directly threatens territories whose security to the United States is of very great importance." [Emphasis added] The language of this document appears to me to be an attempt to restrain a President who was already known to favor the strategy espoused in Commander McCollum's memo of October 7, 1940---that is, inciting Japan to commit an overt act of war. Roosevelt had to consider more than purely military considerations---he had to keep foremost

---

[270] Greaves, Jr., *Pearl Harbor,* 120.

field."

Greaves writes in *Pearl Harbor: The Seeds and Fruits of Infamy (p.118-119):*

"One by one they [Marshall and Stark] pointed out the various reasons why the United States should ***not*** issue an ultimatum to Japan that might force her to take drastic action involving the United States in a Pacific war:

1. The U.S. fleet in the Pacific was inferior to the Japanese Fleet…

2. U.S. military forces in the Philippines were not yet strong enough. They were being reinforced, however, and it was expected that air and submarine strength would be built up by mid-December and that the air forces would reach their projected strength by February or

in his mind <u>the politics of entering the war</u>: **how to get a *united* America into the war against Germany.** Endless delay in confronting the Japanese in the Pacific would only allow Germany more time to prosecute its war against Britain and the Soviet Union, unchallenged by the United States. Roosevelt surely kept two things in mind when deciding how to evaluate this type of narrow military advice: (1) the United States was rapidly building a two-ocean Navy and tooling up to build 50,000 airplanes per year, so it could afford to absorb initial losses once hostilities began; (2) the ABC-1 report, conscious of the greater danger of Nazi Germany and aware of Japan's limited industrial capability, had decided to allocate 85% of America's war material to the war against Germany and only 15% of its resources to the coming war against Japan, <u>and to fight a holding action in the Pacific until Germany was defeated</u>. (Therefore, there was ***no need*** for the Pacific Fleet to conduct an immediate offensive in the event of war with Japan.) Keeping this "big picture" in mind no doubt allowed Roosevelt to deal appropriately with the continued calls, made from a narrow military perspective, to delay war with Japan as long as possible while the Far East was slowly strengthened. **FDR knew that it would do no good to delay the inevitable war with Japan if, as a result, Hitler meanwhile won his war against the Soviet Union and then turned upon Great Britain and finished her off, while the U.S. waited**

	March of 1942. 3. British naval and air reinforcements were expected to reach Singapore by February or March… The memo to FDR also stated that: '…We should not send troops to China, but we should give all aid short of actual war…to the Chinese Central Government.' …It closed with a strong recommendation: **'That no ultimatum be delivered to Japan.'** " [Emphasis added]	**on the sidelines.** His view was global, and more far-reaching, than that of his military chiefs at this time. Therefore, his pressure on Japan would soon be ratcheted-up, in spite of his realistic appreciation of the relative weakness of the Pacific Fleet, when compared with the assembled might of the entire Imperial Japanese Navy. It would soon be time to stop "babying Japan along" (i.e., taking the middle road in U.S.-Japanese diplomacy), in spite of the warnings in this joint Army-Navy report. *Japan did not have the industrial base to win a long war with the United States, and FDR kept this in mind, while continuously pondering how much longer he could afford to delay fighting Nazi Germany.*
November 5, 1941	CNO Harold R. Stark informs CINCPAC (ADM Kimmel) and CINCAF (ADM Hart) that the IJN had ordered the complete withdrawal of all Japanese merchant ships from Western Hemisphere waters.	This step was correctly viewed by the leadership in the U.S. Navy as a presage of Japanese hostilities in the Pacific. An island nation that is crucially dependent on its merchant marine lifeline does not want significant numbers of its merchant fleet interned in foreign ports once hostilities begin. It was one indicator, among many, that Japan would soon initiate war in the Western Pacific.
November 7, 1941	The CinC, Combined Fleet (ADM **Yamamoto**)	This was a one page document, and it

Continued in Volume II,

On page 365;

Volume II also contains the Bibliography,

Afterword, Appendices, and Index.

CPSIA information can be obtained
at www.ICGtesting.com
Printed in the USA
LVHW101003290321
682822LV00019B/305